Critical Thinking in Psychology

Edited by

ROBERT J. STERNBERG
Tufts University

HENRY L. ROEDIGER III
Washington University in St. Louis

DIANE F. HALPERN
Claremont McKenna College

CAMBRIDGE
UNIVERSITY PRESS

CAMBRIDGE UNIVERSITY PRESS
Cambridge, New York, Melbourne, Madrid, Cape Town, Singapore, São Paulo

Cambridge University Press
32 Avenue of the Americas, New York, NY 10013-2473, USA

www.cambridge.org
Information on this title: www.cambridge.org/9780521845892

© Cambridge University Press 2007

First published 2007

Printed in the United States of America

A catalog record for this publication is available from the British Library.

Library of Congress Cataloging in Publication Data

Critical thinking in psychology / edited by Robert J. Sternberg, Henry L. Roediger III,
Diane F. Halpern.
    p.   cm.
Includes index.
ISBN 0-521-84589-0 (hardcover) – ISBN 0-521-60834-1 (pbk.)
1. Critical thinking.   I. Sternberg, Robert J.   II. Roediger, Henry L.
III. Halpern, Diane F.   IV. Title.

BF441.C755   2006
150.1 – dc22   2006016308

ISBN-13   978-0-521-84589-2 hardback
ISBN-10   0-521-84589-0 hardback

ISBN-13   978-0-521-60834-3 paperback
ISBN-10   0-521-60834-1 paperback

Critical Thinking in Psychology

Good scientific research depends on critical thinking at least as much as on factual knowledge; psychology is no exception to this rule. And yet, despite the importance of critical thinking, psychology students are rarely taught how to think critically about the theories, methods, and concepts they must use. This book is an introductory text on critical thinking for upper-level undergraduates and graduate students. It shows students how to think critically about key topics such as experimental research, statistical inference, case studies, logical fallacies, and ethical judgments.

Robert J. Sternberg is Dean of Arts and Sciences at Tufts University. Prior to that, he was IBM Professor of Psychology and Education in the Department of Psychology, Professor of Management in the School of Management, and Director of the Center for the Psychology of Abilities, Competencies, and Expertise (PACE) at Yale. He continues to direct the PACE Center from Tufts. He is the author of more than 1,000 journal articles, book chapters, and books, and he has received more than $18 million in government and other grants and contracts for his research. Sternberg served as president of the American Psychological Association in 2003.

Henry L. Roediger III is the James S. McDonnell Distinguished University Professor and the Dean of Academic Planning in Arts and Sciences at Washington University in St. Louis. He received his bachelor of arts degree from Washington & Lee University and his doctorate from Yale University. His research has centered on human learning and memory, with a recent focus on the application of basic cognitive research to educational applications. In 2003, he was named to the Institute of Scientific Information's list of Highly Cited Scientists. Roediger served as president of the American Psychological Society (now the Association for Psychological Science) in 2003–2004.

Diane F. Halpern is Professor of Psychology and Director of the Berger Institute for Work, Family, and Children at Claremont McKenna College. Her most recent books include *Thought and Knowledge: An Introduction to Critical Thinking* (4th ed.); *Sex Differences in Cognitive Abilities* (3rd ed.), a special two-volume edited issue of the *American Behavioral Scientist* titled *Changes at the Intersection of Work and Family* (edited with Heidi R. Riggio, 2006), and *From Work–Family Balance to Work–Family Intersection: Changing the Metaphor* (edited with Susan Murphy, 2005). Halpern was 2004 president of the American Psychological Association. In addition, she has served as president of the Western Psychological Association, the Society for the Teaching of Psychology, and the Division of General Psychology of the American Psychological Association.

Contents

List of Illustrations and Tables

List of Contributors

Robert A. Bjork
University of California –
  Los Angeles

Judy DeLoache
University of Virginia

Simon Dennis
University of Adelaide

Celia B. Fisher
Fordham University

Adam L. Fried
Fordham University

Thomas Gilovich
Cornell University

Elena L. Grigorenko
Yale University

Diane F. Halpern
Claremont McKenna College

Ray Hyman
University of Oregon

Rachel Hull
Rice University

Christian H. Jordan
Wilfrid Laurier University

Walter Kintsch
University of Colorado

E. David Klonsky
Stony Brook University

Jessica K. Masty
Fordham University

Randi Martin
Rice University

David P. McCabe
Washington University in St. Louis

Kathleen B. McDermott
Washington University in St. Louis

Gregory E. Miller
University of British Columbia

Thomas F. Oltmanns
Washington University in St. Louis

Anthony R. Pratkanis
University of California –
  Santa Cruz

Jane Risen
Cornell University

Henry L. Roediger, III
Washington University in St. Louis

David J. Schneider
Rice University

Norbert Schwarz
University of Michigan

William R. Shadish
University of California – Merced

Barbara A. Spellman
University of Virginia

Robert J. Sternberg
Tufts University

Mark P. Zanna
University of Waterloo

Preface

One day, the president of the American Psychological Association (Bob Sternberg), the president-elect of the APA (Diane Halpern), and the president of the American Psychological Society (now the Association for Psychological Science) (Roddy Roediger) got together to discuss ways in which these two large national associations, both concerned with psychology, might collaborate in a joint venture. Partly we wanted to show the ability of our sometimes rival organizations to collaborate, but partly, the three of us, friends of long standing, wanted to work together on a project. Eventually, we found ourselves talking about a topic that was of great interest to all three of us, and that also was, we thought, important for the field – the nature and development of critical thinking in psychology.

Our concern was that, although psychology curricula were pretty consistently strong in teaching students the main facts, theories, and research done in psychology, these curricula were more variable in the extent to which they fostered critical thinking in the discipline. Part of the reason for this variability, we thought, was that although some texts mentioned or even had exercises in critical thinking, the development of critical thinking in psychology was always secondary to their main purpose. Usually, the purpose of the books was primarily to convey subject matter, and only secondarily, at best, to promote critical thinking about this subject matter.

Of course, there are also books that teach for critical thinking, including books that we have written. But these books are domain general, focusing on critical thinking in general rather than critical thinking in psychology in particular. And if there is anything research in psychology has shown, it is that people often have difficulty applying domain-general principles, especially when they are learned in a decontextualized way, to thinking within a particular domain.

So we decided that what the field needed was a textbook prepared for undergraduates and beginning graduate students that would focus on the nature and development of critical thinking skills and attitudes in psychology. We realized that we would need to edit rather than write such a book. Psychology is a multifaceted and broad discipline, and it would be hard for any one person to have all the knowledge needed for a written book. We decided to ask the people we considered the leading experts in different areas of psychology, including the psychology of critical thinking, to write about the different aspects of critical thinking in psychology. This book is the result.

We are grateful to our sponsoring organizations, the APA and the APS, for their sponsorship of this book. To affirm the editors' and authors' gratitude, all royalties earned by this book will be split between these two organizations and the funds made available for projects undertaken by future presidents. We are also grateful to Cheri Stahl for her help in collating the manuscript and for her invaluable assistance at all stages of the book. We believe the book is unique in its approach to critical thinking in taking different areas of psychology and discussing critical thinking in each of them. But we acknowledge that there have been and continue to be many other fine books on critical thinking in psychology; we believe that, together, they will help the students of tomorrow become not just knowledgeable about the field but able to think critically about and within it.

Finally, we wish to point out that the development of the book did show that our two organizations could work together seamlessly. Never in the course of its development did we have the slightest problem pertaining to collaboration. All three of us are now done with our organizational presidencies. But we continue to value the importance of our organizations – APA and APS – and their role in developing critical thinking in students of psychology – today, tomorrow, and always.

1

The Nature and Nurture of Critical Thinking

Diane F. Halpern

It was during a presentation on ways to enhance critical thinking in college classes that a jaded faculty member shot back at me, "What kind of thinking do you think I teach – noncritical thinking?" I assured this faculty member that no offense had been intended, although certainly it had been taken. In fact, often there is noncritical, or more appropriately labeled, rote memorization or lower level thinking that is taught and tested in many classrooms at all levels of education at the expense of higher order or critical thinking.

NONCRITICAL THINKING

Consider, for example, typical questions that might be found on tests given in developmental psychology classes. There is the ubiquitous question that asks students to list each stage of Piaget's theory of cognitive development, along with the age range for each stage, and an example of a cognitive task that can be accomplished at each stage. This is a basic recall question, even though there is an opportunity to provide an example, which allows for the application of the knowledge of what cognitive abilities become possible at each stage of development. The example given is almost always the same as an example that was presented in class or in the text. If this is the extent of students' knowledge, they are unlikely to be able to use Piaget's conceptualization of cognitive development in any applied setting (such as designing an age-appropriate toy or activity for a preschool) or in a novel or useful way. The information remains available in memory for repetition, but it is not likely to be used.

In a similar vein, consider what most students know about Freudian theory at the end of a course where this is one of several topics covered. Most students can define terms like *id, ego,* and *superego,* but these are disconnected concepts that are, at best, loosely related to other Freudian terms like *penis envy* and *projection.* For the most part, students can define these terms in a few words, see little or no connection among them, and have the general idea that Freudian theory is something to be giggled at and rejected. Few students can see how Freudian theory is related to other theories or personality or development, or are able to recognize the parts of Freudian theory that have survived for almost a century, or know how to think about Freudian theory from the context of a different sociohistorical period, and so on. Even though I have not yet defined critical thinking, I believe most people would recognize this sort of thinking as noncritical. These are examples of memorization or recall, the ability to remember what was learned. Knowledge about a content area is critical to critical thinking; no one can think critically about any topic without the necessary background information, but the facts alone are not enough. In the language of math and logic, they are necessary but not sufficient.

FIRST, SOME EXAMPLES

Critical thinking: everyone thinks it's a good idea, and everyone agrees that we want a workforce and a citizenry that can do more of it. When college and university faculty were asked about "the basic competencies or skills that every college graduate [should] have," they listed critical thinking (and problem solving) along with communicating and interpersonal skills, and computer literacy (Diamond, 1997). If you read the classified ads for executive positions of all sorts – regardless of whether the job is in accounting, law, trade, government, education, technology, or some other area – the top job skill listed is almost always some variant of critical thinking, and if it missing, it is often because it is assumed to be essential for any job where the knowledge base and context in which it is applied are rapidly changing. But, how can someone become a more critical thinker and, more specifically, how does studying psychology help students achieve this goal?

Before answering these questions and considering theories or frameworks of critical thinking that provide a way of thinking about how to get better at thinking, let's start with a few examples of applications of critical thinking skills.

Example 1: Understanding, Shaping, and Communicating Opinions About Complex Topics

Suppose that you are elected to a high-level government office and in that position you are trying to decide whether to support legislation that would provide parents with school vouchers. (If you live in the United States and keep up with its news, you will recognize this as a contemporary issue.) You want to know what your constituents think, so you decide to conduct a poll. You ask two different assistants to each write a question that would accurately assess opinions about school vouchers. Unknown to you, one of your assistants is in favor of vouchers and the other is opposed. Here are the two questions they submit.

1. Do you favor or oppose allowing students and parents to choose a private school to attend at public expense?
2. Do you favor or oppose allowing students and parents to choose any school, public or private, to attend using public funds?

Read these two questions carefully. Do you think that you will get approximately the same percentage of people who say that they favor vouchers in response to both questions? Which question will provide a greater percentage of "favor" responses? (Big hint: This second question should provide a clue as to the correct answer to the first question.)

In fact, in a real poll using these two questions, 41% of respondents answered that they favor school vouchers when they were asked Question 1, compared with 63% who were asked Question 2 (report from the 36th Annual Phi Beta Kappa Wirthlin Gallup Poll of Attitudes Toward Public Education; see "Gallup Poll," 2004).

Look carefully at the way seemingly slight changes in the wording, which might go unnoticed if only one version had been used, can alter the way a proportion of the public thinks about and responds to complex questions with important social ramifications. Of course parents could always choose public schools for their children, but public schools are not explicitly mentioned in Question 1. Question 2 appears to be providing a real choice, whereas there seems to be less choice in the way Question 1 is worded. Results from polls like these are often used to shape and communicate public opinions and to establish laws and policies. Sometimes, the wording is deliberately chosen in ways to sway people who may not be sure what they think and in ways that are not easy to detect. This is just one example of the way we use words to communicate information about thinking and to persuade others. Numerous other examples can be found in texts and workbooks on critical thinking (e.g., Halpern, 2003; Halpern & Riggio, 2003).

Example 2: Thinking With Numbers

Before you go on, answer these two questions:

Is the population of China greater than or less than 2 billion? _____
Now, without consulting any books or looking up the answer, make your best estimate about the population of China. _____

I can imagine that unless you have a particular expertise in Chinese population statistics (an unlikely area of specialization), you are moaning about this question, but go ahead and make your best estimate, even if you are complaining that you have no idea what the population of China is.

It is probably a safe assumption that you answered the first question as "less than," reasoning that although you did not know the population of China, 2 billion is probably too large. (It is interesting to trace how you decided it is probably too large, but that is another topic.) Suppose I had asked instead, "Is the population of China greater than or less than 40 million?" It would probably be a good guess to assume that you would have answered this question as "more than," still assuming that you have no good estimate of the population of China, but 40 million seems far too low.

These are "anchor" questions – not interesting in themselves because most people will "guesstimate" that the population of China is less than 2 billion and more than 40 million, which is still a pretty big range. What happens next is what is interesting. If you are asked the question with the "2 billion" anchor, your estimate for the population of China is likely to be much larger than if you are given the question with the "40 million" anchor. Let's see why and when this can be important. In situations like these, people use the number that is presented, even though they reject it, as an anchor or starting point for their thinking and they then adjust their thinking from there. If I wanted you to think of the population of China as huge – perhaps I wanted to convince you that the Chinese pose a grave threat, or I wanted to convince you to invest in something I plan to market in China – then I would start with some high value. I might start by saying that although the population is less than [insert some high value], it is a huge number of people and therefore you should either be afraid or invest money in my project, depending on what I want you to do.

I could influence how you think without ever giving you the exact numbers or even numbers that are even close to the actual values. Similarly, I could try to persuade you that the population of China is not as large as you might think, and therefore it does not pose a great risk, or that it would not be a good investment opportunity, or whatever it was that I was trying to persuade you about with regard to China. I might say, of course, that it is larger than [insert some value here], but not as large as most people often think, and so on. In this way, and without ever presenting meaningful numbers, one can shape a listener's appraisal of magnitude; your thinking about the relative threat or quality of an investment is manipulated without your awareness.

Now, use this information about anchoring in a totally different context to see if you can transfer this critical thinking skill. Should you suggest a starting salary when you are applying for a job? Answer this question and explain your answer before you continue reading.

If an anchor is a starting point and adjustments are made from the first number that is mentioned, then unless you have some specific information that might prove otherwise for a specific job, it seems to be to your advantage to set the anchor, as long as you do not undersell your own worth. Presumably you would set a higher value than your prospective employer, who would want to negotiate toward the value you set (assuming she recognizes that your critical thinking abilities are worth the high salary!). Anchoring and adjusting values from that anchoring when you are thinking about numbers is a topic that is studied and taught in cognitive and social psychology classes that is useful to understand regardless of your intended future career (Epley, Keysar, Van Boven, & Gilovich, 2004; Galinsky & Mussweiler, 2001). (Just think about all of the cars you are likely to buy!)

Example 3: Applied Research Design and Analysis

An expensive exam preparation program boasts that students who take its course to prepare for the law school entrance exam and who attend classes regularly score higher on the law school entrance exam than do students from the same colleges who do not take this special coursework. Can we conclude that the exam preparation program is an effective way to boost exam scores on the law school application exam?

Although it is tempting to conclude that this program does exactly what its promoters claim that it does, it is likely that students who take the program and attend regularly differ in many ways from those who do not. Those who can afford an expensive exam preparation program probably have many advantages that are associated with higher family income levels – better schools, more educational experiences out of school, larger vocabulary used at home, and so on. These students are, on average, likely to be more motivated, if they attended class regularly, than those who dropped out or attended only sporadically. It would be necessary to sample students and randomly assign them to attend or not attend the special preparation program and then compare scores on these two groups to determine if the program was an effective preparation for the law school examination. It is possible that less affluent but highly motivated students could prepare on their own or with friends by using other materials with the same positive results. Much more extended and elaborate examples of research designs as critical thinking are presented throughout this book.

These three examples are all everyday applications of skills that would be learned and used in psychology courses, although they are applicable in a wide variety of contexts that do not "look like" psychology. They are needed for success in and out of school.

WHAT IS CRITICAL THINKING?

Although many psychologists and others have proposed definitions for the term *critical thinking*, these definitions tend to be similar in content in that they include skills and abilities and the disposition to use those skills and abilities in a careful and thoughtful manner. For example, Ennis proposed a two-part model of critical thinking with the disposition to care about "getting it right" and "care about presenting positions honestly and clearly" (Ennis, 2001).

In a recent review of the critical thinking literature, Fischer and Spiker (2000) found that most definitions for the term *critical thinking* include reasoning or logic, judgment, metacognition, reflection, questioning, and mental processes. Jones and his colleagues (Jones, Dougherty, Fantaske, & Hoffman, 1997; Jones, 1995) obtained consensus from among 500 policy makers, employers, and educators, who agreed that *critical thinking* is a broad term that describes reasoning in an open-ended manner and with an unlimited number of solutions. It involves constructing a situation and supporting the reasoning that went into a conclusion. Paul, Willson, and Binker (1993) have a similar conceptualization of critical thinking as self-directed and "fair-minded," with clarity about the nature of the problem, the way generalizations are made, the evidence, and conclusions.

Here is a simple definition that captures the main concepts: *Critical thinking is the use of those cognitive skills or strategies that increase the probability of a desirable outcome. It is used to describe thinking that is purposeful, reasoned, and goal directed – the kind of thinking involved in solving problems, formulating inferences, calculating likelihoods, and making decisions, when the thinker is using skills that are thoughtful and effective for the particular context and type of thinking task.* Critical thinking is more than merely thinking about your own thinking or making judgments and solving problems – it is using skills and strategies that will make "desirable outcomes" more likely.

There are many different taxonomies of critical thinking skills, and although they differ in the way skills are grouped, and sometimes in the vocabulary used to describe the skills or groups of skills, the differences among the various authors in this field are not important in this context. Critical thinking skills are often referred to as "higher order cognitive skills" to differentiate them from simpler (i.e., lower order) thinking skills. Higher order skills are relatively complex; require judgment, analysis, and synthesis; and are not applied in a rote or mechanical manner. Higher order thinking is thinking that is reflective, sensitive to the context, and self-monitored. Computational arithmetic, for example, is not a higher order skill, even though it is an important skill, because it involves the rote application of well-learned rules with little concern for context or other variables that would affect the outcome. By contrast, deciding which of two information sources is more credible is a higher order cognitive skill because it is a judgment task in which the variables that affect credibility are multidimensional and change with the context. In real life, critical thinking skills are needed whenever we grapple with complex issues and messy, ill-defined problems.

A list of generic skills that can be important in many situations would include these: recognizing that a problem exists; developing an orderly, planful approach so that tasks are prioritized and problems are recognized as differing with regard to how serious and urgent they are; generating a reasoned method for selecting among several possible courses of action;

relating new knowledge to information that was previously learned; using numerical information, including the ability to think probabilistically and express thoughts numerically; understanding basic research principles; and presenting a coherent and persuasive argument about a controversial, contemporary topic. These are all examples that are useful across a wide variety of contexts and that can easily be understood by a broad range of audiences. In my own work (Halpern, 2003), I have suggested 5 to 10 groupings of skills, depending on the context, because I believe that various groupings are possible and groups can contain different numbers of skills, again depending on the reason for the grouping.

A 10-category taxonomy with some examples of the critical thinking skills that apply in each category is shown in Table 1.1.

An alternative way of categorizing thinking skills was proposed by Sternberg (1996) in a tripartite model of the thinking skills that collectively make up "successful intelligence." Most school settings teach and test for the first skill set: analytical thinking skills, which includes analyzing, critiquing, judging, evaluating, comparing and contrasting, and assessing. These thinking skills are valued in school settings (i.e., book learning), and people who are good at these sorts of thinking tasks also tend to score high on traditional measures of intelligence, which are heavily weighted with analytical thinking tasks. The other two components of successful intelligence are creative thinking skills, which include creating, discovering, inventing, imagining, supposing, and hypothesizing; and practical thinking skills, which include applying, using, and practicing the other thinking skills. According to Sternberg, creative and practical thinking skills are largely independent of the sort of thinking skills that are assessed in traditional measures of intelligence, which are overweighted with the thinking skills that are needed for success in school. This conceptualization is a skills-based approach, with three broad groupings of skills.

In an empirical test of his theory, Sternberg and his coauthors (Sternberg, Torff, & Grigorenko, 1998) found that students tend to have a preference for one of these three types of thinking skills; when they were taught predominantly with their preferred thinking skill, they learned better than when the primary teaching method did not match their preferred learning skill. In a later extension of his theory to the topic of wisdom, Sternberg (2003) added a value component that emphasizes the importance in wisdom of using successful intelligence as well as creativity and knowledge for the goal of attaining common good.

CAN CRITICAL THINKING BE LEARNED?

Is the ability to think critically an inherited or natural ability that is relatively immune to the effects of learning, or is it an ability that can be developed or enhanced with appropriate instruction? This is a familiar question for psychologists – it is a variant of the age-old question of nature versus nurture

TABLE 1.1. *A Short Taxonomy of Critical Thinking Skills*

Grouping	Skills
1. Critical Thinking Framework: A General Set of Questions to Guide Thinking	What is the goal? Which thinking skill(s) will help you reach your goal? Have you reached your goal?
2. Memory: The Acquisition, Retention and Retrieval of Knowledge	How to make abstract information meaningful. How you can use overlearning, cognitive interviewing techniques, and memory triggers to recall and organize information. How to develop an awareness of biases in memory.
3. The Relationship Between Thought and Language	How to understand and use questioning and listening strategies. How to recognize and defend against the use of inappropriate, emotional language. How to choose and use graphic organizers.
4. Reasoning: Drawing Deductively Valid Conclusions	How to discriminate between deductive and inductive reasoning. How to understand the differences between truth and validity. How to properly use quantifiers in reasoning.
5. Analyzing Arguments	How to diagram the structure of an argument. How to examine the credibility of an information source. How to judge your own arguments.
6. Thinking as Hypothesis Testing	How to understand the limits of correlational reasoning. How to isolate and control variables in order to make strong causal claims. How to know when causal claims can and cannot be made.
7. Likelihood and Uncertainty: Understanding Probabilities	How to use probability judgments to improve decision making. How to compute expected values in situations with known probabilities. How to avoid overconfidence in uncertain situations.
8. Decision Making	How to reframe decisions to consider alternatives. How to prepare a decision-making worksheet. How to understand the distinction between the quality of a decision and its outcome.

Grouping	Skills
9. Development of Problem-Solving Skills	How to plan and monitor a strategy for finding a solution. How to use graphs, diagrams, hierarchical trees, matrices, and models as solution aids. How to select appropriate problem-solving strategies.
10. Creative Thinking	How to visualize the problem. How to brainstorm productively and create alternatives. How to gather additional information.

that underlies virtually every discussion of intelligence. Critical thinking is similar to intelligence in many ways, so it is subject to many of the same debates. Fortunately, the term *critical thinking* carries less "baggage" than the word *intelligence*, so the debates are a little less acrimonious. For those who are still arguing this question, one way to think about the response is that there is no reason why critical thinking could *not* be improved with instruction. Writing classes are taught in the belief that, on average, across a variety of contexts and disciplines, writing will improve when students learn the skills taught in these classes. Similarly, math classes are taught in the belief that students will be better at math wherever they need to perform math – that is, across settings and domains of knowledge – when they learn basic transcontextual math skills. Sometimes the skills that are taught in these classes transfer to other contexts and sometimes they do not, but individual failures do not mean that success is not possible. There are many examples of improvement in critical thinking as a result of appropriate instruction.

Critical thinking instruction is predicated on two assumptions: (a) that there are clearly identifiable and definable thinking skills that students can be taught to recognize and apply appropriately, and (b) if the skills are recognized and applied, the students will be more effective thinkers. There is ample evidence that this is true, but better thinking is not a necessary outcome of traditional, discipline-based instruction. However, when thinking skills are explicitly taught for transfer, using multiple examples from several disciplines, students can learn to improve how they think in ways that transfer across academic domains. Rubinstein's highly successful course in problem solving (Rubinstein & Firstenberg, 1987) and Woods' use of deliberate planning and monitoring (Wood, 1987) are among the earlier models of successful instruction in critical thinking that eventually swayed even the staunchest critics.

After an exhaustive review of the literature, the Thinking Skills Review Group (2005, p. 6) concluded that "the majority of studies report positive impact on pupils' attainment across a range of noncurriculum measures" (such as reasoning or problem solving). No studies reported a negative impact on such measures. This conclusion was based on a review of 23 "highly relevant studies": 6,500 chapters, articles, and papers were initially identified as relevant, from which 800 were identified as potentially having sufficient information for a review; 191 of these actually had all of the necessary information, and finally 23 allowed in-depth analyses.

Additional strong support for beneficial outcomes from critical thinking instruction comes from a collection of studies by Nisbett (1993) and his colleagues. For example, in one study, Nisbett and his coauthors phoned students at their home after the coursework was completed, under the guise of conducting a survey. They found that students spontaneously applied the thinking skills that they had been taught in school when they encountered novel problems, even when the school-related context cues were absent (Fong, Krantz, & Nisbett, 1986). In a different study, inductive reasoning tasks were taught to college students by using realistic scenarios from many different domains. Students were able to use these skills on a later test. The authors concluded that critical thinking is "a skill" and that "it is transferable" (Jepson, Krantz, & Nisbett, 1993, p. 82). Nisbett's edited book contains 16 chapters that show that rules of logic, statistics, causal deduction, and cost–benefit analysis can be taught in ways that will generalize to a variety of settings. Similar conclusions were found in a recent study conducted at Universidad de Salamanca in Spain, which is available online with learning materials in Spanish (Nieto & Saiz, 2006). There is a solid body of research to support the strong conclusion that specific instruction in thinking skills with diverse types of contexts (to encourage transfer across domains of knowledge) will enhance critical thinking skills.

A PEDAGOGY FOR CRITICAL THINKING

In addition to (a) explicitly teaching the skills of critical thinking, critical thinking instruction needs to (b) develop the disposition for effortful thinking and learning, (c) direct learning activities in ways that increase the probability of transcontextual transfer, and (d) make metacognitive monitoring explicit and overt.

Critical thinking is effortful; it requires a concern for accuracy and the willingness to persist at difficult tasks and suppress immediate and easy responses. It requires an openness to new ideas, which some people find to be the most difficult component. Many people find it easier to reject any new idea with an automatic response like "If it ain't broke don't fix it," instead of considering whether a new approach to an old problem or a new look would change how we think about old problems. Similarly, it often seems easier to stay away from learning or trying anything new where there is the chance of failure. The familiar is comfortable and safe, but not always the best response.

One of the components of critical thinking is conscious reflection on the process of thinking and the evaluation of one's own thinking process. Metacognition is personal knowledge or understanding of one's cognitive processes; for example, making judgments about the likelihood of remembering a fact or event at some time in the future, or deciding how well a problem has been solved, or estimating one's performance on a test of comprehension of complex prose. The underlying idea is that everyone needs to be able to assess how well they are thinking or how much they know about a topic to make reasoned decisions. Research has shown that when people have little knowledge of a content area (e.g., logical reasoning), they will misperceive their ability and rate themselves to be much higher in ability than they actually are, which can explain why some people never seem to learn anything from their mistakes – they do not see their mistakes.

For example, in one study, low-ability participants tested at the 12th percentile on knowledge in a content area, but they judged themselves to be well above average – at the 62nd percentile (Kruger & Dunning, 1999). In the words of the researchers, most people who are unskilled are also unaware of their deficiencies, which is an obvious barrier to improvement. Without the metacognitive skill of knowing what one knows and what needs to be learned, people will make unfortunate choices. The authors of the research found that by improving the skill of the participants, and most importantly their *metacognitive skills,* they were better able to recognize their own level of competence. This is an important step toward planning and evaluating one's own thinking and learning because it is a more accurate awareness of one's knowledge and skill level.

Students can become better thinkers and learners by developing the habit of monitoring their understanding and by judging the quality of their learning. It is the executive or "boss" function that guides how adults use different learning strategies and make decisions about the allocation of limited cognitive resources. Consider another example from the research literature. It is a well-established principle in learning that spaced practice, which means spacing study intervals over time, instead of massed practice, better known as cramming or doing all of one's studying in one block of time (often the night before the exam), leads to better long-term retention. Students who cram will find that they remember little of what they studied even a few days after the cram session. When college students were given options of how to study – whether to space their study time over two sessions, immediately repeat a study session (massed practice), or stop after one study session, they used massed practice for difficult materials and spaced practice for easy materials (Son, 2004). This sort of study choice shows the opposite of what they should have done; in other words, they had poor knowledge of how to enhance long-term retention. Massed practice provides a more immediate "feeling or illusion of knowing" than spaced practice, but it does not provide the same benefit for long-term retention that spaced practice does. Critical thinking instruction that includes some basic instruction on learning about learning and memory will have ancillary benefits for any cognitive processing, because students will make better judgments about what and how much they know and be better able to learn in ways that will help them remember information over longer intervals.

Instruction to enhance the development of critical thinking skills should include a metacognitive component. Sometimes instructors model their own thinking out loud and via other symbol systems, and by making the thinking processes public, explicit, and overt, and by modeling the thinking process, the habit of thinking about one's thinking (progressing toward a goal, quality of the outcomes, accuracy) becomes conscious, automatic, and available for improvement.

DEVELOPING CRITICAL THINKING SKILLS IN PSYCHOLOGY CLASSES

The chapters in this book all demonstrate how critical thinking skills are developed in psychology classes, using a broad range of topics and formats, yet they share a basic assumption – that the subject matter of psychology, the study of how people (and other animals) think, feel, behave, and learn, is a natural context for developing critical thinking skills. The emphasis on thinking in psychology dates back to the generally acknowledged "father of psychology," Wilhelm Wundt, who studied how people think. This emphasis was developed along more contemporary lines by educational psychologist John Dewey, who may have been the first 20th-century psychologist to argue for an education for thinking. As readers look through the following chapters, the topics will suggest the types of skills being developed – evaluating evidence, making causal analyses, using word choices to sway emotions, and so on. These are all topics in psychology that will help readers become better thinkers.

In his (2004) recent review of thinking frameworks, Moseley concluded that thinking skills approaches are effective when learners are engaged, when they think about their own thinking, and when they learn to strategically manage their thinking. The following chapters all offer components of effective thinking frameworks. Moseley concluded, "If learners are to benefit from thinking skills approaches they need to develop a deeper understanding of learning and instruction and appreciate the value of thinking skills in daily life" (p. 1). The following chapters are designed to achieve exactly these goals.

References

Diamond, R. M. (1997). *Curriculum reform needed if students are to master core concepts* [Web Page]. Retrieved December 28, 2000, from http://chronicle.com/search97cgi/s97_cgi?.
Ennis, R. (2001). Goals for a critical thinking curriculum and assessment. In A. Costa (Ed.), *Developing minds* (3rd ed., pp. 44–46.) Alexandria, VA: ASCD Publications.

Epley, N., Keysar, B., Van Boven, L., & Gilovich, T. (2004). Perspective taking as egocentric anchoring and adjustment. *Journal of Personality and Social Psychology, 87,* 327–339.

Fischer, S. C., & Spiker, V. A. (2000). *A framework for critical thinking research and training* (Report prepared for the U.S. Army Research Institute, Arlington, VA).

Fong, G. T., Krantz, D. H., & Nisbett, R. E. (1986). The effects of statistical training on thinking about everyday problems. *Cognitive Psychology, 18,* 253–292.

Galinsky, A. D., & Mussweiler, T. (2001). First offers as anchors: The role of perspective-taking and negotiator focus. *Journal of Personality and Social Psychology, 81,* 657–669.

Gallup Poll of attitudes toward public education. (2004, August 27). *Wall Street Journal,* p. A12.

Halpern, D. F. (2003). *Thought and knowledge: An introduction to critical thinking* (4th ed.). Mahwah, NJ: Erlbaum.

Halpern, D. F., & Riggio, H. R. (2003). *Thinking critically about critical thinking: Workbook to accompany Thought and knowledge: An introduction to critical thinking* (4th ed.). Mahwah, NJ: Erlbaum.

Jepson, C., Krantz, D. H., & Nisbett, R. (1993). Inductive reasoning: Competence or skill? In R. E. Nisbett (Ed.), *Rules for reasoning* (pp. 70–89). Hillsdale, NJ: Erlbaum.

Jones, E. A., Dougherty, B. C., Fantaske, P., & Hoffman, S. (1997). *Identifying college graduates' essential skills in reading and problem-solving: Perspectives of faculty, employers and policymakers* (Contract No. R117G10037/CDFA84.117G). University Park, MD: U.S. Department of Education/OERI.

Jones, E. A., Hoffman, S., Moore, L. M., Ratcliff, G., Tibbetts, S., & Click, B. A. (1995). *National assessment of college student learning: Identifying college graduates' essential skills in writing, speech and listening, and critical thinking* (NCES Publication No. 95-001). Washington, DC: U.S. Government Printing Office.

Kruger, J., & Dunning, D. (1999). Unskilled and unaware of it: how difficulties in recognizing one's own incompetence lead to inflated self-assessments. *Journal of Personality and Social Psychology, 77,* 1121–1134.

Moseley, D. (2004). *Thinking skill frameworks for post-16 learners: An evaluation.* Research report submitted to the Learning and Skills Research Centre, University of Newcastle upon Tyne, England.

Nieto, A. M., & Saiz, C. (2006). *Development and evaluation of a program designed to improve critical thinking.* Manuscript submitted for publication (available at http://web.usal.es/emid/pips/pips.htm).

Nisbett, R. (1993). *Rules for reasoning.* Hillsdale, NJ: Erlbaum.

Paul, R. W., Willson, J., & Binker, A. J. (1993). *Critical thinking: What every person needs to survive in a rapidly changing world.* Dillon Beach, CA: Foundation for Critical Thinking.

Rubinstein, M. F., & Firstenberg, I. R. (1987). Tools for Thinking. In J. E. Stice (Ed.), *Developing critical thinking and problem-solving abilities* (pp. 0–0). New Directions for Teaching and Learning, no. 30. San Francisco: Jossey-Bass.

Son, L. K. (2004). Spacing one's study: Evidence for a metacognitive control strategy. *Journal of Experimental Psychology: Learning, Memory, and Cognition, 30,* 601–604.

Sternberg, R. J. (1996). *Successful intelligence: How practice and creative intelligence determine success in life.* New York: Simon & Schuster.

Sternberg, R. J. (2003). *Wisdom, intelligence, and creativity synthesized.* Cambridge, UK: Cambridge University Press.

Sternberg, R. J., Torff, B., & Grigorenko, E. L. (1998). Teaching triarchically improves school achievement. *Journal of Educational Psychology, 90,* 374–384.

Thinking Skills Review Group. (2005, December). The impact of the implementation of thinking skills programmes and approaches on teachers. Newcastle, UK: University of Newcastle, Learning and Research Center.

Woods, D. R. (1987). How might I teach problem solving? In J. E. Stice (Ed.), *Developing critical thinking and problem-solving abilities* (pp. 0–0). New Directions for Teaching and Learning, no. 30. San Francisco: Jossey-Bass.

2

Evaluating Experimental Research

Critical Issues

Henry L. Roediger III and David P. McCabe

[T]he application of the experimental method to the problem of mind is the great outstanding event in the study of the mind, an event to which no other is comparable.

The author of this quote is Edwin G. Boring (1886–1968), one of the great psychologists of the 20th century and author of *A History of Experimental Psychology* (1929; the quote comes from p. 659). Contemporary psychologists take "the psychology experiment" as a given, but it is actually a relatively recent cultural invention. Although fascination with human behavior is doubtless as old as the emergence of *Homo sapiens*, the application of experimental methods to the study of the human mind and behavior is only 150 or so years old. Scientific methods, with heavy reliance on experimental technique, arose in Western civilization during the time of the Renaissance, when great insights and modes of thoughts from the ancient Greek, Roman, and Arab civilizations were rediscovered. The 17th century witnessed the great discoveries of Kepler, Galileo, and Newton in the physical world. Interest in chemistry and biology arose after the early development of physics. Experimental physiology arose as a discipline in the late 1700s and early 1800s. Still, despite great advances in these fields and despite the fact that scientists of the day usually conducted research in many different fields, no one at that time performed experiments studying humans or their mental life. The first physiologists and anatomists mostly contented themselves with the study of corpses. The idea of conducting experiments on mental phenomena in people would doubtless have seemed exotic, if not deemed utterly impossible.

Of course, philosophers and scientists of the time were keenly interested in the mind and mental happenings. The topics of perception, learning, memory, thinking, and reasoning were widely discussed in scholarly writings. Just among British philosophers, John Locke, Thomas Hobbes, George Berkeley, David Hume, and David Hartley all wrote treatises that were concerned with the issues that today occupy psychologists. Despite the fact that these men were all aware of the great scientific advances of their time, none of them did experiments to illuminate or to test their ideas about the mind. Why? The idea of an experimental science of the human mind had not yet taken hold; no one had yet shown that it could be done. It was not until the period between 1850 and 1900 that bold thinkers turned their experimental techniques to the study of mental life and human behavior.

Consider the following quote from Sir Francis Bacon (published in *Novum Organum* in 1620, as translated in 2000) in making a point about human memory: "If you read a piece of text through 20 times, you will not learn it by heart so easily as if you read it ten times while attempting to recite it from time to time and consulting the text when your memory fails" (p. 143). Give this quote to any competent student of experimental psychology today and it immediately calls forward a hypothesis that could be converted into a psychology experiment. The hypothesis is that learning and memory will be improved during repeated attempts to learn if tests are interspersed with study periods, relative to a condition in which only study periods are given.

Here is a possible experiment: Imagine that passages are created that take about 2 minutes to read. People could be asked to read the passage 20 times (with 2 minutes provided per time) or they could be asked to read the passage, take a test for 2 minutes, read it again, take a test, and so on. The hypothesis predicts that the study–test condition (10 study periods and 10 tests) would lead to better learning and retention than would 20 study periods. If tested a week later, people should show greater retention if they have received 10 study and 10 test trials than if they had received 20 study trials (despite the fact that people tested in the latter condition would have actually studied the material more often). Of course, other possible arrangements are possible, too, such as 15 study periods and 5 tests or 5 study periods interspersed with 15 tests. The point here is simply that Francis Bacon made an assertion about memory, probably based on his own experience, that was open to empirical test. However, he did not test his ideas. It took another 300 years for Bacon's idea to be put to experimental test, when Gates (1917) did so. The psychology experiment had not been invented in Bacon's time. Gates showed that Bacon's idea was essentially correct, and other studies conducted over the years have confirmed the conclusion that testing can be more beneficial to long-term retention than is repeated studying (e.g., Roediger & Karpicke, 2006; Tulving, 1967). Critical thinking – converting hypotheses into experimental tests – is at the heart of experimental methods.

THE EXPERIMENTAL METHOD

The heart of the experimental method is straightforward. A theory or hypothesis suggests the relation between two (or more) variables that exist in nature. For example, Bacon's aforementioned hypothesis could be stated this way: Tests of memory interspersed with study periods improve later retention relative to only studying (all other things being equal). A *variable* in an experiment is any factor that can be manipulated or measured. In the experiment outlined here, the number of test periods would be what is called the independent variable, so there might be 0, 5, 10, or 15 tests interspersed among study intervals for this experiment. When there are zero tests, this is a pure study condition. An *independent variable* is the factor that is manipulated in the experiment; the researcher wants to determine how its manipulation affects some outcome or behavior, the dependent variable. The *dependent variable* in an experiment is what is measured; the name indicates that, in most circumstances, variation in the measure of interest will depend upon the level of the independent variable. Of course, this is not always the case, because manipulation of the independent variable may not affect the dependent variable. The hypothesis under test may be wrong or, alternatively, the independent variable may not be manipulated over a wide enough range to affect the dependent variable. (In the sample experiment outlined here, the dependent variable would be the recall of the passages on a delayed test a week later.) How might "recall of prose" be measured? The usual method is for passages to be divided into idea units (small units of text that constitute an idea, as judged by people rating the text). Therefore, the dependent measure would be the number of idea units recalled or the percentage of idea units recalled.

Another set of factors in an experiment is called control variables (although the name is a bit of a misnomer). In our version of Bacon's hypothesis, the phrase "all other things being equal" appeared in parentheses and these "things" are the control variables. *Control variables* are factors that the experimenter could manipulate, but instead holds constant as much as possible. If they cannot be held constant, they are randomized across conditions. The idea behind an experiment is to determine what effect the manipulation of the independent variable has on the dependent variable. It is critical to hold all other conditions as constant as possible to ensure that if an effect is found on the dependent variable, it was caused by the independent variable. If other variables are allowed to change over conditions, then they might be causing change in the dependent variable and not the independent variable of interest. If some other factor varies along with the independent variable, the experiment is said to be *confounded*, because any effect observed on the dependent variable may have been caused by the independent variable or the other, confounded variable. A *confounding* exists whenever some other factor varies with, or is correlated with, the independent variable of interest. The problem of confounding undermines the rationale for experimental research, so great effort and care are taken in experimental research to hold other factors constant so as not to permit confoundings. However, this is sometimes difficult to accomplish because when a researcher manipulates what seems to be one variable, that variable may actually be composed of several features (unbeknownst to the researcher). Therefore, the researcher might believe that Feature A is causing the experimental effect, but Features B and C vary with A. Further research might show that Feature C is actually causing the effect and A is not.

Control variables may not seem so important to research, because they are the features of the experiment held constant. However, they are actually critical, because the level at which the control variables are held constant may determine the outcome of the research. Suppose, for example, that an experiment is conducted testing some hypothesis about human memory by having various groups of college students learn lists of words. Some independent variable is manipulated and the number of words recalled (the dependent variable) is measured. Control variables in this experiment are the types of subjects (college students) and materials (the word lists). These factors may or may not turn out to be important. If later research is done with elementary school children and the results turn out differently, then clearly the control variable (type of subjects used in the original research) was important. Similarly, if different effects occur with materials besides words lists, such as prose passages, then the type of materials also would turn out to be an important variable. We return to this issue later in the chapter when we consider generality of experimental research. The point here is that selection of control variables (of features of the experiment that are not varied) may have as great a consequence in the long run as the features that are varied.

Between-Subjects and Within-Subjects Designs

Another critical decision in designing experiments is whether to use different sets of people (or other animals) in the various experimental conditions or whether to use the same people (or animals). This constitutes a difference in using between-subjects or within-subjects experimental designs. In a *between-subjects design*, a different group of subjects is assigned to each level of the independent variable. So, in the example used here, one group of subjects would be assigned to study the passage 20 times and a different group of subjects would study the passage 10 times and be tested 10 times in alternating sequence. Then both groups would be tested a week later. But wait – hasn't this experimental design produced a problem, a factor that differs between the two conditions and so is a potential confounding factor? Yes, that is so – different groups of people are being tested in the two conditions, so how do we know that any difference we find might not be a difference in level of ability between the two groups of subjects? A critical factor in between-subjects experimental designs is that people (or animals) must be *randomly assigned* to conditions (or some other measures must be taken to ensure that they are equal, on average, in ability and other characteristics). For example, when a new subject appears at the laboratory to be tested, a coin flip (or a random number table, or some other means) should be used to assign the person to either the pure study or to the study–test condition. This step should ensure that the two groups of people are, on average, about the same in ability and in other qualities. Thus "people in the two conditions" would not literally be held constant as a control variable, but because any differences between subjects would presumably be small ones caused by random assignment, any variation observed in the dependent variable could safely be attributed to the independent variable and not to differing levels of subjects' abilities.

Another type of between-subjects design is the *matched groups design*, in which some relevant ability of people is measured before the experiment. Then subjects are assigned to groups in the experiment so that they are matched on the relevant dimension. For example, if middle-aged and older adults were compared in an experiment on memory or some other cognitive ability, they might be matched on years of education or on level of vocabulary (a proxy for verbal IQ). In this way, even though different groups of people are tested, the researcher can be relatively assured that there are no important intellectual differences between the groups.

Now let us consider the *within-subjects experimental design* in which the same individuals serve in all experimental conditions. For example, in our experiment on testing, on the first day of the experiment the subjects would study one particular passage 20 times and then, after doing that, they would study a second passage 10 times with 10 tests interspersed. A week later they would come back and receive a test on both passages. Thus the two conditions would be compared with the particular subjects participating in the conditions held constant. Although the participants do not differ, other complications are introduced in the within-subjects design. For one thing, there are now two passages and not one (as in the between-subjects design). Does that matter? It probably does, but there are several ways of making sure the passage type is controlled. One strategy is to pretest both passages and make sure they can be read and recalled at about the same level on an immediate test (i.e., the passages are matched). A second strategy is to use both passages (call them A and B) equally often in both conditions, so that passage A is included as often in the pure study condition as it is in the study–test condition across the subjects in the experiment. Using these strategies can convert a problematic situation (two different passages in the two experimental conditions) into one that is well controlled. The trick is making the type of passage a control variable.

The within-subjects design produces other complications, too. One is *practice effects*, or the fact that the subjects will be participating in both conditions and thus practice on one condition might affect how they perform in the next condition. Thus practice can introduce a confounding with the independent variable of interest. The way to minimize this problem is *counterbalancing* the order of conditions across subjects. That is, if the conditions are X and Y, half the subjects will get them in the order X then Y, whereas the other half would get them in the order of Y then X. Thus, on balance, each condition would be tested at the same (average) stage of practice, and therefore stage of practice would not be confounded with the variable of interest. Of course, counterbalancing is easy when there are two conditions in an experiment, but in certain types of research there may be many conditions and counterbalancing becomes much more difficult. Various strategies for counterbalancing can be found in textbooks on experimental design (e.g., Kantowitz, Roediger, & Elmes, 2005).

A problem in within-subject designs that is more difficult to overcome is the *differential carryover effect*. Unlike general practice effects, in this case participation in one condition can greatly change performance in the other condition. Suppose, for example, that a researcher is interested in whether creating mental images is a good strategy for memorizing relative to simple repetition. If a within-subjects design is used, the order of the two conditions must be counterbalanced, with subjects instructed to learn materials in one condition by rehearsing (mentally repeating) them and in the other by forming mental images that would depict the materials (e.g., if they had to learn the pair of words *clock–tree*, they might imagine a giant clock hanging from a tree). However, if subjects are first tested in the imagery condition and they discover that it works really well (which it does), then when they are switched to the repetition condition, they might still use imagery, in the interest of performing their best. (The problem would probably be less severe for subjects tested in the repetition-then-imagery order, because they would be less likely to carry over the repetition strategy, as it is less effective.) In this case, counterbalancing of conditions will not eliminate practice effects, because there might be differential carryover from the imagery to the repetition condition that would create a confounding in the experiment. Of course, in this kind of experiment, the researcher can always just examine the half of the subjects given each treatment first. That is, because half the subjects would get the repetition-then-imagery condition and the other half the imagery-then-repetition one, the experimenter could examine the first condition for both groups. In doing this, the researcher would essentially be treating the study as having a between-subjects design with one group of subjects in one condition and the other group in the other condition. If the results do not differ between the first condition and the overall experiment, the experimenter can conclude that there were no serious carryover effects.

Which type of experimental design is generally the best, between-subjects or within-subjects? There can be no general answer to this question, because the design selected to answer a particular question can depend on many factors. An advantage of within-subjects designs is that the same people (or animals) are used in both conditions, which often reduces variation in performance that is due to having different people in the groups. That is, even if people are randomly chosen to be in the two conditions in a between-subjects design, the groups may differ in small ways and this feature is eliminated from within-subjects designs. Put another way, the power of an experiment (the ability to detect an effect of the independent variable if there really is one) is usually greater in within-subjects designs. Yet, as just discussed, there are drawbacks to within-subjects designs, too, because the same people are tested in each condition, and serving in one condition can affect performance in the other condition. If a differential carryover effect is likely to occur and to cloud the results, then a between-subjects design may be preferred. In the hypothetical experiment comparing an imagery to a repetition strategy for improving memory, a between-subjects design would probably be best. In general, if one condition being tested is likely to greatly influence the other conditions in the experiment, then a between-subjects design is preferred.

Subject Variables

We have distinguished among independent variables, dependent variables, and control variables. We need to introduce one more type of variable, the subject variable, because much psychological research uses this sort of variable. When individual differences among people are examined on some task or set of tasks, the factor is referred to as a *subject variable*. It is somewhat like an independent variable – its effect on the dependent variable is the factor of interest in the experiment – but there are also important differences between independent and subject variables. For example, a researcher may be interested in some behavior of younger children (3–5 years of age) or older children (7–9), or the investigator may be interested in people with high IQs (scores of 120 and up) or those in the normal range (85–115), or the interest may be in older adults (65–90 years of age) and younger adults (20–30), or people who have an anxiety disorder (say, phobias to snakes and spiders) and those who do not have such phobias, and so on. The study of differences among people is a staple of psychology. However, this is a variable that cannot be manipulated like a true independent variable and, by definition, subject variables cannot be randomly assigned to conditions – people are assigned by nature to the variable. The great danger with subject variables is that some other factor might be correlated with the factor of interest and therefore introduces a confounding in the experiment. Because of this problem, great care is taken in such research to try to match people in the various conditions, as already described. For example, in a study of age differences between young, middle-aged, and older adults, subjects in the three groups would be matched as closely as possible on at least several features, which would typically include education, eyesight (corrected to normal), self-reported health, and often vocabulary (as assessed on standardized tests). Matching in this way reduces the risk that the findings from the study may be due to some factor other than the variable of interest, age in this case.

These considerations provide a summary of critical features of experimental methods. To recap briefly, independent variables are those that are manipulated; dependent variables are those that are measured; control variables are features that are held constant; and subject variables are features of people or animals assigned by nature, so that when they are examined care must be taken to match the individual on other characteristics as much as possible. Experimental methods seek to study effects of one or several variables on some behavior while holding others constant.

A SAMPLE EXPERIMENT

We present a sample experiment that we use to discuss the critical evaluation of experimental research for the remainder of the chapter. The experiment is on the issue of false memories. A false memory occurs when a person remembers an event differently from the way it actually happened or, in the most extreme case, remembers an event that never happened at all. Usually we do not know when our own recollections are false because we believe them; if someone else has a different recollection, we tend to believe our own and assume the other person is mistaken. However, consider the following anecdote from Jean Piaget (1962, pp. 187–188), the great Swiss psychologist, about a cherished memory from his childhood:

There is also the question of memories which depend on other people. For instance, one of my first memories would date, if it were true, from my second year. I can still see, most clearly, the following scene, in which I believed until I was about fifteen. I was sitting in my pram, which my nurse was pushing in the Champs Elysees, when a man tried to kidnap me. I was held in by the strap fastened round me while my nurse bravely tried to stand between me and the thief. She received various scratches, and I can still see vaguely those on her face. Then a crowd gathered, a policeman with a short cloak and a white baton came up, and the man took to his heels. I can still see the whole scene, and can even place it near the tube station. When I was about fifteen, my parents received a letter from my former nurse saying that she had been converted to the Salvation Army. She wanted to confess her past faults, and in particular to return the watch she had been given as a reward on this occasion. She had made up the whole story, faking the scratches. I, therefore, must have heard, as a child, the account of this story, which my parents believed, and projected into the past in the form of a visual memory.

Psychologists interested in this issue have developed laboratory paradigms to create and study various types of false memories. Many different paradigms have been developed (see Roediger & Gallo, 2002, for a review). Here we consider one straightforward paradigm developed by Roediger and McDermott (1995), which was based on earlier work by Deese (1959) and is now known as the converging associates or DRM paradigm (for Deese–Roediger–McDermott). The basic paradigm involves presenting lists of related words such as *door, glass, pane, shade, ledge, sill, house, open, curtain, frame, view, breeze, sash, screen,* and *shutter.* After hearing the list presented once (at a rate of about 1.5 seconds per word), subjects recalled the list on a blank sheet of paper by writing down the presented words. They were warned against guessing and told be as accurate as possible. Usually students recalling lists of words are highly accurate and make few errors, especially on immediate tests. However, that was not the case in this experiment.

The basic finding from the Roediger–McDermott experiment was that the subjects were highly likely to recall or to recognize a particular associated word that was not in the list (*window* in the case of the list given here). The 15 presented words were taken from word association norms; when subjects were given the word *window* and asked to write down the first word that came to mind, the 15 words listed here were the most probable responses. When subjects recall *window* just after the list is presented, they are (according to the definition given here) having a false memory: They are recalling an event (the occurrence of a word in a list) that did not happen. Of course, this type of laboratory false memory probably arises for different reasons from those for Piaget's false memory recounted in the previous paragraph, but in both cases there is a firm recollection of an event that never occurred. The basic idea as to why DRM false memories occur is that the presented words are associated to other words (like *window*) and these associations are activated when people hear the list (Underwood, 1965). Such implicit associative responses (which the subject may or not become conscious of during the study presentation) give rise to the DRM false memory effect, because during the test the subjects have difficulty in distinguishing activation that arose from actually encountering presented words (*frame, screen*) from that which arose from activation spreading through the cognitive system (*window*). They often judge strongly activated words such as *window* as having actually occurred and report them in a recall test or endorse them on a recognition test (e.g., Roediger, Balota, & Watson, 2001; McDermott & Watson, 2001).

Let us consider some specifics of one of Roediger and McDermott's (1995) experiments to help us critically evaluate it. They developed 24 lists like the one already given here, all containing 15 words that were associates of a particular word (the critical item) that was not presented. In the experiment, students heard 16 lists one at a time for 1.5 seconds per word. After 8 lists they recalled as many words as they could for 2 minutes, whereas after the other 8 lists they did arithmetic problems for 2 minutes. The rationale here was to determine the effect of whether or not a list was recalled on a recognition test to be given later, but of course false recall just after the list could be examined, too, on the 8 recalled lists. The subjects were cued after each list as to whether they would do arithmetic or recall the list, so they probably listened to the lists expecting to recall them in all cases. They never knew until after the list was over whether or not they would have to recall it.

After studying the 16 lists and recalling half of them, students were given a final recognition test at the end of the experiment. In this test, 96 words were presented and students had to decide whether or not each one had been previously presented (was it old or new?). Further, if they judged that the word was old (that is, had been presented), they were asked if they could remember specific details about the moment the word occurred in the list (a Remember judgment) or if they just knew it had been presented but could not actually remember any details about its occurrence in the list (a Know judgment; this Remember–Know procedure was developed by Tulving, 1985, to study states of awareness accompanying recognition of past events). Of the 96 words on the recognition test, half had been presented and half had not. The 48 presented words included 3 each from the 16 studied lists. The 48 nonpresented words (called lures or distracters in the context of recognition testing) consisted of 16 critical items from the presented lists (the words like *window* that had been used to generate the lists) and 32 new words taken from the 8 lists that had not been studied. Recall that 24 lists were developed but only 16 were presented, so the other lure items on the recognition test were the 8 critical items and 24 list items from the lists that *had not* been presented. The reason for having these items is to examine the general false alarm (or false memory) levels on the test when the relevant lists had not been studied.

On the initial recall tests given for 8 lists just after they had been studied, students recalled 62% of the list words. However, they also recalled the critical (nonstudied) items from those lists 55% of the time! That is, the words like *window* that were not presented were recalled with nearly the same probability as the words like *glass* and the others that were presented. Keep in mind that this occurred despite the fact that the tests were given immediately after presentation and that subjects were instructed to be sure to write down only words that they had just heard.

The recognition test results are provided in Table 2.1. At the top half are results for list words (from lists studied and recalled, from those studied but not recalled, and from those that were not studied at all). The proportions given under the Overall column are for the proportion of items judged to be "old." This number is then decomposed into those old responses that were judged to be remembered and those judged to be known in last two columns. The data in the top half of the table show that prior recall boosted later recognition (the effect of testing that we have already discussed) and that this effect occurred because of increases in remembering (Know judgments for the two conditions were about equal). Notice that the subjects were much more likely to say that they *remembered* than *knew* the words if the lists had been studied. For the nonstudied lists, the false alarm rate (probability of calling an item studied) was quite low (.11), and in this case almost all the

TABLE 2.1. *Recognition Results for the Roediger–McDermott Experiment*

Item Type and Condition	Proportion of "Old" Responses		
	Overall	Remember	Know
List Words			
Study + Recall	.79	.57	.22
Study + Arithmetic	.65	.41	.24
Nonstudied	.11	.02	.09
Critical Lures			
Study + Recall	.81	.58	.23
Study + Arithmetic	.72	.38	.34
Nonstudied	.16	.03	.13

Source: From Roediger and McDermott (1995).

responses are said to be *known* and not *remembered*. This last finding makes sense: How could someone remember an event that never happened?

The answer to this question is in the bottom half of Table 2.1: If a person has experienced events that are associated to (and strongly imply) another event, they may remember the event as actually having occurred. The data for the critical items showed that people falsely recognized them at high levels for the studied lists (.81 if the list had been recalled and .72 if it had not), but if the list had not been studied the false alarm rate was low (.16). Even more surprisingly, people not only recognized the nonpresented words as having been heard, but they judged that they remembered the moment of occurrence of the words at the same levels as for the presented words! That is, the *Remember* judgments for the critical (nonpresented) items in the bottom half of Table 2.1 are of the same magnitude as for the presented items at the top, so this outcome truly represents false remembering.

The Roediger and McDermott (1995) results show that even in the simple task of recalling a list of words, people can suffer from false recollections. These results have been studied and debated for the past 11 years, so we use this paper as a target to critically evaluate experimental research.

GENERALITY AND LIMITATIONS OF EXPERIMENTAL RESULTS

Critics of experiments like to point to their artificial nature and their limitations. The issue of false memories arises in many critical situations: in congressional testimony, in legal settings, in recountings of important meetings of interest to historians or other scholars, or eyewitness testimony of all sorts. How accurate are recollections? Can what we learn in laboratory paradigms inform larger issues outside the lab?

Discussing these issues gets to the heart of reasons for experiments, both their benefits and their limitations. The benefit of an experiment is to isolate one factor or several factors and hold others constant to examine the effect on the critical measures of interest. The drawback is that in creating a simple setting to isolate one factor, we may reduce the ability to generalize the result back to a complicated setting in which many other factors vary willy nilly. Of course, this issue is not unique to psychological research but occurs in all types of research. If massive doses of some substance (say, saccharin) are shown in controlled experiments to cause cancer in laboratory mice, should the substance be banned from human consumption? Can we generalize across a different species and a different dose?

The DRM false memory paradigm can be (and has been) criticized as artificial and of little relevance to the development of false memories outside a laboratory setting (Freyd & Gleaves, 1996). However, often laboratory conditions (being carefully constructed and holding other events constant) can actually make it more difficult to observe a particular result. Experiments are conducted to test hypotheses and to determine causality, which are different goals from immediate generalization (Mook, 1983). In discussing this issue, Roediger and McDermott (1995, p. 812) made this comment:

A critic might contend that because these experiments occurred in a laboratory setting, using word lists, with college students, they hold questionable relevance to issues surrounding more spectacular occurrences of false memories outside the laboratory. However, we believe that these are all reasons to be more impressed with the relevance of our results to these issues. After all, we tested people under conditions of intentional learning, with very short retention intervals, in a standard laboratory procedure that usually produces few errors, and we used college students – professional memorizers – as subjects. In short, despite conditions much more conducive to veridical remembering than those that typically exist outside the lab, we found dramatic evidence of false memories. When less of a premium is placed on accurate remembering, and when people know that their accuracy in recollecting cannot be verified, they may even be more easily led to remember events that never happened than they are in the lab.

The issue of artificiality of experimental research is a difficult one, and certainly researchers should strive as hard as they can to capture the important aspects of a phenomenon of interest and to bring them into the lab. Experiments are designed to provide internal validity of a result; internal validity is whether the independent variable affected the dependent variable. Is the cause and effect conclusion being drawn from the experiment valid (true)? Experiments are usually high in internal validity. External validity refers to generalizability to other settings. Does the effect observed in an experiment generalize to other settings?

The issues of internal and external validity are critical in research, but there is a priority to these considerations that may not be obvious. Internal validity of research must be established before one can begin to worry about external validity (Mook, 1983). Stated another way, one must have a secure finding (manipulating X causes Y to vary) before it is even worth worrying about whether this finding occurs in other settings outside the lab. Banaji and Crowder (1989) argued that experimental research (with tight controls) is the best way to guarantee that research is potentially generalizable. Thus, rather than conducting research in "natural" settings in which many factors vary uncontrollably, researchers usually must develop careful laboratory methods to establish firm findings before asking whether these findings can be generalized. Scientists have no inherent fascination with artificial settings, but rather they create these settings as a means to the end of providing conclusions with internal validity.

Assume that scientists have conducted an experiment and obtained a result that they and other scientists deem to be interesting and important. What are the next steps? The critical first step is always replication of the result: Can other researchers conduct the same experiment and get the same result? Of course, the original scientists may already have replicated their finding, but the critical test is whether others, using the same procedures, will find it as well. A *direct replication* refers to performing the experiment in as similar a way as possible in attempting to repeat the result. We hazard the guess that most experimental results in psychology can be directly replicated (although there are some notable exceptions to this claim). A conceptual replication is the next step. A *conceptual replication* refers to seeking the same general pattern of results but using somewhat different methods from the original procedure. Can the basic concept of the experiment be replicated? Will the experimental effect survive when the independent variable is manipulated slightly differently or when the measure (the dependent variable) is somewhat different? If a conceptual replication experiment obtains the same results as the original experiment, then the phenomenon has at least some generality. If the effect is not found, then the investigator may have found *boundary conditions* for the phenomenon, or variables beyond which the experimental effect will not generalize. Establishing boundary conditions is quite important in many contexts, both for developing theories of the phenomenon and for practical purposes. For example, if huge doses of saccharin cause cancer in mice but small doses do not cause cancer in human beings, then the generalization that "saccharin causes cancer" does not hold over important conditions.

JENKINS'S APPROACH TO GENERALIZABILITY OF RESEARCH

James Jenkins (1979) provided a useful way to think about issues of generality in research. Although Jenkins was concerned with memory research, the points he made apply to all types of research and can therefore be generalized to all areas of psychology. Jenkins pointed out that any single experiment or finding should be considered in the context of the factors that were held constant but that could have potentially been varied. That is, that every experiment occurs in the context of control variables or factors that were held constant in the research, but that could have been

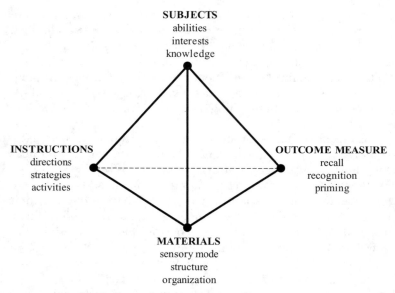

FIGURE 2.1. Jenkins' tetrahedral model of memory experiments. Adapted from J. J. Jenkins (1979).

manipulated. To what extent is the phenomenon of interest determined by the setting of the control variables? Posing the question a different way, when other variables are manipulated, will the experimental effect still generalize to these conditions? This is one way of thinking about the issue of conceptual replications.

Jenkins' basic idea of *contextualism* is represented in Figure 2.1, in what he called a tetrahedral model, where it can be seen that four sets of factors are considered. (The model gets its name from the fact that if all the vertices are connected, the resulting shape is a tetrahedron). One dimension is the type of *subjects* tested: children, white rats, college students, older adults, people with schizophrenia, and so on. If a finding is obtained with samples of one type, will it generalize to other groups? Only future experimentation can say for sure. Similarly, on a different dimension, if some memory phenomenon is obtained by using lists of words, will the results hold when the *materials* are switched to prose passages, to pictures, to poetry, to scientific texts? Another critical issue is the *instructions* given to subjects in an experiment. What strategies do people use and how do the instructions influence strategies? Might the results be affected if these were changed? Finally, there is the *outcome measure* itself, the dependent variable. Most any psychological construct can be measured in at least several different ways. Would the same results be obtained if a different dependent measure had been selected?

All these questions are good ones, and no firm answers can be given in the abstract. Rather, further research examining these factors must be conducted to see over what variables the findings will generalize. As we already noted, discovering boundary conditions for some experimental finding – discovering conditions under which the finding does not hold – is often critically important for understanding a phenomenon and developing an accurate theory about it. So in considering any particular experimental finding, one should keep in mind the control variables that were not studied in the experiment. Many may turn out not to be critical and the result will generalize across them; however, others may be critical and their manipulation will show limitations to the observed result. We will now consider how each of the four factors that Jenkins mentioned – subjects, materials, instructions, and outcome measures – affects false memories in the DRM converging associates paradigm as an example of how researchers have critically approached this topic.

Subjects

Different groups of subjects often vary considerably in their level of memory performance, and subject variables turn out to be particularly important in influencing false memories. Some subjects, like children and people with amnesia, typically show a smaller proportion of false memories than do the college students who were originally used in the DRM paradigm (see Brainerd & Reyna, 2005, chapter 5). Other subject groups, such as older adults and people with Alzheimer's disease, typically show more false memories compared with college students (e.g., Balota et al., 1999).

As mentioned earlier, the converging associates paradigm has been criticized as unnatural, and unlikely to generalize to the real world (Freyd & Gleaves, 1996), but of course this is an empirical question and one could argue the converse point, too (Roediger & McDermott, 1996). One approach to verifying that similar processes are important in the laboratory and the real world of memory distortion is to examine whether people who are susceptible to memory errors in the real world are also more susceptible to false memories in the laboratory. One particularly interesting group of people that fit the criteria of being susceptible to memory distortions is people who claim to have been abducted by aliens and to remember their experiences.

Clancy, McNally, Schacter, Lenzenweger, and Pitman (2002) examined whether alien abductees – people who believe they have been abducted by aliens – were more likely to falsely remember related lures in the DRM converging associates paradigm, as compared with people who did not claim to be abducted. The alien abductees and control subjects were recruited by using a newspaper advertisement, and were matched on age and education. Subjects were brought into the lab and participated in an experiment similar to that of Roediger and McDermott (1995). In the Clancy et al. study, subjects studied lists of 3, 6, 9, 12, or 15 associates, each of which was related to a lure that was not presented. Previous research had shown that false recall increases with increasing list length (Robinson & Roediger, 1997), so this new experiment represented a direct replication of that previous study. After each list, subjects completed math problems for 30 seconds and then tried to recall the words they had heard. Following study and recall of all lists, subjects took a recognition test for all the lists. Because the number of words in a list did not interact with the subject variable, the results will be presented as an overall average across all list lengths. The primary finding of interest was that alien abductees were more than twice as likely as control subjects to falsely recall related lures (.29 vs. .14, respectively). A similar result was found for false recognition, with abductees falsely claiming to recognize related lures more often (.67) than did control subjects (.42). Because there were no differences between the groups in terms of their memories for the actual studied words or for the other distracters on the recognition test, it appears that the alien abductees were more likely to have difficulty differentiating words that were studied from those that were only implicitly activated. Of course, as mentioned previously, when examining subject groups who differ on some important dimension like their likelihood of reporting false memories in the real world, we should be careful to examine what other ways these subjects differ as well. For example, the alien abductees were also more likely than controls to report feeling depressed and exhibiting other symptoms of mental illness, and these reports were positively related to the likelihood that they would exhibit false memories. Thus, it is unclear if depression causes increases in false memories, or whether it is actually a difference in the memory processes of alien abductees that causes this difference. Nonetheless, this study verifies that people who likely have experienced false memories in the real world are also more susceptible to false memories in the laboratory, which suggests that the memory processes involved in false memories in the laboratory are similar to those involved in false memories in the real world.

Outcome Measures

In discussing the Clancy et al. study on false memories in the previous section, we mentioned that the results were similar for both false recall and false recognition. This is an example of a result generalizing across another critical factor mentioned in Jenkins' contextual model of memory: the outcome measure or the dependent variable. Memory research, like other areas of experimentation, has different types of outcome measures that are sensitive to different types of manipulations. For example, one ubiquitous finding in memory research is that words that are used less frequently in the English language are identified better on recognition tests than words that are used more frequently but are not recalled better. These lower frequency items are likely better recognized because they are more distinct than higher frequency items, making them "stand out" on recognition tests. By contrast, on recall tests this type of distinctiveness is apparently not as beneficial to memory, so these lower frequency words are not better recalled. Thus, it is often the case that different memory tests need to be used to generalize results across a variety of measures. With respect to false memories, does the type of memory test matter?

For the most part, research indicates that both measures of recall and recognition show similar patterns of results in most false memory experiments; manipulation of an independent variable or subject variable usually affects false recall in the same manner as it affects false recognition (as in the study by Clancy et al., 2002). For example, false recall and false recognition both decrease after a delay. However, if people must think about the meaning of the words while studying lists rather than thinking about letter characteristics (e.g., number of vowels in the word), both measures of false memory (recall and recognition) increase (Thapar & McDermott, 2001). Also, repeating studied words several times decreases false recall and recognition (Kensinger & Schacter, 1999), as does having subjects generate the words from anagrams (McCabe & Smith, in press). Finally, aging and amnesia usually affect false recall and false recognition in similar ways (Kensinger & Schacter, 1999; Schacter, Verfaellie, & Pradere, 1996). Thus, although recall and recognition tests sometimes lead to different results depending on the nature of the independent variables manipulated in an experiment, this is not typically the case with false memories.

Materials

Jenkins also raised the issue of whether an effect would generalize across varying materials and methods of presentation. Would the DRM false memory effect generalize when different materials, modalities (visual vs. auditory), and organization were used to present the materials? The converging associates illusion has actually been found to be unusually robust, and generalizes across most conditions that have been studied, but the strength of the effect is influenced by the specific materials used and their organization. For example, in the original study (Roediger & McDermott, 1995), all the words associated with a particular related lure were studied together. Previous research using words from different categories shows that presenting words from the same category together enhances memory for those words relative to a condition in which words from several categories are mixed together. This is probably because the organization of the lists in a blocked format allows subjects to relate the words to one another, which provides effective retrieval cues on a memory test. Therefore, this "blocked" presentation of the studied words in the original Roediger and McDermott (1995) study likely supported good memory for the studied words, but did it affect false memories?

McDermott (1996) first showed that blocked presentation increased both correct and false recall relative to random presentation. We discuss a follow-up experiment by Mather, Henkel, and Johnson (1997) that conceptually replicated the Roediger and McDermott (1995) and McDermott studies with a subset of their lists and a recognition memory procedure. Their design was a bit complicated, so we restrict our discussion to the simplest condition. In one condition, 10 lists were used and the words associated to a particular nonstudied word were blocked together. The 10 lists were studied successively, and this was followed by a final recognition test. In the other condition, studied words associated with all 10 related lures were randomly mixed together on the study list. Mather et al. (1997) found, as expected, that the identification of studied words on the recognition test was better when the words were blocked (.84) than it was when they were randomly mixed together (.69). However, blocking the studied words also led to more false recognition (.86) than when the words were randomly intermixed (.66). Thus, the studies by McDermott (1996) and by Mather et al.(1997) show that the organization of materials can affect both false recall and false recognition in the same manner, and these effects parallel the effect on accurate recognition.

Interestingly, this outcome is not always obtained when other independent variables are manipulated. Some variables enhance accurate recall or recognition while reducing false recall and false recognition. For example, reductions in false memories are found when studied words are presented visually as opposed to auditorily, or when studied words are presented in distinctive fonts, or as anagrams (see McCabe, Presmanes, Robertson, & Smith, 2004 for a review). In each of these cases, making the studied words more distinctive appears to lead to reduced levels of false memories and increased levels of accurate retention.

Instructions and the Experimental Setting

Another critical issue in determining generality is, for lack of a better term, the general setting of the experiment – the instructions used, the particular experimenter, the room where it is conducted, the expectations the subjects are given, and the strategies they use. Some of these factors do turn out to be important in determining how often subjects will falsely remember related lures. In one example, different groups of subjects were trained to use one of two different encoding strategies while they were studying the words (McCabe et al., 2004). The question of interest was whether increasing the distinctiveness of the studied words would decrease the likelihood that people would falsely recognize related lures. In the item-specific rehearsal condition, which was intended to encourage distinctiveness, subjects were told to think about one unique characteristic of each studied word, some feature that made each word different from the other words in that list. The other group, the relational encoding group, was told to think about what the words had in common. The hypothesis was that the item-specific encoding group would be better able to distinguish the studied words from each other compared with the relational group, and would also be better able to distinguish the related lures from the studied words. The results were consistent with the hypothesis that making studied words more distinctive led to reductions in false recognition. Related lures were falsely endorsed only 64% of the time in the item-specific encoding group, but 84% of the time following relational encoding. This outcome was replicated in a within-subjects design, when half of the lists were studied under either encoding strategy, indicating that the results were not due to strategy differences between the two groups on the tests, but rather were the result of differences in memory for the studied words themselves. This outcome (and others like it) shows that false recall and false recognition in the DRM converging associates paradigm can be reduced (although not eliminated) by using different encoding strategies created by different instructional sets (McCabe & Smith, in press).

Summary of Jenkins' Contextual Approach

The examination of false memory research from the Jenkins perspective was revealing with respect to how these effects generalize. First, we can conclude that the converging associates memory illusion is quite robust, having never been eliminated across the different subjects, outcome measures, materials, or instructions we considered. Second, we found that false memories differed across subject groups, types of materials, and instructions, but they were relatively unchanged by the type of outcome measure used to assess memory performance. On the basis of the data reviewed we can conclude that false memories are difficult to eliminate, but they can be reduced when memory for the studied items is distinct and subjects are willing and able to discriminate what is real from what is not. The important point to note is that these conclusions can only be made after a careful examination of the contextual factors that can affect memory performance. The basic idea of the contextual approach is to take a phenomenon and try to greatly affect it by manipulating factors held constant in the original work. Only by doing this can researchers get a full picture of the phenomenon they are studying.

CRITICAL QUESTIONS TO ASK ABOUT EXPERIMENTS: A SUMMARY

We conclude the chapter with a set of critical questions that you should ask about experimental research. Keeping these issues in mind while reading experimental reports will aid your critical analysis of the experimental literature. Similarly, keeping these questions in mind while designing your own experiments should help you become a better researcher, too.

1. What hypothesis is the research testing? Is it clearly stated?
2. Does the experiment follow from the assumptions in the hypothesis? Can you think of more effective methods to use in testing the hypotheses?
3. What are the independent variables being manipulated? Does the manipulation seem to be an effective one? Will it permit a fair test of the hypothesis?
4. Are other variables confounded with the independent variable that is being manipulated?
5. What dependent measures are being examined? Do they actually measure the construct of interest? Can you think of other measures that should be used?
6. What variables are being controlled? Are there others that should be controlled?
7. Did the author use a within-subjects or between-subjects design? Why do you think this choice was made? Is it the right choice?
8. If the author used a within-subjects design, were practice effects controlled by appropriate counterbalancing? Did the author consider differential carryover effects?
9. If a between-subjects design was used, did the author use an appropriate procedure (randomization, matching) for ensuring that the subject groups did not differ?
10. How would you rate the probable internal validity of the experiment? Why?
11. What generality might the experiment have, what external validity? Do you think the same effects would be obtained with (a) different types of subjects; (b) different experimental settings; (c) different materials, examples, or procedures; and (d) different dependent measures?
12. Does the experiment make a contribution to knowledge?

References

Bacon, F. The new organon. (L. Jardine & M. Silverthorne, trans.). Cambridge: Cambridge University Press. (Original work published in 1620).
Balota, D. A., Cortese, M. J., Duchek, J. M., Adams, D. A., Roediger, H. L., McDermott, K. B., & Yerys, B. E. (1999). Veridical and false memories in healthy older adults and in dementia of the Alzheimers type. Cognitive Neuropsychology, 16, 361–384.
Banaji, M. R., & Crowder, R. G. (1989). The bankruptcy of everyday memory. American Psychologist, 44, 1185–1193.

Boring, E. G. (1929). *History of experimental psychology.* London: Century/Random House.

Brainerd, C. J. & Reyna, V. F. (2005). *The science of false memory.* Oxford: Oxford University Press.

Clancy, S. A., McNally, R. J., Schacter, D. L., Lenzenweger, M. F., & Pitman, R. K. (2002). Memory distortion in people reporting abduction by aliens. *Journal of Abnormal Psychology, 111,* 455–461.

Deese, J. (1959). On the prediction of occurrence of particular verbal instructions in immediate recall. *Journal of Experimental Psychology, 58,* 17–22.

Freyd, J. J., & Gleaves, D. H. (1996). "Remembering" words not presented in lists: Relevance to the current recovered/false memory controversy. *Journal of Experimental Psychology: Learning, Memory, and Cognition, 22,* 811–813.

Gates, A. I. (1917). Recitation as a factor in memorizing. *Archives of Psychology, 26,* 1–104.

Jenkins, J. J. (1979). Four points to remember: A tetrahedral model of memory experiments. In L. S. Cermak & F. I. M. Craik (Eds.), *Levels of processing in human memory* (pp. 429–446). Hillsdale, NJ: Erlbaum.

Kantowitz, B. H., Roediger, H. L., & Elmes, D. (2005). *Experimental psychology* (8th ed.). Belmont, CA: Wadsworth.

Kensinger E. A., & Schacter D. L. (1999). When true memories suppress false memories: Effects of aging. *Cognitive Neuropsychology, 16,* 399–415.

Mather, M., Henkel, L. A., & Johnson, M. K. (1997). Evaluating characteristics of false memories: Remember/know and memory characteristics questionnaire compared. *Memory & Cognition, 25,* 826–837.

McCabe, D. P., Presmanes, A. G., Robertson, C. L., & Smith, A. D. (2004). Item-specific processing reduces false memories. *Psychonomic Bulletin & Review, 11,* 1074–1079.

McCabe, D. P., & Smith, A. D. (in press). The distinctiveness heuristic in false recognition and false recall. *Memory.*

McDermott, K. B. (1996). The persistence of false memories in list recall. *Journal of Memory and Language, 35,* 212–230.

McDermott, K. B., & Watson, J. M. (2001). The rise and fall of false recall: The impact of presentation duration. *Journal of Memory and Language, 45,* 160–176.

Mook, D. G. (1983). In defense of external invalidity. *American Psychologist, 38,* 379–387.

Piaget, J. (1962). *Play, dreams and imitation in childhood.* New York Norton.

Robinson, K. J., & Roediger, H. L. (1997). Associative processes in false recall and false recognition. *Psychological Science, 8,* 231–237.

Roediger, H. L., Balota, D. A., & Watson, J. M. (2001). Spreading activation and the arousal of false memories. In H. L. Roediger, J. S. Nairne, I. Neath, & A. M. Surprenant (Eds.), *The nature of remembering: Essays in honor of Robert G. Crowder* (pp. 95–115). Washington, DC: American Psychological Association.

Roediger, H. L., & Gallo, D. A. (2002). Processes affecting accuracy and distortion in memory: An overview. In M. L. Eisen, G. S. Goodman, & J. A. Quas (Eds.), *Memory and suggestibility in the forensic interview* (pp. 3–28). Mahwah, NJ: Erlbaum.

Roediger, H. L., & Karpicke, J. D. (2006). Test-enhanced learning: Taking memory tests improves long-term retention. *Psychological Science, 17,* 249–255.

Roediger, H. L., & McDermott, K. (1995). Creating false memories: Remembering words not presented in lists. *Journal of Experimental Psychology: Learning, Memory, and Cognition, 21,* 803–814.

Roediger, H. L., & McDermott, K. B. (1996). False perceptions of false memories. *Journal of Experimental Psychology: Learning, Memory, and Cognition, 22,* 814–816.

Schacter, D. L., Verfaellie, M., & Pradere, D. (1996). The neuropsychology of memory illusions: False recall and recognition in amnesic patients. *Journal of Memory and Language, 35,* 319–334.

Thapar, A., & McDermott, K. B. (2001). False recall and false recognition induced by presentation of associated words: Effects of retention interval and level of processing. *Memory & Cognition, 29,* 424–432.

Tulving, E. (1967). The effects of presentation and recall of material in free-recall learning. *Journal of Verbal Learning and Verbal Behavior, 6,* 175–184.

Tulving, E. (1985). Memory and consciousness. *Canadian Psychology, 26,* 1–12.

Underwood, B. J. (1965). False recognition produced by implicit verbal responses. *Journal of Experimental Psychology, 70,* 122–129.

3

Critical Thinking in Quasi-Experimentation

William R. Shadish

All experiments are about discovering the effects of causes. In this sense, humans always have been experimenters, from early man seeing whether striking a stone against another stone would start a fire, to the modern cook trying out new ingredients in a recipe to see how it changes the taste. All experiments have in common the deliberate manipulation of an assumed cause (striking a stone, adding a new ingredient), followed by observation of the effects that follow (fire, taste). This common thread holds for all modern scientific experiments, including the randomized experiments discussed in the previous chapter, and the quasi-experiments described in the present chapter.

This chapter focuses on critical thinking about causation in quasi-experiments. The reason for this focus on causation is not that other kinds of critical thinking are unimportant in quasi-experiments. To the contrary, every bit of critical thinking that was described in the previous chapter for randomized experiments also has to be done in quasi-experiments, such as choosing good independent and dependent variables, identifying useful populations of participants and settings to study, ensuring that the assumptions of statistical tests are met, and thinking about ways in which the results might generalize. However, the quasi-experimenter also has one more task to do – the critical thinking that takes the place of random assignment.

All tasks in life are easier when you have the proper tools. This chapter describes some of the basic tools we use for the task of critical thinking about causation in quasi-experiments. Those tools teach us to recognize causes, effects, and causal relationships between causes and effects. The tools of causal inference consist of a few simple, abstract concepts that researchers must learn to apply to practical problems in quasi-experimentation.

AN EXAMPLE OF A QUASI-EXPERIMENT

In the late 1960s, when the Head Start program first enrolled disadvantaged children, the Westinghouse Learning Corporation, through Cicirelli and Associates (1969), began a study to see whether Head Start was effective. However, Head Start is an entitlement program, so that all children who applied and were eligible had to be enrolled. Assigning them randomly to a control group would deprive them of their legal right to receive Head Start. So Cicirelli and Associates did a quasi-experiment, that is, an experiment that does not use random assignment to conditions. They compared Head Start children with a matched set of control group children. In principle, the idea was a good one. After all, one of the main purposes of random assignment is to create a control group that is as much like the treatment group as possible. Matching tries to do the same thing, to create a control group that is the same as the treatment group, at least the same on the matching variables. So the researchers matched the Head Start children to other children who were not in Head Start but who were in the same grade in school, who were the same gender, and who had applied for Head Start but were not eligible.

The results of the study were surprising. At the end of the study, Head Start children scored lower than matched control children on educational achievement tests. What does this result mean? Does Head Start work? Does it hurt children? Did Cicirelli and Associates design a good quasi-experiment? Consider these questions from the perspective of the critical thinking tasks that are salient in quasi-experimentation.

CAUSATION

Most people intuitively recognize causal relationships in their daily lives. For instance, you may say that another automobile's hitting yours was a cause of the damage to your car; the number of hours you spent studying was a cause of your test grades; or the amount of food a friend eats is a cause of his weight. You may point to more complex causal relationships, noting that a low test grade was demoralizing, which reduced subsequent studying, which caused even lower grades. Here the same variable (low grade) can be both a cause and an effect, with a reciprocal relationship between two variables (low grades and studying) that cause each other.

Despite this intuitive familiarity with causal relationships, a precise definition to cause and effect has eluded philosophers for centuries. Indeed, the definitions of terms like *cause* and *effect* depend partly on each other and on the causal relationship in which both are embedded. As the 17th-century philosopher John Locke said, "That which produces any simple or complex idea, we denote by the general name *cause*, and that which is produced, *effect*" (1975, p. 324). He also said that "A *cause* is that which makes any other thing, either simple *idea*, substance, or mode, begin to be; and an *effect* is that, which had its beginning from some other thing" (p. 325). Since then, other philosophers and scientists have given us useful definitions of the three key ideas – cause, effect, and causal relationship – that are more specific and better illuminate how experiments work.

What is a Cause?

The canonical analysis of causation in philosophy is by Mackie (1974) in his book *The Cement of the Universe*. Consider the case of the cause of a forest fire. We know that fires start in different ways – a match tossed from a car, a lightning strike, or a smoldering campfire. None of these causes is, by itself, necessary because a forest fire can start even when, say, a match is not present. Also, none of them is sufficient to start the fire. After all, a match must stay hot long enough to start combustion; it must contact combustible material such as dry leaves; there must be oxygen for combustion to occur; and it also helps if it is not raining so that the leaves are dry and the match is not doused. So, the match is part of a constellation of conditions without which a fire will not result, although some of these conditions usually can be taken for granted, as with the availability of oxygen. A lighted match is, therefore, what Mackie (1974) called an *inus condition* – "an *insufficient* but *non-redundant* part of an *unnecessary* but *sufficient* condition" (p. 62; italics in original). It is insufficient because a match cannot start a fire without the other conditions. It is nonredundant if it adds something firepromoting that is uniquely different from what other factors in the constellation (e.g., oxygen, dry leaves) contribute to starting a fire; after all, it would be harder to say if the match caused the fire if someone else simultaneously tried starting it with a cigarette lighter. It is part of a sufficient condition to start a fire in combination with the full constellation of factors, but that condition is not necessary because other sets of conditions can also start fires.

A research example of an inus condition is a potential treatment for cancer. In the late 1990s, researchers at Folkman's laboratory in Boston reported that a new drug called endostatin shrank tumors by limiting their blood supply (Folkman, 1996). Other respected researchers could not replicate the effect even when using drugs shipped to them from Folkman's lab. Scientists eventually replicated the results after they had traveled to Folkman's lab to learn how to properly manufacture, transport, store, and handle the drug, and how to inject it in the right location at the right depth and angle. One observer labeled these contingencies the "in-our-hands" phenomenon, meaning "even we don't know which details are important, so it might take you some time to work it out" (Rowe, 1999, p. 732). Endostatin was an inus condition. It was an insufficient cause by itself. Its effectiveness required it to be embedded in a larger set of conditions that were not even fully understood by the original investigators.

Most causes are more accurately called inus conditions. Many factors are usually required for an effect to occur, but we rarely know all of them and how they relate to each other. This is one reason why most causal relationships are not deterministic, but only increase the probability that an effect will occur (Eells, 1991). It is also why a given causal relationship will occur under some conditions, but not universally across time, space, human populations, or other kinds of treatments and outcomes that are more or less related to those studied. To different degrees, all causal relationships are contextually dependent, so the generalization of experimental effects is always at issue.

Experimental causes have one other crucial feature – they are manipulable. In the intuitive understanding of experimenting that most people have, it makes sense to say, "Let's see what happens if we require welfare recipients to work"; however, it makes no sense to say, "Let's see what happens if I change this adult male into a 3-year-old girl." Experiments explore the effects of things that can be manipulated, such as the dose of a medicine, the amount of a welfare check, the kind of psychotherapy, or the number of children in a class. Nonmanipulable events (the explosion of a supernova) or attributes (people's ages, their raw genetic material, or their biological sex) cannot be causes in experiments because we cannot deliberately vary them to discover what happens.

This is not to say that *all* causes must be manipulable, only that *experimental* causes must be so. Many variables that we correctly think of as causes are not directly manipulable. Thus, it is well established that a genetic defect causes phenylketonuria (PKU), a metabolic disease that causes mental retardation unless treated during the first few weeks of life. However, that defect is not (yet) directly manipulable, so we cannot experiment to see if introducing the defect, or fixing it, would affect mental retardation.

In quasi-experiments, the cause is whatever was manipulated, which may include many more things than the researcher realizes were manipulated. Head Start is not just a set of educational and social interventions. In any given quasi-experiment, it is also the experience and background of the teachers, the characteristics of the building in which Head Start is given, and the socioeconomic status of the neighborhood where the building is located. Descriptions of these parts of the cause help readers know the full set of conditions that were manipulated as part of Head Start. In quasi-experiments, especially if the researcher is not the person manipulating the treatment, it is easy to make mistaken claims about what was manipulated, and the context in which it occurred.

What is an Effect?

We can better understand what an effect is through a counterfactual model that goes back to the 18th-century philosopher David Hume (Lewis, 1973, p. 556), and that has been popularized in the past few decades by statisticians

(Rubin, 1974; Holland, 1986). A counterfactual is something that is contrary to fact. In an experiment, we observe what *did happen* when people receive a treatment. The counterfactual is knowledge of what *would have happened* to those same people if they simultaneously had not received treatment. An effect is the difference between what did happen and what would have happened.

We can never observe the counterfactual. For example, in PKU an enzyme is absent that would otherwise prevent a buildup of phenylalanine, a substance toxic to the nervous system. When a restricted phenylalanine diet is begun early and maintained, retardation is prevented. In this example, the cause could be thought of as the underlying genetic defect, as the enzymatic disorder, or as the diet. Each implies a different counterfactual. For example, if we say that a restricted phenylalanine diet caused a decrease in PKU-based mental retardation in infants who are phenylketonuric at birth, the counterfactual is whatever would have happened had these same infants not received a restricted phenylalanine diet. The same logic applies to the genetic or enzymatic version of the cause. However, it is impossible for these very same infants *simultaneously* to both have and not have the diet, the genetic disorder, or the enzyme deficiency.

Experiments try to create reasonable approximations to this physically impossible counterfactual. For instance, if it were ethical, we might contrast phenylketonuric infants given the diet with other phenylketonuric infants not given the diet but who were similar to them in many ways. Or, we might (if it were ethical) contrast infants without the diet for the first 3 months of their lives to those same infants when they received the diet starting in the fourth month. Neither of these approximations is a true counterfactual. In the first case, the individual infants in the treatment condition are different from those in the comparison condition; in the second case, the identities are the same but time has passed and many changes other than the treatment have occurred to the infants (including permanent damage done by phenylalanine during the first 3 months of life).

So, two central tasks in experimental design are creating a high-quality but necessarily imperfect source of counterfactual inference, and then understanding how this source differs from the treatment condition. Sometimes we can use a within-subjects design, for example, in which each person is exposed to both the treatment and the control condition. The person's response under the control condition can sometimes be a good source of counterfactual inference for what would have happened had he or she not been exposed to treatment; however, it is still not perfect because order effects can occur as a result of fatigue, carryover, practice, or similar influences (Poulton, 1982). Some of these problems can be minimized with counterbalanced designs.

Random assignment forms a control group that is often the best approximation to this counterfactual that we can usually obtain, though even that control group is imperfect because the persons in the control group are not identical to those in the treatment group. However, we do know that participants in the treatment and control groups differ from each other only randomly. Centuries of work in probability theory provide researchers with very good practical and conceptual tools about how random events behave. Using those tools, we can make statements about the probability that those differences are likely to be due to chance. If the differences would only rarely occur because of chance, we say that the differences are an effect of the treatment.

The problem in quasi-experiments is that differences between treatment and control are usually systematic, not random, so nonrandom controls may not tell us much about what would have happened to the treatment group if they had not received treatment. Much of quasi-experimentation is concerned with creating good sources of counterfactual inference. In general, quasi-experiments use two different tools to do so. The first tool is observing the same unit over time, as in time series designs or single subject designs. In the Head Start example, the researchers could have measured the academic achievement of each child many times over many years before and many years after the child received Head Start. Then they could have used the pretests to estimate the counterfactual, to estimate what would have happened to the child if he or she had not received Head Start. What would the answer be if we compared all the pretests to all the posttests? Almost certainly it would show that children's achievement after Head Start was greater than before, which might tempt us to conclude that Head Start works. This conclusion has some obvious flaws, which we will describe more in later paragraphs. For example, children's academic achievement improves as a result of many things over time, including reading books, watching Sesame Street, and talking to friends, so we would expect posttests to show higher scores than pretests even if Head Start had no effect at all.

The second tool for estimating the counterfactual in quasi-experiments is to try to make nonrandom control groups as similar as possible to the participants in the treatment group. This is what Head Start did, using matching to make the control group similar to the treatment group on grade, gender, and the fact that the children applied to Head Start (thus trying to equate groups on motivation to achieve). However, matching equates groups only on the matching variables, which would not be a problem if we knew all variables on which Head Start children differ from control group children. Problematically, there are nearly always unknown and unmeasured systematic differences between control and treatment children in quasi-experiments, so nonrandom controls are not as good an estimate of the counterfactual as are random controls (where we know that the only differences between groups are random). Children who are not eligible for Head Start differ in many more ways from Head Start children than just their grade, gender, and motivation to achieve, and some of those differences could be the real cause of the posttest differences between treatment and control groups.

It is possible to improve both these sources of counterfactual inference. For example, sometimes time series statistics allow us to measure the rate of children's academic maturation before Head Start to predict where they would be after Head Start, and then we can compare that prediction to their actual posttest scores. If actual posttests exceed predicted posttests, Head Start might be effective. Sometimes we can make nonrandom controls more similar to treatment by using statistics such as propensity score analysis or selection bias modeling, or by using design features such as improved matching techniques. It is also possible to combine these two tools into one study that measures the same units many times before and after treatment and adds a nonrandom control group that is also measured at the same times. Part of the art of quasi-experimentation lies in a researcher's ability to make these improvements well.

Even then, effects from quasi-experiments are rarely as trustworthy as those from randomized experiments. Critical thinking about effects from quasi-experiments focuses on the quality of the source of counterfactual inference, on understanding how that source differs from the treatment group, and on whether those differences can be measured well so the effect can be adjusted for them.

Causal Relationship

How do we know if cause and effect are related? In a classic analysis formalized by the 19th-century philosopher John Stuart Mill, a causal relationship exists if (a) the cause preceded the effect, (b) the cause was related to the effect, and (c) we can find no plausible alternative explanation for the effect other than the cause. The second condition is easily met by using any valid statistical analysis that shows whether variation in the presumed cause is related to variation in the presumed effect, such as a correlation between treatment and outcome, or a *t* test. However, in many correlational studies it is impossible to know which of two variables came first. Imagine that you find a correlation between scores on test of positive mood and the number of jokes a person can remember. If you were interested in a causal relationship, you would have to know if mood came before or after the memory for jokes, which is nearly impossible in the typical correlational study in which both variables are assessed simultaneously. Even if you could tell which variable came first, Mill's third condition requires that you rule out third variables that could cause both positive mood and memory for jokes, such as whether the person's siblings told jokes frequently.

Quasi-experiments improve over correlational studies in two ways. First, quasi-experiments force cause to precede effect by first manipulating the presumed cause and then observing an outcome afterward. For example, if I ask a person to tell as many jokes as he or she can remember, and then measure the person's mood, I have forced one variable to occur before the other. Second, quasi-experiments allow the researcher to control some (but not all) of the third-variable alternative explanations. For example, I could control for sibling humor by studying singletons, that is, only children who do not have siblings. If I still found a relationship between mood and jokes, it could not be due to variation in sibling humor because sibling humor was held constant. In theory, correlational studies could also limit the study to singletons to obtain the same control, but in practice most correlational studies are simply observational and rarely use the degree of control found in most quasi-experiments. However, quasi-experiments can almost never control for all third variables because the researcher almost never knows what those third variables are.

Campbell's Threats to Valid Causal Inference

We have already seen that nonrandom controls are not a very good source of counterfactual inference because they usually are too different from the treatment group in systematic ways. We have also said a key problem is that we do not know all those differences, so we cannot measure them and then adjust for them. We would benefit, therefore, from having a conceptual tool to help us identify such differences. Campbell (1957) provided such a tool (see also Campbell & Stanley, 1963; Cook & Campbell, 1979; Shadish, Cook, & Campbell, 2002). He codified some of the most commonly encountered group differences into a more general system of threats to valid causal inference, that is, reasons why researchers might make a mistake when saying that a treatment like Head Start may have caused an outcome like lowered academic achievement. For each of these threats, the subsequent list provides the label, the definition, and an example from Head Start (the reader should decide whether each of these examples is plausible, a key point discussed shortly). In thinking about these examples, remember that the Cicirelli and Associates study found that Head Start children performed worse than control group children at the end of the study, so we are looking to see if there are other reasons that could explain that worse performance.

History: This refers to events occurring concurrently with treatment that could cause worse performance. An example might be that children in the Head Start condition were moved into different classrooms halfway through the year; or that a high-profile hate crime or a race riot occurred in the neighborhood where the Head Start center was located; or that a budget cut disproportionately affected the school district in which the Head Start program was located. Any of these could have hurt the performance of Head Start children.

Maturation: This refers to naturally occurring changes over time that could be confused with a treatment effect. For example, students whose parents do not read to them often develop vocabulary at a slower rate than other children. If this happened disproportionately to Head Start children, those children might mature at a slower rate than control group children in such academic skills, falling further behind even if Head Start had no effect at all.

Selection: This refers to systematic differences over conditions in respondent characteristics that could also cause the observed effect. Is it likely that the criteria used to select children for Head Start made them disadvantaged compared with control children on many other variables as well? For example, is it plausible that Head Start children came from homes that had more family stress in them than the homes of control group children, and so Head Start children performed worse because of that stress? Perhaps Head Start children are more poorly nourished, or live in higher crime neighborhoods, and this negative situation affects their performance.

Attrition: A loss of respondents to treatment or to measurement can produce artifactual effects if that loss is systematically correlated with conditions. Suppose, for example, that the most accomplished children were more likely to drop out of Head Start because their parents were able to get them placed in a magnet school or on a scholarship in a private school. If so, then the remaining Head Start children would perform less well than control children even if both groups started off the same.

Instrumentation: The nature of a measure may change over time or conditions in a way that could be confused with a treatment effect. For example, the researcher might have trained observers who rate the student's performance in the classroom both before and after treatment on such variables as time on task or number of questions asked of the teacher. If those raters change the standards they apply as a result of practice, or they become fatigued or bored, this could result in lower scores for children over time.

Testing: Exposure to a test can affect scores on subsequent exposures to that test, which could be confused with a treatment effect. For example, students who take a very difficult vocabulary test at pretest might become discouraged and give up on the next administration of the test, or if students were tested an unusually high amount for research purposes, they could become fatigued and do less well on subsequent tests.

Regression to the mean: When units are selected for their extreme scores, they will usually have less extreme scores on other variables, which can be confused with a treatment effect. For example, the person who scores highest on the first test in a class is not likely to score highest on the second test; and the person who is tallest is often not the heaviest person. This happens whenever two variables are not perfectly correlated with each other. In the case of Head Start, the highest scoring Head Start children were selected to be in the Head Start quasi-experiment. Naturally, their scores were not as high the second time they took the test, on average, making it look like they did worse over time.

This is a long list of threats. However, it is neither feasible nor desirable to rule out all *possible* alternative interpretations of a causal relationship. Instead, only *plausible* alternatives are of concern. This serves partly to keep matters tractable because the number of possible alternatives is endless, but it also recognizes that many alternatives have no serious empirical or experiential support and so do not warrant special attention. For example, it is possible that Head Start children had systematically different eye and hair color from control group children, but even if this were the case, it is not plausible that this would have anything to do with academic achievement. The list of possible threats to validity is nearly endless. Part of the critical thinking inherent in quasi-experimentation is to identify these alternative explanations, sort out the plausible from the merely possible, and then demonstrate with logic and data whether or not these alternative explanations occurred and could explain the effect.

However, plausibility judgments are inherently fallible. For example, the cause of stomach ulcers was long thought to be a combination of lifestyle (e.g., stress) and excess acid production. Few scientists seriously thought that ulcers were caused by a pathogen (e.g., virus, germ, bacteria) because it was assumed that an acid-filled stomach would destroy all living organisms – that is, pathogens were thought to be a possible but not a plausible explanation. However, in 1982, Australian researchers Barry Marshall and Robin Warren discovered spiral-shaped bacteria, later named *Helicobacter pylori* (*H. pylori*), in ulcer patients' stomachs. With this discovery, the previously possible but implausible became plausible. By 1994, a U.S. National Institutes of Health Consensus Development Conference concluded that *H. pylori* was the major cause of most peptic ulcers. So, labeling rival hypotheses as plausible depends not just on what is logically possible, but on social consensus, shared experience, and empirical data. Thus, the focus on plausibility is a two-edged sword: It reduces the range of alternatives to be considered in quasi-experimental work, yet it also leaves the resulting causal inference vulnerable to the discovery that an implausible-seeming alternative may later emerge as a likely causal agent. Further, Campbell's list is very general, but threats are often context specific, so that different substantive areas develop their own lore about the alternatives that are so important they need to be controlled, even developing their own methods for doing so. Sackett (1979), for example, developed a list of threats that are common in epidemiology. So each researcher needs to think specifically about threats that may apply particularly much, or not at all, in their own context.

CRITICAL THINKING IN QUASI-EXPERIMENTS MEANS SHOWING ALTERNATIVE EXPLANATIONS ARE UNLIKELY

Showing that alternative hypotheses are implausible is closely related to a logic popularized by Popper (1959). Prior to Popper, many philosophers emphasized the importance of using data to confirm hypotheses, to show that a hypothesis has support. Popper criticized this approach, giving the following example. If my hypothesis is that all swans are white, which I claim is confirmed because all the swans I have ever seen are white, my hypothesis may still be wrong because someday I may see a black swan. Even very large amounts of supporting data, therefore, cannot prove a hypothesis is true. By contrast, Popper noted, it is easy to prove a hypothesis is not true – observing a single black swan is sufficient. Popper urged scientists to try deliberately to falsify the conclusions they wish to draw rather than only seek information corroborating them. Conclusions that withstand falsification are treated as plausible until shown otherwise. Quasi-experimentation follows this same logic, requiring experimenters to identify a causal claim (Head Start hurts children), and then to generate and examine plausible alternative explanations that might falsify the claim (Head Start children did worse because of regression to the mean).

Unfortunately, falsification can never be as certain as Popper hoped because it depends on two assumptions that cannot be fully tested. The first is that the causal claim is clear, complete, and agreed upon in all its details. That is never the case. Many features of both the claim and the test of the claim are debatable – for example, which outcome is of interest, how it is measured, how much treatment must be given, who needs treatment, and all the other decisions that researchers make in testing causal relationships. As a result, when data suggest the hypothesis is wrong, theorists often respond by making a small adjustment to their causal theory while maintaining that the overall theory is still correct. Second, falsification requires observational procedures that perfectly reflect the theory that is being tested, but our observations are never that perfect. Rather, observations usually reflect only part of the question of interest, and they also reflect the experimenters' wishes, hopes, aspirations, and broadly shared cultural assumptions and understandings. If so, then our tests can never provide fully definitive results, whether of what seems to confirm a causal claim or of what seems to disconfirm it.

Nonetheless, a more cautious version of Popper's logic is possible. It argues that causal studies are useful even if we have to change the initial hypothesis repeatedly to accommodate our results and the criticisms of others. After all, those changes are usually minor in scope. It also argues that, even though perfect tests of our hypotheses are impossible, we can put more trust in those tests when they have been repeatedly made across different researchers using different procedures in different places and times. Indeed, observations that repeatedly occur despite different biases being built into them often warrant special trust. In summary, then, the critical thinking involved in quasi-experimentation is more than just seeing whether a single test suggests that a threat to validity can explain the results of a quasi-experiment. It involves a complex quasi-experiment with many tests, each having different biases, and a program of research that combines the results of many quasi-experiments done by different authors in different times and place with different biases.

How would this apply to Head Start? Earlier we said that a likely alternative explanation for why Head Start children had poor outcomes was regression to the mean. Campbell and Erlebacher (1970) showed how this could be caused by matching if the populations being matched do not overlap completely on the matching variable. Because Head Start children were more disadvantaged than control group children, the distribution of their pretest achievement test scores was lower than the distribution of test scores for the control group children. The researchers could only obtain matches from the parts of the two distributions that overlapped. So Head Start children were selected from the highest end of the distribution of Head Start children's test scores, and they were matched to control group children from the lower end of the distribution of control group children's test scores. At posttest, Head Start children performed worse than they first did because their scores regressed back to the overall Head Start distribution mean, and control group children performed better than they first did because their scores regressed up toward the overall control group mean, making it look like Head Start hurt the test scores of children. So the theory of how to test hypotheses about Head Start had to be modified to say that the test must use reliable measures so that differential treatment and control group regression to the mean would not occur as a result of measurement error. Magidson (1977, 2000) conducted such a respecified test on the same data, and the apparently harmful effects of Head Start went away, replaced by small but positive effects.

THE FALLIBLE PSYCHOLOGY OF QUASI-EXPERIMENTATION

In quasi-experimentation, ruling out plausible threats to validity in experiments depends on knowing the relevant threats. This knowledge depends on the quality of the relevant methodological and substantive theories available, and on the extent of background information available from experience with the topic on hand. It also depends on the existence of a widely accepted theory of plausibility, so that we know which of the many possible threats are plausible in this particular context. However, we mostly lack all this theory.

Without such a theory, most researchers rely on their own all-too-fallible judgment (Cordray, 1986; Mark, 1986; Rindskopf, 2000). Unfortunately, we humans are not always very good at this kind of critical thinking. Social and cognitive psychologists have documented the many cognitive biases and limitations to which all humans are susceptible (e.g., Faust, 1984; Tversky & Kahneman, 1974). Of particular relevance to falsificationism is confirmation bias, which is the tendency of people to notice and recall evidence in favor of their preferred hypotheses and theories more than they do evidence that undermines them. For example, imagine you are studying the effects of psychotherapy among clients who come to you for help because they are in distress. You measure their level of distress first, then give them psychotherapy, and finally measure their level of distress again – a simple quasi-experimental design. If your results show that their level of distress is lower after therapy than before it, you may be prone to take this as a confirmation of your hypothesis that psychotherapy works. After all, you may have devoted decades to gaining the education and credentials to be a psychotherapist, and surely that effort was not wasted on a therapy that did not work. You will be biased to see evidence that it does work. Yet it is well established in the psychotherapy literature that clients come to psychotherapy when they are most distressed, and that the particular combination of distressing events that caused them to come is unlikely to continue over time. So clients become less distressed over time even if psychotherapy has no effect at all – another example of regression to the mean (notice the clients self-selected into therapy when they were at the extreme of distress). If you did not know about this artifact ahead of time, would you have searched for it as a falsification, or simply taken the original result as a confirmation that psychotherapy works? Scientists, being human, are all too prone to take the confirmation, but the critical thinking demanded by quasi-experimentation demands that they do exactly the opposite, to design their research to falsify their preferred hypotheses, or to show that the falsification is not plausible.

Scientists may, by virtue of our training, have some advantage in overcoming such limitations. Today, for example, it is common to teach budding psychology researchers about the most common threats that can falsify their conclusions, and about how to design research that prevents such threats from interfering with causal inference. But scientists clearly still suffer from enough cognitive biases that it is in our interests to reduce the amount of critical thinking we have to do. One of the best features of the randomized experiment is that it does exactly this: In both the Head Start and psychotherapy examples, if participants had been randomly assigned to conditions, then any regression to the mean would have occurred equally in both treatment and control groups, making regression much less plausible as an explanation for the difference between treatment and control participants at posttest. More generally, with random assignment we know we have the best source of counterfactual inference, we know that cause preceded effect, and we know that most alternative explanations for an effect are not plausible (except for attrition, which we can measure). Random assignment is, ironically, a substitute for critical thinking about many of the issues discussed in this chapter, allowing us to apply our limited cognitive capacities to other scientific tasks.

CONCLUSION

Critical thinking in quasi-experimentation involves knowing what a cause is, what an effect is, what a causal relationship is, and then applying that knowledge to causal claims. If you know how to distinguish between a good source of counterfactual inference and a bad one, how to tell if a study shows whether cause preceded effect or not, and how to identify and even rule out plausible alternative explanations for the effect, you will have the tools it takes to think critically about quasi-experiments.

TEST QUESTIONS

1. What is a quasi-experiment? (Answer: An experiment that does not use random assignment.)
2. What is the counterfactual when we give a treatment to people and then observe their outcome? (Answer: Knowledge of what *would have happened* to those same people if they simultaneously had not received treatment.)
3. Experiments are about
   a. inventing new measurement instruments;
   b. confirming correlations that are predicted by theory;
   c. discovering the causes of effects; or
   d. discovering the effects of causes (CORRECT).
4. If something cannot be manipulated, then
   a. it cannot be a cause;
   b. it cannot be an experimental cause (CORRECT);
   c. it cannot be measured; or
   d. it cannot be studied.
5. Under the counterfactual model, how is an effect defined? (Answer: An effect is the difference between what *did happen* when people received a treatment and what *would have happened* to those same people if they simultaneously had not received treatment.)
6. What does the word *inus* stand for? (Answer: an *insufficient* but *non-redundant* part of an *unnecessary* but *sufficient* condition.)
7. In the Cicirelli and Associates (1969) Head Start quasi-experiment, how did the researchers create a source of counterfactual inference? (Answer: They matched Head Start children to other children who were in the same grade, had the same gender, and applied for Head Start but were not eligible.)
8. The outcome of the original Cicirelli and Associates (1969) Head Start quasi-experiment was as follows.
   a. Head Start children had higher achievement scores than did control children at the end of the study.
   b. There was no difference between Head Start children and control group children at the end of the study.
   c. Head Start children had lower achievement scores than did control children at the end of the study (CORRECT).
   d. The study was ended prematurely because of a lack of funds, so there was no outcome.

9. According to the philosopher John Stuart Mill, what are the three conditions that must hold in a causal relationship? (Answer: a, the cause precedes the effect; b, the cause is related to the effect; and c, we can find no plausible alternative explanation for the effect other than the cause.)

10. When people are selected to be in an experiment because they have extreme scores, their scores on any subsequent occasion are likely to be less extreme. This is the threat to validity called
    a. history;
    b. maturation;
    c. regression (CORRECT); or
    d. testing.

11. Campbell's method of ruling out threats to validity is an example of which more general logical method?
    a. confirmation;
    b. falsification (CORRECT);
    c. logical positivism; or
    d. existentialism.

12. Give one reason why random assignment to conditions can be a substitute for critical thinking about causation. (Answer: Random assignment creates a good source of counterfactual inference so that we do not have to think about all the ways in which the control group may differ from the treatment group. Answer: Random assignment makes most alternative explanations for the observed effect implausible.)

13. In the genetic disorder called PKU, what is the cause of mental retardation?
    a. a genetic defect;
    b. an enzyme is absent that would otherwise prevent a buildup of the neurotoxin phenylalanine;
    c. a failure to follow a diet low in phenylalanine; or
    d. all of the above (CORRECT).

14. Counterfactual models of causation go back to which philosopher?
    a. Donald Campbell
    b. David Hume (CORRECT);
    c. John Stuart Mill; or
    d. Aristotle.

15. Discuss the difference between possible and plausible alternative explanations. (Answer: This discussion can take many forms, but it should somehow refer to the fact that plausible explanations are a subset of possible ones that the researchers judge are likely to be the case.)

16. Define confirmation bias. (Answer: The tendency of people to notice and recall evidence in favor of their preferred hypotheses and theories more than evidence that undermines them.)

17. Random assignment to treatment and control groups
    a. prevents attrition from occurring;
    b. prevents regression to the mean from occurring;
    c. ensures that regression to the mean, if it occurs, happens equally in both groups (CORRECT); or
    d. does little to aid causal inference.
18. Describe one of the two methods that are used in quasi-experiments to create a source of counterfactual inference. (Answer: Either a, observing the same units over time with pretests used to estimate the counterfactual, or b, making nonrandom control groups as similar as possible to the participants in the treatment group through techniques like matching.)
19. Describe why matching is not a good substitute for random assignment. (Answer: Matching equates groups only on the matching variables, but random assignment equates groups on all possible variables.)
20. Describe how regression to the mean caused the negative effects in the Head Start experiment. (Answer: Because Head Start children were more disadvantaged than control group children, the distribution of their pretest achievement test scores was generally lower than the distribution of test scores for the control group children. The researchers could only obtain matches from the parts of the two distributions that overlapped. So Head Start children were selected from the highest end of the distribution of Head Start children's test scores, and they were matched to control group children from the lower end of the distribution of control group children's test scores. At posttest, Head Start children performed worse than they first did, and control group children performed better than they first did, making it look like Head Start hurt the test scores of children.)

References

Campbell, D. T. (1957). Factors relevant to the validity of experiments in social settings. *Psychological Bulletin, 54,* 297–312.
Campbell, D. T., & Erlebacher, A. E. (1970). How regression artifacts can mistakenly make compensatory education programs look harmful. In J. Hellmuth (Vol. Ed.), *The disadvantaged child: Vol. 3. Compensatory education: A national debate* (pp. 185–225). New York: Brunner/Mazel.
Campbell, D. T., & Stanley, J. C. (1963). *Experimental and quasi-experimental designs for research.* Chicago: Rand McNally.
Cicirelli, V. G., and Associates. (1969). *The impact of Head Start: An evaluation of the effects of Head Start on children's cognitive and affective development, vols. 1 and 2. A Report to the Office of Economic Opportunity.* Athens: Ohio University and Westinghouse Learning Corporation.

Cook, T. D., & Campbell, D. T. (1979). *Quasi-experimentation: Design and analysis issues for field settings*. Chicago: Rand McNally.

Cordray, D. W. (1986). Quasi-experimental analysis: A mixture of methods and judgment. In W. M. K. Trochim (Ed.), *Advances in quasi-experimental design and analysis* (pp. 9–27). San Francisco: Jossey-Bass.

Eells, E. (1991). *Probabilistic causality*. New York: Cambridge University Press.

Faust, D. (1984). *The limits of scientific reasoning*. Minneapolis: University of Minnesota Press.

Folkman, J. (1996). Fighting cancer by attacking its blood supply. *Scientific American, 275*, 150–154.

Holland, P. W. (1986). Statistics and causal inference. *Journal of the American Statistical Association, 81*, 945–970.

Lewis, D. (1973). Causation. *Journal of Philosophy, 70*, 556–567.

Locke, J. (1975). *An Essay Concerning Human Understanding*. Oxford, England: Clarendon Press.

Mackie, J. L. (1974). *The cement of the universe: A study of causation*. Oxford, England: Oxford University Press.

Magidson, J. (1977). Toward a causal model approach for adjusting for preexisting differences in the nonequivalent control group situation. *Evaluation Quarterly, 1*, 399–420.

Magidson, J. (2000). On models used to adjust for preexisting differences. In L. Bickman (Ed.), *Research design: Donald Campbell's legacy* (Vol. 2, pp. 181–194). Thousand Oaks, CA: Sage.

Mark, M. M. (1986). Validity typologies and the logic and practice of quasi-experimentaton. In W. M. K. Trochim (Ed.), *Advances in quasi-experimental design and analysis* (pp. 47–66). San Francisco: Jossey-Bass.

Popper, K. R. (1959). *The logic of scientific discovery*. New York: Basic Books.

Poulton, E. C. (1982). Influential companions: Effects of one strategy on another in the within-subjects designs of cognitive psychology. *Psychological Bulletin, 91*, 673–690.

Rindskopf, D. (2000). Plausible rival hypotheses in measurement, design, and scientific theory. In L. Bickman (Ed.), *Research design: Donald Campbell's legacy* (Vol. 1, pp. 1–12). Thousand Oaks, CA: Sage.

Rowe, P. M. (1999). What is all the hullabaloo about endostatin? *The Lancet, 353*, 732.

Rubin, D. B. (1974). Estimating causal effects of treatments in randomized and nonrandomized studies. *Journal of Educational Psychology, 66*, 688–701.

Sackett, D. L. (1979). Bias in analytic research. *Journal of Chronic Diseases, 32*, 51–63.

Shadish, W. R., Cook, T. D., & Campbell, D. T. (2002). *Experimental and quasi-experimental designs for generalized causal inference*. Boston: Houghton Mifflin.

Tversky, A., & Kahneman, D. (1974). Judgment under uncertainty: Heuristics and biases. *Science, 185*, 1124–1131.

4

Evaluating Surveys and Questionnaires

Norbert Schwarz

Much of what we know about human behavior is based on self-reports. When we want to learn about individuals' health behaviors, consumer habits, family problems, media consumption, values, or political beliefs, we ask appropriate questions. The answers provided to these questions serve as input into scientific analyses and provide the basis of statistical indicators used to describe the state of a society. Obviously, these data are only as meaningful as the questions we ask and the answers we receive. Moreover, whom we ask is of crucial importance to our ability to draw conclusions that extend beyond the particular people who answered our questions. Accordingly, the processes underlying question answering and the appropriate selection of respondents are of great importance to many areas of social research.

This chapter provides an introduction to these issues for consumers of published survey results. The first part introduces the concept of a survey, describes elements of survey design, and addresses *who* to ask. The second part addresses *how* to ask. It reviews key components of the question-answering process that apply to all self-reports, whether collected in a survey or in the psychological laboratory. Other elements of survey research, like interviewer behavior and training or the questionnaire pretesting, will only be touched upon in passing. Most reports of survey results provide little information about these components, rendering it impossible for readers to assess their quality.

ELEMENTS OF SURVEY DESIGN

The term *survey* refers to systematic data collection about a sample drawn from a specified larger population. If data are obtained from every member of the population, the study is called a *census*. The best known form of a survey is the opinion poll, in which information is gathered from a sample of individuals by asking questions. However, surveys may also be conducted of organizations or events (e.g., court sentences) and they do not necessarily imply question asking. This chapter, however, deals exclusively with surveys of individuals.

Like any other study, a survey must begin with a statement of its objectives: What does one want to study? The objectives determine the population of interest, from which the sample is to be drawn; the design of the survey (e.g., are respondents to be interviewed repeatedly or only once?); and the questions to be asked. The questions may be asked in face-to-face or telephone interviews, or by means of a self-administered questionnaire, which may be mailed to respondents or administered on the Web. Following data collection, the answers must be coded for data analysis. Data analysis, interpretation of the results, and dissemination of the findings complete the research process. Next, we consider some of the key elements in more detail (for more extended treatments see Bradburn & Sudman, 1988; Schwarz, Groves, & Schuman, 1998; Visser, Krosnick, & Lavrakas, 2000).

Survey Designs

Most surveys collect data from a sample at a single point in time. These *cross-sectional surveys* allow researchers to estimate the prevalence of an opinion or behavior in the population and to estimate differences between subgroups of the population, provided that the sample is representative. In addition, cross-sectional surveys provide information about associations between variables, although the causal nature of these associations is difficult to assess. When representative cross-sectional surveys are *repeated* with different respondents from the same population, researchers can examine changes in the attitudes and behaviors of the population over time. The resulting time series allow for causal conclusions by examining the covariation of variables over time. A better way to assess causality is provided by *panel surveys*, in which the same respondents are interviewed several times. These surveys allow researchers to assess the covariation of variables over time at the individual level and to trace changes to particular elements of the sample, thus providing more insight into the underlying processes. Unfortunately, panel surveys are particularly expensive because the respondents have to be tracked so they can be recontacted. Moreover, panel surveys are plagued by sample attrition as many of the initial respondents may drop out in later waves. Finally, *experimental surveys* include experimental variations embedded in a (usually cross-sectional) survey. For example, a researcher may assess the influence of racial prejudice on attitudes toward welfare by asking respondents about a welfare case in which the described person is either African American or European American (e.g., Sniderman & Tetlock, 1986). Experimental surveys combine the power of experiments with the ability to address differences in the population, which provides a major advantage over experiments with college students for some research topics.

Who to Ask: Populations and Samples

The research objectives determine the population from whom data are to
be collected. This may be the adult population of a country (as is the case
for national opinion polls), the members of an organization, or patients
suffering from a particular illness. In most cases, it will not be possible to
collect data from all members of the population and a sample will be drawn
instead. To allow valid inferences from the sample to the larger population,
the sample has to be *representative* of that population. At a basic level, we can
distinguish probability and nonprobability samples.

Probability Samples

A *probability sample* requires that each member of the population has a speci-
fiable likelihood of being included in the sample. Its most basic form is
simple random sampling, which requires a complete list of all members of the
population from which the sample can be drawn with the help of a random
number table. This list is often referred to as the sampling frame. If the
list is incomplete, it results in *coverage error*, that is, discrepancies between
the population and the sampling frame used. Simple random sampling
is feasible for some populations (like the members of an organization),
but not for surveys of a whole nation. Instead, nationally representative
surveys are usually based on cluster sampling when personal interviews
are intended or on random digit dialing when telephone interviews are
intended.

    Cluster sampling often begins by the drawing of a random sample of coun-
ties, followed by a random sample of census tracks within these counties, and
blocks within these census tracks. Next, the households within these blocks
are enumerated and a random sample of these households is drawn. Once
the interviewer contacts the household, a further randomization scheme
determines which household member is interviewed. In practice, many face-
to-face surveys of the adult population of the United States are based on
clusters of about 80 households within randomly selected neighborhoods.
This reduces the cost of data collection and the likelihood of coverage error,
except for people who are homeless, institutionalized, or otherwise not living in a household. But cluster sampling comes at the expense of more
complicated analyses, which need to take the clustered nature of the sample into account.

    Today, however, most nationally representative surveys are conducted by
telephone, which is more cost efficient. For this purpose, a sample could be
drawn from telephone directories. Unfortunately, unlisted numbers result in
incomplete directories and the population's high mobility renders the directories often outdated within a short time after their publication. *Random
digit dialing* avoids these problems. Researchers randomly select area codes
and exchanges (the first three numbers of the seven-digit phone number),

and a random number generator supplies the missing four numbers. Properly applied, this results in a representative sample of the roughly 95% of American households with working telephones. Obviously, the 5% of households without working telephones are missed, and how much this coverage error is a matter of concern depends on the issue under study. Residents in households without working phones tend to be poorer, less educated, and younger, and are more often racial minorities (e.g., Thornberry & Messey, 1988).

Nonresponse

No matter how well a sample is drawn, its representativeness can be compromised by low *response rates*. Those who cannot be reached, or who refuse to participate when reached, may differ in unknown ways from those who willingly participate. Accordingly, survey researchers attempt to maximize the response rate through repeated calls when respondents cannot be reached and through particularly persuasive interviewers or the offer of incentives when respondents refuse to participate. For example, Traugott (1987) observed in a telephone interview survey that 39% of the sample could be successfully interviewed on the first or second call, and that this proportion increased to 57% after 3 calls, 68% after 4 calls, 92% after 10 calls, and 96% after 15 calls. In Traugott's study, for example, individuals aged 30 years or younger were underrepresented after the first call, reflecting that they were more difficult to reach at home. Hence, the proportion of young respondents increased from 23% after the first call to 30% after 15 calls. When surveys are conducted very quickly, for example, to capture the nation's response to breaking news in time for tomorrow's newspaper, numerous callbacks are not feasible, which results in low response rates that can compromise representativeness.

In most countries, response rates have been continuously declining over the past few decades (Steeh, 1981), and the response rates obtained in most high quality academic surveys hover around 70% for face-to-face surveys and 60% for telephone surveys. For cost reasons, the response rates are usually considerably lower (often around 20 to 30%) in commercial market research. Unfortunately, the media often fail to include response rates when they report on surveys. Investigating the determinants of respondents' decision to (not) participate in a survey provides a challenging agenda for psychological research (see Groves, Cialdini, & Couper, 1992).

Nonprobability Sampling

The high cost of probability sampling and the problem of low response rates are avoided by *nonprobability sampling*, which renders it attractive to many market research companies – with negative implications for the study's representativeness. In the worst case, researchers interview whoever is readily available. Such *convenience samples*, be they college students who voluntarily sign up for a study, readers who respond to a questionnaire printed in a magazine, or Web users who follow a link posted at an Internet discussion board, do not allow inferences to any population because their representativeness is unknown. For example, readers who decide to complete and mail a questionnaire printed in a magazine are likely to do so because they find the topic particularly important – and those who don't find it important may never bother. Hence, such studies only tell us about the people who, for whatever reason, volunteered their opinions. But they are useless if we are interested in learning about some specified population, even the population of all readers of the particular magazine. Convenience samples are very useful, however, in experimental research designed to explore the impact of some experimental treatment, as we shall see.

A somewhat more meaningful way of nonprobability sampling is *quota sampling*. In this case, a sample is selected on the basis of a set of characteristics in the population. For example, if the population of interest contains 40% married people, 18% Black, and 35% over the age of 45, one can select a sample that will conform to these characteristics. To accomplish this, interviewers are not given a specified list of respondents or addresses but are provided with the quota criteria and are free to select any respondent who fits these criteria. Although quota sampling results in a better cross section of the population than can be provided by a convenience sample, it still does not allow strong conclusions about the population because the probability with which a member of the population is selected remains unknown. This precludes the calculation of sampling error, which is addressed in the next section.

How Many?

Media reports of surveys usually include a reference to the survey's *margin of error* or *sampling error*, often in form of the comforting assurance that the reported values have a margin of error of plus or minus 3 percentage points. Unfortunately, the sampling error is only one component of a survey's *total error*. We have already encountered coverage error (discrepancies between the population and the list of population members used for sampling, i.e., the sampling frame) and *nonresponse error* (resulting from those who can't be reached or refuse to participate). In the second part of this chapter, we will encounter *measurement error*, that is, distortions that arise in the question-answering process. Measurement error is often the largest, and most difficult to assess, component of total survey error.

None of these sources of error is considered in the calculation of sampling error. Technically, this term refers to the discrepancies between the results obtained from a particular sample and the true population values that can be attributed to random differences between the sample and the sampling frame. Put more simply, people differ and randomly drawing different people from the same sampling frame would result in somewhat different results – how different can be calculated when the probability of selection is known, which is only the case for probability samples.

Suppose that a survey based on simple random sampling indicates that 70% of the sample would vote for Candidate A. With a sample size of $N = 500$ and a desired confidence interval of 95%, sampling error would be around 4%. Hence, one may conclude that between 66% and 74% of the population would vote for Candidate A. Sampling error decreases with increasing sample size, but the decrease is nonlinear. For the example given here, sampling error declines from 9% for a sample of 100 to 4% for a sample of 500. However, doubling the sample size from 500 to 1,000 further decreases sampling error only modestly to 3%, and to reduce sampling error to 1% we would need a sample of approximately 10,500. For most national surveys, researchers aim for a sampling error of 3%, requiring a sample of approximately 1,000 respondents.

Because sampling error depends on sample size, the sampling error for any subgroup – such as the residents of a particular state, African Americans, or 18- to 20-year-olds – is much larger than the sampling error for the sample as a whole. Hence, it is misleading to apply the margin of error of a national survey to the results reported for a particular state (or any other subgroup). If it is important to obtain accurate estimates for specified subgroups, we need to increase their representation through *oversampling*. Accordingly, surveys with an interest in a particular social category often include a larger number of category members than is warranted by their percentage in the population. Results from these overrepresented groups are then adjusted through weighting procedures when statistics for the general population are estimated.

The most counterintuitive aspect of survey sampling is certainly that the results from a probability sample of $N = 500$ are more informative than the results of a convenience sample with a seemingly impressive $N = 50,000$. Such high total numbers in a sample can be obtained when questionnaires are printed in magazines or when Web sites offer a button to allow readers to express their opinion. The readers of the magazine and users of the Web site are likely to differ from the population in the first place. It would not be surprising to observe, for example, that over 90% of the readers of a gun magazine oppose gun regulation, whereas a majority of the population may support it. Moreover, those readers who responded probably found the topic more important than those who did not respond, and their answers may not even be representative of the majority of readers. Finally, in the absence of random sampling, sampling error cannot be calculated, further undermining population estimates. Accordingly, the reader surveys printed in magazines, or Web surveys offered at news sites, have mostly entertainment value.

Surveys and Experiments: What Can We Learn From Each?

The major strength of a representative survey is that it allows us to draw conclusions from a sample to a specified population. For example, we may infer, within the margins of sampling error, which percentage of the population is likely to vote for a given candidate. Accordingly, surveys provide an excellent source of descriptive data. Their major weakness, on the other hand, is that the resulting data are purely correlational, thus limiting our ability to draw causal inferences (unless the survey follows a panel design). We may observe, for example, that individuals who are concerned about inflation are less likely to vote for the candidate – but we can't tell if this reflects a causal impact of their concern about inflation or a causal impact of some other variable that covaries with inflation concerns. We may control for the possible influence of such third variables with appropriate statistical techniques (see Weisberg, Krosnick, & Bowen, 1989, for an introduction to survey analysis), but this requires that we know which variables may be relevant and that we have assessed these variables in our study.

In contrast, the major strength of experiments is that they allow causal inferences (see Chapter 8, this volume). By randomly assigning participants to different conditions of an experiment, the experimenter can ensure that variables other than the ones manipulated in the experiment cannot exert a systematic influence. If we wanted to know, for example, if inflation concerns influence voting intentions, we could assign participants to conditions that do or do not raise these concerns and could subsequently assess their voting intentions. The major weakness of most experiments, however, is that they are usually conducted with a small number of volunteers, comprising a convenience sample of unknown representativeness. Hence, they do not allow us to draw inferences to any specified population. Moreover, the usually homogeneous nature of the volunteers (often college sophomores enrolled in psychology classes) renders it impossible to assess if the influence of the experimental manipulation varies with participants' background characteristics (like age, social class, or political orientation).

These shortcomings of experiments can sometimes be overcome if we include experiments in representative surveys. Let's return to the earlier inflation example; researchers could randomly assign half of a representative sample to a condition in which questions designed to raise concerns about inflation precede questions about voting intention. A comparison with a condition in which the inflation questions follow the voting intention question would bear on the causal influence of inflation concerns, and the representative sample would allow for more detailed analyses bearing on how this causal influence is moderated by background characteristics.

Summary

In sum, good surveys are based on representative probability samples, and how the sample was drawn is more important than the number of respondents per se. Probability samples allow the calculation of sampling error, which is needed for computing population estimates. For many purposes, a sample of 500 is fine, although most national surveys are based on samples of approximately 1,000, resulting in a sampling error of about plus or minus 3%. But keep in mind that this sampling error only pertains to the sample as a whole; analyses of subgroups are based on a smaller number of respondents and are hence associated with considerably larger sampling error. Finally, sampling error is only one component of total survey error. The other components are coverage error (were parts of the population missed by the sampling frame used?) and nonresponse error (did many of those sampled not participate in the survey?). Nonresponse error is particularly likely when the field time of the survey is very short (as is the case for many news surveys), thus precluding numerous callbacks when respondents cannot be reached. Good survey reports include information about the response rate. The final component of survey error is measurement error, which refers to distortions introduced by the question-answering process, addressed next.

HOW TO ASK: COGNITIVE AND COMMUNICATIVE PROCESSES

Historically, survey researchers assumed that people know what they do and believe and can hence report on their behaviors and opinions with "candor and accuracy" (Campbell, 1981). This gave rise to extensive research into the interviewing process to identify the conditions that allow for candid answers and to develop rules for appropriate interviewer behavior. Subsequent research showed, however, that characteristics of respondents' tasks – like the wording of a question or the order in which response alternatives are presented – exert much more influence on respondents' answers than do variations in interviewer behavior (for a short history see Sudman, Bradburn, & Schwarz, 1996, chapter 1). In response to these findings, survey researchers turned to psychological theories of language comprehension, memory, and judgment to understand the processes underlying the question-answering process. This gave rise to a burgeoning interdisciplinary field that investigates the cognitive and communicative underpinnings of survey research (for reviews see Sirken et al., 1999; Sudman et al., 1996; Tourangeau, Rips, & Rasinski, 2000). Its key findings are consistent with psychological research that emphasizes the constructive nature of human judgment and memory. We often form our opinions on the spot, when needed, and we often don't know what we did in the past and need to "reconstruct" what we might have done. The underlying cognitive processes are highly context dependent and profoundly influenced by the nature of the question asked. For example, consider the following:

- When asked what they consider "the most important thing for children to prepare them for life," 61.5% of a representative sample chose the alternative "To think for themselves" when it was offered on a list. Yet, only 4.6% volunteered an answer that could be assigned to this category when no list was presented (Schuman & Presser, 1981).
- When asked how successful they have been in life, 34% of a representative sample reported high success when the numeric values of the rating scale ran from −5 to +5, whereas only 13% did so when the numeric values ran from 0 to 10 (Schwarz, Knäuper, Hippler, Noelle-Neumann, & Clark, 1991).
- Whether we conclude that marital satisfaction is a major or a minor contributor to general life satisfaction depends on the order in which both questions are asked, with correlations ranging from $r = .18$ to $r = .67$ as a function of question order and introduction (Schwarz, Strack, & Mai, 1991).
- When asked how often they experience a variety of physical symptoms, 62% of a sample of patients reported symptom frequencies of twice a month or more when the response scale ranged from "twice a month or less" to "several times a day." Yet, only 39% reported frequencies of more than twice a month when the scale ranged from "never" to "more than twice a month" (Schwarz & Scheuring, 1992).

Quite obviously, respondents' answers are strongly influenced by how we ask the question. Survey researchers refer to such influences as *context effects* or *response effects*. In scientific surveys, researchers try to guard against such effects through extensive pretesting. However, not everything presented as a "survey" serves the purpose of collecting information. Political parties and interest groups, for example, conduct "push polls" that are designed to lead respondents to a desired conclusion (like voting for a particular party). Similarly, companies may design questionnaires for shoppers with the intention to advance their products. Such endeavors often make deliberate use of questions that are likely to lead respondents to the "right" answer.

To understand how questions shape respondents' answers, we need to consider respondents' tasks. These tasks apply to question answering in surveys as well as in any other research situation, including the psychological laboratory.

Respondents' Tasks

As a first step, respondents need to interpret the question to understand what information is asked for. Next, they need to retrieve this information from memory. If the question is an opinion question, respondents may sometimes be able to retrieve a previously formed opinion. In most cases, however, a previously formed opinion may not be accessible or may not match the specific aspects addressed in the question. Hence, respondents' third task is to form a judgment based on the information they have available at the time. If the question is a behavioral question, they need to recall or reconstruct relevant instances of this behavior from memory. If this proves difficult, or if respondents are not sufficiently motivated to engage in the effort, they may rely on their general knowledge or other salient information that may bear on their task to compute an estimate. Once a "private" judgment is formed in respondents' minds, they have to communicate it to the researcher. In most studies, they cannot do so in their own words but need to format their judgment to fit the response alternatives provided as part of the question. Depending on the behavior or opinion under study, respondents may be concerned that their answer is socially undesirable. If so, they may "edit" their answer before they communicate it to avoid a negative self-presentation.

Accordingly, *understanding* the question, *retrieving* relevant information, *forming* a judgment, *formatting* the judgment to fit the response alternatives, and *editing* the answer are the main components of a process that starts with participants' exposure to a question and ends with their overt report (for a more detailed discussion see Sudman et al., 1996, chapter 3).

Question Comprehension

Not surprisingly, survey textbooks urge researchers to write questions that are easy to understand. This includes the use of simple grammar and familiar, unambiguous terms. Bradburn, Sudman, and Wansink (2004) provide much useful advice in this regard. Even familiar terms, however, vary in interpretation. For example, Belson (1981) asked respondents if they had "read" a certain magazine and observed that their interpretation of "reading" spanned the whole range from having seen the magazine at a newsstand to having read it cover to cover.

Moreover, understanding the words, that is, the *literal meaning* of a question, is often not enough to provide a meaningful answer. When asked "What have you done today?," all participants will understand the words, but they still need to decide what the researcher is interested in. Should they report, for example, that they took a shower, or not? This decision requires inferences about the *pragmatic meaning* of the question: What does the researcher want to know? To infer the question's pragmatic meaning, respondents draw on contextual information, including the content of adjacent questions and the nature of the response alternatives (Clark & Schober, 1992; Schwarz, 1996).

Question Context

In general, respondents assume that adjacent questions are meaningfully related to one another, unless otherwise indicated. Hence, a term like *drugs* acquires different meanings when it follows questions about respondents' medical history rather than questions about crime in the neighborhood. Similarly, German students inferred that a question about an ambiguous "educational contribution" referred to fellowships that students receive when it was preceded by fellowship questions, but to tuition they have to pay when it was preceded by tuition questions (Strack, Schwarz, & Wänke, 1991). It is therefore important to know in which context a given question was asked. Unfortunately, few reports include this information.

Response Alternatives

Most questions are presented with a fixed set of response alternatives, which facilitates administration and data analysis. Far from being "neutral" measurement devices, however, response alternatives influence question interpretation (Schwarz & Hippler, 1991). First, consider the differences between *open* and *closed* response formats. When asked in an open response format "What have you done today?," respondents are likely to omit activities that the researcher is obviously aware of (e.g., "I gave a survey interview") or may take for granted anyway (e.g., "I took a shower"). But if these activities were included in a closed list of response alternatives, most respondents would endorse them. At the same time, such a list would reduce reports of activities that are not represented on the list, even if an "other" option were provided, which respondents rarely use. Both of these question form effects reflect that response alternatives can clarify the intended meaning of a question by specifying what the researcher is interested in. When a closed response format is used, it is therefore very important to ensure that the list of response alternatives covers the full range of behaviors or opinions.

As another example, suppose respondents are asked how successful they have been in life along an 11-point rating scale, ranging from "not at all successful" to "extremely successful." Does "not at all successful" refer to the absence of outstanding success or to the presence of failure? Respondents can resolve such ambiguities by attending to contextual information, including the *numeric values* of the rating scale. When these values range from 0 (not at all successful) to 10 (extremely successful), the respondents infer that "not at all successful" refers to the absence of success; yet when the values range from −5 (not at all successful) to +5 (extremely successful), they infer that "not at all successful" refers to the opposite of success, namely failure. Hence, endorsing a value in the lower range of the 0 to 10 scale amounts to saying "I'm doing OK, but don't have any outstanding successes to report," whereas endorsing a similar value on the −5 to +5 scale amounts to saying, "I really failed." Accordingly, 34% chose a value below the midpoint of the 0 to 10 scale, whereas only 13% did so on the

−5 to +5 scale (Schwarz, Knäuper, et al., 1991). In general, rating scales with positive numeric values suggest that the researcher has a unipolar dimension in mind (pertaining to the presence of a single attribute, e.g., success), whereas a combination of negative and positive numeric values suggests that the researcher has a bipolar dimension in mind (pertaining to the presence of a given attribute or its opposite, e.g., success vs. failure).

In sum, apparently formal differences in the response alternatives can profoundly influence respondents' interpretation of the question. Far from reflecting superficial responding, such effects indicate that respondents do their best to make sense of the question asked by drawing on the full range of information available to them – including information the researcher never intended to provide. To safeguard against unintended interpretations, researchers have developed pretesting procedures that can identify these problems at the question development stage (for a review see Sudman et al., 1996, chapter 2). Respondents' other tasks are best discussed in the context of opinion and behavior questions, to which we turn next. Before you read on, however, you may want to use the material already given to design questions that would increase or decrease support for a policy issue of your choice.

Opinion Questions: The Emergence of Context Effects

The key goal of opinion polls is to learn about the distribution of opinions in a population by collecting reports from a representative sample. Unfortunately, respondents answer the researchers' questions in a context to which the population is never exposed, namely, the context of the research instrument. If the wording of the question, or the content of preceding questions, draws respondents' attention to aspects they would otherwise not consider, the obtained answers do not reflect what the population thinks. As we discussed earlier, these influences are referred to as context effects and they are a major threat to the validity of population inferences.

Question Wording and Issue Framing

How a question is worded can profoundly affect the obtained answers. Whereas blatantly biased questions with loaded wordings are easy to detect and avoid, other wording issues pose tricky judgment calls. For example, one survey (Herbers, 1982) asked respondents, "Suppose the budgets of your state and local governments have to be curtailed, which of these parts would you limit most severely?" When "public welfare programs" was offered as one of the choices, 39% of the respondents opted for cutting welfare; but when the term "aid to the needy" was used instead, only 8% opted for cuts. These discrepancies reflect that the two terms bring different associations to mind (Smith, 1987), which enter into respondents' judgments. On the substantive side, they show that public opinion about welfare (and any other issue) depends on how the issue is *framed*. On the methodological side, framing effects pose the problem that we cannot tell which version of a question captures the prevalent opinion without knowing in which terms the population spontaneously thinks about the issue. It is therefore important to scrutinize survey questions for their implied issue framing – and wise to use multiple question versions whenever more than one frame is common in public discourse. To become sensitive to this problem, you may want to design a few questions that frame a policy issue in ways that increase or decrease its likely support.

Question Order Effects

Many psychological experiments show that people are unlikely to retrieve all information that may potentially bear on a judgment. Instead, they truncate the search process as soon as enough information has come to mind to form a judgment with sufficient subjective certainty (see Bodenhausen & Wyer, 1987, for a review). Accordingly, their judgments are based on the information that is most accessible in memory at that point in time, e.g. because it has just been brought to mind by a preceding question. For example, Schwarz, Strack, and Mai (1991) asked respondents to report their marital satisfaction and their general life satisfaction. When the general life-satisfaction question preceded the marital-satisfaction question, the answers correlated $r = .32$, but when the marital satisfaction question was asked first, this correlation increased to $r = .67$. This reflects that respondents can draw on a wide range of information to evaluate their lives and are more likely to consider their marriage when it has just been brought to mind by the preceding question. Accordingly, happily married respondents reported higher, and unhappily married respondents lower, mean life satisfaction in the marriage–life order than in the life–marriage order. The observed increase in correlation was attenuated to $r = .43$ when questions about three different life domains (job, leisure time, and marriage) preceded the general question. These questions brought a more diverse range of relevant information to mind, thus limiting the impact of marriage-related information.

Complicating things further, a survey interview is not only a cognitive event but also a communicative event to which respondents bring the rules that govern the conduct of conversation in daily life (Clark & Schober, 1992; Schwarz, 1996). One of these rules holds that speakers should provide new information, instead of reiterating information that the recipient already has. Hence, respondents may disregard information that they have already provided when they perceive related questions as potentially redundant. Whether they see questions as closely related depends, in part, on how the questions are presented. In one condition of the aforementioned study, the marital-satisfaction and life-satisfaction questions were introduced with a joint lead-in, which read, "We now have two questions about your life. The first pertains to your marriage and the second to your life as a whole." With this lead-in, the correlation dropped from the previously observed $r = .67$ to $r = .18$, when the questions were asked in the same marriage–life order. Apparently, respondents interpreted the general life-satisfaction question as if it were worded, "Aside from your marriage, which you already told us about, how satisfied are you with other aspects of your life?" Supporting this assumption, a condition in which the life-satisfaction question was reworded in this way resulted in a highly similar correlation of $r = .20$. Once respondents disregarded their marriage, happily married respondents reported lower, and unhappily married respondents higher, general life satisfaction, thus reversing the previously observed influence.

These findings illustrate an important general principle: Information (here, about one's marriage) that is included in the representation of the attitude object (here, "my life") results in *assimilation effects*. That is, happily married respondents report higher, and unhappily married respondents lower, life satisfaction. Conversely, information that is excluded from the representation formed of the attitude object results in *contrast effects*. On the one hand, excluding one's happy marriage from consideration leaves one with a less positive representation of one's life, resulting in a less positive judgment. On the other hand, one's happy marriage may now serve as a high standard of comparison, further hurting the evaluation of other life domains. Numerous variables can influence whether information is used in forming a representation of the target or in forming a representation of the standard. Sudman et al. (1996, chapter 5) provide a detailed discussion and present a model that predicts the emergence, direction, and size of question order effects.

To increase your awareness of question order effects, you may want to consider which preceding questions would increase or decrease support for a policy issue of your choice.

Response Order Effects

Respondents' answers can also be influenced by the order in which a given set of response alternatives is presented. Suppose, for example, that respondents are asked in a self-administered questionnaire if divorce should be "easier to obtain" or "more difficult to obtain." When they first think about the "easier" option, they may quickly come up with a good reason for making divorce easier and may endorse this answer. But had they first thought about the "more difficult" option, they might as well have come up with a good reason for making divorce more difficult and might have endorsed that answer. In short, the order in which response alternatives are presented can influence the mental representation that respondents form of the issue (see Sudman et al., 1996, chapter 6).

Which alternative respondents are more likely to elaborate on first depends on the presentation order and mode (Krosnick & Alwin, 1987). In a visual format, like a self-administered questionnaire, respondents think about the response alternatives in the order in which they are presented. In this case, a given alternative is more likely to be endorsed when presented first rather than last (referred to as a *primacy effect*). In an auditory format, like a telephone interview, respondents can't think about the details until the interviewer has read the whole question. In this case, they are likely to begin with the last alternative read to them and a given alternative is more likely to be endorsed when presented last rather than first (a *recency effect*). Response order effects are particularly likely when respondents have mixed beliefs, are not particularly motivated, or find it difficult to keep all response alternatives in mind.

Summary

As these examples illustrate, the associations evoked by question wording and the thoughts brought to mind by previous questions or response alternatives can profoundly affect the results of opinion surveys. Although the question wording is often included in media reports, readers rarely learn about the broader context in which a question was presented. Without context information, however, it is difficult to assess to what extent the obtained answers were shaped by the research instrument.

Asking Questions About Behaviors: Memory and Estimation

In survey research, many questions about respondents' behavior are frequency questions, pertaining, for example, to how often they bought something or drank alcohol during some specified time period. Researchers typically hope that respondents will identify the behavior of interest, scan the reference period, retrieve all instances that match the target behavior, and finally count these instances to determine the overall frequency of the behavior. However, respondents are unlikely to follow such a "recall and count" strategy, unless the events in question are highly memorable and their number is small (see Brown, 2002, for a discussion). In fact, several factors render this strategy unsuitable for most behaviors.

First, memory decreases over time, even when the event is relatively important and distinctive. For example, Cannell, Fisher, and Bakker (1965) observed that only 3% of their respondents failed to report an episode of hospitalization when interviewed within 10 weeks of the event, yet a full 42% did so when interviewed 1 year after the event.

Second, when the question pertains to a frequent behavior, respondents are unlikely to have detailed representations of numerous individual episodes of a behavior stored in memory. Instead, the various instances of closely related behaviors blend into one global, knowledge-like representation that lacks specific time and location markers (see Strube, 1987). As a result, individual episodes of frequent behaviors become indistinguishable and irretrievable.

Third, our autobiographical knowledge is not organized by categories of behavior like "drinking alcohol" or the like. Instead, these behaviors are embedded in memories of other events, like dinners or parties, and are difficult to access by searching for "drinking alcohol" (see Belli, 1998). Moreover, successful memory search takes time, whereas survey interviews follow a fast pace, with usually less than 1 minute allocated to a question.

As a result of these difficulties, respondents usually need to resort to inference and estimation strategies to arrive at a reasonable answer. Which strategies they use, and at which answers they arrive, is again strongly influenced by the research instrument (for more detail see Schwarz & Oyserman, 2001).

Reconstructing the Past

A particularly important inference strategy is based on subjective theories of stability and change (see Ross, 1989, for a review). In answering questions about the past, respondents often use their current behavior or opinion as a benchmark and invoke an implicit theory of self to assess whether their past behavior or opinion was similar to, or different from, their present behavior or opinion. The resulting reports are correct to the extent that the implicit theory is accurate.

In many domains, people assume a rather high degree of stability, resulting in underestimates of the degree of change that has occurred over time. Accordingly, retrospective estimates of income or of tobacco, marijuana, and alcohol consumption were found to be heavily influenced by respondents' income or consumption habits at the time of interview (Ross, 1989). On the other hand, when respondents have reason to believe in change, they will detect change, even though none has occurred. Assuming, for example, that one's political beliefs become more conservative over the life-span, adults (erroneously) infer that they held more liberal political attitudes when they were young than they do now (Markus, 1986). Hence, retrospective reports are unsuitable for assessing actual change over time.

Frequency Scales

Another important source of information that respondents use in arriving at an estimate is provided by the questionnaire itself. In many studies, respondents are asked to report their behavior by checking the appropriate alternative on a frequency scale, like the ones shown here:

Low Frequency
( ) never
( ) about once a year
( ) about twice a year
( ) twice a month
( ) more than twice a month

High Frequency
( ) twice a month or less
( ) once a week
( ) twice a week
( ) daily
( ) several times a day

Assuming that the researcher constructed a meaningful scale, respondents use the scale as a source of information in computing an estimate. Specifically, they assume that values in the middle range of the scale reflect the "average" or "usual" behavioral frequency, whereas the extremes of the scale correspond to the extremes of the distribution. Hence, they use the range of the scale as a frame of reference in estimating their own behavioral frequency. This strategy results in higher estimates along scales that present high rather than low frequency values. For example, Schwarz and Scheuring (1992) asked patients to report their physical symptoms on one of the aforementioned scales. They found that 39% of the patients reported a symptom frequency of twice a month or more on the low frequency scale, whereas 62% did so on the high frequency scale. Similar results have been obtained across a wide range of behaviors (see Schwarz, 1999, for a review).

In addition, respondents extract comparison information from their placement on the scale. For example, checking "twice a month" on the low frequency scale suggests that one's symptom frequency is somewhat above average; in contrast, checking "twice a month" on the high frequency scale suggests that it is far below average. As a result, the patients who were given the high frequency scale reported higher health satisfaction, despite having just reported a higher symptom frequency. To avoid such complications, frequency questions are best asked in an open response format that requests a numeric answer without providing a frequency scale that biases respondents' frequency estimates and subsequent judgments.

To familiarize yourself with the logic of these scale effects, you may want to design a frequency question that elicits either a high or a low report of newspaper reading. How would these questions influence respondents' inferences when they are later asked whether they follow the news more or less closely than others do?

Vague Quantifiers

As another alternative, researchers are often tempted to assess behavioral reports with vague quantifiers, such as *sometimes, frequently,* and so on. This, however, is the worst possible choice (see Pepper, 1981, for a review). Most important, the same expression denotes different frequencies in different content domains. Thus, frequently suffering from headaches implies higher absolute frequencies than frequently suffering from heart attacks. Moreover, different respondents use the same term to denote different objective frequencies of the same behavior. For example, suffering from headaches "occasionally" denotes a higher frequency for respondents with a medical history of megrim than for respondents without that megrim history. Accordingly, the use of vague quantifiers reflects the objective frequency relative to respondents' subjective standard. *Frequently* or *sometimes* is always relative to something, rendering vague quantifiers inadequate for the assessment of objective frequencies, despite the popularity of their use.

Threatening Questions and Response Editing

Additional complications arise when the behavior under study is highly undesirable and respondents engage in it, or highly desirable and respondents do not engage in it. In this case, respondents may hesitate to report their estimate to the researcher and may instead "edit" their answer to make it more acceptable. Such self-presentation concerns decrease with increasing anonymity of the interview situation. They are smallest in self-administered questionnaires and most pronounced in face-to-face interviews, with telephone interviews falling in between (see DeMaio, 1984, for a review). Fortunately, however, influences of social desirability are typically modest in size and limited to highly threatening questions. Survey researchers have developed a variety of techniques that ensure the confidentiality of respondents' answers, and these techniques reduce social desirability bias (see Bradburn et al., 2004, for advice).

Summary

In sum, retrospective behavioral reports are rarely based on adequate recall of relevant episodes. Rather, the obtained reports are to a large extent theory driven: Respondents are likely to begin with some fragmented recall of the behavior under study and apply various inference rules to arrive at a reasonable estimate. Moreover, if frequency scales are presented, respondents are likely to use them as a frame of reference, resulting in systematic biases. Although researchers have developed a number of strategies to facilitate recall (which are reviewed in Schwarz & Oyserman, 2001, and Sudman et al., 1996, chapters 7–9), it is important to keep in mind that the best we can hope for is a reasonable estimate, unless the behavior is rare and of considerable importance to respondents.

CONCLUDING REMARKS

As the discussion of the question-answering process indicates, the hope that respondents know what they believe and do and can hence report on their opinions and behaviors with candor and accuracy has seen many challenges. The picture that emerges is consistent with basic psychological research that emphasizes the constructive nature of human judgment and memory. Far from retrieving previously formed opinions, respondents usually need to form a judgment when asked. And far from recalling relevant behavioral episodes and counting their number, respondents need to rely on complex inference and estimation strategies to reconstruct what their behavior plausibly might have been. The answers at which respondents arrive depend on the information that comes to mind at that point in time. Unfortunately, some of this information may only come to mind because of previous questions or other features of the research instrument. In this case, the answers that respondents provide may not reflect the opinions or behaviors of the population to which we want to generalize. Hence, the emergence of context effects is a major threat to the validity of population inferences. Although the underlying cognitive and communicative processes are increasingly well understood (Sudman et al., 1996; Tourangeau, Rips, & Rasinski, 2000), they are often difficult to avoid. Moreover, the way in which the media report on survey results typically renders it impossible to form an informed opinion about these problems.

The representativeness of the sample is comparatively easier to evaluate. As discussed, only probability samples allow the calculation of sampling error, which is required for population estimates. Even the representativeness of well-designed probability samples, however, can be threatened by low response rates, which should be part of every survey report. In contrast, nonprobability samples do not allow population estimates. Convenience samples, as their worst form, have merely entertainment value, no matter how impressively large the number of respondents is.

References

Belli, R. (1998). The structure of autobiographical memory and the event history calendar: Potential improvements in the quality of retrospective reports in surveys. *Memory, 6,* 383–406.

Belson, W. A. (1981). *The design and understanding of survey questions.* Aldershot, England: Gower.

Bodenhausen, G. V., & Wyer, R. S. (1987). Social cognition and social reality: Information acquisition and use in the laboratory and the real world. In H. J. Hippler, N. Schwarz, & S. Sudman (Eds.), *Social information processing and survey methodology* (pp. 6–41). New York: Springer-Verlag.

Bradburn, N. M., & Sudman, S. (1988). *Polls and surveys: Understanding what they tell us.* San Francisco: Jossey-Bass.

Bradburn, N. M., Sudman, S., & Wansink, B. (2004). *Asking questions* (2nd ed.). San Francisco: Jossey-Bass.

Brown, N. R. (2002). Encoding, representing, and estimating event frequencies: Multiple strategy perspective. In P. Sedlmeier & T. Betsch (Eds.), *Etc. Frequency processing and cognition* (pp. 37–54). New York: Oxford University Press.

Campbell, A. (1981). *The sense of well-being in America.* New York: McGraw-Hill.

Cannell, C. F., Fisher, G., & Bakker, T. (1965). Reporting on hospitalization in the Health Interview Survey. *Vital and Health Statistics* (PHS Publication No. 1000, Series 2, No. 6). Washington, DC: U.S. Government Printing Office.

Clark, H. H., & Schober, M. F. (1992). Asking questions and influencing answers. In J. M. Tanur (Ed.), *Questions about questions* (pp. 15–48). New York: Russell Sage Foundation.

DeMaio, T. J. (1984). Social desirability and survey measurement: A review. In C. F. Turner & E. Martin (Eds.), *Surveying subjective phenomena* (Vol. 2, pp. 257–281). New York: Russell Sage Foundation.

Groves, R. M., Cialdini, R. B., & Couper, M. P. (1992). Understanding the decision to participate in a survey. *Public Opinion Quarterly, 56,* 475–495.

Herbers, J. (1982, February 14). Polls find conflict in views on aid and public welfare. *New York Times*, p. 19.

Krosnick, J. A., & Alwin, D. F. (1987). An evaluation of a cognitive theory of response order effects in survey measurement. *Public Opinion Quarterly, 51*, 201–219.

Markus, G. B. (1986). Stability and change in political attitudes: Observed, recalled, and explained. *Political Behavior, 8*, 21–44.

Pepper, S. C. (1981). Problems in the quantification of frequency expressions. In D. W. Fiske (Vol. Ed.), *New Directions for Methodology of Social and Behavioral Science, Vol. 9. Problems with language imprecision* (pp. 0–0). San Francisco: Jossey-Bass.

Ross, M. (1989). The relation of implicit theories to the construction of personal histories. *Psychological Review, 96*, 341–357.

Schuman, H., & Presser, S. (1981). *Questions and answers in attitude surveys.* New York: Academic Press.

Schwarz, N. (1996). *Cognition and communication: Judgmental biases, research methods, and the logic of conversation.* Mahwah, NJ: Erlbaum.

Schwarz, N. (1999). Self-reports: How the questions shape the answers. *American Psychologist, 54*, 93–105.

Schwarz, N., Groves, R., & Schuman, H. (1998). Survey methods. In D. Gilbert, S. Fiske, & G. Lindzey (Eds.), *Handbook of social psychology* (4th ed., Vol. 1, pp. 143–179). New York: McGraw-Hill.

Schwarz, N., & Hippler, H. J. (1991). Response alternatives: The impact of their choice and ordering. In P. Biemer, R. Groves, N. Mathiowetz, & S. Sudman (Eds.), *Measurement error in surveys* (pp. 41–56). Chichester, England: Wiley.

Schwarz, N., Knäuper, B., Hippler, H. J., Noelle-Neumann, E., & Clark, F. (1991). Rating scales: Numeric values may change the meaning of scale labels. *Public Opinion Quarterly, 55*, 570–582.

Schwarz, N., & Oyserman, D. (2001). Asking questions about behavior: Cognition, communication and questionnaire construction. *American Journal of Evaluation, 22*, 127–160.

Schwarz, N., & Scheuring, B. (1992). Selbstberichtete Verhaltens- und Symptomhäufigkeiten: Was Befragte aus Anwortvorgaben des Fragebogens lernen [Frequency reports of psychosomatic symptoms: What respondents learn from response alternatives]. *Zeitschrift für Klinische Psychologie, 22*, 197–208.

Schwarz, N., Strack, F., & Mai, H. P. (1991). Assimilation and contrast effects in part–whole question sequences: A conversational logic analysis. *Public Opinion Quarterly, 55*, 3–23.

Smith, T. W. (1987). That which we call welfare would smell sweeter by any other name. *Public Opinion Quarterly, 51*, 75–83.

Sniderman, P. M., & Tetlock, P. E. (1986). Symbolic racism. *Journal of Social Issues, 42*, 129–150.

Sirken, M., Hermann, D., Schechter, S., Schwarz, N., Tanur, J., & Tourangeau, R. (Eds.). (1999). *Cognition and survey research.* New York: Wiley.

Steeh, C. (1981). Trends in nonresponse rates. *Public Opinion Quarterly, 45*, 40–57.

Strack, F., Schwarz, N., & Wänke, M. (1991). Semantic and pragmatic aspects of context effects in social and psychological research. *Social Cognition, 9*, 111–125.

Strube, G. (1987). Answering survey questions: The role of memory. In H. J. Hippler, N. Schwarz, & S. Sudman (Eds.), *Social information processing and survey methodology* (pp. 86–101). New York: Springer-Verlag.

Sudman, S., Bradburn, N., & Schwarz, N. (1996). *Thinking about answers: The application of cognitive processes to survey methodology.* San Francisco: Jossey-Bass.

Thornberry, O. T., & Massey, J. T. (1988). Trends in United States telephone coverage across time and subgroups. In R. M. Groves, P. P. Biemer, L. E. Lyberg, J. T. Massey, W. L. Nichols, & J. Waksberg (Eds.), *Telephone survey methodology* (pp. 25–50). New York: Wiley.

Tourangeau, R., Rips, L. J., & Rasinski, K. (2000). *The psychology of survey response.* New York: Cambridge University Press.

Traugott, M. W. (1987). The importance of persistence in respondent selection for preelection surveys. *Public Opinion Quarterly, 51,* 48–57.

Visser, P. S., Krosnick, J. A., & Lavrakas, P. J. (2000). Survey research. In H. T. Reis & C. M. Judd (Eds.), *Handbook of research methods in social and personality psychology* (pp. 223–252). New York: Cambridge University Press.

Weisberg, H. F., Krosnick, J. A., & Bowen, B. D. (1989). *An introduction to survey research and data analysis* (2nd ed.). Glenview, IL: Scott, Foresman.

5

Critical Thinking in Designing and Analyzing Research

Robert J. Sternberg and Elena L. Grigorenko

If you are like most students, you prefer an easy test to a hard test. "Who wouldn't?" you might ask. But if you are a good student, you probably should prefer a hard test to an easy one, for reasons to be discussed. Our intuitions in these matters are not always correct: Sometimes what seems less preferable is actually more preferable, by far.

In this chapter, we consider 21 basic lessons of critical thinking as applied to designing and analyzing research. We do not discuss sophisticated issues, but rather the fairly simple ones that we learn in elementary statistics and design courses, but that nevertheless often trip us up.

MATTERS OF DESIGN

Lesson 1: Make Sure Your Research Question Is Worth Answering
in the First Place

We have spent some portion of our careers editing journals. The Number 1 problem we found was not exactly one of design or analysis, but one of whether it was even worth it to design a study in the first place. Always start by asking whether the question is indeed worth asking. Are you *really* interested in the answer to the question you pose? Would anyone else be? Why? Is the question a big one or a little one? If it is a little one, is it too little to be worth asking? Think critically about your question before you start to answer it!

The senior author's undergraduate mentor, Endel Tulving, taught the author to divide research questions in articles into three groups: those you wish you had thought of yourself, those you are perfectly happy to see someone else answer, and those that were not asking in the first place (Tulving, personal communication, January, 1972). Ask yourself this question: Is the question really worth your time?

It is important to keep in mind that questions cannot only be too small, but also too big! For example, a question such as "What makes people happy?" may lead to answers that are so broad and diffuse that it may not lend itself to empirical analysis. So find questions that are large enough to be meaty, but not so large as to be diffuse.

Lesson 2: Make Sure That Your Research Actually Addresses
and Potentially Can Answer the Question You Set Out to Answer

In our years of editing, we also confronted a number of studies in which the study did not actually answer the question it set out to address. So it is important to think critically about whether the study you have designed actually addresses the question you think it is addressing. Seeking guidance and counsel from others can be helpful in this regard, because often, others see things that we do not see ourselves.

Early in his career, the senior author was determined to answer the question, What is intelligence? He designed a number of studies over a period of years (summarized in Sternberg, 1985) that analyzed the information-processing components underlying responses to questions on conventional intelligence tests. By the mid-1980s, however, he began to question whether such tests actually measured all of intelligence. He realized that his answer to the question – What is intelligence? – assumed, first, that conventional intelligence tests measured all of intelligence, and, second, that the question of what intelligence is would be answered by parsing mental functioning on these tests into constituent information-processing components. Later, he decided that these assumptions were not entirely justified.

Lesson 3: Ask Whether the Methods You Are Using Are Well Suited
to the Type of Question You Are Asking

In psychology, as in all fields, there is a status hierarchy of methods, at least according to some investigators. Experimental and neuroscientific methods are typically viewed today as high in this hierarchy, case studies of single individuals not as high. But a better question to ask than where a method stands in the status hierarchy is how appropriate the method is to the research question you are asking. For example, Gruber and Davis (1988) were interested in the detailed workings of the minds of scientists who have done extraordinarily creative work, such as Darwin and Piaget. What good would experimental or neuroscientific methods have been? None. Darwin, for example, is long gone, so it would be difficult to study him experimentally or neuroscientifically. Moreover, there are so few scientists of the repute of Darwin or Piaget that it would be hard to get a sufficiently large sample to study them experimentally. And it is unlikely (although not impossible) that the greatest scientists of their time would be willing to become participants in studies examining their brains.

Early in the senior author's career, he believed that one particular method, factor analysis, was a flawed method (Sternberg, 1977). He wrote what he thought was a critique of the method. Within a few years, he realized that his critique was not of the method per se, but rather of how the method had been used in particular research studies. He realized that the appropriate question was not one of how "good" or "bad" a method was, but rather of how well or poorly and how appropriately or inappropriately the method was used.

MATTERS OF ANALYSIS

Lesson 4: Scores Mean Little or Nothing in the Absence of Information About Central Tendency

To interpret a score, one needs to know how it compares with others. Too often, this comparison information is missing.

Among the most notorious of current examples is grade inflation. Suppose a student has a college grade-point average (GPA) of 3.7. At one time, when the average was 2.0, the 3.7 GPA would have been impressive. Today, in many schools, the average is 3.5 or even higher. A 3.7 average obviously means a very different thing, depending on whether the mean is 2.0 or 3.5.

Consider a second example. Suppose one of us writes a letter saying that a student we have taught is "excellent." Someone else writes a letter saying her student is "excellent." But we are comparing the student to the average at Yale, and the other letter writer is comparing the student to the average at Stinkbomb U. Clearly, *excellent* will have different meanings, depending on the mean above which the student excels.

Lesson 5: Means Mean Little or Nothing in the Absence of Variability Information

In everyday life, one sees tables of averages all the time. These averages (means) are supposed to tell us something useful. They rarely do. The reason is that, except in journal articles – and even sometimes in journal articles – they are presented without variability information, such as a standard deviation. They then tell you nothing. Consider three examples.

It is common to see average gross per capita earnings across a variety of countries. These figures tell us how well various countries are doing in their respective levels of affluence. The United States usually fares reasonably well – but tell this to a poor person living in Appalachia, or rural North Dakota or Mississippi, or inner-city Detroit, or Harlem. The dirt-poor resident may be almost next door to the billionaire living a few blocks south in Manhattan, but their levels of income and wealth could hardly be more different. The billionaire may earn more in a day than the Harlem resident will in a lifetime. The mean for the United States hid tremendous variability.

Consider a second example. Someone we knew took a test for entrance into an organization of individuals with high IQ. He scored 178 on the IQ test that the organization gave. This is an extremely high score. Compared with the mean score of 100, it would place the individual in the stratosphere of human intellectual abilities. There was one catch, however. The test had a standard deviation of 24 points rather than the usual 15 or 16 points. This means that his score on a typical test with a standard deviation of 15 would have been about 147, still very high, but a far cry from 178.

Now consider a third example, with which you may be familiar. Bob, the first author, usually feels warm, regardless of the room temperature. Elena, the second author, usually feels cold. On average, we both feel fine in almost any room, but neither of us individually feels fine! Our average temperature does not reflect that either of us is comfortable!

Lesson 6: Shapes of Distributions Matter: Do Not Jump to Conclusions From Parametric Statistics Without First Making Sure the Underlying Distribution With Which You Are Working Is at Least Roughly Normal

Let's return to the question of average income. Without knowing variability, one could and probably would draw conclusions that are inadequate and perhaps wholly wrong. But without knowing the shape of the distribution, one can only draw conclusions that are wrong as well.

Distribution of incomes is extremely right skewed. There is a very long right tail. As a result, the mean is substantially higher than the median. People with yearly incomes in the tens and even hundreds of millions bring the mean way up beyond the median. If one were to look at standard scores (z scores) for income, well more than half of the population of the United States would have a negative score, because the mean is so much higher than the median.

When the news media talk about economic conditions, they typically talk about means. So we may hear that incomes are rising, or that spending is increasing, or that people's general financial well-being is increasing. Keep in mind, in listening to these statistics, that they hide poverty in plain sight. Without knowing how people are doing at all income levels, one may draw generalized conclusions that apply to some hypothetical average person who does not exist, much as in the case of the two individuals who were either too hot or too cold, so, on average, were comfortable with the temperature.

Lesson 7: The Significance Level of a Statistical Test Does Not Tell You the Strength of an Effect

Surprisingly often, the significance of a statistical test is taken, incorrectly, to be an assertion of the magnitude of an effect. For example, a researcher may write in a paper that an effect was "very significant." Such statements show a misunderstanding of how statistical significance testing works. The strength of a test of statistical significance indicates not how strong an effect is, but how likely a set of data is to have occurred if the null hypothesis were true. Thus, successive levels of significance refer not to strength of effects, but rather to likelihoods of obtaining data under the null hypothesis.

Consider an example. Two different investigators examine effects of two different reading programs on groups of students drawn from the same population. In each case, the treated children are compared with those in a comparable control group. Which program was more effective, the one that showed an effect at the .001 level or the one that showed an effect at the .05 level? The answer is that one cannot tell from these data. Why? Because we do not know enough about the two studies. Suppose that the study that displayed an effect at the .001 level of statistical significance had 1,000 participants per group, and the study displayed an effect at the .05 level, only 75 students per group. It is possible that the effect size in the smaller experiment was larger, but that the statistical significance of that effect was smaller because of the lesser power of the study. Without sample-size or effect-size information, one simply cannot draw any conclusion about which program was more effective, based merely on the magnitudes of p values.

Now consider a second example. An investigator does an experiment, shows an effect at the .001 level, and the journal editor dismisses the effect as uninteresting. How could this happen? Because statistical significance addresses only the question of whether there is any effect at all, not the question of how strong the effect is. It is possible to get an effect that is statistically significant but trivial in magnitude. Some investigators work with extremely large data sets that may contains sample sizes in the thousands, ten thousands, or more. At these levels of power, almost any effect, no matter how small, will be statistically significant. The question then becomes one of whether it is practically significant – large enough to make a difference in real life. An effect may be statistically, but not practically, significant. Ideally, you should always report effect sizes as well as significance levels.

Lesson 8: Always Know the Power of the Tests You Are Conducting

Our training in statistics courses tends to emphasize the danger of Type 1 errors, or false alarms. When we use significance testing, we are trying to avoid Type 1 errors where we go beyond our data in making claims that the data do not support. But Type 2 errors are also important, and arguably, equally important. Recall that, in a Type 2 error, one makes a miss – one misses a phenomenon that exists. In designing your research, it is important to ensure that your group size and total sample size are adequate to ensure that, if there is an effect, you have a reasonable chance of detecting it.

We sometimes do not do power calculations, either because they are extra work to do or because, perhaps, we are afraid of what they will show. However, if you have low power, you may put a lot of effort into a research study that has little chance of showing any except the largest effects. So make sure you know your power, and report it, so that readers also will know how likely you were to detect an effect of a reasonable magnitude.

Lesson 9: You Need to Consider the Scale Properties of Your Data Before Operating on Them

Suppose you have participants in a survey study rank order how much they like four products. Participant A ranks Product 1, 1, Product 2, 2, Product 3, 3, and Product 4, 4. Participant B ranks Product 1, 1, Product 2, 3, Product 3, 2, and Product 4, 4. So the only disagreement about rank orders is with respect to Products 2 and 3, which come out tied. But suppose we also look at Likert scale ratings of the four products. Asked to rate the products, suppose the ratings for the four respective products on a 1 (low) to 10 (high) scale are 10, 9, 8, 1 for Participant 1, and 10, 3, 9, 1 for Participant 2. The averaged ratings for the four products are 10, 6, 8.5, and 1. Note the following: First, Products 2 and 3 are neither tied nor particularly close. Product 3 is, on average, substantially preferred to Product 2. Second, Product 3 is quite close to Product 1 and also to Product 3, but Product 4 is further away from even Product 2 than Product 1 is from Product 2. In other words, the rank orders do not show how much more Product 1 is disliked than the other products. In general, the averaged ratings give a rather different picture for the four products.

Rankings are ordinal data, meaning that the distances between them hold no meaning. Three products can be ranked 1, 2, and 3, but they are not necessarily at equal distances from each other on a preference scale. Someone may like Products 1 and 2 almost equally, but detest Product 3. When one "averages" rank orders, one assumes interval properties to the scale (that is, that arithmetical operations on them make sense) that one is not allowed to assume. One should therefore be careful in remembering that rank-order data do not have scale properties that properly lend themselves to averaging or other arithmetical operations.

Lesson 10: Correlation Does not Imply Causation – Really

Everyone who studies statistics learns that correlation does not imply causation. Relatively few people seem to take this lesson to heart. There are several reasons why.

First, sometimes, intuitively, they want to believe in a certain direction of causation, and so they do. For example, data show that people with less education have lower IQs. But why? Some theorists have argued that people enter into lower socioeconomic classes because their IQs are lower (e.g., Herrnstein & Murray, 1994). Other theorists (e.g., Ceci, 1996) have argued that lesser levels of education lead to lower IQs. Still others have argued that other forces may affect both IQ and education level, such as socioeconomic status, with lower socioeconomic status leading to fewer educational opportunities (Sternberg, 1997). We do not know, for sure, which of these explanations of the original relationship between less education and IQ is correct, and it may be that the relationship is multidirectional. But the example points out the hazards of inferring causation from correlation, even when one tries to take confounding variables into account.

Sometimes the design of a study is correlational, but it is not obvious from the design because there are no actual correlations. For example, suppose you divide two groups of students into "high achievers" and "low achievers" and compare their scores on a test of motivation. You find that the high achievers score higher on the test of motivation than do the lower achievers, and you conclude that students who are more motivated achieve at higher levels. Although no correlations were reported – only mean differences on the motivation scale between the higher and lower achievers – the design is nevertheless a correlational one. Instead of correlating scores on the achievement measure with scores on the motivation measure, differences on the achievement measure are dichotomized (high versus low) and then correlated with the motivation measure. This is a correlational design, even without correlations. And there is no way of knowing that higher motivation in the sample led to higher achievement. It may be that higher achievers became more motivated because of their high achievement, or that both achievement and motivation were dependent on some other factor or factors, such as parental support.

In recent times, a particularly frequent source of correlational evidence is in cognitive and affective neuropsychological studies. The investigators do functional magnetic resonance imaging studies relating performance on some cognitive task to patterns of activation across the brain. When people perform a certain task, a certain portion of the brain "lights up." One then concludes that the lighted portion of the brain "causes" the cognitive or affective activity.

In fact, despite the neuropsychological twist, this is just another variant of a correlational design. There is a correlation between performance on a task and the lighting up of a depiction of brain function. How one gets to the point even getting this correlation is a procedure fraught with hazards, in that it involves a subtractive methodology that makes assumptions that are not always fully met. But keep in mind that the correlation does not tell us anything about direction of causation. It might be that, for a different population, a different portion of the brain would light up on the same task. Indeed, this often happens, as when a task can be done either by spatial visual or verbal processing (such as the linear syllogism, "John is taller than Jane. Jane is taller than Jean. Who is tallest?"). So the lighted area of the brain is not uniquely causal. It might be that some other area of the brain not being studied actually causes the light up in the part that is being studied, so that the part of the brain that is lighting up is merely a way station. The bottom line is that one has to be very careful about drawing causal inferences.

Lesson 11: Experimental Studies Without Control Groups, or at Least Comparison Groups, Usually Give Uninterpretable Results

Here is a design we see frequently in the educational literature. Students who are poor readers, or poor mathematical problem solvers, or whatever, are given an intervention to improve their reading or mathematical skills. Before the intervention they are given a pretest. After the intervention they are given a posttest. The investigator finds that after the program, scores are significantly higher on the posttest than on the pretest. The investigator then concludes that the program resulted in enhanced reading or mathematical skills.

The problem is that one can conclude nothing of the kind, because there could have been many reasons for the increase from the pretest to the posttest that had nothing to do with the intervention program. Perhaps the posttest was the same as the pretest and students remembered items that they had taken before, as well as their answers. Or perhaps the students would have improved equally even without the program, simply by virtue of being in school. Perhaps the posttest was merely easier than the pretest. The list of potential confounds goes on. One can conclude essentially nothing.

To draw any conclusions about the efficacy of the program, one would need some kind of control group or, better, control groups. One control group might give the students just regular instruction with no special program at all. One then compares the amount of gain in the experimental program with that in the no-program control. This new group controls for having the program, but it does not control for having any program. Perhaps there is what is referred to as a Hawthorne effect – the mere fact of being in a program – any program – improved achievement. Students, by virtue of being singled out and given attention, did better. So use of an alternative program might serve as a better control group. One compares one program with another. But the problem here is that one's program might truly be better than nothing but not than an alternative program. So it might actually be best to have both control groups.

In general, one always wants to have strong control groups so that one ensures that the conclusion one wishes to draw truly follows from the data.

Lesson 12: Beware of Ceiling and Floor Effects

Recall that, in the introduction to this chapter, we said that good students should never prefer an easy to a harder test. Here is why.

Suppose your teacher gives a very easy test. The average score, say, is 95. This test penalizes good students, because there is a low ceiling, making it difficult for them to differentiate themselves. Many students may come close to or achieve 100%, and there is no differentiation among them. What's worse, if you are a good student but just happen not to know the answers to one or two of the items, you may find yourself with a score that does not much distinguish you from the other students, because you were unlucky enough not to know the answers to those few questions.

Floor effects tend to penalize weaker but not terrible students. If the test is quite hard, and the average score is, say, only 10% correct, there will be little range among the weaker students, so that students who are not among the better ones, but certainly not among the worst ones, may have trouble differentiating themselves. You should design measures so that they have neither ceiling nor floor effects.

Lesson 13: Partial Correlation and its Analysis-of-Variance Analogue – Analysis of Covariance – Do Not Always Do What They Are Supposed to Do – Eliminate Effects of Irrelevant Variables

Partial correlation and analysis of covariance are intended to eliminate effects of irrelevant variables, but sometimes they are used in ways that give the appearance of doing something they are not doing. Consider an example.

You want to understand the relationship between IQ and achievement. So you give an intelligence test, such as the Wechsler Intelligence Scale for Children, and an achievement test, such as the Stanford Achievement Tests, to a group of students, and you discover a high correlation, say, .6. Then you realize there is a problem. Both tests contain very similar problems involving word knowledge. Someone with poor word knowledge will be handicapped on both tests. But word knowledge is clearly achievement. So you give a vocabulary test, hold vocabulary constant, and now find the partial correlation to be much lower, say, .3. You conclude that intelligence and achievement are not so highly related after all.

The problem is that it is often hard to know exactly what is "irrelevant variance." Most theorists of intelligence would argue that verbal skills are not irrelevant to intelligence, but rather are part of it. Indeed, the Wechsler Intelligence Scale for Children–III involves vocabulary items. Verbal skills are also part of achievement. In holding them constant, you remove not irrelevant but rather relevant variance. But certainly, leaving in the verbal components inflates the correlation because the same kinds of items are used in both tests. A different way of defining the problem would be to say that measures of intelligence are, at least in part, measures of achievement. It is hard to measure intelligence without somehow tapping into achievement. Even abstract-reasoning problems, such as those requiring reasoning with geometric shapes, require achievement of skills in handling abstracted forms, with which one rarely reasons in one's everyday life.

Lesson 14: Always Plan Your Statistical Analysis *Before* You Do Your Research

Many students design studies, figuring that they will work out the details of the data analysis later. They later discover that the study was designed in a way that makes adequate statistical analysis difficult or even impossible. Because students often do not look forward to the statistical analysis, they may want to postpone thinking about it as long as possible. In our experience, it is far better to plan it in advance, and thereby to ensure that one later has data that one can, in fact, analyze.

Lesson 15: After You Have Written up Your Analysis and Interpreted Your Results, Read What You Have Written With the Mindset of Your "Worst Enemy"

All of us are susceptible to confirmation bias, whereby we tend to look to confirm rather than disconfirm our beliefs through our data. Although science proceeds best when scientists seek to disconfirm their own hypotheses through their research, in fact, few scientists follow this idealized model. Rather, the large majority of them use their research to attempt to confirm what they already believe. In interpreting data, we are all susceptible to reading it in the best possible light.

It is for this reason that we recommend that when you are done writing up a talk or a paper, you read what you have written as though you were your own worst enemy. What might an opponent say? How might he or she criticize your design, your analysis, or the conclusions you draw from your analysis? You should then write into your talk or paper your answers to the questions your opponents are likely to raise. In our experience, it is a mistake to "hope for the best," for example, that referees will not discover flaws in your experimental or other design. Most often, reviewers do discover the weaknesses. It is better if you discover them first, and respond to them in your paper or talk before your critics do.

Lesson 16: Always Look for Outliers

Outliers are points with extreme values that are judged to be outside the distributions one is analyzing. For example, if one is evaluating reaction times, almost all of which are between 500 and 900 milliseconds, and one finds a participant with reaction times of 50 to 80 milliseconds, this participant's data will appear as outliers. There is a good chance, in this case, that the reaction times were so fast because the participant responded at random. His data are not systematic and should not be counted. Or if one is analyzing four-option multiple-choice test scores, almost all of which have percentages correct of 60 to 90, and someone has a percentage correct of 24, the chances are that these data represent an outlier and that the participant was responding at random. People presenting such data need not respond at random: They may not have understood the test instructions, they may have been ill and unable to function properly, they may have misunderstood how to use the testing equipment, and so on. Nevertheless, including their data distorts one's statistical analyses.

When one of the authors was younger, he was reading an article by a distinguished scientist in which the scientist was touting a high correlation between two variables. In the article, he gave the scatterplot on which the correlation was based. It was clear from the scatterplot that the high correlation was due in large part to two outliers, one at the high end of the distribution, the other at the low end. Take out the two outliers, and there would not be all that much correlation left.

Outliers can make data look much better or worse than they really are. In the example given here, they made the data look better. Linear correlations are quite affected by values at the extremes, and not much by values in the middle of distributions. So if there are even small numbers of outliers at the extremes, then they can affect the correlations, either for better or worse. In this particular case, they raised the correlations; had they been in different places, they might have lowered them. Outliers can also affect statistical significance tests between means. A few extreme values can change the results one way or the other. So always check your data for outliers before interpreting them.

Lesson 17: Always Take Into Account Confidence Intervals

Occasionally, one sees reports of differences between correlations that appear to be very large, and that are interpreted as different, without a significance test. Be wary of such reports. The same applies, of course, to mean differences for which significance is not tested. The problem is that without taking into account confidence intervals, it is very hard to interpret differences. Two correlations may differ by a substantial amount, but the difference may not be statistically significant. Correlations tend to have very large confidence intervals (i.e., large standard errors), and unless one has a great deal of power, it is difficult to get a difference between correlations to be statistically significant. You always need to view differences in terms of the confidence intervals associated with them. Do not assume that merely because two means or correlations "look" different, they really are.

Lesson 18: Consider the Relative Costs of Type I Versus Type II Errors, and Consider Effect Sizes in Relation to Costs and Benefits

We have a tendency to think of Type I errors in a rigid way. We set a minimum significance level – say, .05 – and then call anything below that "significant." If we are using multiple tests, we may use a Bonferroni correction, which makes it more difficult to achieve significance for any one test, as with multiple tests, more results will appear to be significant when they really are not.

We need to think in a more critical and flexible way. The costs of Type I and Type II errors vary, depending on the circumstances. Suppose, for example, you have a new drug that has the potential to cure a certain type of cancer. You do a clinical trial and find a result significant at the .10 level. It would be foolish to give up on the drug because the effect was only marginally significant. Certainly it would be worthwhile to consider doing further tests of greater power.

Consider a second example. When aspirin was studied as a possible preventative measure against heart attacks, the effect size for its preventative efficacy was very low. But the drug came to be widely used nevertheless, because even an effect size of .01 could save thousands of lives per year. You always need to consider effect sizes in relation to the question being asked.

Lesson 19: When You Are Done, Ask Yourself Whether the Way You Framed Your Research Is Still the Best Way to Frame It

As often as not, we have found, results of studies do not conform to predictions. Sometimes, they end up giving different answers to questions than we had originally expected. Other times, they somehow end up answering questions different from those we had originally posed. One of the most exciting aspects of research is that it often leads us down paths that we never anticipated when we designed it.

Do not feel straitjacketed by the answers you originally expected or even the questions you originally posed. It is perfectly fine to reframe your study in terms of what you have found, as long as you make it clear that you have done so. But in saying you have done so, do not give a long song and dance as the explanation. Merely say what happened, briefly, and leave it at that. You may even say so in a footnote. Readers are not interested in the autobiography of your research attempts, but rather, in the questions the research actually addresses and how it answers them. Of course, if the research has led you in a direction different from that you originally set out on, then replication of your results will be all the more important.

In analyzing his dissertation data many years ago, the senior author discovered, to his chagrin, that fits of the alternative cognitive models he had proposed to the data were not very good (Sternberg, 1977). He was horrified. He had spent a year collecting the data, and now it appeared that the data had turned out poorly. Because his data were correlational, he was able to look at residuals observed from predicted values. He discovered that the errors in prediction were systematic. By changing the models to include a "preliminary scan" of the stimulus materials, he was able to improve his model fits dramatically. Had he felt bound to the models he originally proposed, he would have had a set of rather poor dissertation data. Rather, he attempted to figure out what was wrong with his models, discovered inadequacies in them, and then modified them to encompass his findings. He then, in his write-up, explained how incorporating a preliminary scan improved the model fits because it better described how participants actually processed the test items.

Lesson 20: Figure Out What Story Your Study Tells, and Then Tell It

Novices often view empirical reports as mere presentations of "facts." Such presentations of facts are the sign of a novice presenter, however, not an expert. An expert applies critical thinking to his or her work: The expert figures out what story his or her data have to tell, and then tells the story. The story is not like a short story, because it is not fiction, but it is a story nevertheless. You should write up your empirical paper so that it tells the story your design and data, in combination, have to tell readers. As you write up an article, or even earlier, as you do data analyses, you should be guided by the story you have to tell. There are always an infinite number of possible ways of analyzing and then writing up data. The best ways are ones that tell a story, at the same time pointing out gaps and even inconsistencies in the story that may need to be worked out in the future.

So, in the end, it is important to apply critical thinking in one's interpretation of statistics. An effect size of .01 might be trivial in some circumstances, but quite important in others. Statistics are merely numbers. Numbers do not tell a story; you do. It is up to you to use statistics critically and effectively, telling the right story about the numbers you produce in your research.

Lesson 21, the Last Lesson: Never, Ever, Violate Ethical Standards or Cheat in Your Data

Over the course of a career, you will invest time and effort in studies that either do not turn out as well as you had hoped, or that yield data that are, on the whole, disappointing, given your investment in them. Especially when you are young and future hiring and promotions depend in part on your data, you may feel the temptation to cheat. You must resist it at all costs. Both of the authors of this chapter have done reasonably well in their careers, despite recalcitrant data sets that just did not come out as either had hoped. But that is the cost of doing business. It is like a tax. It would be the rare researcher indeed who never has a disappointment.

At the time we were writing this chapter, there was a major scandal in the scientific world. A South Korean researcher and his colleagues published data in a highly prestigious journal, *Science*, that proved to be, at least in part, falsified. First, it appeared that data had been obtained unethically. Then it came out that some of the data were simply fake. The authors have had to retract their article. Ethical breaches in data collection or analysis are bad for three reasons. First, they are bad because behaving unethically is bad. Second, they are bad because they give science a black eye, and lead people both inside and outside the field to question the integrity of the people doing research. Third, they are bad because they are career enders. There is no better way to end your career than to behave in an unethical, and hence unprofessional, way. The lead scientist who had faked the data was forced to resign his university position in disgrace, and will end up spending much of his time as a target of scientific and possibly legal probes.

The point is simple. If you are ever tempted to behave unethically in science, just don't. There are no benefits. Even if you get away with it in the short term, you well may not in the long term. People may investigate your data, or worse, you, even years after you turn in and possibly publish falsified results. If you fail to obtain informed consent, or engage in study procedures that violate ethical standards, not only your own research, but that of others as well, may be shut down by the university or the federal government. Engaging in unethical behavior is something that not only may, but very likely will, stalk you the rest of your life.

In this chapter, we have reviewed some of the main aspects of critical thinking as they apply to experimental design and statistical analysis. We cannot possibly list every kind of problem you might encounter. Hence, your best bet is always to be vigilant, and to review critically the analyses you do and the conclusions you draw in your research.

AUTHOR NOTE

Preparation of this essay was supported by Grant R206R00001 from the Javits Act Program administered by the Institute for Educational Sciences, U.S. Department of Education. This article does not necessarily represent the position or policies of the IES or the U.S. Department of Education, and no official endorsement should be inferred.

References

Ceci, S. J. (1996). *On intelligence* (Exp. rev. ed.). Cambridge, MA: Harvard University Press.

Gruber, H. E., and Davis, S. N. (1988). Inching our way up Mount Olympus: The evolving-systems approach to creative thinking. In R. J. Sternberg (Ed.), *The nature of creativity* (pp. 243–270). New York: Cambridge University Press.

Herrnstein, R., & Murray, C. (1994). *The bell curve.* New York: The Free Press.

Sternberg, R. J. (1977). *Intelligence, information processing, and analogical reasoning: The componential analysis of human abilities.* Hillsdale, NJ: Erlbaum.

Sternberg, R. J. (1985). *Beyond IQ: A triarchic theory of human intelligence.* New York: Cambridge University Press.

Sternberg, R. J. (1997). *Successful intelligence.* New York: Plume.

6

The Case Study Perspective on Psychological Research

Randi Martin and Rachel Hull

The case study approach has a rich history in psychology as a method for observing the ways in which individuals may demonstrate abnormal thinking and behavior, for collecting evidence concerning the circumstances and consequences surrounding such disorders, and for providing data to generate and test models of human behavior (see Yin, 1998, for an overview). Nevertheless, the most typical methods for scientifically studying human cognition involve testing groups of healthy people – typically, college undergraduates. In their statistics and research methods courses, psychology students are trained to study the effects of manipulations that are significant across groups of participants despite considerable variation at the level of the individual. They are trained to be skeptical of reasoning from an individual case that goes against the general trend, and to be suspicious of the compelling anecdote that may be introduced to defend some position about how cognition or social interactions might work. Given this state of affairs, are the practitioners of the case study approach misguided, or can valid conclusions be drawn from findings with one patient? Can case reports that detail a client's symptoms and reactions to psychotherapy constitute scientific data? What about case studies that investigate how brain damage affects particular cognitive processes? The goal of this chapter is to demonstrate how single-case-study approaches in clinical psychology and cognitive neuropsychology have contributed to the advancement of theories and models of human cognition and to address the common concerns that researchers often have about case study methodology. First, we provide a brief discussion of the clinical case study approach, followed by a lengthier discussion of the cognitive neuropsychology case study approach, in which a large body of evidence from single case studies has been used to test and develop cognitive theory.

The Clinical Case Report Approach

Case reports in clinical psychology are fundamentally different from neuropsychological case studies in a number of ways. Note that we use the term *report* to refer to the clinical case, and the term *study* for the neuropsychological case. Although these terms are often used interchangeably, we draw the distinction because of the type of data provided by each. Specifically, clinical case reports are typically observational, providing detailed reports about the characteristics of various types of abnormal thinking and behavior, and they focus on the treatment of such mental disorders in individual patients and provide descriptions of the outcomes of this treatment. The case study in neuropsychology, on the other hand, depends on the contrast of performance, using standard dependent measures, across a variety of experimental manipulations and the convergence of findings from these manipulations. The patients are tested at a point where their symptoms are stable. In contrast, the clinical case study typically cannot be carried out in a fashion that would allow for experimental manipulation of treatment approaches. For instance, it is unlikely that a psychotherapist would try treatment approach X for a certain number of weeks, and then switch to treatment approach Y for the next several weeks as a means of assessing relative efficacy. Even if this were practical or ethically valid, the conclusions one could draw would be tenuous because of the possible interaction of treatment X with treatment Y and the difficulty in obtaining reliable dependent measures for improvement from one individual. Of course, the therapist hopes that the patient is changing as a result of treatment, but if change is observed, one cannot directly attribute the change to the treatment because of the possibility of spontaneous recovery or the influence of uncontrolled outside events (Campbell, Stanley, & Gage, 1963). Even so, clinical case reports can help bring to light new areas of investigation that researchers in psychology can subsequently use to scientifically test the mechanisms that may underlie disordered thought processes, and to improve psychological theories about them accordingly.

An example of the interplay between clinical case reports and experimental research can be found in the literature on recovered memories. As early as the 17th century, clinicians have argued that mental illnesses may arise from blocked, highly emotional memories (Stein, 1970). Freud (1935) asserted that at least some mental illness cases he had observed were a result of blocked memories about childhood sexual abuse (now called CSA). Other case reports documented by Sargant and Slater (1941) observed a significant positive correlation between severity of stress and amnesia in World War II soldiers. These clinicians argued that bringing the repressed memories to consciousness through psychotherapy was essential for the patient's recovery.

These early case reports of repressed memories have been supplemented by numerous contemporary reports of recovered memories of CSA (e.g., Briere & Conte, 1993; Loftus, Polonsky, & Fullilove, 1994). In these cases, a patient typically seeks professional help with some condition, such as persistent insomnia, for which the patient cannot identify the cause, and for which no biological cause can be identified. Sometimes during the course of treatment, the patient may spontaneously remember being sexually abused as a child. Such memories are traumatic for the patient to recall, but some clinicians think that acknowledging the memories and dealing with the resulting emotions, such as anger, betrayal, guilt, and fear, will promote a catharsis that will allow the patient to overcome other problems, such as insomnia or generalized anxiety, that have presumably developed secondarily to the repression of the traumatic memories (Brewin, 1989; Eyre, 1991).

Although recovered memories of CSA may seem quite real to patients, and they undoubtedly are accurate in some cases (e.g., Briere & Conte, 1993; Brown, Scheflin, & Hammond, 1998; Taylor, 2004), an important caveat to recovered memories of this sort is their general lack of verifiability (Gleaves, Smith, Butler, & Spiegel, 2004; Lief, 2003; McNally, 2003; Smith et al., 2003). That is, although the memories could be quite real, it is almost impossible to verify this through objective means or corroborative evidence because many years have often elapsed, making medical examinations useless, and the patient had rarely told anyone of the experiences at the time of their occurrence. Moreover, because the clinical methodology relies on the therapeutic orientation of the clinician, which may range from interviews to hypnosis to self-report inventories, each approach may differentially constrain the problems that are detectable, as well as the subsequent diagnosis and treatment (Perrotto & Culkin, 1993). In fact, it has been argued that recovered "memories" of CSA may be false recollections resulting from misinterpretations or suggestive questions by the therapist (see Bowman & Mertz, 1996; Ceci & Loftus, 1994). Indeed, the recent rash of such clinical reports has been called a "time-limited craze of therapy-induced incest accusations" (McHugh, Lief, Freyd, & Fetkewicz, 2003, p. 525).

Another possibility is that the patient may have experienced a source monitoring failure, in which so-called memories may include a confabulation of people and events from different times and places, or events that actually happened to someone else (Dodson & Johnson, 1993; Johnson, Hashroudi, & Lindsay, 1993; Kolb, 1988). At least one other alternative that has been suggested is that people who report recovering previously blocked memories may suffer from a cognitive deficit that affects their ability to distinguish memories of real versus imagined events (Clancy, 2001; Kaplan & Manicavasagar, 2001; McNally, 2003).

Although the reports of recovered CSA memories may in most cases be impossible to verify, these clinical case reports have introduced new directions for memory researchers to investigate the mechanisms that may underlie forgetting and remembering, and specifically those that should support repression followed by memory recovery versus those supporting false memory formation. For instance, it has been hypothesized that people who recover CSA memories may have an increased ability to divert attention away from and repress trauma-related material, as compared with controls; however, the opposite effect was revealed in controlled experiments with CSA individuals (McNally, Metzger, Lasko, Clancy, & Pitman, 1998). Another experiment showed that CSA individuals experienced more than two times the number of false memories than did controls (Clancy, McNally, & Schacter, 1999). These outcomes suggest that the cognitive mechanisms for remembering and forgetting among people reporting recovered CSA memories may not operate in the same way as for nonclinical controls.

Concern over the accuracy of blocked and recovered memories with clinical populations (Loftus, 1993; Ofshe & Watters, 1993) has also spawned a slew of experimental memory studies with *nonclinical* populations (e.g., Gleaves et al., 2004; McDermott, 1996; Robinson & Roediger, 1997; Smith et al., 2003). The *comparative memory paradigm* developed by Smith et al. represents one such methodology for addressing the debate about the veracity of clinically recovered memories, as it has been used to experimentally induce both false and accurate recovered memories in nonclinical populations, and it has shown that the two types of memories may be distinguishable to some degree, as participants expressed a "feeling of knowing" that the correctly recalled items were more accurate than the falsely recalled ones. These results thus highlight the relationship between the introduction of misleading cues and the generation of false memories. Consequently, clinical techniques, such as guided imagery, that involve cuing patients to visualize abusive episodes in order to "unblock" suspected suppressed memories may need to be rethought.

Clearly, clinical case reports offer valuable directions for research and spur critical thinking about the origins of disrupted cognition. In what follows, we focus on advances stemming from one particular area that relies heavily on individual case studies, namely, neuropsychology.

THE NEUROPSYCHOLOGICAL CASE STUDY APPROACH

Single Cases versus Group Studies

In studies of neurally intact individuals, questions about the relation between individual characteristics and cognitive function are often addressed by identifying group membership, then relating group membership to performance on some experimental manipulation. For instance, one might be interested in whether individual differences in working memory (WM) capacity are related to the ability to understand complex sentences. Individuals would be tested on some measure of WM capacity, and performance measures on this task could be used to assign participants to groups with low and high WM capacity. Next, an experiment could be carried out to assess comprehension for simple versus complex sentences. An analysis of variance could be used to determine at least three things: (a) whether there was a main effect of sentence complexity such that all participants performed better on simple than complex sentences, (b) whether there was a main effect of WM capacity such that the high WM capacity group performed better overall on both sentence types, and (c) whether there was an interaction between sentence complexity and WM capacity such that the effect of sentence complexity was greater for the low WM capacity group. Although some participants would likely diverge from the general group trends uncovered in such an experiment, the results would inform the investigator of the way high versus low WM capacity was related to sentence comprehension in this sample of participants, which, in turn, would serve as an indicator of the role of WM in sentence comprehension in the general population.

Based on the group study example just given, it may seem that the proper way to study the relation, or lack thereof, among symptoms resulting from brain damage would be to assign brain-damaged patients to groups and then look at group differences, either between the patient group and matched controls or among different patient groups. Group assignment might be made on the basis of clinical classification, lesion localization, or the result of an assessment on some experimental measure (as in the WM example). For instance, in the area of language deficits, the researcher might be interested in the relation between deficits in language production and language comprehension, with the goal of determining the extent to which the same grammatical knowledge is involved in both. To address this question, patients might be assigned to groups on the basis of (a) the outcome of a standardized test battery that categorizes patients into groups such as Broca's, Wernicke's, or conduction aphasia, as such classifications are highly related to features of language production, (b) lesion localization data that sort patients into those with frontal versus posterior left hemisphere damage, as different production patterns are correlated with anterior and posterior damage, or (c) a combination of performance on experimental measures of semantic and grammatical aspects of language production.

Once groupings have been determined, patients in this hypothetical study might be tested on their comprehension of sentences, where comprehension depends on processing the syntactic information in the sentence (e.g., determining who was doing the carrying and who was being carried in a sentence such as, "The girl that the boy carried had red hair"). The issue would be whether a deficit in grammatical aspects of sentence *production*, which has been noted in Broca's aphasics (who tend to have frontal lesions), is related to a deficit in *comprehending* syntactic information. If so, it would suggest that the same grammatical abilities are involved in production and comprehension, and that left frontal brain regions support this grammatical knowledge.

In fact, hundreds of studies along these lines have been carried out over the past 25 years since a seminal study of Caramazza and Zurif (1976), which demonstrated just such a pattern. Specifically, a group of Broca's aphasics (characterized by good single-word comprehension but various syntactic errors in sentence production) showed deficits specific to comprehending the syntax of sentences. The same study showed that a group of Wernicke's aphasics (who typically produce speech that is more grammatically correct, but semantically garbled) seemed to have deficits related to comprehending the meaning of individual words in the sentences. However, the avalanche of studies on these patient groups has not resulted in major steps forward in understanding the relation between language production and comprehension. A major obstacle to progress has been the group approach; that is, although Broca's aphasics as a group may have difficulty with comprehending syntactic information in sentences, many individual cases show intact sentence comprehension for at least some types of sentence structures, indicating that deficits in production and comprehension may derive from separate sources rather than a single syntactic module (e.g., Caramazza & Hillis, 1989; Kolk, van Grunsven, & Keyser, 1985; Linebarger, Schwartz, & Saffran, 1983; Martin, Wetzel, Blossom-Stach, & Feher, 1989).

In a meta-analysis of 15 studies involving a total of 42 Broca's aphasics, Berndt, Mitchum, and Haendiges (1996) addressed the persistent notion that all Broca's aphasics should be "agrammatic" for syntactic comprehension as well as production. Berndt et al. reported that 30% of cases showed above-chance performance on *both* actives and passives, and 4 of these were close to ceiling in accuracy on both sentence types. Only 4 cases showed high performance on the active sentences and chance performance on passives. Finally, of the 22 cases that showed chance performance on active sentences, 4 were actually better at comprehending *passive* sentences. Berndt et al.'s results also clearly challenged the claim that the agrammatic production of Broca's aphasics is necessarily accompanied by an inability to comprehend syntactically complex sentences such as passives. Moreover, the results showed that, even for those who do show comprehension difficulty, the pattern of breakdown is far from uniform. Importantly, the heterogeneity of results from Berndt et al.'s meta-analytic breakdown of group studies with patients shows that the operation of a single syntactic impairment cannot account for the comprehension pattern of all Broca's aphasics, providing a strong argument against assumptions that patients compartmentalized into one clinical category (e.g., Broca's aphasics) will all show comparable language deficits. Other evidence has also shown that the production deficits of Broca's aphasics are far from uniform (see review by Badecker & Caramazza, 1985). At least two different subtypes of "agrammatism" in Broca's aphasics have been well documented (e.g., Miceli, Mazzucchi, Menn, & Goodglass,

1983; Saffran, Berndt, & Schwartz, 1989; see also Howard, 1985; Linebarger, Schwartz, Romania, Kohn, & Stephens, 2000). Thus, both on the production and the comprehension sides there is heterogeneity of deficit within this clinically defined group, undermining conclusions that can be drawn about the relation between comprehension and production.

The failure of the group study approach to advance knowledge of sentence processing (and of other cognitive domains) can be contrasted with the successes of the case study approach in helping to delineate models of cognitive function in areas such as short-term memory (STM), number processing, reading, writing, and object recognition (for overviews, see Rapp, 2001 and Shallice, 1988). Whereas group studies have left gaps in our knowledge about the range and types of cognitive impairments that can arise from particular brain damage, case studies with a single brain-damaged individual have provided insights into the mechanisms that may underlie intact cognitive processing by identifying how it can be disrupted.

To understand the neuropsychological case study perspective, one must start with an understanding of some general assumptions. The first is the *modularity assumption*, that is, the assumption that the cognitive system in a particular domain consists of a set of interconnected components, which carry out specific functions (Coltheart, 2001; Fodor, 1983). For example, in the domain of word production, the components involved might be those shown in Figure 6.1a (adapted from Roelofs, 1992), which starts with a conceptual representation of the word to be produced, followed by access to a lexical representation for the conceptual representation (termed a *lemma*), and then to a word form, which can finally be articulated. Importantly, it is not necessary to assume that these components are noninteractive. The model shown in Figure 6.1b from Dell and O'Seaghdha (1992), which assumes feedforward and feedback connections between semantic and lexical and between lexical and phonological levels of representation, has been the basis of a fruitful line of research using cognitive neuropsychological data (Dell, Schwartz, Martin, Saffran, & Gagnon, 1997).

A second assumption to the neuropsychological case study perspective, the *universality assumption*, is that prior to brain damage, all individuals with similar developmental backgrounds will have a similar cognitive architecture. A third important assumption is the *subtractivity assumption*, that is, that after brain damage, the remaining components of the cognitive system will function as they would have prior to damage. Therefore, following damage, one may assess the functioning of the preserved components in the absence of the damaged components. By assessing precisely which cognitive functions are spared and which ones are impaired in brain-damaged patients, we can infer the underlying modules and how they are interconnected in a given domain such as word production or STM.

Because of the complexity of the cognitive architecture in any given domain, and given the possibility that any combination of modules might

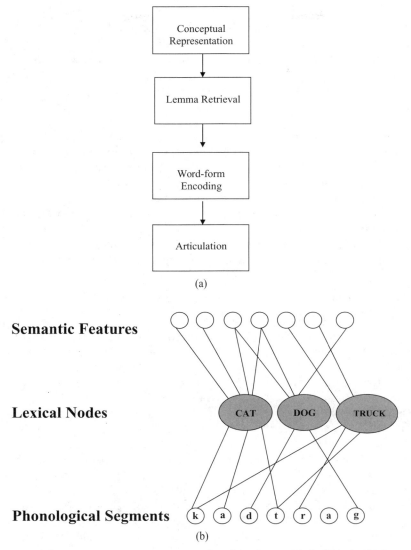

(a)

Semantic Features

Lexical Nodes

CAT   DOG   TRUCK

Phonological Segments   k a d t r a g

(b)

FIGURE 6.1.   (a) Model of word production based on Roelofs (1992). (b) Interactive model of word production based on Dell & O'Seaghdha (1992).

be affected by brain damage, the variety of different disorders that might be observed is immense, even within a limited domain such as word production. Consequently, it is highly unlikely that one will find a group of patients who are identical in the cognitive components that have been affected or spared. Any strategy for grouping patients together will thus likely involve grouping together patients with different underlying deficits. Consequently, because of the heterogeneity of deficits within any group of brain-damaged patients, group data from this source can be highly misleading. That is, the validity of group averaging for drawing conclusions about some process depends upon the assumption that all members of the group are the same in terms of their cognitive abilities, and, therefore, the distribution of individual scores around the true group mean will be a reflection of sampling error, that is, unbiased and unsystematic (e.g., Caramazza & McCloskey, 1988). However, as we have seen in the example with Broca's aphasics, some patients are consistently unable to comprehend certain types of sentences while others consistently perform normally on these same sentence types. Consequently, the distribution of scores around the mean will be a function of true differences among these patients, rather than random error; therefore, a valid inference about the particular impairment to the cognitive system following brain damage can only be drawn at the level of the individual.

With these points in mind, in the following section we describe the neuropsychological single case approach to investigating human cognition.

Case Studies as Facilitators of Cognitive Theory Development

One might justifiably wonder how studying a single individual with a particular syndrome could provide more meaningful information than studying a group of such individuals. First, it must be recognized that the case study approach does not entail the selection of one person as representative of some syndrome, followed by the testing of that individual through the few experimental manipulations that might be done in a group study. In fact, syndrome classification is not seen as an important aspect of case study procedures at all. Instead, when well done, the case study approach involves evaluating a case with respect to a theory in a particular domain, then carrying out a number of assessments to determine what aspects of cognitive function in that domain are spared and which are impaired, the assumption being that the kinds of impairments that might arise will aid in describing the way an intact system would operate. In this way, inferences about normal cognitive function drawn from each single case study can be aggregated with outcomes from unimpaired people to illustrate a more detailed picture of the mechanisms that underlie cognition.

A striking example of the utility of the case study for promoting cognitive research and theory, in this case in the domain of memory, comes from the famous case of patient HM, who was only 27 when both of his medial temporal lobes were removed in an effort to control his epilepsy (e.g., Scoville & Milner, 1957). Although his long-term memory (LTM) for events before the surgery and his intellectual functioning remained intact, the operation left HM with profound *anterograde amnesia*, meaning that he could not remember new information learned or experienced after the surgery event in 1953.

This included his age, where he lived, and the names and identities of the medical and psychological professionals who worked with him on a regular basis (see Searleman & Herrmann, 1994). Imagine waking up and looking in the mirror and being unable to recognize yourself!

Interestingly, however, HM's severe amnesia for new declarative memories did not extend to his procedural memory. That is, he could acquire and remember how to perform perceptual-motor tasks, such as mirror tracing, even though he could not remember learning them. These case study outcomes with HM have, in part, led to theories about the functional separation of the declarative and procedural memory systems (e.g., Cohen & Squire, 1980; Squire, Knowlton, & Musen, 1993), as well as the anatomical separation of their neural bases (e.g., Ullman, 2001). Many other new hypotheses have, in turn, emerged from these cognitive theories. For instance, it has been proposed that the processing of syntactic information may rely on procedural memory, whereas the processing of semantic word features may involve the declarative memory system (e.g., Faust & Chiarello, 1998; Ullman, 2001).

Although HM's case represented unexpected outcomes that ultimately gave rise to new theories about the functional properties and neural bases of memory, most case studies involve experiments that are both driven by a given cognitive theory *and* used to provide a test of the theory. A series of case studies concerning another remarkable case of brain damage, found in patient EA, took this approach to evaluate the functional relationship between STM and language deficits, as well as the neural substrates that support it.

In 1975, EA suffered a stroke that damaged her left temporal and parietal lobes (Martin & Breedin, 1992; Martin, Shelton, & Yaffee, 1999). In conversation, EA shows fluent speech production and good comprehension. In fact, research assistants who first meet her tend to think that she is one of the control subjects rather than a brain damaged patient. Standardized testing bears out this impression of good language abilities, as she scores above the mean for control subjects her age on comprehension measures. Her spontaneous speech output is quite normal in terms of speech rate and morphological and structural complexity. However, EA shows a conspicuous inability to repeat word lists that she hears or reads. This task requires the maintenance in STM of phonological information in a temporary *input* phonological buffer, so that it can be retrieved for repetition. Overall, EA has a word span of about 1.0 to 1.5 items. EA's difficulties with word list recall are not limited to situations in which she has to repeat the list orally. She performs very poorly on matching span tasks, where a decision is required with regard to whether two lists are the same or different. This task also requires the maintenance of phonological input in STM. Across many different tests of STM, EA shows evidence of having a very restricted ability to maintain phonological information. This difficulty can be attributed neither to a difficulty in perceiving words (Martin & Breedin, 1992) nor to a difficulty in articulating words (Martin et al., 1994), but instead seems to be specific to a deficit in maintaining phonological information.

The contrast between EA's very reduced STM capacity and her excellent speech production in both spontaneous speech and controlled experimental tasks (Martin & Freedman, 2001; Martin, Miller, & Vu, 2004) and seemingly normal language comprehension may come as quite a surprise to many, given the common assumption that whatever is tapped by serial list recall is also used to support language processing (e.g., Crowder, 1982; Hitch, 1980). If one assumes that some type of STM buffer is used to hold phonological representations in preparation for speech output, then the dissociation demonstrated by EA between list memory and production suggests that different buffers are involved on the input and output sides (Martin, Lesch, & Bartha, 1999). With regard to comprehension, it is clear that EA can comprehend a range of sentence types, even when such comprehension depends on linking words across several intervening words in a sentence (Martin, 1993). She does demonstrate some difficulty comprehending certain types of syntactically complex sentences (e.g., "The boy that the girl carried had red hair"); however, other patients with similar STM deficits have been reported who do not show these comprehension difficulties.

The contrast between EA's poor STM and preserved language production has suggested that there are separable input and output stores for phonological information. Importantly, other patients have been reported who show the reverse pattern – that is, they do well on matching span tasks that tap input retention but poorly on list repetition, and they show disruptions of spontaneous speech (e.g., Romani, 1992). The double dissociation illustrated by the contrast between these case studies allows the kind of inference about normal cognition that has traditionally been the bread and butter of cognitive neuropsychology (but see Rapp & Goldrick, 2000, for a different approach). That is, the double dissociation can be interpreted to mean that damage to one system does not impair performance of the other. In turn, this functional independence tells us that independent input and output phonological buffers most likely function to support normal phonological processing.

Challenges to the Neuropsychological Case Study Approach

Despite the obvious value of case study outcomes for providing evidence on a range of language and memory disorders, the generalizability of such data to neurally healthy individuals has been challenged on several grounds. One objection concerns the assumptions about modularity that cognitive neuropsychology often makes, as illustrated by the conclusions drawn from the double dissociation between deficits in input and output phonological storage described in the previous section. It has been argued that at least some cognitive processes may arise from a diffuse network of systems rather than some isolated module; thus, damage to any one of these systems or to any of the connections between them could result in impairments that are subsequently misattributed to damage to a single module located at the particular lesion site (Coltheart, 2001; Green & Price, 2001). Indeed, some functional neuroimaging studies have shown widespread activation during certain language tasks (see Hickok, 2001; Price, 1998; and Vaid & Hull, 2002 for reviews).

In light of the integral relationship between impaired cognitive function and brain damage, it is especially important to point out that cognitive neuropsychology does not claim that functional modularity necessitates anatomical modularity (Coltheart, 2001). However, if all mental processes involved vast networks of neural regions, we would expect that even mild brain damage to any area would result in the disruption of a variety of cognitive functions (Coltheart, 2001). Instead, there exists a huge body of case study and animal study evidence for consistent relationships between damage to particular brain areas and subsequent systematic disruptions to cognition, although differences in lesion size and location may certainly give rise to differences in the degree and range of deficits (see Coltheart, 2001; Martin, 2001; Poeppel & Hickok, 2004; and Shallice, 1988 for reviews).

A second challenge to the case study approach is that case studies are difficult to carry out, because of a host of methodological and strategy issues (Cupples & Inglis, 1993). Both of these concerns raise important issues for neuropsychological researchers. First, a patient cannot be realistically evaluated until he or she has reached a stable plateau in terms of cognitive processing. Certainly, many patients experience an emotional crisis after a life-threatening injury or illness that impairs their ability to function normally, making it imperative that neuropsychological testing is postponed until the patient is fully prepared to undertake the process. During the first few months after the brain insult, patients frequently experience short-lived physical impairments that are ameliorated with time. Cognitive impairments tend to spontaneously recover, at least to some extent, during this time period as well. If the patient has not reached a stable plateau, then poor performance on one test at an early time point and better performance on another test at a later time point could simply reflect general recovery, rather than a dissociation.

Once a patient has been identified for neuropsychological testing, it is critical that patients are placed within a universal platform that is accessible and understandable to other researchers in order for comparisons to be meaningful across outcomes with the same patient as well as among different patients. One can accomplish this by evaluating each patient on a wide variety of standardized psychological and neuropsychological tests, such as the Psycholinguistic Assessments of Language Processing in Aphasia (Kay,

Lesser, & Coltheart, 1992) or the Wechsler Memory Scale (Wechsler, 1987). In addition to making inter-patient and control comparisons more meaningful, correspondence across several assessment measures for the same patient bolsters confidence that the impairment profile is valid.

Also of importance when comparing patient and control scores is that the controls should be matched to the patient as closely as possible, such as in terms of age and education level and other relevant variables. As mentioned earlier with respect to neuroimaging outcomes, standard baseline tests prevent the misattribution of symptoms, such as when perceptual impairment is misinterpreted as a picture-naming deficit (see Shallice, 1988). Thus, as with any scientific discipline, careful attendance to participant characteristics, study design, and assessment measures can alleviate methodological concerns about the case study approach.

Another complaint that is often raised against drawing conclusions from case studies is that the patients may have developed particular strategies that give rise to their pattern of performance, and thus do not reflect the operation of the normal system in the absence of the damaged component. Often, interesting cases are followed for years, and the issue of strategy development in such patients is a real one. For instance, it is possible that a patient could develop some strategy for accomplishing a given neuropsychological assessment task that he or she has performed multiple times, so researchers must be vigilant in detecting and explaining considerable changes in a patient's performance. As the patient anticipates what is expected to achieve a "normal" score, he or she may develop an idiosyncratic technique that has nothing to do with the cognitive process of interest. In our own lab, patient EA developed just such a strategy for repeating a list of letters designed to test the capacity of her phonological input buffer. EA had consistently performed poorly on this task, and then her performance suddenly and inexplicably improved. Careful questioning revealed that, as she heard each letter, she matched it to the first letter of the name of a member of her family, and she constructed a mental image of these people from left to right as she heard the list. She was then able to use this mental image to produce the first letter of their names in order. Clearly, this "miraculous" recovery of letter repetition ability had nothing to do with the return of EA's phonological STM capacity!

In this example, we had one discordant result that failed to fit with numerous others and, consequently, raised the suspicion of strategy usage. What the critics of case studies typically have in mind, however, is a situation in which a patient has developed a strategy in some domain that results in consistent results across various tests tapping this domain. For instance, one might hypothesize that developmental cases of phonological STM deficits with excellent sentence comprehension (Butterworth, Campbell, & Howard, 1986; Hanten & Martin, 2001) have invented processes for understanding sentences that allow for excellent performance despite the absence of the phonological store, that most unimpaired individuals use. However, this should be a testable hypothesis. To test it, one would have to come up with a possible strategy that these individuals could be using that would allow them to syntactically and semantically analyze the wide variety of sentence constructions that one encounters in everyday life. It should be noted that it is often much more difficult to actually devise a plausible strategy to account for the patient's behavior than to simply raise the criticism that a strategy might be in place.

Another related concern about lesion-deficit case studies is the issue of reallocation of neural tissue. Specifically, it has been argued that lesion data do not allow for a separation of effects stemming from the injury and those that may arise from the reallocation of healthy cortical tissue to language functions lost as a result of the brain injury. Given that the brain retains at least some plasticity, even later in life, it is possible that, over time, a patient's performance on some cognitive task may improve as a result of reorganization of function; thus, it is important to distinguish between strategy development and neural reorganization. But what is the nature of reorganization? Does it mean that new cortical tissue simply "takes over" the lost function, or does it entail a new way of processing the same material?

If reorganization of function simply means that new brain areas assume the lost function, then performance continues to reflect the cognitive process of interest, even though it is supported by a new neural architecture. If, however, reorganization of function means that an entirely new way of processing some task has emerged, then performance that appears "normal" would not reflect the process of interest. That is, the patient's performance, no matter how good, would not be comparable to the same process that we are measuring in other patients and healthy controls, or even in that same patient before the neural reallocation. Consequently, conclusions about normal function in such a patient would be compromised. The implication of this would be that one would have to test whether the seemingly normal patient performance differs in its detail from that of normal subjects. That is, more subtle measures than just accuracy would be needed to determine if the patient's performance derived from new mechanisms. Various measures in the domain would need to be obtained to determine whether the patient was affected in the same or a different fashion as controls by a variety of experimental manipulations.

Another concern about the case study approach has been how to determine "abnormal" performance. As any student of psychology knows, variability within neurally healthy people on a given task can be quite high. Therefore, neuropsychologists, like other scientists, use statistical procedures to identify some cutoff point beyond which scores are considered abnormal. Statistical procedures have been developed for comparing the data from a single case against that from a sample of control participants (Crawford & Howell, 1998). In some instances, however, although the patient value is significantly outside of the range of controls, there are a few controls who show equally deviant performance. What makes patient scores different? Here, again, we see the importance of a multitude of consistent and converging measures. Whereas a control participant may supply the occasional outlying score, perhaps as a result of a temporary loss of concentration, or because he or she failed to follow study directions, a patient showing a cognitive deficit will consistently score in the outlying range on additional tasks of the same kind, thus making clear the importance of replication.

Researchers who work solely with unimpaired individuals sometimes comment that the assumption of a deficit based on a patient failing to show a normal effect in some task is not compelling because some of these researchers' normal undergraduate participants also fail to show the effect. For instance, patient EA does not show a phonological similarity effect on memory span tasks with visually presented words. No doubt, some undergraduate participants will also fail to show this effect in a group administration of STM tasks. However, with a well-done case study, the conclusion of a deficit to a particular cognitive component (such as phonological STM) is not based on the outcome of one test with a few items. Rather, what is demonstrated is a consistent pattern across a variety of tests. For instance, EA has been shown to have very reduced span, an absence of word length effects with auditory and visual presentation, no recency effect, and an extremely poor ability to repeat individual nonwords if they have more than three phonemes, *in addition to* her failure to show a phonological similarity effect. Certainly, if only one of these outcomes had been obtained on a single testing administration, the claim that she had a phonological STM deficit would have a weak basis; she may just have had a bad day and been distracted during testing. However, when the whole complex of results is considered, the odds that the entire set of findings could be attributed to random variation would be small indeed. Typically, normal individuals are not tested extensively on a whole range of tests. If they were, most individuals who performed differently from the control pattern on one test would nonetheless show a normal pattern on the rest, and might, on retesting, show a normal pattern on the one deviant task. Some individuals might, however, show an abnormal pattern, similar to EA, across the whole battery of tasks, even if their span deficit were not quite as dramatic as EA's (e.g., see Hanten & Martin, 2001). If such were to occur, it would seem that the conclusion would *not* be that it is invalid to claim that EA has a phonological STM deficit, but rather that there is individual variation within the normal population for this capacity, and some individuals are far below the mean in terms of their abilities in this domain. If these individuals were nonetheless good at language production and comprehension, that would provide further evidence supporting the conclusions drawn from dissociations like those noted in EA rather than undermining them (Hanten & Martin, 2001).

SUMMARY

The goal of this chapter was to illustrate the methods of the case study approach and the connection between case studies and psychological research with the general population. We have seen that clinical case reports can spur important discoveries in cognitive research with healthy individuals, as evidenced by promising new research in the area of blocked and recovered memories. We have further seen that neuropsychological case studies have been increasingly important to the development of cognitive theory, as such case studies have provided insights into the mechanisms that may underlie normal cognition. Specifically, the case study approach can help elucidate the neural and functional architecture of cognition by identifying the brain structures that are damaged in a given patient and thoroughly assessing the capabilities of that patient. Comparison with other patients with similar or different lesions and impairments can help identify associations and dissociations that, in turn, help determine which cognitive functions may or may not be isolable. Moreover, some consistent relationships between lesion sites and certain disruptions of cognition have been documented, thereby further contributing to the development of new and improved cognitive models. In all, we have seen that the single case approach can provide a valuable contribution to the study of human psychology.

AUTHOR NOTE

Preparation of this manuscript was supported in part by grant NIH-DC00218 to Randi Martin at Rice University.

References

Badecker, W., & Caramazza, A. (1985). On consideration of method and theory governing the use of clinical categories in neurolinguistics and cognitive neuropsychology: The case against agrammatism. *Cognition, 20*, 97–126.

Berndt, R. S., Mitchum, C., & Haendiges, A. (1996). Comprehension of reversible sentences in "agrammatism": A meta-analysis. *Cognition, 58*, 289–308.

Berndt, R. S., Mitchum, C., & Haendiges, A. (1996). Comprehension of reversible sentences in "agrammatism": A meta-analysis. *Cognition, 58*, 289–308.

Bowman, C. G., & Mertz, E. (1996). A dangerous direction: Legal interventions in sexual abuse survivor therapy. *Harvard Law Review, 109*, 549–639.

Briere, J., & Conte, J. (1993). Self-reported amnesia for abuse in adults molested as children. *Journal of Traumatic Stress, 6*, 21–31.

Brewin, C. R. (1989). Cognitive change processes in psychotherapy. *Psychological Review, 96*, 379–394.

Brown, D., Scheflin, A. W., & Hammond, D. C. (1998). *Memory, trauma treatment, and the law.* New York: Norton.

Butterworth, B., Campbell, R., & Howard, D. (1986). The uses of short-term memory: A case study. *Quarterly Journal of Experimental Psychology: Human Experimental Psychology, 38*, 705–737.

Campbell, D. T., Stanley, J. C., & Gage, N. L. (1963). *Experimental and quasi-experimental designs for research.* Boston: Houghton Mifflin.

Caramazza, A., & McCloskey, M. (1988). The case for single-patient studies. *Cognitive Neuropsychology, 5*, 517–528.

Caramazza, A., & Hillis, A. (1989). The disruption of sentence production: Some dissociations. *Brain and Language, 36*, 628–650.

Caramazza, A., & Zurif, E. (1976). Dissociation of algorithmic and heuristic processes in language comprehension: Evidence from aphasia. *Brain and Language, 3*, 572–582.

Ceci, S. J., & Loftus, E. F. (1994). 'Memory work': A royal road to false memories? *Applied Cognitive Psychology, 8*, 351–364.

Clancy, S. A. (2001). Memory distortion in individuals reporting recovered memories of trauma. *Dissertation Abstracts International, 62*, 2098B.

Clancy, S. A., McNally, R. J., & Schacter, D. L. (1999). Effects of guided imagery on memory distortion in women reporting recovered memories of childhood sexual abuse. *Journal of Traumatic Stress, 12*, 559–569.

Cohen, N. J., & Squire, L. R. (1980). Preserved learning and retention of pattern analyzing skill in amnesia: Dissociation of "knowing how" and "knowing that." *Science, 210*, 207–209.

Coltheart, M. (2001). Assumptions and methods in cognitive neuropsychology. In B. Rapp (Ed.), *The handbook of neuropsychology* (pp. 3–22). Philadelphia: Psychology Press.

Crawford, J. R., & Howell, D. C. (1998). Comparing an individual's test score against norms derived from small samples. *The Clinical Neuropsychologist, 12*, 482–486.

Crowder, R. (1982). The demise of short-term memory. *Acta Psychologica, 50*, 291–323.

Cupples, L., & Inglis, A. L. (1993). When task demands induce "asyntactic" comprehension: A study of sentence interpretation in aphasia. *Cognitive Neuropsychology, 10*, 201–234.

Dell, G. S., & O' Seaghdha, P. G. (1992). Stages of lexical access in language production. *Cognition, 42*, 287–314.

Dell, G. S., Schwartz, M. F., Martin, N., Saffran, E. M., & Gagnon, D. A. (1997). Lexical access in aphasic and nonaphasic speakers. *Psychological Review, 104*, 801–838.

Dodson, C. S., & Johnson, M. K. (1993). Rate of false source attributions depends on how questions are asked. *Journal of Psychology, 106*, 541–557.

Eyre, D. P. (1991). Therapy with a sexually abused woman. *International Journal of Psycho-Analysis, 72*, 403–415.

Faust, M., & Chiarello, C. (1998). Constraints on sentence priming in the cerebral hemispheres: Effects of intervening words in sentences and lists. *Brain and Language, 63*, 219–236.

Fodor, J. A. (1983). *The modularity of mind.* Cambridge, MA: MIT Press.

Gleaves, D. H., Smith, S. M., Butler, L. D., & Spiegel, D. (2004). False and recovered memories in the laboratory and clinic: A review of experimental and clinical evidence. *Clinical Psychology: Science and Practice, 11*, 3–28.

Freud, S. (1935; reprinted in 1960). *A general introduction to psychoanalysis*. New York: Washington Square Press.

Green, D. & Price, C. 2001. Functional imaging in the study of recovery patterns in bilingual aphasia. *Bilingualism: Language and Cognition, 4*, 191–201.

Hanten, G., & Martin, R. (2001). A developmental phonological short-term memory deficit: A case study. *Brain and Cognition, 45*, 164–188.

Hickok, G. (2001). Functional anatomy of speech perception and speech production: Psycholinguistic implications. *Journal of Psycholinguistic Research, 30*, 225–235.

Hitch, G. (1980). Developing the concept of working memory. In G. Claxton (Ed.), *Cognitive psychology: New directions*. London: Routledge & Kegan Paul.

Howard, D. (1985). Introduction to "On agrammatism" (Ueber Agrammatismus), by Max Isserlin, 1922. *Cognitive Neuropsychology, 2*, 303–307.

Johnson, M. K., Hashroudi, S., & Lindsay, D. S. (1993). Source monitoring. *Psychological Bulletin, 114*, 3–28.

Kaplan, R., & Manicavasagar, V. (2001). Is there a false memory syndrome? A review of three cases. *Comprehensive psychiatry, 42*, 342–348.

Kay, J., Lesser, R., & Coltheart, M. (1992). *Psycholinguistic assessments of language processing in aphasia*. New York: Psychology Press.

Kolb, L. C. (1988). Recovery of memory and repressed fantasy in combat-induced post-traumatic stress disorder of Vietnam veterans. In H. M. Pettinati (Ed.), *Hypnosis and memory* (pp. 265–274). New York: Guilford Press.

Kolk, H., van Grunsven, M., & Keyser, A. (1985). On parallelism between production and comprehension in agrammatism. In M. L. Kean (Ed.), *Agrammatism* (pp. 347–384). New York: Academic Press.

Lief, H. I. (2003). Questions raised by the controversy over recovered memories of incest. *Journal of the American Academy of Psychoanalysis & Dynamic Psychiatry, 31*, 381–395.

Linebarger, M. C., Schwartz, M. F., Romania, J. R., Kohn, S. E., & Stephens, D. L. (2000). Grammatical encoding in aphasia: Evidence from a "processing prosthesis." *Brain and Language, 75*, 416–427.

Linebarger, M., Schwartz, M., & Saffran, E. (1983). Sensitivity to grammatical structure in so-called agrammatic aphasics. *Cognition, 13*, 361–392.

Loftus, E. F. (1993). The reality of repressed memories. *American Psychologist, 48*, 518–537.

Loftus, E. F., Polonsky, S., & Fullilove, M. T. (1994). Memories of childhood sexual abuse: Remembering and repressing. *Psychology of Women Quarterly, 18*, 67–84.

Martin, R. C. (2001). Sentence comprehension deficits. In B. Rapp (Ed.), *Handbook of cognitive neuropsychology* (pp. 349–374). Philadelphia: Psychology Press.

Martin, R. C. (1993). Short-term memory and sentence processing: Evidence from neuropsychology. *Memory and Cognition, 12*, 176–183.

Martin, R. C., & Breedin, S. (1992). Dissociations between speech perception and phonological short-term memory. *Cognitive Neuropsychology, 9*, 509–534.

Martin, R. C., & Freedman, M. L. (2001). Short-term retention of lexical-semantic representations: Implications for speech production. *Memory, 9*, 261–280.

Martin, R. C., Lesch, M., & Bartha, M. (1999). Independence of input and output phonology in word processing and short-term memory. *Journal of Memory and Language, 41*, 3–29.

Martin, R. C., Miller, M., & Vu, H. (2004) Lexical-semantic retention and speech production: Further evidence from normal and brain-damaged participants for a phrasal scope of planning. *Cognitive Neuropsychology, 21,* 625–644.

Martin, R. C., Shelton, J. R., & Yaffee, L. S. (1994). Language processing and working memory: Neuropsychological evidence for separate phonological and semantic capacities. *Journal of Memory and Language, 33,* 83–111.

Martin, R. C., Wetzel, F., Blossom-Stach, C. & Feher, E. (1989). Syntactic loss versus processing deficit: An assessment of two theories of agrammatism and syntactic comprehension deficits. *Cognition, 32,* 157–191.

McDermott, K. B. (1996). The persistence of false memories in list recall. *Journal of Memory and Language, 35,* 212–230.

McHugh, P. R., Lief, H. J., Freyd, P. P., & Fetkewicz, J. M. (2003). From refusal to reconciliation: Family relationships after an accusation based on recovered memories. *Journal of Nervous and Mental Disease, 192,* 525–531.

McNally, R. J. (2003). Recovering memories of trauma: A view from the laboratory. *Current Directions in Psychological Science, 12,* 32–35.

McNally, R. J., Metzger, L. J., Lasko, N. B., Clancy, S. A., & Pitman, R. K. (1998). Directed forgetting of trauma cues in adult survivors of childhood sexual abuse with and without posttraumatic stress disorder. *Journal of Abnormal Psychology, 107,* 596–601.

Miceli, G., Mazzucchi, A., Menn, L., & Goodglass, H. (1983). Contrasting cases of Italian agrammatic aphasia without comprehension disorder. *Brain and Language, 19,* 65–97.

Ofshe, R., & Watters, E. (1993, March/April). Making monsters. *Society,* 4–16.

Poeppel, D., & Hickok, G. (2004). Towards a new functional anatomy of language. *Cognition, 92,* 1–12.

Perrotto, R. S., & Culkin, J. (1993). *Exploring abnormal psychology.* New York: Harper Collins.

Price, C. (1998). The functional anatomy of word comprehension and production. *Trends in Cognitive Science, 2,* 281–288.

Rapp, B. (2001). *Handbook of cognitive neuropsychology.* Philadelphia: Psychology Press.

Rapp, B., & Goldrick, M. (2000). Discreteness and interactivity in spoken word production. *Psychological Review, 107,* 460–499.

Robinson, K. J., & Roediger, H. L., III. (1997). Associative processes in false recall and false recognition, *Psychological Science, 8,* 231–237.

Roelofs, A. (1992). A spreading activation theory of lemma retrieval in speaking. *Cognition, 42,* 107–142.

Romani, C. (1992). Are there distinct input and output buffers? Evidence from an aphasic patient with an impaired output buffer. *Language and Cognitive Processes, 7,* 131–162.

Saffran, E. M., Berndt, R. S., & Schwartz, M.F. (1989). The quantitative analysis of agrammatic production: Procedure and data. *Brain and Language, 37,* 440–479.

Sargant, W., & Slater, E. (1941). Amnestic syndromes of war. *Proceeding of the Royal Society of Medicine, 34,* 757–764.

Scoville, W. B., & Milner, B. (1957). Loss of recent memory after bilateral hippocampal lesions. *Journal of Neurology, Neurosurgery, and Psychiatry, 19,* 252–259.

Searleman, A., & Herrmann, D. (1994). *Memory from a broader perspective.* New York: Mcgraw Hill.

Shallice, T. (1988). *From neuropsychology to mental structure.* New York: Cambridge University Press.

Smith, S. M., Gleaves, D. H., Pierce, B. H., Williams, T. L., Gilliland, T. R., & Gerkens, D. R. (2003). Eliciting and comparing false and recovered memories: An experimental approach. *Applied Cognitive Psychology, 17,* 251–279.

Squire, L. R., Knowlton, B., & Musen, G. (1993). The structure and organization of memory. In L. W. Porter & M. R. Rosenzweig (Eds.), *Annual review of psychology* (Vol. 44, pp. 463–495). Palo Alto, CA: Annual Reviews.

Stein, J. (1970). *Neurosis in contemporary society.* Belmont, CA: Wadsworth.

Taylor, S. (2004). Amnesia, folklore and folks: Recovered memories in clinical practice. *Cognitive Behaviour Therapy, 33,* 105–108.

Ullman, M. (2001). The neural basis of lexicon and grammar in first and second language: The declarative/procedural model. *Bilingualism, 4,* 105–122.

Vaid, J., & Hull, R. (2002). Re-envisioning the bilingual brain using functional neuroimaging: Methodological and interpretive issues. In F. Fabbro (Ed.), *Advances in the neurolinguistics of bilingualism: A festschrift for Michel Paradis* (pp. 315–355). Udine, Italy: Forum.

Wechsler, D. (1987). *Wechsler Memory Scale Revised.* San Antonio, TX: Psychological Corporation.

Yin, R. (1998). The abridged version of case study research: Design and method. In L. Bickman and D. J. Rog (Eds.), *Handbook of applied social research methods* (pp. 229–259). Thousand Oaks, CA: Sage.

7

Informal Logical Fallacies

Jane Risen and Thomas Gilovich

> Premise 1: All good chapters begin with a pithy quote.
> Premise 2: We do not begin with a pithy quote.
> Conclusion: This is not a good chapter.

Is this a valid conclusion? According to formal logic, it is. Formally, an argument is valid if the conclusion follows from the premises (whether or not the premises are true) and is invalid if it does not. Thus, formal logic is only concerned with the rules for drawing conclusions from a given set of premises (Baron, 1994). It does not specify a standard for evaluating the premises themselves (except, of course, to the extent that the premises were derived as conclusions from other premises).

This chapter focuses on informal logic. Unlike formal logic, informal logic seeks standards for the generation and evaluation of premises. Thus, if Premise 1 is not supported by sufficient evidence, then, according to informal logic, the conclusion about the chapter is not valid. So don't despair: This chapter may have more promise than our opening syllogism would compel you to conclude.

A second difference between formal logic and informal logic is that formal logic deals with certainty, and therefore does not offer a way to weigh the reasonableness of multiple valid or invalid conclusions (Baron, 1994). For instance, if the first premise were, "Some good chapters begin with pithy quotes," the conclusion would be invalid. The conclusion would also be invalid if the first premise read, "Almost every good chapter begins with a pithy quote." The conclusion surely seems more reasonable in the latter case than in the former, but formal logic deems them equally invalid. Formal logic has the desirable properties of objectivity and precision. And although some of that objectivity and precision is lost with informal logic, much is gained in applicability and utility.

Informal logic, then, involves standards for evaluating the reasonableness of conclusions, starting with the search for pertinent evidence and ending with the inferences drawn from the evidence. Thus, an informal logical fallacy is a misconception that results from faulty reasoning at any point in that process. The goals of the present chapter are to describe the most common informal logical fallacies and to offer ways to avoid them. Of course, any claim that our discussion covers all informal logical fallacies would be a fallacy itself. Therefore, we present the fallacies that we see as the most important, and encourage you to read other compilations of fallacies if you want a different take on this important topic (see Baron, 1994; Dawes, 2001; Vos Savant, 1996).

But before describing the most common informal fallacies and discussing strategies to avoid them, it is important to take a moment to explore why you should strive to spot and overcome such fallacies. Many of you, to be sure, are likely to take it as a given that it is important to avoid logical fallacies and think rationally. But if you're of a skeptical bent and are disinclined to accept such a proposition, it is worth considering the issue in a bit more detail. The arguments for why it is important to avoid informal logical fallacies are the same as why, more generally, it is important to think critically. But it is particularly important, we believe, to be able to spot and resist informal logical fallacies because they are unusually seductive. That is, the fallacies to be examined in this chapter are not the fallacies made by woefully uneducated people or by mentally challenged people. They are the fallacies made by nearly all people. One reason for this is that many informal logical fallacies, as we shall see, resemble or are based on useful heuristics. A heuristic is an implicit strategy of judgment that converts a complex inferential problem to a simpler mental assessment. We benefit by using heuristics because they allow us to solve problems efficiently and they typically lead to the correct answer, or a close approximation to the correct answer. However, when a heuristic is stretched too far and is applied too liberally, predictable errors result. And because there is a fine line between a helpful heuristic and an informal logical fallacy, even very educated, very rational, and generally very effective thinkers are vulnerable to such errors.

But why is it important to think critically and, by extension, particularly important to avoid informal logical fallacies? For one thing, in daily life a great deal rides on the quality of our thinking and the validity of our conclusions. The benefits of more rewarding decisions belong to those who think most clearly. Second, as a student of behavioral science, it is imperative to think critically about evidence to be able to discern what conclusions can and cannot be drawn from a body of evidence – whether one's own or someone else's. Finally, as a citizen with the power and obligation to elect effective leaders and to contribute to the public debate on the issues of the day, it is important that you be able to accurately evaluate candidates, policies, and evidence, and not be hoodwinked by sloganeering and demagoguery. Our political system is based on the Enlightenment promise that reason is the surest guide to human progress. But that promise can only be fulfilled if we reason soundly.

FALLACIES OF EVIDENCE SEARCH AND INTERPRETATION

Confirmation Bias

For conclusions to be valid, the premises on which they are based must be valid, and that requires the accumulation of accurate and probative evidence, a task rendered quite difficult by a common and particularly powerful bias known as the *confirmation bias*. The confirmation bias is the inclination to recruit and give weight to evidence that is consistent with the hypothesis in question, rather than search for inconsistent evidence that could falsify the hypothesis (Bassok & Trope, 1984; Skov & Sherman, 1986; Snyder & Swann, 1978).

In some sense, it is the most natural thing in the world to entertain a proposition by looking for evidence to support it. Thus, the tendency to search for consistent evidence is based on the very valid belief that, "If the hypothesis is true, there must be some evidence for it." However, this belief rests on the very premise (that the hypothesis is true) that one is supposed to be testing. Thus, it is also necessary to base one's search on the equally valid belief that, "If the hypothesis is not true, there must be some evidence against it" and search for evidence inconsistent with the hypothesis. In other words, the confirmation bias consists of the natural tendency to gather consistent evidence, without supplementing it with the less natural, but equally necessary, process of gathering inconsistent evidence.

The confirmation bias is evident both when searching for new evidence and when recruiting evidence from memory. For example, take a moment to think about your best friend from high school. What evidence comes to mind when you think about whether your friend is shy? Does that same evidence come to mind when you think about whether your friend is outgoing? If you assume that shy and outgoing are opposite ends of the same dimension, then, logically, the same set of evidence should be recruited to answer both questions. But the confirmation bias leads to the recruitment of two distinct sets of evidence. When thinking about whether your friend is shy, you probably thought of several examples of when she or he acted in an introverted manner (e.g., she always gets nervous around guys and is really quiet in large groups). However, when thinking about whether your friend is outgoing, you most likely recalled the times when she or he tends to be extroverted (e.g., she is goofy when we hang out with the girls and she loves meeting new people). The evidence that your friend likes meeting new people should factor into your evaluation of whether she or he is shy, and if you don't overcome the confirmatory bias to recruit that evidence, your conclusion is unlikely to be valid.

Although the confirmation bias is often described as a cognitive bias, it is especially pronounced and problematic when one is motivated to believe the hypothesis in question (Gilovich, 1991). For example, if you have to determine whether a stranger is kind, the cognitive component of the confirmatory bias might lead you to search for examples of kindness rather than for examples of unkindness. However, if you must determine whether *you* are kind, the motivation to answer "yes" will likely exaggerate the tendency. Similarly, if you have to decide whether to rent a small, cheap apartment or a large, lavish apartment and you have your heart set on the larger one, you may be motivated to confirm your opinion by asking your most extravagant friends for advice rather than asking your more thrifty friends for their thoughts. Therefore, you need to be most careful to seek evidence that could disconfirm the hypothesis in precisely those instances in which you hope not to find any.

Assimilation Bias

Overcoming the confirmation bias and gathering balanced evidence is the first step toward reaching a valid conclusion. The second step is interpreting that evidence in an unbiased manner. To do that, one must overcome the *assimilation bias,* or the inclination to interpret ambiguous evidence in a manner that supports an initial hypothesis or supposition. Because people give more weight to evidence that confirms their initial supposition, new evidence that is objectively equivocal can actually bolster the initial belief.

A well-known study by Lord, Ross, and Lepper (1979) offers perhaps the best example of how ambiguous evidence can be interpreted differently by those with opposing prior beliefs. Participants who were either for or against the death penalty were recruited to participate. After indicating their attitudes toward capital punishment, participants read evidence from two studies: one study offered empirical evidence in support of the death penalty and one offered evidence in opposition. Although both groups read the same mixed evidence, both felt that on balance, the weight of evidence supported their own position. This led to the problematic finding whereby the very same body of ambiguous evidence created final attitudes that were even more polarized than the attitudes the participants brought with them to the experiment.

Perhaps the most familiar example of the assimilation bias is demonstrated every 4 years in the United States, when political partisans watch the Presidential debates, and both sides come away claiming that their candidate won. To be sure, some of these claims are pure political spin. But often, both sides truly believe that their own candidate won, in part because they attend to different features of the debate and quite literally see a different contest (Hastorf & Cantril, 1954).

In addition to a tendency to search for confirmatory evidence and inter-pret ambiguous evidence in support of a favored hypothesis, people are also plagued by the tendency to ignore, filter out, or get around evidence that flatly disconfirms the hypothesis. If one draws a conclusion based on evidence and later finds out that the evidence was fabricated, then logically, the conclusion should change. Back to square one. However, many studies have demonstrated pronounced *belief perseverance*, whereby beliefs remain even after the evidence on which they were based is revealed to be false (Anderson, Lepper, & Ross, 1980; Ross, Lepper, & Hubbard, 1975). This tendency has particularly important implications for beliefs about govern-mental policy. For example, when citizens of the United States were told that there were weapons of mass destruction in Iraq and ties between Sad-dam Hussein and Al Qaeda, many formed the belief that the U.S. should go to war with Iraq. Once those two pieces of evidence were discredited, how-ever, the belief that the U.S. should invade Iraq remained strong for a large percentage of the population. Certainly there were other reasons for going to war that had not been discredited and were still logically valid. But it is far from clear that such pro-invasion sentiments would have been formed initially if everyone knew that there were no weapons of mass destruction or ties to Al Qaeda.

Naïve Realism

A final obstacle to achieving an unbiased interpretation of evidence is the basic failure to recognize that you *are* interpreting the evidence. *Naïve real-ism* refers to the conviction that one perceives objects and events as they are, rather than as they appear in light of one's particular vantage point, prior beliefs, and expectations (Ross & Ward, 1996). Among other things, naïve realism helps to explain why it is that people think that informal logical fallacies – and biases in general – are more often something that plagues someone else's thinking. That is, people suffer from something of a "bias blindspot," detecting bias in other people's judgments that they fail to detect in their own (Pronin, Lin, & Ross, 2002). Suppose Bill and Ted disagree about the threat posed by global warming. Because each thinks he understands the pertinent evidence as it is, each will attribute their dif-ference of opinion to the other (Pronin, Gilovich, & Ross, 2004). And the handiest, most generally applicable interpretation of the other's divergent opinion is that the other is biased. Interestingly, this same tendency also leads the two sides to perceive a neutral third party as biased toward the other side (Vallone, Ross, & Lepper, 1985).

The problem of naïve realism can be particularly pronounced when the pertinent information is secondhand. Secondhand information tends to be more streamlined and less variable than firsthand information (Gilovich, 1987; Thompson, Judd, & Park, 2000). When we hear about someone who walked away from the negotiating table without making a counteroffer, someone who cursed at a student in class, or someone who drove everyone crazy with incessant talking, it is all too easy to construct a particular mental representation that seems every bit as real and vivid as a direct experience of these events – and yet bears little resemblance to what actually transpired. For these reasons, one ought to be more wary of drawing conclusions from secondhand sources. Failing to take account of the uncertainties inherent in secondhand information often leads to invalid conclusions. Thus, like informal logical fallacies more generally, reliance on secondhand information can give rise to premises that seem more sound than they really are.

FALLACIES OF INFERENCE

Non Sequiturs

Democrat Debbie: George W. Bush said that new tax cuts will improve the economy, but since he hasn't proved it, I know he's wrong. Everyone I read about in Hollywood says that Bush's approach to North Korea is wrong-headed, so I agree. You're either against Bush or you're for oppression and torture.

Republican Rachel: Why did I vote for George W. Bush? For one thing, I believe in strong and stable marriages so I'm against efforts to extend marriage rights to homosexuals. Besides, the majority of the country supported Bush's decision to go to war against Iraq, so it must have been the right thing to do. Since each member of the President's cabinet is smart and informed, the cabinet must make smart and informed decisions.

These arguments should sound familiar. Although the flaws may be more unadorned and more obvious than those you hear in everyday life, they are the same fallacies that have been made on countless occasions by supporters and opponents of Bush's policies. We trust that most of these statements struck you as illogical. In fact, all six statements are examples of non sequitur fallacies of inference. A *non sequitur fallacy* literally means one in which the conclusion does "not follow" from the given evidence (and hence is the province of both formal and informal logic). Specifically, the term is used for fallacies in which the premise is irrelevant to the conclusion, rendering the conclusion arbitrary from a logical standpoint. Arguments such as these are made quite often in everyday life, and so one needs to guard against their seductive appeal (however obvious and unseductive they may appear in the caricatured form shown here).

In her mock conversation with Democrat Debbie, Republican Rachel started by making a *zero-sum* or *fixed pie fallacy*. Her argument against gay marriage rests on the assumption that marriage on the part of homosexual and heterosexual couples is a zero sum game: whatever gains are realized by gay and lesbian couples must translate into losses for the heterosexual "institution of marriage." But as advocates of homosexual marriages point out, marriage is not zero sum: Encouraging long-term homosexual relationships by allowing homosexual couples to marry need not detract from the strength of the institution of marriage; indeed it may even strengthen it. This type of zero-sum fallacy has been shown to be particularly costly in negotiation situations because it can blind the two sides to the possibility of mutually beneficial compromises (Bazerman, 1998).

Democrat Debbie ended her comments with a related fallacy known as an *invalid disjunction*. An invalid disjunction is the tendency to assume that something must be one extreme or the other, not something in between. Certainly it is possible to support Bush's position in the war and also be against torture. Debbie's statement paints a black-and-white world without allowing for shades of gray.

A third common type of non sequitur fallacy occurs when one assumes that an argument made by a likable source is valid (*argumentum ad verecundiam*) or an argument made by an unlikable source is invalid (*argumentum ad hominem*). The stars of Hollywood may dazzle Debbie, but that does not mean their beliefs can be accepted as valid. Similarly, an argument by a disliked individual is not automatically invalid. An extreme (and common) form of argumentum ad hominem is known as "playing the Hitler card." In this form, one claims that an idea lacks validity by citing Hitler's support of it (i.e., euthanasia is wrong because Hitler was in favor of it). Other fallacies in this family of errors involve claims that something is good because it is natural (*naturalistic fallacy*), new (*argumentum ad novitatem*), or the way it's always been done (*argumentum ad antiquitatem*).

Republican Rachel also falls prey to the *bandwagon fallacy* (*argumentum ad populum*), the tendency to assume that the majority opinion is the valid opinion. The bandwagon fallacy is another example of how a generally useful heuristic can nevertheless lead to errors. The majority opinion *is* valid most of the time. Most people believe that tigers do not make good household pets, and that toddlers shouldn't drive. Thus, if one sees people giving a wide berth to an animal with which one is unfamiliar, it's wise to give it a wide berth oneself (and not personally test the validity of the belief). Nonetheless, there are times when the majority opinion is not valid, and following the majority will set one off track. There was a time when everyone believed the world was flat, and a more recent time when the majority condoned slavery. As we gather new information and our cultural values change, so too does the majority opinion. Therefore, even though the majority is often right, the fluctuation of the majority opinion implies that a logically valid conclusion cannot be based on the majority alone. Thus, even if the majority of the country did support going to war with Iraq, the majority opinion is not sufficient for determining whether the decision was correct.

Another fallacy that results from a generally useful heuristic being taken too far is the *fallacy of ignorance* (*argumentum ad ignorantiam*). The fallacy of ignorance can take one of two forms: (a) assuming that if something has not been proven false, it must be true; (b) assuming that if something has not been proven true, it must be false. Debbie incorrectly assumes that tax cuts will not improve the economy because Bush has not shown that they will. Of course, it would be equally invalid to conclude that tax cuts will improve the economy simply because no one has proven that they will not. The truth or falsity of a claim is determined by evidence that supports or refutes the claim, not by the lack of support for a contradictory claim. This fallacy often rears itself in dorm room discussions about the existence of God. Despite what people sometimes claim, a lack of evidence for God's existence does not prove that there is no God and a lack of evidence against God's existence does not prove that there is one.

Finally, Rachel is also guilty of the *fallacy of composition*, the assumption that the properties of the whole are the same as the properties of its parts. Even if all of the individual cabinet members are smart and well informed, it does not follow that the cabinet as a whole will make wise and well-informed decisions. Group decision making has its own set of influences that can lead to nonoptimal decisions (Janis, 1972; Kerr, MacCoun, & Kramer, 1996; Levine & Moreland, 1998). Similarly, in athletics, having good individual players does not guarantee a good team because the teamwork among the players is sometimes as vital as the individual talent. As emphatic supporters of the underdog, we feel compelled to offer the 2003–2004 Los Angeles Lakers as a case in point. The basketball world assumed that if you added two superstars, in this case Karl Malone and Gary Payton, to an already formidable Laker team, you would have a virtually unstoppable team. The 2003–2004 Champion Detroit Pistons proved otherwise.

Inferential Errors in Frequency Estimation

Another common set of fallacies arise when people try to determine the likelihood of events or the size of different categories. These fallacies demonstrate better than any other the fine line between useful heuristics and informal logical errors. Kahneman and Tversky (1973) introduced the *availability* and *representativeness* heuristics to explain some of people's systematic departures from normative judgment. These two heuristics are the most well documented and researched heuristics in the judgment and decision-making literature and offer great insight not only into the errors that people make, but also into the ways in which people think.

Availability
The availability heuristic involves an assessment of the probability of an event or the size of a category by the ease with which relevant instances are brought

to mind. It is thus based on a logical fallacy. Because instances of large categories or likely events are relatively easy to call to mind, one assumes that instances that easily come to mind must belong to large categories or likely events. But other factors also influence the ease of imagination. Salient, distinctive features and emotionally laden events are also easily imagined, and the availability heuristic leads those features and events to be overestimated. For instance, people tend to overestimate the number of deaths caused by car accidents and homicide and underestimate the number caused by diabetes and heart disease (Lichtenstein, Slovic, Fischoff, Layman, & Combs, 1978). People's willingness to pay for insurance is also influenced by the ease of imagining disastrous events and thus offers a telling example of how the availability heuristic can lead to a logical error. In a study by Johnson, Hershey, Meszaros, and Kunreuther (1993), participants reported being willing to pay an average of $14.12 for flight insurance that paid $100,000 in case of death due to terrorism, but they were only willing to pay an average of $12.03 for a policy that paid $100,000 in case of death due to any reason (including, of course, terrorism). Logically, this doesn't make sense, but psycho-logically it does. Because it is more difficult to imagine death due to "any reason" than death due to terrorism, death due to any reason feels less likely, and participants are less willing to pay for the policy that provides more protection.

Representativeness

The representativeness heuristic involves substituting a simple similarity computation for a much more difficult assessment of probability, causality, or category membership. For instance, if Ben has long hair and wears sandals, it seems more likely that he is from California than Kansas, more likely liberal than conservative, and more likely young than old because of his resemblance to the prototypical Californian, liberal, or young person. The representativeness heuristic typically pays off, but it can lead to a variety of errors.

First, representativeness can lead to misconceptions about random sequences. Imagine the sequence of coin flips: heads, tails, tails, heads, tails, heads. That sequence looks representative of a fair coin because there are equal numbers of heads and tails and there is no easily summarized pattern to their occurrence (Falk & Konold, 1997). The sequence HTHHHH does not look as representative of a fair coin because it contains substantially more heads than tails, and the sequence HHHTTT likewise does not look representative because the location of the three heads and three tails is too structured. These latter two sequences are therefore seen as less probable than the first sequence, even though all three are equally likely. The tendency to believe that even short sequences should be representative of the underlying characteristics of the chance process leads to the well-known *gambler's fallacy*, whereby people believe that if a particular outcome has not occurred for a while, it is "due" (Tversky & Kahneman, 1974). For example, after a string of reds on a Roulette wheel, people expect a black. Similarly, because an extra tails on the end of the second sequence shown here would make it more representative of a fair coin, people erroneously believe that tails is more likely to occur than a sixth heads. In this way, people misconceive chance as self-correcting rather than truly random.

The reliance on representativeness also contributes to the *regression fallacy*, the tendency to be blind to instances of regression to the mean and to create unnecessary explanations for simple regression effects (Gilovich, 1991; Nisbett & Ross, 1980). Elementary statistics teaches that when two variables are imperfectly correlated, extreme values of one variable are accompanied by less extreme values on the other. For instance, a 7-foot tall father will likely have a tall son, but not as tall (on average) as he is. Similarly, a student who aces a midterm will tend to do well on the final, but not as well (on average) as she did on the midterm. Although regression to the mean is a basic rule of statistics, people's use of the representativeness heuristic leads to the intuition that inputs should match or "fit" outputs. When this intuition is taken too far or applied blindly, it leads to the assumption that an output variable should deviate from the average just as much as the input variable. Thus, people tend to expect students to ace the final if they aced the midterm. And when a student doesn't, people often create unnecessary explanations (she got cocky and didn't study as hard) for the natural regression to the mean.

The regression fallacy leads to numerous unsubstantiated conclusions. For example, children who behave exceptionally well are often rewarded and those who behave exceptionally badly are often punished. Regression to the mean dictates that good children will not be as well behaved the next time and bad children will not behave quite as badly. However, because people are often blind to the regression effect, they can erroneously conclude that punishments, and not rewards, are most effective in shaping desired behavior (Kahneman & Tversky, 1973; Schaffner, 1985). Thus, to see relationships in the world as they really are, it is essential to recognize the natural fluctuations that ensue because of regression to the mean.

The *conjunction fallacy*, a third error due to representativeness, occurs when people believe that the conjunction of two events is more probable than either of its constituent elements. It seems obvious to most people that the chance of winning two lotteries is less than the chance of winning one of the two, and the chance of Dan's being able to drive a boat and fly a plane is less than the chance of his having only one of those skills. However, when the conjunction of two events "fits" a familiar category better than one of the constituent events, logical errors are often made. The most famous demonstration of the conjunction fallacy was built around Linda, the feminist bank teller (Kahneman & Tversky, 1973). Participants read that "Linda is 31 years old, single, outspoken, and very bright. She majored in

philosophy. As a student, she was deeply concerned with issues of discrimination and social justice, and also participated in antinuclear demonstrations."
Participants then ranked a variety of statements of careers and interests in
terms of how likely it was that Linda would have them. The key finding was
that participants thought it was more likely that Linda was a bank teller AND
active in the feminist movement than that she was simply a bank teller. Thus,
although it is illogical for the conjunction to be more probable (because a
feminist bank teller is also a bank teller), people relied on their assessment
of goodness of fit and incorrectly judged that Linda the feminist bank teller
was more likely than Linda the bank teller.

Inference from Samples

When people make inferences from samples of data, the most common
and problematic mistake is *over-inference* from small samples. We can only
be confident that a sample is representative of a population if the sample is
large enough (and is drawn by using an acceptable sampling procedure).
A particularly pronounced (and particularly common) version of this error
involves the tendency to draw firm conclusions from a single instance or
event. "My dad has smoked a pack a day for 40 years, and is extremely
healthy, so all this talk about the hazards of smoking is overblown." "*U.S.
News and World Report* claims that Princeton has a high faculty-to-student
ratio compared with that of other colleges, but my neighbor is a Princeton
student and she has had mostly big classes, so I don't think I'm going to
apply." "I have a friend who tried that diet, and she lost 40 pounds. I can't
wait to see myself 40 pounds lighter." All such conclusions are based on
single data points and therefore should not be given much credence. To
be sure, single data points are not uninformative. A neighbor who has had
many large classes may inspire you to do a larger poll of Princeton students,
but the experience of that one neighbor should not negate the research
that went into the ranking by *U.S. News and World Report*. In other words,
single anecdotes may serve an important role as "existence proofs," they
may inspire you to do more research, and they can be satisfying to tell (and
hear) at cocktail parties. But only rarely can they serve as the basis of a sound
broad inference.

Correlation and Causality

One of the most common fallacies of informal logic is the tendency to
confuse correlation with cause (*cum hoc ergo propter hoc*). As is true of many
other fallacies, this logical error may stem from the tendency to apply a
perfectly valid belief too liberally. Causation does imply correlation, but that
does not mean that correlation implies causation. People often mistakenly
assume that if there is a relationship between two variables, one must have

caused the other. This is often not the case, however. Sometimes, a third variable caused both. One reason it is so easy to confuse correlation with causation is that once you assume that the relationship is causal, it is very easy to create an explanation for how one variable causes the other (Gilovich, 1991).

For instance, if you read in the newspaper that an increase in beer prices cut the rate of gonorrhea, you would probably have little trouble creating an interesting story for why that was the case. The more expensive beer is, the less people will buy, and the less drunk people are, the less likely it is that they will have unsafe sex. Although such a link is possible, a simple correlation between the two variables is not sufficient evidence of that interpretation. It is just as likely (if not more so) that the passage of time is the common cause. Over time, while beer prices have steadily climbed because of inflation, gonorrhea rates have steadily declined because of sex education, creating a completely spurious correlation. In order to determine whether beer prices and consumption do indeed influence the transmission rate of gonorrhea, of course, one would need to randomly assign increased beer prices to certain locations and compare the change in gonorrhea rates in those locations with the change in gonorrhea rates in locations in which there was no increase in price. So, next time you avoid chocolate out of fear of acne, think about whether eating chocolate causes acne or whether something else, such as stress, causes both.

Many instances of invalid causal inference are based on various types of *magical thinking*. Magical thinking is the tendency to think that two events that "go together" – either in time, distance, or similarity of features – are causally linked. The key difference between magical thinking and the confusion of correlation and causation is that magical thinking does not require that there be any actual statistical connection between the two events. For instance, if on a few occasions you notice that soon after you cross your fingers, something good happens, you might incorrectly infer that crossing your fingers leads to favorable outcomes, even if the actual correlation between crossing your fingers and the occurrence of good events is zero.

One principle of magical thinking, *the law of similarity*, is based on the representativeness heuristic and involves the tendency to believe that "like causes like" or that causes resemble effects (Gilovich & Savitsky, 2002). For instance, many craps players believe that rolling the dice softly will produce low numbers (small cause equals small effect) and rolling the dice with more vigor will produce higher numbers (large cause equals large effect; see Hanslin, 1967).

Tunnel Vision

If you are able to avoid all the informal logical fallacies associated with evidence search and inference, and have managed to form a logically sound conclusion, you still have one set of fallacies with which to contend. Once a conclusion has been generated, people often fail to recognize the possibility or the reasonableness of other conclusions. This general penchant for ignoring alternative conclusions can lead to several specific fallacies.

First, once an event has occurred, a decision is made, or an uncertainty has been resolved, people are often subject to the *hindsight bias*, or the tendency to exaggerate the likelihood that one would have predicted the outcome in advance (Fischhoff, 1975). As President George W. Bush often points out, September 11 changed everything. It didn't just change our approach to the future, though, it also changed our perceptions of the past. In hindsight it seems obvious that America should have paid more attention to Osama Bin Laden and Al Qaeda operatives and that there should have been better communication between the different intelligence-gathering branches of the government. It seems so obvious, in fact, that a commission was created to determine who was at fault for not knowing on September 10 what we all learned on September 11. And while Democrats point to the current administration's failures and Republicans point to lax efforts by the Clinton administration, most people forget how they felt beforehand. When people reflect back, they may assume that an attack on American soil was bound to occur and fail to consider, given all of the information that was correctly pursued and all of the information that was correctly ignored, the inherent vulnerability of an open society to terrorist attacks. More broadly, the hindsight bias may lead one to focus too much on the links in a causal chain that led to a particular outcome, and too little on the varied causal forces that might give rise to a broader range of outcomes.

The hindsight bias can also be seen as one example of the *curse of knowledge*, the inability of an informed person to accurately reproduce the judgments of a less informed person. In the case of the hindsight bias, individuals are unable to reproduce their own uninformed, pre-event expectations. However, the curse of knowledge can also extend to an inability to anticipate the judgments of uninformed others. For example, if you know what tune Jon is thinking when he taps his pencil on the desk, you will be able to hear the tune in your head as he taps. This knowledge is likely to lead you to incorrectly assume that other people would be able to recognize the tune from the tapping or that you would have been able to recognize it if you hadn't been told the tune ahead of time (Newton, 1990, as cited by Griffin & Ross, 1991). Similarly, if you knew that Beth was being sarcastic when she thanked a friend for a restaurant recommendation because you knew that she did not like the restaurant, you are likely to incorrectly assume that her friend would also know she was being sarcastic (Keysar, 1993, 1994).

Finally, the tendency to be blind to alternative conclusions is partly responsible for the *sunk-cost fallacy*. The sunk-cost fallacy occurs when people continue to spend time, money, or energy in one endeavor simply because they have already invested time, money, or energy in it. Although economic theory prescribes that only future costs and benefits should be weighed when making a decision, people do not treat historical costs as irrelevant (Arkes & Blumer, 1985; Thaler, 1980). For example, imagine that Jack and Jill each bought a $4,000 used car last year. Imagine that while they are driving up the hill, both of their cars break down and, stretching credulity still further, it will cost exactly $2,500 for each of them to have their engine rebuilt. In addition, imagine that Jack's car broke down once before and he invested $1,000 in fixing the car at that time. Both Jack and Jill are in a position where they must weigh different options to decide whether to have their car fixed. For instance, it may be more profitable to sell the car for parts or to sell it to a mechanic who could fix it at his leisure rather than pay for the car to be fixed. However, because Jack had already invested $1,000 in fixing his car on a prior occasion, he may decide to fix it again, after devoting scant attention to his other options. Choosing to give up on the car now can make the original expenditure seem like a waste. Thus, Jack's original decision could blind him to other more productive courses of action (and other, more enlightening ways of framing his choice), and thus may lead to an unwise decision based on historical costs.

AVOIDING INFORMAL LOGICAL FALLACIES

Having completed our tour of the most common informal logical fallacies, the obvious next step is to consider how they might be avoided. That, in turn, requires a more basic consideration of how and why these errors occur.

System 1 and System 2

In recent years, a great many psychologists have put forward various "dual process" accounts of everyday cognition. Each of these accounts involves the idea that there is one set of mental processes that operates quickly and effortlessly and another that operates in a deliberate and effortful manner. Some of these dual process models are essentially either–or accounts that rest on the assumption that people typically rely on the quick and effortless mental processes when a judgment is not too important, and switch to the more deliberate mental processes for consequential judgments (Bodenhausen, 1990; Chaiken, Liberman, & Eagly, 1989; Fiske & Neuberg, 1990; Petty & Cacioppo, 1986). A second set of dual process models, in contrast, rests on the assumption that the two sets of mental processes work in parallel (Kahneman & Frederick, 2002; Sloman, 1996; Stanovich & West, 2002). Although we will focus our discussion on this second set of models (and use the same termonology), similar conclusions and recommendations would follow from the first set.

Among those who champion the idea that the two systems work in parallel, the quick and effortless set of mental processes is often referred to simply as "System 1" (Stanovich & West, 2002). System 1 renders quick, holistic judgments that are typically based on associative connections. The products of System 1 are often evaluative in nature and are responsible for our rapid positive–negative, approach–avoid reactions to stimuli (Cacioppo, Priester, & Berntson, 1993; Zajonc, 1980). The quick, associative output of System 1 is often sufficient to guide effective action. Occasionally, however, the output of System 1 needs to be supplemented or corrected. "System 2," a deliberate, rule-based system, is responsible for overriding System 1 if there is an error detected in the original, automatic assessment, or the output seems inadequate to guide one effectively through the task at hand.

As you might suspect from the descriptions of the two systems, System 1 is responsible for most of the informal logical fallacies that people commit. For instance, many of the informal fallacies described in this chapter follow from the fallacy of *affirming the consequent* – that is, incorrectly assuming that "if X, then Y" is the same as "if Y, then X." An associationist system, such as System 1, encourages such an error because it largely just connects X and Y. Consider once again the availability heuristic. Although it is true that common events tend to come to mind easily, this does not logically imply that events that come to mind easily are common. However, an associative system will have trouble with the distinction, having simply learned – and represented – that common events "go with" events that come to mind easily. The fallacy of ignorance follows from this same associationist error. If a belief is true, then it hasn't been proven false. That does not logically imply, however, that a belief that hasn't been proven false must be true. But again, an associative system that learns the connection without learning the logical rule sets one up for the fallacy of ignorance.

It is not possible (nor would you ever want) to turn off System 1. Therefore, to best avoid informal logical fallacies, which are largely the product of System 1, it is important to do everything possible to encourage the operation of System 2. It is in the rule-based System 2 that most principles of logic are represented, and therefore it is up to System 2 to spot the very natural, seductive fallacies committed by the associationist system. Engaging System 2 is therefore the surest route to fallacy-free reasoning.

Engaging System 2

Congratulations! You have already taken an important step toward readying System 2 and becoming a better thinker. System 2 is engaged when it "catches" an error made by System 1. Therefore, one of the best ways to ensure that System 2 engages is to learn about the most common fallacies made by System 1. Thus, simply by reading this chapter, you should find it easier to recognize the kinds of problems and contexts in which the output of System 1 is likely to mislead. Reading the chapter will not change the associative nature of System 1, and the output of System 1 will still encourage predictable errors. But the errors are just that, predictable, and the knowledge you have gained should make it easier for System 2 to recognize an incipient error and step in to correct it. In a telling program of research, Richard Nisbett and his colleagues have demonstrated that people can be trained to be better reasoners (Krantz, Fong, & Nisbett, 1983; Lehman, Lempert, & Nisbett, 1988; Nisbett, Fong, Lehman, & Cheng, 1987). Specifically, they found that people with statistical backgrounds were less likely to commit fallacies similar to those described in this chapter. For example, compared to individuals untrained in statistics, those who had received statistical training were much more likely to treat a single instance appropriately and not over-infer from it. Importantly, Nisbett and colleagues demonstrated that even very brief training was effective in substantially reducing logical and statistical errors. Reading about the most common fallacies, as you have done in this chapter, can be considered one form of training that you have already successfully completed. To learn about the most common fallacies is to encourage the future operation of System 2. In this case, knowledge truly is power.

System 2 is also activated when a person doesn't like the product of System 1. You are much more likely to make an error by believing something that you want to believe than by believing something that you don't want to believe. People invoke different standards of evidence and burdens of proof for hypotheses that they want to believe than for those that they do not want to believe. When evaluating a proposition they do not want to believe, people tend to ask themselves, "Must I believe this?," but when evaluating a proposition they are motivated to accept, they tend to ask themselves, "Can I believe this?" (Gilovich, 1991). In other words, when motivated to believe something, people tend to adopt relatively lax standards for evaluating the pertinent evidence, and too easily accept the desired hypothesis (Ditto & Lopez, 1992; Gilovich, 1991). In contrast, the skeptical mindset accompanied by the question, "Must I believe this?" tends to promote more sound reasoning (Gilovich, 1991). Indeed, a skeptical mindset has been shown to protect people from a variety of errors, many of which were covered in this chapter. Approaching a problem skeptically makes a person less likely to fall prey to the confirmation bias (Dawson, Gilovich, & Regan, 2002), to over-infer from small samples (Doosje, Spears, & Koomen, 1995), and to detect a correlation between two variables that are not actually related (Schaller, 1991).

Motivated skepticism, in other words, tends to make people think more critically and effectively. The key question, then, is how to encourage this same healthy skepticism when evaluating propositions one would be perfectly happy to accept as true. How can we engage the oversight functions of System 2 when we are pleased by the output of System 1? The best way to do so, as advocated by virtually all proponents of critical thinking, is to play the role of someone who is staunchly opposed to the proposition in question. Be your own devil's advocate. That can be difficult to do, but as the origin of the term indicates, it is not impossible. The term *devil's advocate* comes from the Catholic Church. When the Church must decide whether or not to make someone a saint, they appoint a Church official to dig up all the dirt he can on the potential saint and use that information to argue the devil's position that this person is not worthy of sainthood. In this way, the Church can be sure that they have a balanced body of evidence before making their decision. Similarly, when you evaluate propositions yourself, especially propositions you are motivated to believe, you should act as your own devil's advocate and dig up all the dirt you can for why your preferred conclusion may not be sound.

Beyond activating a skeptical mindset, another way to encourage effective oversight by System 2 is to invoke an audience to which you may need to justify your thinking. Phillip Tetlock and his colleagues have shown that a sense of "accountability" to others can help people avoid a number of common errors of reasoning (for a review, see Lerner & Tetlock, 1999). For example, Tetlock, Skitka, and Boettger (1989) found that participants thought in more complex, flexible, and multidimensional ways when they expected to justify their positions to an unknown audience. The authors suggest that accountability generates preemptive self-criticism as a way to anticipate potential critics. Therefore, when trying to reach an important conclusion, you may catch otherwise unnoticeable errors by imagining that you are highly accountable for your thinking. For instance, you can imagine that you have to present your ideas to the entire faculty in your department. (And while you're at it, you can invoke the devil's advocate by trying to anticipate what questions and concerns might be raised by the department's crankiest skeptic).

Finally, questions that encourage deliberate, methodological thinking will activate System 2. Therefore, in order to engage System 2, you should ask yourself these questions throughout every step of the reasoning process.

1. Did I gather evidence that could both support and refute the hypothesis that I am testing?
2. Would someone who was trying to refute the hypothesis interpret the evidence in the same way, or is the evidence ambiguous?
3. Does my conclusion necessarily follow from the premises?
4. Am I answering the question that I was asked, or am I answering a question that was easier to answer?
5. Is the sample large enough to make valid inferences?
6. Is there truly a relationship between the variables? Am I sure that the relationship is causal?
7. Are there any other conclusions that could be reasonably drawn from the evidence?

In summary, there are several methods for encouraging the activation of System 2 and avoiding the common informal logical fallacies laid out in the first part of the chapter. First, learning about the most common fallacies will make it easier for System 2 to recognize potential errors and step in and correct them. Second, approaching hypotheses with a skeptical mindset will increase the likelihood of spotting errors. When you don't want to believe a hypothesis, the skepticism tends to come naturally. However, when you do want to believe it, try imagining yourself as a devil's advocate in order to encourage your skeptical mindset. Third, accountability encourages a tendency to anticipate potential critics and thus detect one's errors. So, try imagining that you will need to justify your conclusions as a method for engaging System 2. Finally, to be sure that you have engaged in deliberate mental processing, you should ask yourself questions that require deliberate, effortful answers.

These suggestions should help you avoid informal logical fallacies and think more critically as a budding social scientist and in your everyday life. And to overcome this chapter's opening deficiency, we leave you with a pithy quote attributed to Voltaire: "A witty saying proves nothing."

References

Anderson, C. A., Lepper, M. R., & Ross, L. (1980). Perseverance of social theories: The role of explanation in the persistence of discredited information. *Journal of Personality and Social Psychology, 39,* 1037–1049.

Arkes, H. R., & Blumer, C. (1985). The psychology of sunk cost. *Organizational Behavior and Human Decision Processes, 35,* 124–140.

Baron, J. (1994). *Thinking and deciding* (2nd ed.). Cambridge, England: Cambridge University Press.

Bassok, M., & Trope, Y. (1984). People's strategies for testing hypotheses about another's personality: Confirmatory or diagnostic? *Social Cognition, 2,* 199–216.

Bazerman, M. H. (1998). *Judgment in managerial decision making* (4th ed.). New York: Wiley.

Bodenhausen, G. V. (1990). Stereotypes as judgmental heuristics: Evidence of circadian variations in discrimination. *Psychological Science, 1,* 319–322.

Cacioppo, J. T., Priester, J. R., & Berntson, G. G. (1993). Rudimentary determinants of attitudes. II. Arm flexion and extension have differential effects on attitudes. *Journal of Personality and Social Psychology, 65,* 5–17.

Chaiken, S., Liberman, A., & Eagly, A. H. (1989). Heuristic and systematic processing within and beyond the persuasion context. In J. S. Uleman & J. A. Bargh (Eds.), *Unintended thought* (pp. 212–252). New York: Guilford Press.

Dawes, R. M. (2001). *Everyday irrationality.* Boulder, CO: Westview Press.

Dawson, E., Gilovich, T., & Regan, D. T. (2002). Motivated reasoning and performance on the Wason selection task. *Personality and Social Psychology Bulletin, 28,* 1379–1387.

Ditto, P. H., & Lopez, D. F. (1992). Motivated skepticism: Use of differential decision criteria for preferred and nonpreferred conclusions. *Journal of Personality and Social Psychology, 63*, 568–584.

Doosje, B., Spears, R., & Koomen, W. (1995). When bad isn't all bad: Strategic use of sample information in generalization and stereotyping. *Journal of Personality and Social Psychology, 69*, 642–655.

Falk, R., & Konold, C. (1997). Making sense of randomness: Implicit encodings as a basis for judgment. *Psychological Review, 104*, 301–318.

Fischhoff, B. (1975). Hindsight is not equal to foresight: The effect of outcome knowledge on judgment under uncertainty. *Journal of Experimental Psychology: Human Perception and Performance, 1*, 288–299.

Fiske, S. T., & Neuberg, S. L. (1990). A continuum of impression formation, from category-based to individuating processes: Influences of information and motivation on attention and interpretation. In M. P. Zanna (Ed.), *Advances in experimental social psychology* (Vol. 23, pp. 1–74). New York: Academic Press.

Gilovich, T. (1987). Secondhand information and social judgment. *Journal of Experimental Social Psychology, 23*, 59–74.

Gilovich, T. (1991). *How we know what isn't so: The fallibility of human reason in everyday life*. New York: The Free Press.

Gilovich, T., & Savitsky, K. (2002). Like goes with like: The role of representativeness in erroneous and pseudo-scientific beliefs. In T. Gilovich, D. Griffin, & D. Kahneman (Eds.), *Heuristics and biases* (pp. 617–624). Cambridge, England: Cambridge University Press.

Griffin, D., & Ross, L. (1991). Subjective construal, social inference, and human misunderstanding. In M. P. Zanna (Ed.), *Advances in experimental social psychology* (Vol. 24, pp. 319–359). San Diego: Academic Press.

Hanslin, J. M. (1967). Craps and magic. *American Journal of Sociology, 73*, 316–330.

Hastorf, A., & Cantril, H. (1954). They saw a game: A case study. *Journal of Abnormal and Social Psychology, 49*, 129–134.

Janis, I. (1972). *Victims of groupthink: A psychological study of foreign-policy decisions and fiascoes*. Boston: Houghton Mifflin.

Johnson, E. J., Hershey, J., Meszaros, J., & Kunreuther, H. (1993). Framing, probability distortions, and insurance decisions. *Journal of Risk and Uncertainty, 7*, 35–51.

Kahneman, D., & Frederick, S. (2002). Representativeness revisited. In T. Gilovich, D. Griffin, & D. Kahneman (Eds.), *Heuristics and biases* (pp. 49–81). Cambridge, England: Cambridge University Press.

Kahneman, D., & Tversky, A. (1973). On the psychology of prediction. *Psychological Review, 80*, 237–251.

Kerr, N. L., MacCoun, R. J., & Kramer, G. P. (1996). Bias in judgment: Comparing individuals and groups. *Psychological Review, 103*, 687–719.

Keysar, B. (1993). Common sense and adult theory of communication. *Behavioral and Brain Sciences, 16*, 54.

Keysar, B. (1994). The illusory transparency of intention: Linguistic perspective taking in text. *Cognitive Psychology, 26*, 165–208.

Krantz, D. H., Fong, G. T., & Nisbett, R. E. (1983). *Formal training improves the application of statistical heuristics to everyday problems*. Unpublished manuscript. Murray Hill, NJ: Bell Laboratories.

Lehman, D. R., Lempert, R. O., & Nisbett, R. E. (1988). The effects of graduate training on reasoning: Formal discipline and thinking about everyday life events. *American Psychologist, 43*, 431–432.

Lerner, J., & Tetlock, P. E. (1999). Accounting for the effects of accountability. *Psychological Bulletin, 125*, 255–275.

Levine, J. M., & Moreland, R. L. (1998). Small groups. In D. T. Gilbert, S. T. Fiske, & G. Lindzey (Eds.), *The handbook of social psychology* (4th ed., Vol. 2, pp. 415–469). New York: McGraw-Hill.

Lichtenstein, S., Slovic, P., Fischhoff, B., Layman, M., & Combs, B. (1978). Judged frequency of lethal events. *Journal of Experimental Psychology: Human Learning and Memory, 4*, 551–578.

Lord, C. G., Ross, L., & Lepper, M. R. (1979). Biased assimilation and attitude polarization: The effects of prior theories on subsequently considered evidence. *Journal of Personality and Social Psychology, 37*, 2098–2109.

Newton, E. (1990). *Overconfidence in the communication of intent: Heard and unheard melodies.* Unpublished doctoral dissertation, Stanford University.

Nisbett, R. E., Fong, G. T., Lehman, D. R., & Cheng, P. W. (1987). Teaching reasoning. *Science, 238*, 625–631.

Nisbett, R. E., & Ross, L. (1980). *Human inference: Strategies and shortcomings of social judgment.* Englewood Cliffs, NJ: Prentice-Hall.

Petty, R., & Caccioppo, J. (1986). The elaboration likelihood model of persuasion. In L. Berkowitz (Ed.), *Advances in experimental social psychology* (Vol. 19, pp. 123–205). San Diego: Academic Press.

Pronin, E., Gilovich, T., & Ross, L. (2004). Objectivity in the eye of the beholder: Divergent perceptions of bias in self versus other. *Psychological Review, 111*, 781–799.

Pronin, E., Lin, D. Y., & Ross, L. (2002). The bias blind spot: Perceptions of bias in self versus others. *Personality and Social Psychology Bulletin, 28*, 369–381.

Ross, L., Lepper, M. R., & Hubbard, M. (1975). Perseverance in self perception and social perception: Biased attributional processes in the debriefing paradigm. *Journal of Personality and Social Psychology, 32*, 880–892.

Ross, L., & Ward, A. (1996). Naive realism: Implications for social conflict and misunderstanding. In T. Brown, E. Reed, & E. Turiel (Eds.), *Values and knowledge* (pp. 103–135). Mahwah, NJ: Erlbaum.

Schaffner, P. E. (1985). Specious learning about reward and punishment. *Journal of Personality and Social Psychology, 48*, 1377–1386.

Schaller, M. (1991). Social categorization and the formation of group stereotypes: Further evidence for biased information processing in the perception of group-behavior correlations. *European Journal of Social Psychology, 21*, 25–35.

Skov, R. B., & Sherman, S. J. (1986). Information-gathering processes: Diagnosticity, hypothesis-confirmatory strategies, and perceived hypothesis confirmation. *Journal of Experimental Social Psychology, 22*, 93–121.

Sloman, S. A. (1996). The empirical case for two systems of reasoning. *Psychological Bulletin, 119*, 3–22.

Snyder, M., & Swann, W. B. (1978). Hypothesis-testing processes in social interaction. *Journal of Personality and Social Psychology, 36*, 1202–1212.

Stanovich, K. E., & West, R. F. (2002). Individual differences in reasoning. In T. Gilovich, D. Griffin, & D. Kahneman (Eds.), *Heuristics and biases* (pp. 421–440). Cambridge, England: Cambridge University Press.

Tetlock, P. E., Skitka, L., & Boettger, R. (1989). Social and cognitive strategies for coping with accountability: Conformity, complexity, and bolstering. *Journal of Personality and Social Psychology, 57*, 632–640.

Thaler, R. H. (1980). Toward a positive theory of consumer choice. *Journal of Economic Behavior and Organization, 1*, 39–60.

Thompson, M. S., Judd, C. M., & Park, B. (2000). The consequences of communicating social stereotypes. *Journal of Experimental Social Psychology, 36*, 567–599.

Tversky, A., & Kahneman, D. (1974). Judgment under uncertainty: Heuristics and biases. *Science, 185*, 1124–1131.

Vallone, R., Ross, L., & Lepper, M. R. (1985). The hostile media phenomenon: Biased perception and perceptions of media bias in coverage of the "Beirut Massacre." *Journal of Personality and Social Psychology, 49*, 577–585.

Vos Savant, M. (1996). *The power of logical thinking.* New York: St. Martin's Griffin.

Zajonc, R. B. (1980). Feeling and thinking: Preferences need no inferences. *American Psychologist, 35*, 151–175.

8

Designing Studies to Avoid Confounds

Kathleen B. McDermott and Gregory E. Miller

The ability to design studies that are free from confounded variables is an acquired skill that separates the true psychological scientist from a layperson. The latter might be quite capable of generating interesting questions that could be addressed by psychological research; turning these questions into a study that cleanly tests the hypotheses, however, can be quite a challenge. It is this topic that the present chapter addresses.

Consider the fundamental goal of psychological research: to discover the causes and consequences of behavior. The only way to make such discoveries is to be able to examine data from a study that is free from alternative explanations. Such alternative explanations most often arise when an experiment contains *confounded variables*. Confounded variables involve the "simultaneous variation of a second variable with an independent variable of interest so that any effect on the dependent variable cannot be attributed with certainty to the independent variable" (Elmes, Kantowitz, & Roediger, 2003, p. 436). A well-designed study is one in which the researcher has carefully considered potential alternative explanations and designed the study so that these alternative explanations are no longer viable.

Psychological research can be categorized into two broad classes: experimental studies and correlational studies. In the former case, the researcher manipulates the variable of interest (the independent variable) and observes its effects on the dependent variable. The latter involves examining variation that occurs naturally (e.g., the variation between emotional awareness and happiness) and attempts to draw conclusions regarding this relationship. The experimental design is the preferred approach because it allows the researcher to draw the strongest inferences. The experimental approach can involve a between-subjects (or between-participants) manipulation, in which different participants receive different treatments, or a within-subjects manipulation, in which all subjects receive all treatments. Both classes of research are susceptible to confounding variables, although the specific types of such variables differ for experimental and correlational designs. We begin by considering experimental research studies.

EXPERIMENTAL STUDIES

The specific confounds one needs to worry about often differ for between-subjects and within-subjects experimental designs. Let's consider an example of a simple experimental study with a between-subjects manipulation. Imagine that a health psychologist was interested in the relationship between caffeine intake and memory. She recruited 24 subjects to participate in the study. On the day of the experiment, the first 8 subjects to arrive were assigned to the no-caffeine condition. They were given nothing to drink and were asked to study a list of 50 words for a later memory test. They then sat quietly while the experimenter gathered the next 8 subjects to arrive and assigned them to the low-caffeine condition, in which each person consumed 36 ounces of Jolt Cola and then studied the same 50 words studied by the no-caffeine group. The final 8 subjects were assigned to the high-caffeine condition in which each person consumed 72 ounces of Jolt Cola before studying the 50 words. Once the high-caffeine group finished studying the words, all subjects were gathered together and were asked to write down as many words as they could remember from the earlier study episode. The researcher discovered that the mean number of words recalled was highest in the high-caffeine condition, intermediate in the low-caffeine condition, and lowest in the no-caffeine condition. She concluded from this study that caffeine increases one's memory abilities.

What do you think of this study? If you evaluate it critically, you will notice that there are several explanations for the obtained results, not just the one that the researcher preferred. Specifically, the researcher did manipulate the amount of caffeine consumed (the independent variable) and she did present the same 50 words to each group of subjects (so it is not the case that one set of subjects may have received an easier set of words to remember). At a global level, however, she did not keep the conditions as similar as possible with the sole exception of the independent variable. For example, the retention interval (or time between studying the list and taking the test) differed across the groups. Maybe the high-caffeine group did the best because they had studied the words more recently than the low-caffeine group, who in turn outperformed the no-caffeine group for the same reason. That is, retention interval was a confounded variable.

What else is wrong with this study? Could you imagine that the subjects who showed up first to the study differed in some systematic way from those who arrived last? What if personality type influenced both punctuality (and thus, which caffeine dose a subject received) as well as memory abilities? Or what if the late arrivers were late because they were all having lunch together, whereas the early-arriving group skipped lunch? Degree of hunger could influence the data, as could any number of other potential explanations. In addition, the groups had differing amounts of liquid to drink; consider the possibility that this factor somehow influenced the results.

In short, this researcher inadvertently designed a confounded study. It is impossible to draw firm conclusions from the results because there are other potential explanations of the observed data. Such a situation is said to have *low internal validity*; the researcher did not vary only the independent variable but left other potential important factors uncontrolled (see Campbell & Stanley, 1963; Shadish, Cook, & Campbell, 2002; Whitley, 2002 for extensive reviews). The goal of experimental research should be to identify the factor that you want to manipulate and to manipulate only that factor. (Of course, some studies will contain more than one independent variable, in which multiple factors are manipulated, but the same principle – of tight experimental control – holds true.) The ideal experiment is elegant in that the only difference between conditions is the variable of interest (the independent variable).

How might the researcher have designed a better study? Random assignment of subjects to treatment condition would have been one step toward an internally valid study. Random assignment can overcome any differences between people in the study, at least if enough subjects are tested. Random assignment would mean that early arrivers would not all be placed in the same condition, for example.

Another important change one would want to make in designing this study to be internally valid would be to better equate the conditions during the treatment phase. One approach would be to randomly assign people to treatment conditions (no caffeine, low caffeine, high caffeine) and to give them all an equivalent amount of soda to drink (ensuring that one soda was free of caffeine, one low in caffeine, and one high in caffeine). Ideally, the subjects (and experimenter) would not even know which person was getting which treatment (although these data would, of course, be recorded by a second experimenter). This approach is something called a *double-blind approach*, in that both the experimenter and the participants are unaware of the treatment conditions each participant receives. This approach would help guard against subtle cues that the experimenter might accidentally give with respect to expected results (*experimenter bias*) and against subjects trying to "help" the experimenter by trying to give data that confirm the hypothesis (the problem of *demand characteristics*). After drinking the soda and waiting the appropriate amount of time, all subjects would study the words together and take the test together, without ever knowing which condition they were in (or even the question of interest in the study). An important point here is that the experimenter will want to rule out all reasonable confounds at the design stage, even those that do not actually occur to the experimenter. How on earth do you rule out confounds you haven't thought of? The best approach is to try to equate your groups in all ways reasonably possible except for the variable of interest. In the caffeine example, doing things like giving all subjects equivalent amounts of liquid (and varying the caffeine contained in the liquid) exemplifies a step toward treating groups equivalently. Random assignment to experimental conditions also goes a long way toward achieving this goal; when there are enough subjects in the study, this procedure evenly distributes subject variables like personality, education, and intelligence across levels of the independent variable.

Instead of performing this between-subjects manipulation, the researcher could have tried a within-subject manipulation of the variable of interest (caffeine). This approach would have carried with it another set of potential confounds, however. A within-subjects design gets around person-level variables because each subject participates in each condition and therefore each person serves as his or her own control group. In such a study, people may be given three sets of 50 words to study (and three memory tests) on three different days. Before each encoding and retrieval episode, they would ingest the same amount of liquid; once, though, the liquid would have lots of caffeine, once it would have moderate caffeine, and once it would have no caffeine. A little thought suggests, though, that this design carries with it some other challenges. For example, we would not want the high-caffeine condition to always come first, as maybe people would be more motivated in the first study-test phase than they would be by the end of the experiment. We would want to counterbalance the order of caffeine intake (such that the high-caffeine condition occurred first, second, and third an equal number of times across subjects). In addition, we would now need three lists of 50 words. What if the lists differed in their difficulty? To control for this, we would also counterbalance word lists, such that a given list of 50 words would be used in each condition (no caffeine, moderate caffeine, high caffeine) an equal number of times across subjects. Random assignment of 150 words to the three lists might also be advisable. Finally, another obvious concern would be carryover effects; we would need to design the study such that there was sufficient time between the three treatment periods that any caffeine ingested (say, at the beginning of the study) was washed out of the system by the time the second treatment phase began.

By now, you may be noticing that designing a good experiment is truly a difficult challenge. How does one go about designing an elegant study that places a premium on certainty of the conclusions? Our suggestion is that in thinking through the independent and dependent variables and the operationalization of each, you may want to mentally design both a within-subjects and a between-subjects study, identifying potential confounds in each approach. Which design is better is often a judgment call, but you should at least realize the relative advantages and disadvantages of each when choosing it. How can you design the study such that you can achieve the greatest level of certainty in the conclusions? The answer to this question sometimes needs to be balanced with logistical issues, however, such as care not to place unreasonable demands on subjects (e.g., 12-hour experimental sessions are not typically ideal) and on resources (e.g., paying subjects to stay in the laboratory for many hours may be cost prohibitive).

Let's return to the issue of random assignment that we talked about with respect to between-subjects studies. The idea behind random assignment is to evenly distribute across conditions all factors that might influence memory. Variables such as the age and intelligence of the participant and preexperiment caffeine exposure would be hard to counterbalance across conditions, so the idea is that random assignment will (on average) tend to evenly distribute people with various characteristics across the treatment conditions. This is a great idea in theory, but how will you know if your random assignment worked such that your treatment groups were in fact fairly equivalent with the exception of the treatment variable? Manipulation checks can be built in to test whether random assignment did its job. The idea is to show empirically that on the variable of interest (e.g., free recall of word lists) your subject groups are identical in overall abilities and that any differences you observe across groups are due to your treatment manipulation (and not preexisting differences in the groups). Returning to the caffeine example, you might want to give all subjects a word list and test their memory before ever administering the treatment. This would allow you, the experimenter, to show that the groups were equivalent before the treatment (but differed after the administration of varying levels of caffeine). Such manipulation checks are critical to between-participants designs.

Another possible approach to this issue would be a matched-groups design. Here, subjects might be tested prior to the manipulation of interest, and group assignment would be made such that the three between-subjects groups given the various levels of caffeine were matched for memory abilities prior to administration of the independent variable. Of course, matching in all dimensions of potential consequence is not possible, so matched designs are not as ideal as they might initially seem.

The primary consideration in designing your study is to be able to conclude with reasonable certainty that your treatment variable was the cause of any observed effects and that there are no other potential explanations. Whether a between-subjects or within-subjects design is preferable will depend upon the specific set of circumstances, but our recommendation is to think through how you might design the study in both ways and to choose the one that seems to have a better fit for your question. Given that certainty in one's conclusions is of primary importance in psychological research, replication (with a different set of participants) is desirable, too; often, replicating basic findings from a between-subjects design in a within-subjects design (or vice versa) is a nice way of attaining converging evidence for one's conclusions.

As mentioned previously, the main goal of psychological research is to address the issue of causality. The only way to know with reasonable certainty that an independent variable is having a causal influence on a dependent variable is through experimental research. At times, however, interesting questions arise that are not amenable to experimental approaches. We now turn our attention to such situations.

CORRELATIONAL STUDIES

As we've said at many points in this chapter, most psychological research aims to explain the world in causal terms. Scientists want to be able to conclude that "caffeine improves memory" or that "psychotherapy ameliorates suffering." Carefully designed experiments permit scientists to make claims of this nature, because they use tools like random assignment and counterbalancing to rule out competing explanations.

Unfortunately, scientists do not always have these powerful tools at their disposal. There are many important phenomena that psychologists wish to study, but cannot manipulate experimentally, because re-creating them in the lab would be unethical or impractical. For instance, to study the long-term effects of child abuse, we cannot expose youngsters to parental maltreatment; similarly, to identify the pathways to financial or emotional stability, we cannot randomly assign students to attend public versus private or small versus large colleges.

In situations of this nature scientists must resort to other research designs, such as quasi-experimental, case study, survey or questionnaire, historical, or correlational research designs. Because they are prevalent, we consider correlational designs here. Rather than experimentally manipulate the processes of interest, these designs take advantage of naturally occurring variations in the population. For instance, among any group of adults in society, some will have attended small private colleges, others large public universities, and still others small community colleges. A scientist using correlational methodology would measure features of these institutions (their average class size, faculty-to-student ratio, etc.) and then quantify their relationship with outcomes of interest (say, job prestige, annual salary, subjective happiness). The data would tell us whether certain educational backgrounds maximize the chances a person will live "the good life."

However, as you are likely aware by now, we cannot infer causality from studies that rely on correlational methodology. What prevents us from doing so? Simply put, there are two major alternative explanations for any correlation, and it is difficult (and perhaps impossible) to rule them both out definitively. The first has to do with the direction of causality. In most studies that use correlational methodology, it is unclear whether the first variable has caused changes in the second variable, the second variable has caused changes in the first variable, or yet a third variable (e.g., SAT scores) is related to both variables. This causal ambiguity is especially difficult to resolve in cross-sectional studies, where the variables are measured simultaneously at a single point in time. The problem is more tractable in longitudinal designs, where all variables are measured repeatedly over time. Under these conditions it is possible to establish "temporal precedence" by showing that disparities in one variable preceded disparities in the second variable. For instance, if a study finds that attending a small private college as a young adult relates to higher salary in middle age, we can safely assume that education is shaping income, rather than vice versa. However, some third variable could still be causing selection of a college and later financial stability.

Confounds represent the other major impediment to causal inference in correlational methodology. Whereas experimental studies can eliminate confounds through random assignment and counterbalancing, scientists performing correlational studies do not have such powerful safeguards at their disposal. Any time a relationship is found between two naturally occurring processes, there is always a nagging possibility that it's noncausal, and simply the result of another underlying process. This is known as the *third-variable problem* in correlational research. For instance, in the study of education and salary that we just described, intelligence could be acting as a confound. Bright people are likely to be admitted to selective private colleges, and also succeed in challenging professions that command high salaries. So any association that is observed may not reflect the causal influence of education on salary, but instead the fact that intelligence partly shapes the college people attend and the careers that they select. A similar argument could be made for personality as a potential confound. There is likely to be a certain group of people in the world – those marked by conscientiousness, for example, or family wealth or a strong desire for status – who tend to favor private colleges and achieve economic success. If so, these personality or socioeconomic characteristics may cause education and income to cluster together (correlate), even if the kind of college a person attends has no causal influence on his or her later economic success. These examples illustrate what is perhaps the most irksome feature of correlational research – namely, that there's always a universe of potential confounds that represent compelling alternative explanations for one's findings.

How do psychological scientists grapple with this problem? The most favored strategy, of course, is to use experimental methods. But as we pointed out earlier, manipulation is not always possible because of practical or ethical constraints. In these cases scientists work hard before a study begins to identify variables that might represent confounds. To the extent that such variables are identified up front, their influence can be eliminated though careful design or statistical methods. To get a sense of how this might be done, imagine a scientist is planning a study of children who are mistreated by their parents, and whether or not they have a greater risk of mental health problems in adulthood. In thinking about potential alternative explanations for any association that he or she observes, the scientist realizes that parental history of psychiatric disorder could represent an important confound. The logic is this: If a parent suffers from a severe mental illness, it could adversely impact his or her ability to care properly for offspring. The same parental mental illness could also give rise to psychiatric difficulties for the offspring later in life, as these conditions are often transmitted across generations through genetic and learning mechanisms. So in this scenario, a parent's mental illness is responsible for maltreatment of a child, as well as that offspring's own psychiatric difficulties later in life. However, these latter processes are causally unrelated to each other.

How might the scientist get around this conundrum? If he or she could identify it before the study began, the most elegant solution would be through design. Each subject's parents could be carefully screened for psychiatric difficulties, and those whose mothers or fathers had a history of mental illness could be excluded from participation. With this strategy, parental mental illness would be "taken off the table" as a potential confound. In other words, because none of the subjects in the study has a parent with a history of mental illness, this variable cannot be confounding associations that are later observed between childhood maltreatment and psychiatric difficulties.

Another potential solution would be to collect data on parental mental illness, and then use statistical methods to evaluate (and if necessary, eliminate) its influence. This can be done through a variety of different analytic strategies. Probably the most straightforward and convincing strategy is called a *stratified analysis*, and it involves stratifying (or dividing) subjects into those who do versus do not have the suspected confound. The association between the two variables of interest (parental maltreatment and mental health) is then estimated separately for each cohort of subjects. Returning to our example, this would involve dividing subjects into two cohorts, those with and without parental mental illness, and then separately estimating associations between childhood maltreatment and later mental illness. If significant associations between our variables emerge in both cohorts, we can rest assured that parental mental illness is not operating as a confound in our sample. However, if childhood maltreatment turns out to confer risk of future illness only in subjects with a family history, we are forced to conclude that this association is dependent upon having a mother or father with psychiatric difficulties. In other words, it is a confound, and a viable alternative explanation for our findings.

Though stratified analyses are a convincing way to rule out confounds, they are not always possible to perform. Many potential confounds that scientists wish to examine are measured on a continuum, so subjects cannot easily be divided into those who do versus do not possess the characteristic. Other times the sample size in a study is too small for subgroups to be meaningfully analyzed, or the potential confound is distributed in such a way that only a few subjects do or don't have it. In these cases a procedure known as *covariance analysis* is used instead to gain statistical control. It involves

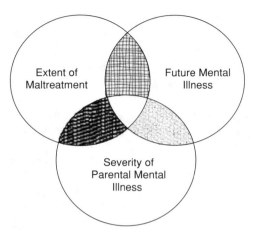

FIGURE 8.1. Venn diagram representing a situation in which covariance analysis would be beneficial. In this example, covariance analysis would allow one to estimate the influence of childhood maltreatment on future mental illness (over and above the influence of parental mental illness).

estimating the association between an independent and dependent variable, after statistically removing any variation that is attributable to the potential confound.

A simple way to imagine how it works is to visualize a Venn diagram with three overlapping circles (as shown in Figure 8.1). Each circle represents a variable that is measured in a study, and regions where two circles overlap indicate an association, where fluctuations in one process are related to fluctuations in another, though not necessarily in any causal sense. In the circles depicted in the figure, you can see that all three variables in our study are interrelated. (Assume for the moment that parental mental illness is on a continuum that ranges from none at all to very severe.) Subjects who have been maltreated have a greater risk of future mental illness (the overlap between the top two circles, hatched area plus clear area); subjects who have been maltreated are more likely to have been reared by parents with severe mental illness (the overlap between the top left and bottom circles, darkly shaded area plus clear area); and subjects who were reared by parents with severe psychiatric difficulties are themselves at greater risk of future mental illness (the overlap between the top right and bottom circles, lightly specked area plus clear area). What a covariance analysis does is estimate the overlap between an independent and dependent variable, apart from what each of them shares with the suspected confound. Going back to the Venn diagram, we see that the covariance analysis estimates the size of the hatched area, that is, the overlap of maltreatment and future mental illness that is separate from parental mental illness. If that area of overlap turns out to be significantly greater than zero, the scientist can safely conclude that the suspected confound is not responsible for his or her findings. However, sometimes the covariance procedure substantially weakens a previously observed association, and diminishes its magnitude to the point that it is no longer significantly different from zero. When that happens, the researcher is forced to conclude that the association was artifactual, or occurred simply because the independent and dependent variables had common overlap with the confounding variable.

In most large-scale studies there are multiple confounds that a scientist must consider. For example, apart from parental history of mental illness, we may want to evaluate the role of sociodemographic variables that are associated with both maltreatment and mental illness, or certain personality characteristics that bias people toward exaggerated symptom reporting. Covariance analysis is able to accommodate as many potential confounds as we can imagine, and tell us whether the association between our variables of interest is independent of them. When used wisely, this strategy can bolster the rigor of correlational research and help us rule out plausible alternative explanations for our findings. Nevertheless, it is important to remember that even when we've controlled for a long list of confounds, we can never be certain that the association between variables is causal in nature. There's always the possibility of other confounds that we haven't considered.

That said, scientists need to be thoughtful and cautious in applying covariance strategies to their research. Adjusting for large numbers of confounds simultaneously can bias statistical procedures, such that they lead us to derive inaccurate conclusions from our data. One way this occurs is through *overfitting* of a model (Babyak, 2004). In any data set, the number of associations that are estimated has to be balanced against the number of subjects, because otherwise spurious findings can emerge. The basic problem is that by estimating a large number of statistical parameters, relative to the number of subjects in the data set, we risk detecting patterns of association that are unique to our sample – in other words, findings that won't replicate in future research with a different sample of subjects. To avoid this problem in our analyses, we need to carefully select potential confounds, and make sure to have enough subjects to get accurate results if they are included. Though the optimal subject–confound balance will vary from study to study, a minimum ratio of 10:1 is usually necessary to achieve accurate parameters estimates. Therefore, unless a study has a very large number of subjects involved, it's unwise to "throw the whole kitchen sink" of confounds into a covariance analysis. Instead, spend time up front deciding which ones are the likely culprits, and then enroll enough subjects so you can rule them out definitively. Or if your study is going to be small in terms of sample size, make sure to design it in a way that eliminates a few potential confounds, so you don't have control for them later.

Another factor to consider when applying covariance strategies is whether certain variables represent *confounds* or *mechanisms*. The distinction between a confound and a mechanism can be subtle, and in many cases it will depend entirely on the theoretical leanings of the person making the judgment. But as you will see, that judgment has important implications for how the results of a study are interpreted. Returning to our example of a study on childhood maltreatment and mental illness, let's imagine that we're concerned with the role that alcohol consumption might play in this association. Some scientists might argue that alcohol represents a confound in this research because it's an established contributor to mental illness. The argument here would be that if the association between maltreatment and later mental illness is totally dependent upon alcohol, then it's no longer interesting, because maltreatment history doesn't tell us anything "new" about a person's risk for mental illness above and beyond what we already know (i.e., that using alcohol enhances this risk). These researchers might have the mindset that only biological mechanisms are theoretically interesting – permanent changes in the structure or function of the brain that result from maltreatment during childhood and cause later mental illness. By contrast, other scientists might view alcohol as a perfectly legitimate mechanism. They'd argue that using alcohol is a way for troubled youngsters to cope with maltreatment, and for a multitude of reasons, doing so leads them to develop psychiatric difficulties when they reach adulthood. From their perspective, the fact that alcohol explains the association between maltreatment and mental illness doesn't make it a confound, but instead a theoretically interesting "mechanism of action."

Interestingly, if these two groups of researchers were to conduct the study we've been discussing, they might arrive at very different conclusions. Those who view alcohol as a confound would treat it as a covariate in statistical analyses, and by doing so would wipe out any association that exists between maltreatment and mental illness. In other words, the findings would lead them to conclude that these processes are unrelated. By contrast, those who view alcohol as a mechanism would not treat it as a covariate, and as a result would end up concluding that being maltreated does heighten later risk of mental illness. In follow-up analyses this latter group may discover that controlling for alcohol eliminates their association. However, because of their theoretical orientation, the researchers would likely interpret these findings as evidence that alcohol is the mechanism of action, rather than a competing explanation to be ruled out.

So what does all this mean for scientists designing a correlational project? The most important take-home message is to do your theoretical homework. Before the study begins, sketch out a model that attempts to explain your phenomenon, and decide what variables constitute legitimate (and theoretically interesting) mechanisms versus nuisance variables that need to be ruled out. This kind of up-front work will enable you to conduct studies that document genuine associations between variables of interest, rule out the obvious competing explanations for them, and perhaps gain some traction on what underlying mechanisms are responsible.

In conclusion, we believe that learning to design studies to avoid confounds is one of the more difficult aspects of advanced psychological training. Here we have discussed some of the issues routinely encountered in designing experimental and correlational studies such that conclusions are unhampered by alternative explanations.

AUTHOR NOTE

Support for the writing of this chapter was provided by the James S. McDonnell Foundation and the Institute of Education Sciences (K. McDermott) and by the Canadian Institutes of Health Research, the Michael Smith Foundation for Health Research, and the Human Early Learning Partnership (G. Miller).

References

Babyak, M. A. (2004). What you see may not be what you get: A brief, nontechnical introduction to overfitting in regression-type models. *Psychosomatic Medicine, 66,* 411–421.

Campbell, D. T., & Stanley, J. C. (1963). *Experimental and quasi-experimental designs for research.* Chicago: Rand McNally.

Elmes, D. G., Kantowitz, B. H., & Roediger, H. L. (2003). *Research methods in psychology* (7th ed.). Belmont, CA: Wadsworth.

Shadish, W. R., Cook, T. D., & Campbell, D. T. (2002). *Experimental and quasi-experimental designs for generalized causal inference.* Boston: Houghton Mifflin.

Whitley, B. E. (2002). *Principles of research in behavioral science* (2nd ed.). New York: McGraw-Hill.

9

Evaluating Theories

Simon Dennis and Walter Kintsch

All theories are false (Popper, 1959). So in one sense evaluating theories is a straightforward matter. However, some theories are more false than others. Furthermore, some theories have characteristics that tend to promote the advance of scientific knowledge. In this chapter, we examine what some of those characteristics are and how one goes about the process of identifying and building useful theories.

A theory is a concise statement about how we believe the world to be. Theories organize observations of the world and allow researchers to make predictions about what will happen in the future under certain conditions. Science is about the testing of theories, and the data that we collect as scientists should either implicitly or explicitly bear on theory.

There is, however, a great difference between theories in the hard sciences and theories in the soft sciences in their formal rigor. Formal theories are well established and incredibly successful in physics, but they play a lesser role in biology, and even less in psychology, where theories are often stated in verbal form. This has certainly been true historically, but some scientists, especially physicists, as well as laypeople, construe this fact to mean that formal theories are restricted to the hard sciences, particularly physics, while formalization is unattainable in the soft sciences. There is absolutely no reason to think so. Indeed, this is a pernicious idea that would permanently relegate psychology to second-class status. If nature is governed by causal laws, they govern both the simplest physical phenomena (which, when analyzed at the level of quantum mechanics, turn out not to be so simple at all) as well as the higher-order phenomena in biology and psychology. Human behavior is neither vague nor indeterminate, and hence should be described with equal rigor as physical phenomena.

Although psychology is dominated by verbal theories, formal mathematical and computational models have become increasingly popular. Hintzman (1991) argues that mathematics "works" in psychology and many other scientific domains because it enforces precision and consistency of reasoning, which, for many reasons (such as working memory restrictions or hindsight biases), is not otherwise guaranteed. In recent years, there has been a great deal of interest in not only how one might formulate models mathematically, but also in how one can formally test theories. This development is particularly important in an area such as psychology, where data are inevitably influenced by many sources of noise, so that model selection is a nontrivial exercise (Pitt, Myung TICS, 2002). In this chapter, we give some of the basic ideas behind these developments and provide pointers for those who are interested in understanding these methods in depth.

At the outset we would like to distinguish between the characteristics that lead a theory to be successful from those that make it truly useful. Although these are not completely disjointed sets, the literature on the philosophy and sociology of science contains many demonstrations of how factors such as social aptitude, rhetorical power, scientific networks, and the sheer unwillingness of proponents to die have led one or another framework to be favored for a time, when in hindsight that has seemed unwise (Gilbert & Mulkay, 1984; Kuhn, 1962). In this chapter, however, we focus on those considerations that there is some consensus *ought* to play a role in theory evaluation.

These characteristics include the following.

1. *Descriptive adequacy*: Does the theory accord with the available behavioral, physiological, neuroscientific, and other empirical data?
2. *Precision and interpretability*: Is the theory described in a sufficiently precise fashion that other theorists can interpret it easily and unambiguously?
3. *Coherence and consistency*: Are there logical flaws in the theory? Does each component of the theory seem to fit with the others into a coherent whole? Is it consistent with theory in other domains (e.g., the laws of physics)?
4. *Prediction and falsifiability*: Is the theory formulated in such a way that critical tests can be conducted that could reasonably lead to the rejection of the theory?
5. *Postdiction and explanation*: Does the theory provide a genuine explanation of existing results?
6. *Parsimony*: Is the theory as simple as possible?
7. *Originality*: Is the theory new or is it essentially a restatement of an existing theory?
8. *Breadth*: Does the theory apply to a broad range of phenomena or is it restricted to a limited domain?
9. *Usability*: Does the theory have applied implications?
10. *Rationality*: Does the theory make claims about the architecture of mind that seem reasonable in light of the environmental contingencies that have shaped our evolutionary history?

In different areas of psychology, these criteria apply to different degrees and in different ways, and it is important to be familiar with the standards in your area. In the following sections, we give an overview of each criterion and illustrate it with examples. These examples are drawn primarily from memory and comprehension research, which are our areas of expertise. Similar considerations, however, apply across the discipline.

CRITERIA ON WHICH TO EVALUATE THEORIES

Descriptive Adequacy

The first and probably most important criterion on which to judge a theory is the extent to which it accords with data. Across psychology, data takes many forms. Traditionally, data have been generated through surveys, laboratory experimentation, or physiological measures. In areas such as discourse studies and corpus psycholinguistics, however, data come primarily in the form of texts or transcripts of conversations. Furthermore, neuroanatomical studies and brain imagining (including event-related potentials, positron emission tomography, and functional magnetic resonance imaging) are playing an increasingly important role in psychological theorizing. What is the "right" type of data is a contentious issue, and different domains of psychology have different rationales for the way they employ data. Across domains, however, the importance of data is realized and theories that are consistent with known data are to be preferred.

In psychology, the most popular way of comparing a theory against data is null hypothesis significance testing. Hypothesis testing involves generating two competing hypotheses, one of which would be true if the theory is correct and one of which would be false. For instance, our theory of recognition memory might suggest that if we increase the number of items in a study list, we will see a decrease in the performance at test. We might then design an experiment in which we present study lists of different lengths to subjects and then ask them to determine which items from a test list appeared on the study list. Using methods of null hypothesis significance testing, we can then decide whether the data we collect support the conclusion that there is a difference or not. In this way, we have tested the theory against data.

The case of list length in recognition memory is an interesting one, because it demonstrates that determining whether a theory is consistent with data is not always as straightforward as it may at first appear. It has long been assumed that a decrease in performance was indeed a necessary result of increasing the number of items on the study list. Most existing models predict that length would have this effect, and several studies seemed to suggest that these predictions are confirmed (Gronlund & Elam, 1994). However, Dennis and Humphreys (2001) proposed a model that did not show a decrement in performance as a consequence of list length. Rather, they proposed that variables that are often confounded with length, such as the time between study and test and differences in the distribution of attention between short and long lists, were responsible for previous results. They conducted experiments that controlled the confounding variables and failed to find any difference between the short and long lists.

This result is controversial (Cary & Reder, 2003), and it will likely be some time before consensus is reached on the actual state of affairs. However, this episode illustrates some of the subtleties involved in determining the extent to which a theory accords with data. One reason that this result continues to be questioned is that, using null hypothesis significance testing, it is not possible to conclude that there is no difference. A proponent of a theory that predicts a list-length effect can always propose that a failure to find the difference was a consequence of lack of power of the experimental design. Perhaps there were not enough subjects to reliably find a result, or perhaps the effect is there but it is small. And the debate remains unresolved.

Another difficulty with null hypothesis significance testing is that it encourages a game of 20 questions with nature (Newell, 1973). A study proceeds by setting up one or more dichotomies, and at the end we have a set of yes–no answers to these questions. The danger is that rather than develop a cohesive theory and use hypothesis testing to evaluate it, researchers will generate an endless set of issues, each of which is only loosely coupled with previous work, and little cumulative progress will be achieved (Newell, 1973). Not everyone agrees that this has actually been a problem for psychology, but Newell certainly makes a strong case for his position.

The dominant role of null hypothesis significance testing in psychological investigation has come under intense scrutiny in recent years (Cohen, 1994), and in 1999 the American Psychological Association published recommendations about how one should conduct statistical analyses that included reducing reliance on the hypothesis test (Wilkinson & the Task Force on Statistical Inference, 1999). Anyone intending to conduct psychological research ought to be familiar with the principles set out in this report.

One of the advantages of formal models of psychological phenomena is that they can be used to derive measures of how well a theory fits the data (Pitt & Myung, 2002) that do not rely on null hypothesis significance tests. Typically, a model defines one or more parameters, which are chosen so that the predictions of the model are as close as possible to the observed data.[1] The advantage of the formal model is that we can say exactly how closely it approximates the data (although see the section on parsimony for a discussion of the difficulties with relying on fit alone). In addition, rather than providing a set of yes–no answers, the use of formal models

---

[1] In some cases, the parameters are varied according to some prior distribution to define a distribution of predicted outcomes.

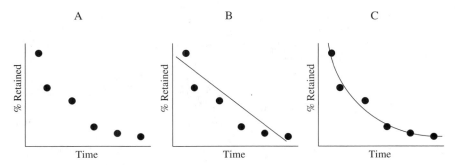

FIGURE 9.1. Hypothetical retention data and fits to two possible models: A, data; B, linear fit; and C, power fit.

gives us additional information about the nature of the relationship between variables as given by the values of the parameters.

To see how such an investigation might proceed, consider how information is retained as a function of time. Figure 9.1A shows hypothetical data that would be collected from a memory test in which subjects are asked to recall a list of items at different intervals poststudy. Performance is measured by the number of items they are able to recall. As time progresses, we would expect performance to decrease as indicated in the figure. If we were to employ hypothesis testing, we could take two of these intervals and ask whether performance decreased.

Using formal models, however, we can ask additional questions. Figures 9.1B and 9.1C show two alternative models of how the retention interval and performance are related. In Figure 9.1B, performance decreases as a linear function of the interval; in Figure 9.1C, performance decreases as a power function. So, now we can ask which of these models better describes the form of the relationship between the variables. In this case, we would choose the power function, as it is, in general, closer to the data. In addition, we can look at the values of the parameters of the best-fitting models to provide an indication of how much we expect performance to decrease across any given interval – that is, we can make quantitative predictions. We now have a much deeper understanding than was afforded by the null hypothesis significance test. In particular, we are able in a much more straightforward way to say what it means for the theory to accord with the data.

Precision and Interpretability

One common criticism of psychological theories is that they are often described in vague and imprecise language. This makes them difficult for independent researchers to apply, as the following quotes attest:

Terms are used such as "access to the lexicon," "automatic processing," "central executive," "resources"; formal definitions of such terms are rare, and even rarer are statements of the rules supposed to be governing their interaction. As a result one is left unclear about exactly what kinds of experimental data would invalidate such theories, and whether or not they are intended to apply to some new experimental situation. (Broadbent, 1987, p. 169)

When a theory does attract criticism, the critic almost always turns out to have misunderstood, and the theory stands as originally proposed. . . . On the rare occasion a criticism demands action, fine tuning will almost always suffice. Thus, the chance[s] of a theory having to be abandoned or even appreciably revised as a consequence of criticism are vanishingly small, and hence researchers can be confident that their theories will stay alive just as long as they continue to nourish them. (Watkins, 1990, p. 328)

When evaluating a theory, pay close attention to how well the constructs in the theory and the relationships between them are defined. Can you be confident that you could apply the theory in a related domain unambiguously? Conversely, when articulating a theory, ask yourself what implicit assumptions you may be making that may not be shared by your readers.

Coherence and Consistency

Another hallmark of a good theory is its coherence and consistency. Although it may seem obvious that theories should be free from logical flaws, it isn't always easy to spot these flaws, particularly when theories are presented in verbal form.

As an example (from Hintzman, 1991), consider the following claim taken from a textbook on learning: "While adultery rates for men and women may be equalizing, men still have more partners than women do, and they are more likely to have one night stands" (Leahey & Harris, 1985, p. 287). On the surface, the statement seems plausible and consistent with our understandings of male and female behavior. However, a more careful consideration reveals a logical flaw. From context, it was clear that the claim did not hinge on homosexual encounters, nor did it rely on small differences in the overall numbers of males and females, which would have rendered it uninteresting. So, as Hintzman points out, given that each liaison will usually involve one man and one woman, there really can't be a substantive difference in either the number of partners or the number of one-night stands between the genders. Of course there may be other differences, such as the willingness to report, but there can't be an actual difference in the total counts for each of the genders.

Another common problem that one must look for in evaluating theories is circularity, and, again, the issue can be quite subtle. One such example is the notion of transfer appropriate processing (TAP) that appears in the memory literature. TAP asserts that "performance is a positive function of the degree of overlap between encoding and retrieval processes" (Brown & Craik, 2000, p. 99). So, the more similar the processes evoked at test are to the processes evoked during encoding of the material, the more likely it is that information will be retrieved. Again, on the face of it, this seems like a reasonable theoretical conjecture. However, the difficulty arises in defining what it means to have overlap in unseen psychological processes. If the only mechanism for determining overlap is performance itself, then the overlap in processes determines performance, but performance is our benchmark for determining if there is an overlap in processes. To the extent that this is actually the case, the TAP claim becomes vacuous.

Beyond ensuring that theories are free from logical flaws of the kind just illustrated, it is also important to ask how consistent a theory is, both with other theories within psychology and also with theory outside psychology. For instance, one might prefer a theory of text comprehension that incorporates the constraints on working memory capacity that have been found by memory researchers (Kintsch, 1998). For the same reason, theories of psi and remote viewing are not preferred because they are inconsistent with physical laws. Of course, it is always possible that our understanding of working memory or even the physical universe will change in ways that would invalidate our theoretical assumptions. However, our current understanding remains our best guess of how the world operates, and so theories that are consistent with this approximation are more likely to endure.

Prediction and Falsifiability

One of the key attributes of a good theory is falsifiability (Popper, 1959). Ideally, one should be able to make unambiguous predictions based on the theory and conduct empirical tests that could potentially bring the theory into doubt. We start this section by giving an example of falsification in action.

Many models of recognition memory, particularly those known as global matching models (SAM, Gillund & Shiffrin, 1984; TODAM, Murdock, 1982; Minerva II, Hintzman, 1984; Matrix model, Humphreys, Bain, & Pike, 1989; see also Humphreys, Bain, Pike, & Tehan 1989), propose that performance is compromised by other items that appear in the same context. Ratcliff, Clarke, and Shiffrin (1990) realized that one of the consequences of this assumption is that as the strength of one item on a study list is increased, either by increasing the time for which it is studied or by increasing the number of times it appears, performance should decrease for the other items on the list. Because the global matching models are mathematical models, it is possible to formally prove this prediction.

In a series of experiments, however, Ratcliff et al. (1990) demonstrated that no such effect occurs. They presented subjects with a list consisting of items that were each presented once, or alternatively with a list in which some items appeared once and some items were repeated. The subjects showed an improved performance on the items that were repeated, but there was no difference between the once-presented items as a function of the strength of the other items. This result immediately falsified this entire class of models and has led to a productive time in the area as researchers look for alternative models that are capable of accounting for these data.

Although falsification provides the most useful information in advancing scientific knowledge, it is sometimes the case that verifying predictions can increase our confidence in a theory. However, not all predictions are equally diagnostic. Predictions that seem to violate our intuitions and yet turn out to be the case provide more support for a theory than predictions that are unsurprising.

A classic example of such a prediction is the phenomenon of overexpectation in fear conditioning. The Rescorla–Wagner model of classical conditioning (Rescorla, 1970) proposes that the amount of learning that occurs on a trial when a tone is paired with a shock is proportional to the difference between the maximum value of associative strength and the current strength of the association between the tone and the shock. This simple model provides a good account of a number of conditioning phenomena, including how responding increases as a function of learning trials, how responding decreases if the tone is presented without the shock (extinction), and the lack of learning when a novel conditional stimulus is presented with another conditional stimulus that has already been associated with the unconditional stimulus (blocking).

Being able to account for these phenomena with such a simple model was impressive in its own right. However, Rescorla (1970) went one step further: He deduced a highly nonintuitive prediction from his model and tested it experimentally. He reasoned that if two stimuli that each by itself was highly associated with the unconditioned stimulus were jointly presented, then the response to this compound cue should decrease in strength because the difference between the total associative strength of the two cues and the maximum strength would be negative. This is a startling prediction, because intuition would suggest that any pairing of the conditional and unconditional stimuli should produce positive learning. However, the model predicted otherwise, and Rescorla's (1970) results confirmed the prediction.

Postdiction and Explanation

In general, clear demonstrations of prediction and falsification like those just given are rare in psychology. "Predictions are hard to make, especially about the future," said the Nobel Prize winner Niels Bohr about physics, and that is even truer of psychology. Prediction is possible under well-controlled laboratory conditions, like those just outlined, but hardly ever under natural conditions. We can predict the responses of subjects in the lab, but not where it really counts, in real life. That does not mean that our theories are no good, only that they do not afford prediction. Our explanations of behavior often are not predictive, but only *postdictive* (the term *retrodictive* is also used). Admittedly, postdictive explanations are weaker than predictive explanations, but they are still explanations. Other sciences, too, rely primarily on postdiction. A good example is meteorology. Meteorologists do predict the weather, but with limited success. That is not because their explanations or theories are not good: It is probably not an exaggeration to say that they understand very well the physical laws that govern the weather, from the molecular level to the macrolevel. Nevertheless, they are often unable to predict what will happen, because to do so perfectly one would have to know the state of the atmosphere with respect to a multitude of variables in exquisite detail and over a huge geographic area. Even knowing what every molecule is doing where, and having a big enough computer to crank out predictions might still not be enough because of chaos effects. A tiny disturbance somewhere – the flutter of a butterfly's wings in Mongolia – could under certain circumstances have system-wide consequences, resulting in a hurricane in Florida. Prediction is hard, indeed, but after the fact the meteorologist can explain quite well what happened and why.

Psychology is in a similar situation: There is no reason to think that we shall ever have available all the information about a person's history and current state that would enable a precise prediction of his or her future acts. Thus, prediction cannot be our goal, except in limited circumstances. But explanation after the fact – postdiction – is both possible and worthwhile. Much the same can be said about linguistics: Linguists have good and formal theories to explain, for instance, phonological change, but the explanation is after the fact. Medicine is another discipline that is basically not predictive, but postdictive: Just how and when a particular person will die is in general not predictable, but the good doctors can very well explain what happened and why once the person is dead. To predict we need to understand what is going on and have sufficient control over the relevant variables; postdiction also implies understanding, though not control. The true goal of science is understanding, not necessarily prediction.

Postdiction can be based on formal theories as much as prediction. Thus, the difference between the hard and soft sciences is not in the degree of formalization and rigor. For psychology formal rigor is a worthwhile and achievable goal, even though prediction is not generally feasible.

Parsimony (Occam's Razor)

The principle of parsimony states that theories should be as simple as possible. This idea was first articulated by the Franciscan friar William of Ockham as *pluralitas non est ponenda sine neccesitate*, which translates as "Plurality should not be posited without necessity." That is, only those causes or constructs that are needed to explain a phenomenon should be posited.

In our discussion of descriptive adequacy, we stated that it is important that a model of a theory be able to fit the existing empirical data. Although this is certainly a desirable quality, it is important to realize that the ability to fit data by itself does not necessarily add a great deal of credibility to a model. It is also important to consider the range of data sets the theory can

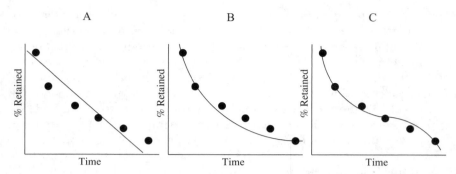

FIGURE 9.2. Fits to retention data: A, linear; B, power; and C, cubic (adapted from lecture slides prepared by Michael Lee).

fit. Some theories are very flexible and are able to fit both data that are observed and data that are not observed. In this case, the ability to fit the data provides little comfort (Roberts & Pashler, 2000).

To appreciate this point, consider the retention data that we already discussed. Figure 9.2 shows this data fit with linear and power functions as above (panels A and B), as well as with a more complicated cubic function (panel C).

In this case, the fit becomes progressively better as we move from linear to power to cubic functions. In general this will be the case because the cubic is a more flexible function and can look similar to the linear and power functions, particularly over a restricted range. It is able to model not only the true underlying function but also the random noise that is part of this data set but that would not appear if we were to run the experiment again. Consequently, when generalizing to new data, the cubic function often does not do well.

Figure 9.3 shows what can happen when we extend the time scale over which we collect data. In the new regions, the power function does a much

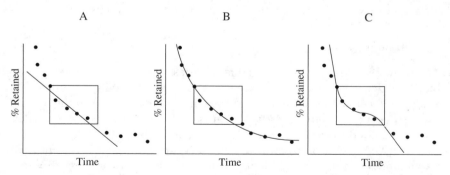

FIGURE 9.3. Generalizing to new data: A, linear; B, power; and C, cubic (adapted from lecture slides prepared by Michael Lee).

better job. So in choosing between models of a given phenomenon, we would like to favor the one that fits the data well *and* is as simple as possible. That is, we would like to fulfill the aims of descriptive adequacy and parsimony at the same time.

A number of techniques have been developed to achieve these objectives (see Pitt, Myung, & Zhang, 2002 and Pitt & Myung, 2002 for summaries). They include the Akaike information criterion (Akaike, 1973), the Bayesian information criterion (Schwarz, 1978), the information theoretic measure of complexity (Bozdogan, 1990), cross-validation (Stone, 1974), minimum description length (Pitt, Myung, & Zhang, 2002), Bayesian model selection (Kass & Raftery, 1995; Myung & Pitt, 1997), the stochastic complexity criterion (Rissanen, 1996), and the geometric complexity criterion (Myung, Balasubramanian, & Pitt, 2000; Navarro & Lee, in press). In addition, techniques such as response surface analysis (Myung, Kim, & Pitt 2000), landscaping (Navarro, Myung, Pitt, & Kim, 2003), and the parametric bootstrap cross-fitting method (Wagenmakers, Ratcliff, Gomez, & Iverson, 2004) provide additional insight into the relationships between models. Outlining these methods is beyond the scope of this chapter, but it is important to be aware that the area of model selection is developing rapidly and is likely to play an increasingly significant role in theory evaluation as it matures.

Breadth

Unlike sciences such as physics, in which providing a unified account of phenomena is seen as the ultimate goal, in psychology efforts at unification are often treated with deep skepticism. The modus operandi in psychology tends to be to continually divide phenomena into smaller and smaller classes – to know more and more about less and less. Instead of general theories in psychology, we have miniature models that are expected to hold under only very specific conditions.

Many psychologists believe that this is simply a consequence of the lack of maturity of the science of psychology, which when coupled with the complexity of psychological phenomena, means that we are simply not ready for broad theories that integrate many different phenomena in different areas of psychology. Newell (1973) argued otherwise, however. He felt that the piecemeal approach hampered progress, and that it was time to begin work on a unified theory of psychology. In cognitive psychology, the push for unification has been led by Newell (1990, the SOAR model) and Anderson (Anderson & Lebiere, 1998, the ACT-R model).

Whether or not one believes that the time for a completely unified theory is upon us, clearly theories should attempt to be as broad as possible, while maintaining the other criteria such as descriptive adequacy and the ability to provide genuine explanations of phenomena.

Originality

Another key characteristic of a theory is its originality. It goes without saying that plagiarism is unacceptable. However, originality goes well beyond issues of plagiarism. Theories may look very different, and indeed be different in their broader implications, but yet with respect to a particular set of data it may not be possible to differentiate them. Thus, great care must be taken when comparing theories against each other, even when they are stated formally. A good example of how tricky even straightforward tests between theories can be comes from the early work on concept identification. The experiments were simple: For instance, subjects saw on each learning trial a five-letter string, and they had to sort the letters into two types, A and B. After they made their response, they were told whether they were correct or not. The experimenter employed an arbitrary classification rule, say, "If the fourth letter is an R, it is type A; if not it, is type B." Researchers already knew that subjects either knew the rule or did not, in which case they guessed. At issue was the question of how they learned the rule. According to the old reinforcement view, learning could occur on every trial since the response was reinforced each time. According to the then-novel more strategic view of learning, learning could occur only when an error was made, because when subjects were told they were correct, they had no reason to change what they were doing. It seemed an easy matter to be decided. One can construct two simple mathematical models, each with two parameters (a learning rate and a guessing probability), perform an experiment, and fit the proportion correct on each learning trial to both models. The one with the better fit wins. Surprisingly, investigators found out that both models fit equally well. Eventually, it was shown that, in spite of the fact that they are based on opposite assumptions about the nature of learning, the two models made exactly the same predictions as far as the learning data in these experiments was concerned. Their mathematical formulations looked very different, but in fact were just different ways to express the same structure.

Fortunately, the story does not end here, but has a happy end: Once researchers knew what the underlying problem was, they could design experiments that looked beyond learning curves to data that actually did discriminate between these two views of learning. (It turned out that the learning-or-errors-only model was the correct one for these simple concept learning problems; for a full discussion of this episode in theory construction, see Kintsch, 1977, chapter 7.)

Usability

Good scientific theories should be useful in addressing societal problems. In the landmark report "Science: The Endless Frontier," Vannevar Bush (1945) outlined a linear model of the relationship between scientific discovery and

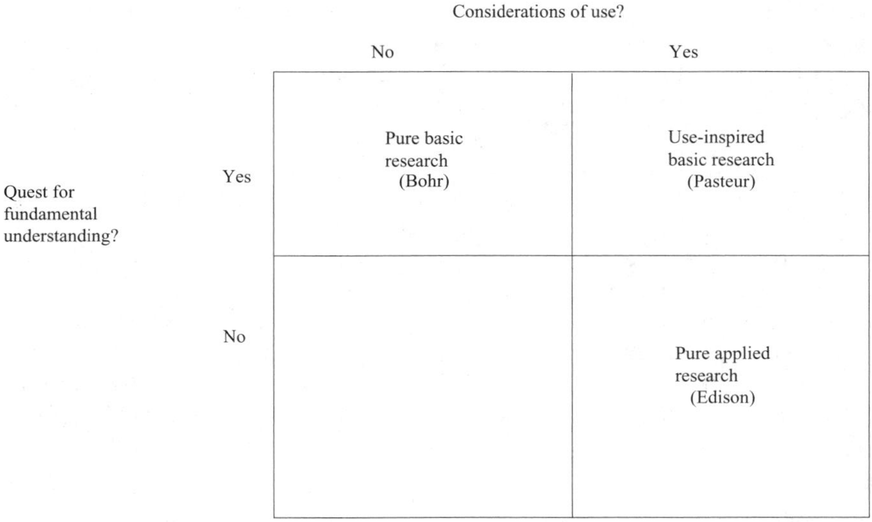

Considerations of use?

		No	Yes
		Pure basic research (Bohr)	Use-inspired basic research (Pasteur)
Quest for fundamental understanding?	Yes		
	No		Pure applied research (Edison)

FIGURE 9.4. A schematic representation of the landscape of scientific research in relation to the search for fundamental understanding and applied significance (adapted from Stokes, 1997).

technological innovation, which saw basic research and applied research at opposite ends of a continuum. Under this model, progress was made by conducting fundamental research without concern for use and then in a quite separate exercise transferring the knowledge gained into technology.

More recently the assumption that research must either be basic or applied has been challenged (Stokes 1997). Figure 9.4 shows schematically the view that has been emerging in scientific communities and among policy makers, namely, that considerations of use and the quest for fundamental understanding are different dimensions in the research landscape (Stokes, 1997).

Under this view the best research (and the best theory) contributes to scientific understanding while fulfilling a societal need. The work of Louis Pasteur is a prime example of this type of research. Pasteur was a key contributor to the development of the field of microbiology in the 19th century. As Stokes (1997) notes, however,

there is no doubt that Pasteur wanted to understand the process of disease at the most fundamental level as well as the other microbiological processes that he discovered, but he wanted that to deal with silk worms, anthrax in sheep and cattle, cholera in chickens, spoilage in milk, wine and vinegar, and rabies in people. (p. 6)

Within psychology, there are many examples of working in Pasteur's quadrant. One such example is the theory of meaning called latent semantic analysis (LSA, Landauer & Dumais, 1997). LSA is a method for taking large text corpora and deriving vector representations of the words in that corpora based on the patterns of word usage. Words with similar meanings tend to have similar locations in the semantic space defined by the model. From a fundamental perspective, then, the model provides a theory of how meaning is represented and acquired.

In addition, however, LSA has been used extensively in educational technologies. One of the most impressive of these technologies is an automated essay grader. LSA makes it possible to represent texts as vectors, so that an essay can be compared against a gold standard essay to assess whether a student has captured the essence of a writing assignment. Furthermore, it can do this with a reliability that is equivalent to human tutors (Landauer, Laham, & Foltz, 2000). So, the LSA theory is advancing our understanding of human cognition and providing a valuable (and commercially viable) service to the community.

Rationality

The final criterion that we will consider is rationality. That is, does the theory make claims about the architecture of mind that seem reasonable in light of the environmental contingencies that have shaped our evolutionary history? Stated in this way, the criterion seems rather vague. Given enough imagination, it is usually possible to envisage evolutionary scenarios to justify most claims about the way the mind should be. However, Anderson (1990) showed that a more precise notion of rationality is possible if one focuses on how information appears in the environment. Anderson argues that the cognitive system is what it is because it is adapted to the way information is distributed in the environment. It is the structure of the environment that over eons of evolution has shaped psychological processes so that they are maximally able to deal with that structure.

As an example, consider the retention curves that we looked at earlier. We concluded at that stage that the power function was the best fit to the data. But why should the memory system be constructed in such a way that performance would degrade as a power function of the retention interval? Anderson and Schooler (1991) showed that the power function is ubiquitous in nature. If you look at the probability that a word or phrase in newspaper articles or child language corpora repeats as a function of the time since its last occurrence, it decreases as a power function of the interval. Forgetting also occurs according to the power law because the memory system has been optimized through evolution to deal with an environment that encapsulates the power law.

It is not always easy to capture the relevant environmental statistics in the way that Anderson and Schooler (1991) did. However, when it is possible, it provides compelling support for a theory.

CONCLUSIONS

We have outlined in this chapter a number of considerations that should be taken into account in the evaluation of theories. We have also tried to provide access to the literature on evaluating theories for those readers who need to know more. Evaluating theories – like science in general – is hard, however, and there are no recipes for doing so. The issues we have raised here are certainly worth serious consideration, but they are no substitute for critical analysis. Every theory, every model is different and makes different demands on the reader. The points we have discussed here are valid ones in general, but how they are to be weighted in a specific case depends on many factors. Surely, parsimony is a worthwhile criterion for evaluating theories, but equally surely there are cases where the less parsimonious theory should be preferred. For example, if parsimony is bought at the expense of dramatically restricting the scope of a theory, that may not be a good bargain because it conflicts with the goal of having a broadly applicable theory. Thus, a highly parsimonious theory of recognition memory may not be as attractive as a less parsimonious one that applies to all of memory. On the other hand, a theory of everything that relies on a host of free parameters is not very interesting either. Where is the fine line that should not be transgressed? There is none; every case must be analyzed on its own merit and conflicting factors must be weighted carefully anew in each instance. Evaluating theories – and even more so, building theories in the first place – cannot do without creative, original thinking. It has rules and principles, as we outlined here, but they cannot be applied thoughtlessly.

AUTHOR NOTE

We thank Michael Lee and Dan Navarro for many valuable suggestions.

References

Akaike, H. (1973). Information theory and an extension of the maximum likelihood principle. In B. N. Petrox & F. Caski (Eds.), *Second international symposium on information theory* (pp. 267–281). Budapest, Hungary: Akadémiai Kiadó.

Anderson, J. R. (1990). *The adaptive character of thought.* Hillsdale, NJ: Erlbaum.

Anderson, J. R., & Lebiere, C. (1998). *The atomic components of thought.* Mahwah, NJ: Erlbaum.

Anderson, J. R., & Schooler, L. J. (1991). Reflections of the environment in memory. *Psychological Science, 2,* 396–408.

Bozdogan, H. (1990). On the information-based measure of covariance complexity and its application to the evaluation of multivariate linear models. *Communications in Statistics: Theory and Methods, 19,* 221–278.

Broadbent, D. (1987). Simple models for experimental situations. In P. Morris (Ed.), *Modeling cognition* (pp. 169–185). London: Wiley.

Brown, S. C., & Craik, F. I. M. (2000). Encoding and retrieval of information. In E. Tulving and F. I. M. Craik (Eds.), *The Oxford handbook of memory* (pp. 93–108). New York: Oxford University Press.

Bush, V. (1945). *Science – The endless frontier, appendix 3*. (Report of the Committee on Science and the Public Welfare). Washington, DC: U.S. Government Printing Office.

Cary, M., & Reder, L. M. (2003). A dual-process account of the list-length and strength-based mirror effects in recognition. *Journal of Memory and Language, 49*, 231–248.

Cohen, J. (1994). The earth is round ($p < .05$). *American Psychologist, 49*, 997–1003.

Dennis, S., & Humphreys, M. S. (2001). A context noise model of episodic word recognition. *Psychological Review, 108*, 452–477.

Gilbert, G. N., & Mulkay (1984). *Opening Pandora's box: A sociological analysis of scientists' discourse.* Cambridge, England: Cambridge University Press.

Gillund, G., & Shiffrin, R. M. (1984). A retrieval model for both recognition and recall. *Psychological Review, 91*, 1–67.

Gronlund, S. D., & Elam, L. E. (1994). List-length effect: Recognition accuracy and variance of underlying distributions. *Journal of Experimental Psychology: Learning, Memory, and Cognition, 20*, 1355–1369.

Hintzman, D. L. (1984). MINERVA2: A simulation model of human memory. *Behavior Research Methods, Instruments, and Computers, 16*, 96–101.

Hintzman, D. L. (1991). Why are formal models useful in psychology? In W. E. Hockley and S. Lewandowsky (Eds.), *Relating theory and data: Essays on human memory in honor of Bennet B. Murdock* (pp. 39–56). Hillsdale, NJ: Erlbaum.

Humphreys, M. S., Bain, J. D., & Pike, R. (1989). Different ways to cue a coherent memory system: A theory for episodic, semantic and procedural tasks. *Psychological Review, 96*, 208–233.

Kass, R. E., & Raftery, A. E. (1995). Bayes factors. *Journal of the American Statistical Association, 90*, 773–795.

Kintsch, W. (1977). *Memory and Cognition.* New York: Wiley.

Kintsch, W. (1998). *Comprehension: A paradigm for cognition.* New York: Cambridge University Press.

Kuhn, T. (1962). *The structure of scientific revolutions.* Chicago: University of Chicago Press.

Landauer, T. K., & Dumais, S. T. (1997). A solution to Plato's problem: The latent semantic analysis theory of acquisition, induction and representation of knowledge. *Psychological Review, 104*, 211–240.

Landauer, T. K., Laham, D., & Foltz, P. W. (2000). The Intelligent Essay Assessor. *IEEE Intelligent Systems, 15*(5), 27–31.

Leahey, T. H., & Harris, R J. (1985). *Human learning.* Englewood Cliffs, NJ: Prentice-Hall.

Murdock, B. B., Jr. (1982). A theory for the storage and retrieval of items and associative information. *Psychological Review, 89*, 609–626.

Myung, I. J., Balasubramanian, V., & Pitt, M. A. (2000). Counting probability distributions: Differential geometry and model selection. *Proceedings of the National Academy of Sciences USA, 97*, 11,170–11,175.

Myung, I. J., Kim, C., & Pitt, M. A. (2000). Towards an explanation of the power law artifact: Insights from response surface analysis. *Memory & Cognition, 28*, 832–840.

Myung, I. J., & Pitt, M. A. (1997). Applying Occam's razor in modeling cognition: A Bayesian approach. *Psychonomic Bulletin & Review, 4*, 79–95.

Navarro, D. J., & Lee, M. D. (in press). Common and distinctive features in stimulus representation: A modified version of the contrast model. *Psychonomic Bulletin & Review.*

Navarro, D. J., Myung, I. J., Pitt, M. A., & Kim, W. (2003). Global model analysis by landscaping. In R. Alterman & D. Kirsh (Eds.), *Proceedings of the 25th Annual Conference of the Cognitive Science Society.* Mahwah, NJ: Lawrence Erlbaum.

Newell, A. (1973). You can't play twenty questions with nature and win. In W. C. Chase (Ed.), *Visual information processing* (pp. 283–308). New York: Academic Press.

Newell, A. (1990). *Unified theories of cognition.* Cambridge, MA: Harvard University Press.

Pitt, M. A., & Myung, I. J. (2002). When a good fit can be bad. *Trends in Cognitive Sciences, 6*, 421–425.

Pitt, M. A., Myung, I. J., & Zhang, S. (2002). Towards a method of selecting amoung computational models of cognition. *Psychological Review, 109*, 472–491.

Popper, K. R. (1959). *The logic of scientific discovery.* London: Hutchinson.

Ratcliff, R., Clarke, S., & Shiffrin, R. (1990). The list strength effect: I. Data and discussion. *Journal of Experimental Psychology: Learning, Memory, and Cognition, 16*, 163–178.

Rescorla, R. A. (1970). Reduction in the effectiveness of reinforcement after prior excitatory conditioning. *Learning and Motivation, 1*, 372–381.

Rissanen, J. (1996). Fisher information and stochastic complexity. *IEEE Transactions in Information Theory, 42*, 40–47.

Roberts, S., & Pashler, H. (2000). How persuasive is a good fit? A comment on theory testing. *Psychological Review, 107*, 358–367.

Schwarz, G. (1978). Estimating the dimension of a model. *The Annals of Statistics, 6*, 461–464.

Stokes, D. E. (1997). *Pasteur's quadrant: Basic science and technological innovation.* Washington, DC: Brookings Institution Press.

Stone, M. (1974). Cross-validatory choice and assessment of statistical predictions (with discussion). *Journal of the Royal Statistical Society Series B, 36*, 111–147.

Wagenmakers, E. J., Ratcliff, R. Gomez, P., & Iverson, G. J. (2004). Assessing model mimicry using the parametric bootstrap. *Journal of Mathematical Psychology, 48*, 28–50.

Watkins, M. J. (1990). Mediationism and the obfuscation of memory. *American Psychologist, 45*, 328–335.

Wilkinson, L., and the Task Force on Statistical Inference APA Board of Scientific Affairs. (1999). Statistical methods in psychology journals: Guidelines and explanations. *American Psychologist, 54*, 594–604.

10

Not All Experiments Are Created Equal

On Conducting and Reporting Persuasive Experiments

Christian H. Jordan and Mark P. Zanna

If you leaf through a standard psychology textbook, it can reveal a wealth of insights into mind and behavior – into how people sense and perceive their environments, for instance, or how they learn, grow, remember, make decisions, or relate to each other. It can also reveal descriptions of the experiments that form an evidentiary basis for such insights. Each of these experiments demonstrates something noteworthy about how people think, feel, or act. Curiously though, if you leaf through a few competing textbooks, you will probably find the same experiments described repeatedly. This is curious because for many topics in psychology, numerous studies exist that demonstrate the same basic effect or reveal the same insight into behavior. Yet some experiments garner attention and citations whereas others that make the same points languish in relative obscurity. This happens, in part, because some experiments are more persuasive than others. That is, some experiments capture people's imaginations and attention more fully, offering especially compelling demonstrations of particular effects. These are the kinds of experiments that you, as a researcher, want to conduct and report. This chapter explores considerations that will, we hope, enable you to do so.

Unfortunately, there are no guarantees. There is no set formula to follow that can ensure that an experiment will be broadly persuasive. Every research problem is unique, with its own attendant issues and complexities. It is impossible to anticipate all of these nuances in advance, so every research problem must be approached from a somewhat different angle. This makes science exciting, but it can also be a source of frustration. Fortunately, there are enough common themes in the art of experimentation that some general advice can be offered. By the end of this chapter, you should have a clearer sense of many issues that can affect the design, analysis, and report of experiments in order to make them more compelling. This is less a how-to manual, then, than a set of guidelines that may be useful.

After some preliminary remarks, we navigate through the organization of a research report – through the introduction, method, results, and discussion sections – highlighting not only how each section can be written to be more persuasive but also many issues to consider while designing and conducting an experiment in order for it to produce more persuasive results.

THREE CAVEATS

Before we begin, however, three caveats are in order. First, both of us are social psychologists. Because of this, our advice may be most germane to other social psychologists. We have, however, striven to offer broadly applicable advice, and we believe our guidelines will be useful to researchers across all areas of psychology.

Second, it is not true that all of our experiments are persuasive. Some of them have been duds. Moreover, they do not always meet the criteria set forth here. Nevertheless, we have analyzed many experiments that are regularly cited, as compared with experiments that are relatively neglected, and we believe there are general principles that can distinguish between the two. In addition, while preparing this chapter, we surveyed some true experts in the art of experimentation to learn their thoughts on this matter, and we incorporate their insights throughout.

Lastly, this chapter does not give extensive instruction on how to write well. Certainly, to be persuasive, writing well is essential. But we do not detail the virtues of repetition, parallel sentence construction, or extensive editing here. Instead, we urge you to read Bem's (1987) classic paper on writing the empirical journal article, which is a valuable resource for nourishing academic prose (see also Bem, 2004). Although we offer a few writing tips, we broaden our focus to consider elements of the development, design, and analysis of an experiment that can contribute to persuasiveness. Our focus thus goes beyond the final writing stage of the research process to consider issues that touch all stages (see also Sternberg, 1995).

BEING PERSUASIVE REQUIRES ARGUING WELL (AND THEN SOME)

Let's start at the end. Once you have conducted an experiment, found some interesting results, and drawn conclusions, you must next persuade others that your conclusions are correct by presenting them in a research report. This goal requires presenting arguments in a clear and compelling manner. To be persuasive requires arguing well; it requires structuring arguments effectively. State your conclusions clearly and explain how they follow logically from the results (cf. Toulmin, 1958). Consider likely counterarguments or rebuttals that critics might level against your conclusions (Toulmin, 1958). Preempt critics by raising alternative explanations first, on your own terms. Then explain why those alternatives are implausible, or else qualify your conclusions appropriately. You will then be in a better position to convincingly draw conclusions and give a clear, take-home message. There is thus a basic framework that you can use to structure the arguments in a research report (i.e., state your position, make your case, raise alternatives, rule out alternatives wherever possible, and conclude you are correct). Your ability to effectively implement this framework hinges on having designed a methodologically sound experiment. This framework can then help you to be more persuasive. We will explore ways to help you implement this structure.

Structuring arguments well, however, is not enough to be persuasive. To be truly persuasive requires having something interesting to say. In other words, being persuasive requires both compelling argument *structure* and compelling argument *content*. You cannot be persuasive unless people pay attention to what you say. And if people can't see the importance of your topic, the relevance of your findings, or the significance of your results, they won't pay much attention. They may read your report, but they might miss the main points or else soon forget them. So think about the content of your arguments long before writing a report. Consider the content of your arguments while choosing topics to study and designing experiments. As much as possible, design and conduct experiments that people can relate to, understand, and recognize as meaningful. It will then be easier for you to report your findings in an engaging and convincing manner. We will also explore ways to help you develop compelling argument content.

PREPARING A PERSUASIVE RESEARCH REPORT

In each section of a standard research report, there are specific issues that must be addressed and specific information that must be described. For full details about the contents of a standard research report, consult the *Publication Manual of the American Psychological Association* (2001). It is precise and detailed. Here, we discuss only select issues. We focus on considerations of experimental design, analysis, and presentation that may enhance the persuasiveness of a report.

Introduction

The major goals of the introduction are to introduce the research problem, to situate the study in the research literature, and to outline the specific hypotheses that were tested. A major part of the introduction is the literature review, which outlines theory and past findings that are relevant to the research goals and hypotheses. Your experiment was informed by, or is at least related to, past research and you should highlight these connections as the introduction unfolds. But save it for later – start big.

Do not open a report by saying, "Several theorists have struggled with the question of what determines whether and how people's self-views are affected by outstanding individuals." Instead, say something like,

It is a cultural cliché that superstars, that is, individuals of outstanding achievement, can serve as role models to others, inspiring and motivating them to do their utmost best. To promote such inspiration, prominent women scientists are often invited to address high school girls, eminent African Americans are introduced to African American children, and outstanding employees are profiled in corporate newsletters and bulletin boards.

Lockwood and Kunda (1997) skillfully opened with the latter quote and saved the former until later in the introduction to their article on how role models affect self-views.

Journalists routinely open their articles with a hook. They are mindful to begin with a pertinent fact or issue raised by their story, or an engaging anecdote that illustrates the importance of the piece. This helps pull in readers. Prospective readers want to know whether they should take the time to read an article or not. A good hook can convince them to read it. Similarly, consumers of research reports are generally busy people, whether they are students or professionals. Many will decide quickly whether to read a report, and so you want to convince them quickly that yours is worth their time. Otherwise, you will have lost the opportunity to persuade.

Open, then, with a hook. Start with the big picture. Situate your research in the world beyond psychology labs and journals. Introduce your topic briefly with an interesting anecdote, some pertinent facts about the problem, or even a hypothetical situation that illustrates the issues that originally got you interested in the problem. It may be useful to begin writing as though you are explaining your research to a nonpsychologist friend or roommate. Doing so can help you to avoid the tendency to start by describing past research. As Bem (1987) wisely suggested, "Whenever possible, try to open with a statement about people (or animals), not psychologists or their research" (p. 176). Do bear in mind that a hook should suit your audience; an appropriate opening for a research report should assume greater familiarity with the topic than may be true for a journalistic piece. But also bear in mind that your work is ultimately about people (or animals), not psychologists or their research. Communicate this fact.

Suppose you have studied a relatively minor aspect of a neural pathway that may be involved in schizophrenia. In the context of ongoing research, you might feel that your work is but a small piece of a large puzzle. But it is an important puzzle, and therefore an important piece. If you open by describing the subtle methodological variations that distinguish your work from past studies, rightly or wrongly, many readers will lose interest. Specialists may continue reading, but others with a passing curiosity may balk. If instead you open by describing how schizophrenia touches the lives of many people, affects their connections to reality, and impacts their loved ones, readers can more clearly situate your research in its proper context. They may thus be encouraged to read on.

A point of clarification: Open your report with an engaging example or anecdote that illustrates the problem you studied and why it is important. Do not open with an amusing story or joke that is only minimally related (or worse, unrelated) to your topic. The point is not to amuse readers. The point is to engage them with the relevance of your research. Stay focused. Your hook should be a genuine introduction to your research.

Incidentally, similar issues bear on the title of a research report. The title must accurately describe the major theoretical issues or variables that were studied. Beyond that, however, a catchy title can make a real difference. Not only can it attract readers, but it can also provide a memorable catchphrase to represent your work. Give careful consideration to your title. It will be the first thing that prospective readers see.

In most cases, the first step toward convincing readers that your work is important is to personally believe that it's important. This might be somewhat surprising. But consider that if *you* don't see the relevance of your research, it will be hard for you to convince anyone else of its merit. It is thus ideal, at the outset of your research program, to choose a problem that interests you. There are many good reasons to study an issue. You might be interested in a problem because of its relevance to an existing, influential theory (in fact, you may be interested in challenging such a theory), or you might be motivated to fill a gap you noticed in the research literature. You might want to address a pressing social issue that concerns you. Or maybe you noticed an interesting aspect of your own or others' behavior that begs explanation. Whatever your reasons, though, be sure you are genuinely interested. Genuine fascination will not only put you in a better position to communicate your enthusiasm (and thus generate interest in your work), it will also sustain you through the long research process. As a consequence, it will surely enhance the quality of your work.

Note that there are other criteria beyond personal interest that can be useful for choosing a research focus. All else being equal, nonobvious or even counterintuitive predictions are preferable. Such predictions, when realized by data, can be extremely persuasive and memorable. Note, however, that counterintuitiveness per se is not the highest virtue of a research hypothesis – many truisms of psychology are actually quite sensible. But if your grandmother could predict the outcome of your study before you conduct it, it may be of limited interest to anyone else (Abelson, 1995). The bottom line, however, is to choose a problem that interests, and hopefully excites, you. Doing so will help you to communicate the reasons why the problem is important.

Once readers are hooked, you can then situate your research in the broader research literature and outline your predictions. As you do so, always work toward introducing your specific hypotheses. Describe past research only to the extent that it helps to explain what you studied and why. Demonstrate how your work is original and extends past research. Demonstrate how your research is relevant to an influential theory or extends the existing literature. Make sure that each point you introduce follows logically from what you have said so far, and that all of your points are moving toward your hypotheses and the goals of your study. When writing the introduction, start by considering the concepts you need to introduce in order to make your hypotheses clear. Introduce and define key variables. Describe past research that supports your predictions. Use examples to introduce unfamiliar concepts and theories. The writing process for the introduction should thus begin at the end, with consideration of the specific hypotheses. The writing itself should start at the beginning and always move toward that end. The beginning is the hook, the anecdote or example that illustrates the basic problem. The end is a clear statement of purpose, a summary of the specific goals and hypotheses of the research. Everything in between should create a logical, smooth transition from the hook to the hypotheses.

Method

The major goal of the method section is to describe how the study was conducted. The method section includes descriptions of the participants, materials and apparatus, and the procedures. It must be detailed enough to allow experts to assess the validity of the design and the significance of the findings, and to allow replication of the study. What you write in the method section is thus tightly constrained by the experiment you conducted. Clearly, your method section must reflect your actual methods. In order to write a persuasive method section, you must conduct a persuasive experiment.

What makes an experiment persuasive? Certainly, it must be technically sound. The logic of experimentation – the combination of manipulation, random assignment to conditions, and control over extraneous variables – when properly implemented, allows clear causal conclusions. Many factors contribute to sound experimental design, too many to detail here. Instead, we focus on two overarching goals that can help to make a technically sound experiment even more persuasive. The first goal is simplicity.

Simplicity

Psychological phenomena are complicated and result from many causes. There is no single factor that determines mood, motivation, circadian rhythms, or the vividness of memory. As you learn about the topic you have chosen to study, you will generate many viable ideas, and identify many factors that could contribute to the behavior or outcome of interest. You must translate these ideas into concrete, testable methods. Because of the complex nature of the phenomena, you may be tempted to work all of your insights into a single experimental design, and we are confident that you could do so. But resist this temptation. For the sake of persuasiveness, keep the design simple.

A useful strategy for determining the overall design of an experiment is to start by outlining a study that could, in principle, test your ideas in their full complexity. Forget practicality and resource constraints for a moment. Map out the full $2 \times 3 \times 4 \times 3$ factorial design that could capture the full complexity of the phenomena. Then start winnowing. Sit down and decide which factors are most important and which are less essential. Decide which conditions are necessary to produce meaningful results. (Do you need success, failure, and neutral conditions? Could you reasonably test your ideas with just success and failure conditions, or with just failure and neutral conditions?) Determine the central issues you want to address, and pare down your experiment to a more straightforward, streamlined design. Strive for the simple elegance of a 2×2 factorial design (or simpler). Not only will your design be easier to conduct in a timely manner, but it will likely be more persuasive. Keep in mind that research problems can, and generally should, be approached programmatically; in an ongoing program of research, you can test other aspects of a phenomenon in further studies. An overly complicated design in any one study can create needless confusion, distract from your central ideas, and undermine the persuasiveness of your research.

Psychological phenomena are complicated and result from many causes. Because of this, there are some research questions that can only truly be addressed by complex research designs. Some theoretical predictions can only truly be captured by a three-way or even a four-way interaction. In our experience, however, this is rare – much rarer than is commonly believed. Most predicted three-way interactions, especially in the early stages of a research program, can be meaningfully parsed and tested as a series of two-way interactions in a series of less complicated designs. Such studies are generally easier to comprehend. Confusion is a multiplicative function of the number of independent variables in an experiment. To be persuasive, you want to minimize confusion. You therefore want to minimize the number of independent variables in experiments. This can normally be accomplished without any significant loss of fidelity in your research.

"Bottling" Experience

The second goal, toward increasing the persuasiveness of an experiment, is to create a situation that engages the psychological processes of interest. Many of the most memorable (and frequently cited) experiments have procedures that distil the essence of situations in which the processes under study naturally occur. A psychological experiment should be a microcosm. It should be a working model of the typical contexts in which phenomena normally occur. In the life sciences, bacteriological experiments are hosted in Petri dishes. First, bacteria cultures are grown. The elements that stimulate bacterial growth – nutrients, oxygen levels, temperature – can be closely monitored and controlled in Petri dishes. Against this backdrop, other factors can be modified and manipulated in order to observe their effects on bacteria. Although human beings are often more sophisticated than bacteria, psychological experiments should similarly be microcosms. They should be carefully monitored and controlled settings, but also incorporate the elements needed to nurture the phenomena of interest. Ideally, the procedures should create a backdrop against which experimental effects can naturally occur. An experiment will then be more ecologically valid (i.e., the research setting better matches the normal environments of the problem). It will also be more likely to attract attention and capture imaginations. The experimental context will be more familiar and identifiable, which can ultimately heighten the impact of the findings.

Some highly persuasive experiments closely parallel familiar situations. Aronson and Mills (1959), for example, explored whether severe initiations increase liking for groups. Their young, female participants hoped to become part of an ongoing discussion group on the psychology of sex. First, however, some of them took a screening test to ensure they could discuss sex openly. Some took a relatively severe test (i.e., reciting obscene words and reading sexually explicit passages in front of the researchers), whereas others took a relatively mild test (i.e., reciting sex-related but not obscene words). Everyone was then admitted to the group and could listen to an ongoing discussion. Those who took the severe test enjoyed the discussion more (though it was actually designed to be quite boring). Although few people have had exactly this experience, it is easy to recognize real world situations that these procedures model. Severe initiations are common for admittance to fraternities and sororities, or to military groups. This experiment distils the main psychological features of these experiences in a controlled setting, thus making the experiment highly representative of these experiences. The parallels between these familiar situations and the procedures of this study surely make the findings more vivid, memorable, and compelling.

An elaborately staged setting is not necessary to capture experience in this way. Much can be accomplished through well-designed stimuli and hypothetical scenarios in studies of judgment and decision making, for example. Consider the following scenario:

Mr. Crane and Mr. Tees were scheduled to leave the airport on different flights, at the same time. They traveled from town in the same limousine, were caught in a traffic jam, and arrived at the airport 30 minutes after the scheduled departure of their flights.
Mr. Crane is told that his flight left on time.
Mr. Tees is told that his flight was delayed, and just left five minutes ago.
Who is more upset? Mr. Crane or Mr. Tees?

Most people intuit that Mr. Tees is more upset. Kahneman and Tversky (1982) used this scenario to demonstrate that people are more upset by near misses than far misses (though the objective outcomes may be the same). Although few people have had exactly this experience, they can easily imagine the situation and how they would react.

The choice between relatively passive stimuli and more elaborate situations should not be made lightly, however. It should be based on consideration of the specific processes being studied. For some processes, such as sensation, perception, and some forms of judgment, carefully designed, passive stimuli can directly engage the processes of interest. In other cases, such stimuli may be less effective. Reading about another person might not engage the same impression formation goals and processes as actually meeting another person. Serious thought should be given to the procedures of an experiment, and how well they capture the processes of interest.

Similar considerations should guide the choice of dependent variable measures. Self-report measures are widely used in psychology, in part because they are easily administered. Although they may often be perfectly valid, and their convenience is appealing, in some cases self-report measures may not fully engage the reactions of interest. They may be distorted by social desirability concerns or may simply be treated lightly. To study impression formation, reports of liking another person can be useful and informative. But they could be considerably enhanced by observing whether participants choose to spend time with another person. Similarly, as a measure of intentions to practice safer sex, self-reports are useful. But they could be considerably enhanced by recording whether participants buy condoms or take pamphlets on safer sex from the study (Stone, Aronson, Crain, Winslow, & Fried, 1994). Behavioral measures and other measures that are more consequential and unobtrusive are often more naturalistic and ecologically valid than self-report scales. As a consequence, they are often more compelling.

Some independent variable manipulations are also more compelling than others. Some manipulations more closely correspond to familiar experiences. As an example, it is often theoretically useful to tax participants' cognitive resources while they perform certain tasks (to see whether those tasks are disrupted). Participants may thus be asked to remember a random nine-digit number while performing another task. This manipulation works well. In some cases, however, more naturalistic manipulations can be equally effective. Participants can be taxed by time pressure, for example. Gilbert, Pelham, and Krull (1988) taxed participants by telling them they had to give a public speech, thus preoccupying them as they mentally prepared and rehearsed. Because they are more familiar, naturalistic manipulations can be more persuasive. They may also be subtler, reducing demand characteristics.

Heavy-handed manipulations can suggest to participants how they "should" respond, leading them to behave unnaturally. More naturalistic manipulations, because they are often subtler, may elicit less artificial responses. Note, though, that the critical issue is not whether a manipulation superficially resembles mundane events, but whether it engages natural responses (Aronson & Carlsmith, 1968). To manipulate fear, a researcher could show participants clips from horror films. This reflects common experiences, but may be an obvious manipulation. On the other hand, participants could be convinced that they will take a painful cold-pressor test later in the study. This is a far less common experience, but may elicit more natural fear responses. In this sense it may be a subtler manipulation, even though it's an otherwise more conspicuous event.

Incidentally, relative to heavy-handed manipulations, it can be more persuasive when subtle manipulations produce large effects. This is related to the idea that counterintuitive predictions, when realized, can be quite compelling. When extremely subtle or minimal manipulations produce results, it can be remarkable (Prentice & Miller, 1992). When people are divided into groups on the basis of trivial criteria (e.g., preferences for one of two abstract painters, or coin flips), for example, they favor members of their own group (e.g., Billig & Tajfel, 1973; Tajfel, Billig, Bundy, & Flament, 1971). This finding is impressive precisely because the manipulation is so slight. An experimental effect is generally more surprising (and impressive) to the extent that it is larger than expected (Abelson, 1995). Large effects are often expected to follow heavy-handed manipulations. But when large effects follow small, subtle manipulations, they can be all the more compelling.

Results

The major goals of the results section are to describe the data that were collected and the statistics used to analyze them. The results must be described in enough detail to justify conclusions. What you write in the results section is thus tightly constrained by the data you collected. In order to write a persuasive results section, you must have persuasive results.

There are a few things you can do to help produce strong, clear results. Design your experiment with an eye to internal and ecological validity. Conscientiously conduct participants through the procedures and carefully record their responses. Then cross your fingers. Prayer might help, but now the results are largely beyond your control. If you find nothing interesting, go back to the drawing board. (But explore the data from every angle before giving up. There could be an unexpected effect that you hadn't considered before. If so, you will want to replicate the finding before making too much of it, but it could be the start of an important discovery.) In the best of all possible worlds, a subtle manipulation will produce a large effect. If so, that's terrific. Breathe a sigh of relief. But you're not done yet. Even when you have impressive data, how you present those data can affect their persuasiveness.

Start by presenting your results with straightforward, transparent inferential statistics. Conduct analyses that test your hypotheses clearly. This can often be accomplished through conventional statistics. If you conducted a 2 × 2 factorial experiment, an analysis of variance testing the two main effects and the interaction will generally be a good place to start, followed by standard simple effects tests. These are widely recognized and accepted analyses, and will thus be persuasive. The bottom line, however, is that your analyses should clearly test your hypotheses. If your hypotheses are better served by a series of planned orthogonal contrasts, by all means conduct and present those analyses. But clearly justify your decision to do so. Do not leave it up to readers (or reviewers) to wonder why you used somewhat unorthodox tests. They might conclude that the data are weak or fishy. Your goal is to make the results clearer and less ambiguous, not more so.

Whatever specific tests you use, describe what they mean in plain English (see also Bem, 1987). Statistics are important, but they won't carry your arguments. For every statistic you report, explain what it tests, how it relates to your predictions, or what it reveals about the behavior being studied. Do not simply say that, "Participants who expected to undergo a cold-pressor test reported more identify confusion ($M = 7.1$) than those who did not ($M = 3.3$), $t(32) = 3.45$, $p < .01$." First remind us that some participants expected to take a painful cold-pressor test, in order to make them feel more anxious, whereas others did not. (It is also useful to demonstrate that your manipulations were successful, so consider using manipulation checks.) Then remind us that you expected anxiety to make people feel less sure of themselves and to question their own personal identities. Now you can present the t test, and explain that it shows that participants' reactions were consistent with your predictions. Statistics serve a purpose. They can reveal patterns of reactions and behavior, and test specific hypotheses. Make sure that your statistics clarify your findings, rather than obscure them.

In addition to reporting inferential statistics, describe your results. Present the data in descriptive, possibly nonparametric terms. Although the percent of participants in each condition who chose a particular response might not be an appropriate focus for inferential tests, it can give a clearer sense of participants' reactions. Report that 81% of participants who expected a cold-pressor test said they felt "moderately" or "extremely" unsure of themselves, compared with only 34% of control participants. Remind readers what specific scale values mean. If you log transformed reaction times to perform inferential tests, convert them back to seconds to describe them. They will then be easier to understand. If you converted raw scores to z scores for analyses, explain that a mean z score of .78 indicates that participants bought an average of three or four condoms. If participants described personal failures, indicate that 63% described poor exam grades and 21% described romantic rejections. Explain that one participant described being left standing alone at the altar. Quote directly from participants' responses if they are revealing (and you can ensure their anonymity). Data describe behavior, thoughts, and feelings. Give a clear sense of how participants behaved in your study.

The results section can also be a good place to rule out obvious alternative explanations. Some alternatives can be ruled out (or made substantially less plausible) through supplementary analyses. In some cases, including good measures of proposed mediating variables is useful. They can demonstrate that the processes you suggest actually do account for observed effects. Similarly, good measures of plausible confounds can be useful. If you threatened self-views by having some participants recall personal failures, a mood measure can demonstrate that the manipulation did not simply depress people (thus explaining your results). Otherwise, you could demonstrate that the findings remain strong after statistically controlling for mood. Additional coding of responses may also be worthwhile. If you are comparing the reactions of high and low self-esteem people to failure, further coding could show that high and low self-esteem individuals described equally severe failures. This could rule out severity of failure as an explanation for self-esteem effects. Similarly, simple follow-up studies designed to rule out plausible alternatives can be presented briefly at the end of the results section or in the discussion section. Such supplementary analyses and measures, assuming they are reliable and valid, can help to rule out many alternatives. This, of course, will make your findings more persuasive.

Discussion

The major goals of the discussion are to interpret the theoretical and practical implications of the results and draw final conclusions. You described the findings in the results section; now consider what they mean. Return to the research literature, and situate your findings in the context of past research. Indicate how your findings qualify or extend existing theory, and how they relate to past results. Try to reconcile any inconsistencies between your findings and past findings. Acknowledge any limitations to the interpretation or generality of the findings. Inspire further research. And give a clear, take-home message.

It is customary to open the discussion with a summary of the main findings and how they relate to the original hypotheses. This is typically a good idea. Not only is it expected, but you want to clearly illustrate that your conclusions follow logically from your results. Because your conclusions will commonly be that your hypotheses were supported, this opening summary is an ideal opportunity to bridge the gap between data and theory. Quickly remind readers of the major findings and how they supported your hypotheses. If your findings deviated from predictions at all, indicate that too. The remainder of the discussion hinges on the primary findings, so make them salient.

Incidentally, the fact that conclusions will commonly be that the hypotheses were supported is no indication that most experiments work out exactly as planned (they do not). It reflects the fact that the theory and hypotheses presented in a report should be informed from the start by the findings of the study (Bem, 1987). This gives greater continuity to the storyline of a report. (We will return to this point later.)

After the summary, explain how your findings extend past research. In the introduction, you outlined the goals of your experiment in relation to past findings. Now remind readers of those goals, and how well your results met them. What distinguishes your study and findings from past research in the area? Do your findings help to resolve conceptual ambiguities in past findings? If so, say so. Did you identify conditions under which an established effect no longer holds? Note that too. Has the effect you uncovered never been documented before? Definitely mention that. This is no time to be modest. If your findings are genuinely novel and original, especially if they change the way people ought to think about a phenomenon, make that clear. Do so first of all because it will improve the odds that your research will be published. Do so also because readers will be better able to appreciate the real contributions your research makes.

In particular, note the theoretical advancements suggested by your findings. How do your results qualify or extend existing theories? Although your findings may hold some interest by themselves, their real value probably lies in their theoretical implications. Science is based on the dynamic interplay of discovery and justification, the discovery of facts, and their theoretical explanation (see Jordan & Zanna, 1999). Simply documenting effects or relations between variables is rarely of broad scientific interest. More commonly, findings are interesting to the extent that they support or refute certain theories. The fact that, after making a difficult decision, people come to value their chosen alternative more and their rejected alternative less is interesting (see, e.g., Brehm, 1956). It is widely cited and influential, however, because it supports cognitive dissonance theory, the theory that people find cognitive inconsistency aversive (e.g., thinking, "I chose to buy a Honda instead of a Volvo," while also recognizing that "Volvos are safer than Hondas"), and will work to resolve it (e.g., by rationalizing their decisions). In your discussion, clearly indicate the theoretical contributions made by your study. Are you advancing a new theory that your findings support? Do your findings cast doubt on an existing theory, or suggest limitations to its scope? Give a clear take-home message about the theoretical contributions of your work.

Acknowledge the limitations of your findings too. Are there interpretational ambiguities? Were there unexpected results that are not easily fit into your theory? If there are obvious alternative explanations for your findings, note them. It is hoped that you have already made them less plausible in your results section, or can do so now on logical grounds. If not, acknowledge the alternatives and appropriately qualify your conclusions, but recognize the difference between possible and plausible alternatives. There are always possible alternative explanations. You are not obliged to document every far-fetched possibility. But acknowledge plausible alternatives. If you do not, critics will. And they will probably be less charitable than you toward your conclusions.

Inspire further research. The limitations you have identified can suggest further studies that could clarify matters. What questions remain unresolved? Do your findings raise new issues that haven't previously been considered? To the extent that your results differ from past findings, could further research help explain these discrepancies? No matter how impressive your findings might be, they are not the end of the story. Science is a cumulative enterprise, with new studies building on past work. Inspire readers with possibilities of where to go next. Suggest novel contexts in which your findings could be further tested. Are there theoretical implications of your findings that could be tested? Can your theory or findings be applied to other areas of study? Do your findings suggest possible resolutions to any practical problems?

Try to build the explanatory coherence of your theory or findings. A theory is generally more credible to the extent that it has broad explanatory coherence, that it can explain a wide variety of phenomena (Thagard, 1989; see also Abelson, 1995). Cognitive dissonance theory is broadly compelling, in part, because it accounts for many disparate effects, from the rationalization of decisions to the fact that people like groups more following severe initiations. Consider how your theory or findings might help explain other phenomena. Be speculative, but consider what your findings and theory might reasonably suggest about past findings in other research areas, or about specific practical problems. Maybe your results can connect past findings that have not previously been considered related. Such unifying power can make your findings and theory more memorable and persuasive.

As you close your report, make a brief but memorable exit. Emphasize an important contribution or implication of your work. It might be theoretical or practical, but be sure it clearly demonstrates the true value of your work. Although the most concrete contribution of your work might be resolving a conceptual ambiguity in the literature, this is probably not the note you want to end on. Your work might be in some sense a small piece of a large puzzle. But remember that it is an important puzzle, and therefore an important piece. Make this fact clear. Remind readers why the problem you studied is important. This is your last chance to make an impression – make it count.

TELL A CLEAR STORY

Research reports tell a story. They tell the story of how a particular research problem was studied; how the researchers formulated specific hypotheses, designed a study to test them, analyzed their results, and drew conclusions. This structure is embodied in the standard format of research reports. It is embodied in the progression from the introduction to the method, results, and discussion sections. Research reports have a linear, narrative structure with a beginning, middle, and end. Elsewhere, we suggested that while reading journal articles, this narrative structure can be used to enhance understanding and memory for the main points in an article (Jordan & Zanna, 1999). The details of an experiment should be generally easier to comprehend, and thus remember, if they are linked together by a coherent story. The narrative structure of research reports can thus guide your reading.

As a writer, exploit this narrative structure. Although the standard format of research reports steers them naturally toward a narrative line, you may sometimes struggle as a reader to draw the story from an article. As a writer, keep readers from needing to exert this effort. Write the story of your research in bold relief. Make it as salient as possible, so the internal logic of the research is clear. The easier you make it for readers to see the story behind your research, the easier it will be for them to understand and remember your main points. This is a major step toward persuading readers that your theory and conclusions are correct and worth caring about.

Note, however, that telling a story is not necessarily the same thing as telling *the* story of how your research actually unfolded (Bem, 1987). Remember, a research report tells the story of how researchers formulated hypotheses, designed a study to test them, analyzed results, and drew conclusions. This is a highly streamlined and romanticized version of the research process. Most research programs do not unfold so neatly. Throughout the research process, ideas are developed and discarded, revised in response to results. Pilot testing may lead to modifications of methods, and so on. Most of these hiccups and missteps will only clutter your storyline. In most cases, you should omit them. Include them only if they are pertinent to the interpretation of your results or conclusions. Your storyline should be shaped from the beginning by the findings of your study (Bem, 1987).

To summarize, tell a clear story. In most cases, this will mean telling a somewhat sanitized story.

EPILOGUE

It is commonly believed that the ultimate goal of science is the accumulation of facts (Sternberg, 1995). Following this line of thinking might suggest that some of the guidelines offered here are plainly unscientific. According to this perspective, science is about documenting facts in as objective a manner as possible. It is not about storytelling or being persuasive. It is about uncovering the truth.

Science certainly is about uncovering the truth. But this goal does not preclude being persuasive. On the contrary, we believe that being persuasive is a central part of conducting good science. Being objective about documenting facts is important. You must describe your method and results faithfully so the basic facts can be weighed by others. But the interpretation and explanation of facts is also central to science. Theory is important. To the extent that multiple interpretations of the same set of facts are possible, it is important to be persuasive in presenting your own interpretation.

Persuasive presentation is one thing, but what about the process of conducting experiments? Experiments are designed to uncover clear causal relations. They should be rigorously designed to control extraneous, potentially confounding factors. Our guidelines are admittedly light on the logic of experimentation, and heavy on the art. This should not suggest that experimental control is unimportant. But neither is it necessarily incompatible with our guidelines. An experiment can be both artfully designed and tightly controlled. In some cases, however, the move toward more naturalistic procedures can entail some loss of control. There can be a trade-off between ecological and internal validity. To some extent, a balance must be struck between the two. Which side of that balance should be favored is a judgment call and depends on the values of individual researchers. Note, however, that both can be achieved, particularly through programmatic research. The two goals can be traded off across studies in a research program, with some studies favoring internal validity and others ecological validity.

Even in cases where persuasiveness entails some loss of experimental control, this loss may be offset by gains in inspirational value. Though there may be more alternative explanations for a particular set of findings, if the experiment on which they are based is persuasive, the findings and theory will garner attention and inspire further research. Some of that attention and research will be critical. The original explanation of the findings may be overturned. Such is the marketplace of ideas. But more familiar, straightforward, simple, naturalistic, and ultimately compelling experiments are more likely to be noticed in this marketplace. Their theories and findings will survive long enough to inspire further work, which is desirable whether they are ultimately upheld or not. In this way, persuasive experiments are good science. So go forth, and be persuasive.

AUTHOR NOTE

Preparation of this paper was facilitated by research grants from the Social Sciences and Humanities Research Council of Canada to both authors. Many thanks to Elliot Aronson, Roy Baumeister, Robert Cialdini, Jennifer Crocker, Alice Eagly, Dan Gilbert, Tom Gilovich, Arie Kruglanski, James Olson, Lee Ross, Mike Ross, and Shelly Taylor, all true experts in the art of persuasive experimentation whose insights were invaluable while the authors were preparing this chapter. Thanks also to Diane Halpern, Mike Ross, Steve Spencer, and Anne Wilson for their helpful comments on a later draft. Correspondence concerning this chapter can be addressed to Christian Jordan, Department of Psychology, Wilfrid Laurier University, Waterloo, Ontario, Canada N2L 3C5. E-mail can be sent to cjordan@wlu.ca.

References

Abelson, R. P. (1995). *Statistics as principled argument.* Hillsdale, NJ: Erlbaum.
American Psychological Association. (2001). *Publication manual of the American Psychological Association* (5th ed.). Washington, DC: Author.
Aronson, E., & Carlsmith, J. M. (1968). Experimentation in social psychology. In G. Lindzey and E. Aronson (Eds.), *The handbook of social psychology* (2nd ed., Vol. 2, pp. 1–79). Reading, MA: Addison-Wesley.
Aronson, E., & Mills, J. (1959). The effect of severity of initiation on liking for a group. *Journal of Abnormal and Social Psychology, 59,* 177–181.
Bem, D. J. (1987). Writing the empirical journal article. In M. P. Zanna & J. M. Darley (Eds.), *The compleat academic: A practical guide for the beginning social scientist* (pp. 171–201). New York: Random House.
Bem, D. J. (2004). Writing the empirical journal article. In J. M. Darley, M. P. Zanna, & H. L. Roediger III (Eds.), *The compleat academic: A career guide* (pp. 185–219). Washington, DC: American Psychological Association.
Billig, M., & Tajfel, H. (1973). Social categorization and similarity in intergroup behavior. *European Journal of Social Psychology, 3,* 27–52.
Brehm, J. (1956). Postdecision changes in the desirability of alternatives. *Journal of Abnormal and Social Psychology, 52,* 384–389.
Gilbert, D. T., Pelham, B. W., & Krull, D. S. (1988). On cognitive busyness: When person perceivers meet persons perceived. *Journal of Personality and Social Psychology, 54,* 733–740.
Jordan, C. H., & Zanna, M. P. (1999). How to read a journal article in social psychology. In R. F. Baumeister (Ed.), *The self in social psychology* (pp. 461–470). Philadelphia: Psychology Press:
Kahneman, D., & Tversky, A. (1982). The simulation heuristic. In D. Kahneman, P. Slovic, & A. Tversky (Eds.), *Judgment under uncertainty: Heuristics and biases* (pp. 201–208). New York: Cambridge University Press.
Lockwood, P. J., & Kunda, Z. (1997). Superstars and me: Predicting the impact of role models on the self. *Journal of Personality and Social Psychology, 73,* 91–103.
Prentice, D. A., & Miller, D. T. (1992). When small effects are impressive. *Psychological Bulletin, 112,* 160–164.
Sternberg, R. J. (1995). *The psychologist's companion: A guide to scientific writing for students and researchers* (3rd ed.). Cambridge, England: Cambridge University Press.
Stone, J., Aronson, E., Crain, A. L., Winslow, M. P., & Fried, C. B. (1994). Inducing hypocrisy as a means of encouraging young adults to use condoms. *Personality and Social Psychology Bulletin, 20,* 116–128.
Tajfel, H., Billig, M., Bundy, R., & Flament, C. (1971). Social categorization and intergroup behavior. *European Journal of Social Psychology, 1,* 149–178.
Thagard, P. (1989). Explanatory coherence. *Behavioral and Brain Sciences, 12,* 435–467.
Toulmin, S. E. (1958). *The uses of argument.* Cambridge, England: Cambridge University Press.

11

Making Claims in Papers and Talks

Barbara A. Spellman, Judy DeLoache, and Robert A. Bjork

Getting stuff published is easier than getting people to read what you've published.

– Dennis Proffitt

INTRODUCTION

So, you've done some research and have some interesting results; perhaps you've even written drafts of your method and results sections. Now you have to write your introduction and discussion and figure out how to present your research to the world outside your lab. In addition to describing what you found, how are you going to frame the contribution of your research to psychology? In other words, what claims will you make?

This chapter is about how to make claims; that is, how to develop and communicate the sorts of arguments that make for informative, interesting, and persuasive papers and talks. In the first part of the chapter, we describe different types of claims and discuss how to assess your claim; that is, how to create an argument of "the right size." In the second part, we discuss when and how to communicate your claim; that is, how to use the standard formats of papers and talks to your best advantage. Although we write in terms of empirical papers, these strategies are also relevant for review papers and talks. In the last part of the chapter, we offer tips specific to giving talks.

We believe that this chapter – focusing on the appropriate way to make research-based claims – will be of particular benefit to fledgling psychologists. We admire Neal Miller's aphorism: "Be bold in what you try, cautious in what you claim." Good science requires bold thinking. Simply taking the next obvious step in a program of research can be important, even necessary, but major advances depend on the Star Trek approach – "to boldly go where no [psychologist] has gone before."

Having been bold in asking a research question and designing relevant tests, it is, as Miller noted, important to be cautious in what you claim. Some researchers consistently overstate the strength or importance of their results – something that does no credit to themselves or to the field. Our concern is not so much with overstatement, however, but with understatement of the value and contribution of one's research. In our experience, psychologists – and especially junior investigators – often err on the side of being overly cautious, taking a defensive approach that (like the overly bold approach) does no credit to themselves or to the field. Thus, a primary focus of this chapter is on suggestions for how to make *appropriately* strong claims for your research.

DEVELOPING AND ASSESSING YOUR CLAIM

What is a "Claim"?

Your claim is your statement of what your research encompasses and what it contributes. It goes beyond just describing what you did and what you found. You want to communicate not only the outcome but also the value of what you have done – how what you have done fits into existing research and adds to existing knowledge.

You should be able to state your claim in two or three sentences when you are explaining your research to someone, even though you might never use those exact sentences in your paper.

Types of Claims

What are some types of claims? In the following subsections, we illustrate five different kinds of claims with sentences from selected abstracts, introductions, and discussions of articles recently published in *Psychological Science*.[1] Our examples are chosen to show the importance of making a clear, explicit, straightforward statement about the contribution of the research.

1. Claims of Novelty or Innovation
Your claim may be that you have devised a new method or approach, discovered a new phenomenon, or generated a new theory. Note that your claim should not be that you have new data – it is assumed that you do. Your job is to situate your new data within the appropriate claim.

---

[1] Citations to articles from *Psychological Science* have the month and year included to facilitate finding them.

We describe a new method for mapping spatial attention that reveals a pooling of attention in the hemifield opposite a peripheral flash. (Tse, Sheinberg, & Logothetis, March, 2003)

We developed a strategy based on classic signal detection theory that combined elements from these three [previously described] approaches in a naturalistic daily experience study. (Gable, Reis, & Downey, March, 2003)

We demonstrate a new bias in children's belief-desire reasoning. (Friedman & Leslie, August, 2004)

2. *Claims of Theoretical Progress or Refinement*
Your claim may be that you have extended a previous theory to cover new data; or that you have found, tested, and verified non-obvious predictions of an old theory; or that your results constrain existing theories.

This finding adds a new perspective to classic theories of interference and recovery. Lustig, Konkel, & Jacoby, November, 2004)

These findings place powerful constraints on theories of object recognition. (Grill-Spector & Kanwisher, February, 2005)

We demonstrate that the compatibility effect depends on people's representation of their selves in space rather than on their physical location. (Markman & Brendl, January, 2005)

For contrast, we provide the following weak example of a claim of theoretical progress. Although we made it up, it is parallel to actual published language.

Weak claim: These findings add to the growing literature indicating that children's preferences for particular facial expressions vary systematically as a function of age and experience.

3. *Claims That Challenge Prevailing Interpretations or Theories*
Your claim may be to challenge or reject an existing theory or interpretation.

Overall, these findings challenge the assumption that all positive emotions share the same expression, and suggest that pride may be added to the pantheon of basic emotions generally viewed as evolved responses. (Tracy & Robins, May, 2004)

These results challenge predictions derived from the presumed superiority of discovery approaches in teaching young children basic procedures for early scientific investigations. (Klahr & Nigam, October, 2004)

4. *Claims That Challenge Conventional Wisdom*
Your claim may be to overturn – or to verify – some "conventional wisdom" about how people think or behave.

We conclude that blind individuals are more accurate than sighted individuals in representing the size of familiar objects because they rely on manual representations, which are less influenced by visual experience than are visual memory representations. (Smith, Franz, Joy, & Whitehead, January, 2005)

[P]olitical ideology influences how the popular press reports research findings and ... such reporting in turn affects readers' beliefs and attitudes. (Brescoll & LaFrance, August, 2004)

5. Claims That Stress the Applied Importance of Your Findings

Your claim may be that your results have implications for an important problem, or that your new theory or an existing theory has relevance to an important applied setting.

Finding the mechanisms that relate psychometric intelligence to mortality might help in formulating effective interventions to reduce inequalities in health. (Deary & Der, January, 2005)

Our findings make it clear that ... children profit from gesture when it conveys information that differs from the information conveyed in speech. ... [T]hese data open the possibility for a heretofore unappreciated technique to improve learning in and out of the classroom. (Singer & Goldin-Meadow, February, 2005)

Our hope is that the current work provides a critical first step toward understanding the factors that influence (and potentially eliminate) racial biases in police officers' responses to criminal suspects. (Plant & Peruche, March, 2005)

We have just shown you examples of strong versions of five types of common claims. We don't mean to imply that these categories are exhaustive; however, most of your claims will be of one of these types.

Thinking Critically About Your Own Claim

It is no accident that this chapter on making claims is positioned late in the book. Making a suitable claim requires many of the critical thinking skills discussed in earlier chapters. Three such skills are particularly relevant: (a) creating a coherent story; (b) analyzing arguments; and (c) communicating effectively to others.

Creating a Coherent Story

Creating a coherent story means pulling together the pieces of what you have done and integrating them with the existing literature. No study stands in isolation; each has to be presented in context. You need to have read the existing literature with a critical eye to know where your research fits. If, for example, you are making a claim of theoretical progress or refinement (Claim 2) or one that challenges prevailing interpretations or theories (Claim 3), you must spend considerable time thinking about the existing theories in order to understand their predictions and limitations. If you are making a claim that stresses the applied importance of your findings

(Claim 5), you must consider the differences between your experimental conditions and the conditions to which you would like to generalize. For example, if you want to claim that your results have strong implications for optimizing learning, you need to consider whether your experiments include materials and retention intervals that are realistic from an educational standpoint.

Analyzing Your Argument

Of all the tools in the successful scientist's toolbox, we believe that the most valuable one is being able to critically analyze one's *own* arguments. Becoming a psychologist means learning to evaluate research – and everyone has plenty of opportunities to read and critique other peoples' research. Unfortunately, it is far less common – and far more difficult – to critique one's own research. Doing so, however, is essential to making a claim that others will take seriously.

Why is it so difficult to evaluate one's own research? For one thing, it is highly likely that you agree with the conclusion. Research has shown that people tend to be more accepting and less critical of arguments with which they agree. In addition, you know more than you have stated in your manuscript; for example, you have read literature that you haven't cited, perhaps run experiments that "didn't work" and aren't included, and probably delved more deeply into your data than your manuscript suggests. You may have, inadvertently, made a coherent argument out of the parts that neatly fit together but left out some of the problematic issues raised along the way.

Communicating Your Argument to Others

The challenges in analyzing one's own arguments are similar to the challenges in evaluating one's own writing. You already know what you have done and why, how it all turned out, and what it means. But your reader does not. You have lots of ideas and information in your head that may not have made their way onto the paper. Your text makes sense and seems to be complete to you because you have automatically filled in gaps in the flow of thought and logic; however, you need to make sure that you have fully communicated your research in orderly steps so that the reader, too, can appreciate what you have done. You need to present the relevant background concisely; motivate and describe your study in the necessary amount of detail, display your data effectively; interpret your results and draw your conclusions in a clear and understandable way; and, finally, anticipate obvious objections to your interpretation – all so the reader can evaluate your argument and assess the validity of your claim.

Getting It Right

What steps can you take to make sure you have done a good job? We have two recommendations. First, after you have written a "full draft" of your manuscript (we don't mean the final draft, we mean the first one that goes from the Introduction through the Discussion and presents your full argument), put it down for a few days. After this break, pick it up and read it as if you were a first-time reader and it were someone else's manuscript. Be as ruthlessly critical of your own manuscript – both argument and writing style – as you would be of manuscripts written by others. Second, when the manuscript is further along, ask knowledgeable and trusted others to read it. Ask them to be ruthlessly critical, too. (Don't hold it against them if they are – it's for your benefit and they are doing you a favor. Cultivate the art of being grateful for tough feedback.) Make sure that one or two such people are from outside your laboratory. People in the same laboratory group often use the same jargon and accept the same assumptions. At least one of your readers needs to be someone who is smart but naïve to your particular topic; that person can represent the anticipated consumers of your research.

On Being the Right Size[2]

So now that you have critically assessed your research, it is time to state your claim. How bold should your claim be? The best claims are not too big, and not too small, but just right. You should portray your contribution to the field accurately. If you are too conservative, readers or listeners may dismiss your results as inconsequential, in which case neither you nor your research will get the credit you deserve. On the other hand, if you are too generous to yourself, readers or listeners may come to question not only your current claim but all of the other claims you make as well.

Most graduate students and junior investigators err by making claims that are too timid (although we have also seen undergraduates make claims that are too bold). There are at least three reasons for this common reticence.

First, graduate students often feel overwhelmed and intimidated by the amount of research already done on their topic. How can you make a claim for novelty if you aren't sure that you have read and understood everything previously written about it? What if you missed some article or paragraph or footnote that has already put forward what you want to claim? The answer is that you need only make a good faith effort to ascertain that the claim has not, in fact, already been made. Searching the relevant literature is an obvious part of such an effort, but talking to knowledgeable researchers can also be invaluable. Once your research gets communicated broadly to others in talks, posters, or manuscripts, the self-correcting nature of science will take over. People who come to your talks or posters will offer you information

---

[2] We take the title of this section from the well-written and widely anthologized essay by J. B. S. Haldane (1927).

about related work – particularly their own. In addition, when you send a manuscript to a journal, the action editor and, especially, the reviewers, will be familiar with the literature and give you guidance.

If, however, someone tells you "that's already been done," or "I've done that," it's important not to take such comments at face value; instead, you should do some rigorous fact checking of your own. Unfortunately, many people claim too much for the field and for themselves. You should always ask where the research is published. You will then often find that the work referred to differs substantially from your own, or that your work goes beyond the previous findings in an important way, or even that the work referred to was never actually published.

A second contributor to an overly timid approach is the (accurate) belief that your data and interpretation cannot withstand all attacks. You are good enough, and concerned enough, to see the flaws in your data, the potential counterarguments to your interpretation, and the issues that you failed to address. How can you make a strong claim when so much is lacking? The answer is to recognize that data are rarely "perfect," that not all questions can be answered in a single manuscript, and that more research is (almost) always needed. (A good point to remember, but not appropriate to state in your paper.) Science usually proceeds in small, rather than earth-shaking, increments, so any increments you contribute are valuable.

The final reason why graduate students often make timid claims is because the language of philosophy of science, especially as adopted by psychologists, has implicitly and explicitly taught them to do so. As philosophers of science, and as scientists, we know that no theory with empirical content can ever be proven true. Even after observing 1,000,000 white swans you may still stumble upon a black swan, disproving your theory that all swans are white. We also know (less explicitly) that scientific theories are almost never disproven – at least not by a single observation or experiment. Were you to find that black swan, you might argue that it was really white but had just fallen afoul of an oil slick. Correspondingly, when you confront others with contradictory findings, their first action will not be to abandon their theory; rather, it will be to question your method or data. Eventually, however, they might modify their theory to fit your new data. (To get a good sense of how difficult it is to get people to modify a theory, even when they have approved of the methods, see Mellers, Hertwig, & Kahneman, 2001. This article is an example of an "adversarial collaboration" – in which researchers on different sides of a controversy design studies together in the hope that their results will resolve the controversy.)

Our language of psychology, however, pressures us to be even more timid than just avoiding claims of proof and falsification. As a field, we have adopted the language of tentativeness. We (correctly) never say "our data *prove* X," which would be both overly bold and scientifically illiterate, but we then go too far in the other direction and use overly timid phrases, such as "our data *seem to suggest* X." Our journals are now rife with that sort of language.

As careful readers of this literature, graduate students, who are trying to absorb the culture of academic psychology, will mirror the language around them. You say it that way because others say it that way. Or, stated in a fashion consistent with the present argument, "It can be inferred that perhaps you say it that way because you might have been influenced by others who have previously said something like it in a similar manner." Do not make that error. If your claim is the right size, you need not be tentative with your language.

COMMUNICATING YOUR CLAIM IN A MANUSCRIPT

As we already mentioned, we believe that good papers are informative, interesting, and persuasive. Those three characteristics are not independent of each other and nowhere are they more interrelated than when you are making your claim.

Your entire paper should be an argument for your claim. You begin, of course, with an issue (a question you are going to answer, a theory you are going to extend or limit, etc.). Your introduction should then motivate why the issue is interesting and important; your method should clarify how you hope to gain leverage on the issue; and your results section should be structured to illustrate clearly how your results bear on the issues of interest. Finally, your general discussion should state your conclusions explicitly; acknowledge and then rebut – if you can – potential counterarguments; show how your conclusions might be even more interesting or applicable than they seem at first glance; and tie up all loose ends. At a minimum, the reader should finish reading your article believing you have said something new and interesting.

Your claim should be made in several sections of your manuscript.

Abstract

Abstracts are your first – and sometimes your only – chance to make it clear to the reader what you have done and why anyone should care.

Your abstract can function successfully in two quite different ways. One is to motivate the reader to go on and read the whole paper. Think of your abstract as an advertisement – a teaser to entice the reader to want more. To achieve that goal, your abstract has to recruit and hold attention. Unfortunately, abstracts are woefully underutilized as advertising. Most follow the guidelines of the *Publication Manual of the American Psychological Association* (2001), describing details from every section of the manuscript (p. 14). What is frequently left out altogether is what the author claims, the very thing most conducive to achieving the author's primary goal – that is, getting others to *want* to read the paper.

The second way an abstract can be successful is to convey such a good sense of the importance and interest value of the research that a casual reader (e.g., someone in a different field who has stumbled upon your abstract) will understand what you did, what you found, and why it is important. Such an abstract is memorable and leaves a good impression of the work and its author. It may even lead that person to recommend your paper to others.

There are many ways to write bad abstracts: they can easily be too vague, too wordy, too timid, and so on. In particular, abstracts often suffer from being, no pun intended, too abstract. We are appalled by the plethora of abstracts in psychology that read something like this: "In several studies, we investigated A. N participants did B. Results showed C. Implications and conclusions are discussed." What a waste of words! Neither the first nor the last sentence contributes anything. Readers do not care what you investigated; they care what you found and what it means. Telling them "implications and conclusions are discussed" is vacuous. An abstract of the type parodied here tells your reader nothing about what your article contributes to psychology.

Instead of the insipid, uninspired, and uninformative type of abstract that is all too common, make your abstract informative by including your claim. It is more important that your abstract communicate what you believe your research shows than it is to communicate the specific details of what you did to show it.

A good, strong abstract uses clear, strong language. Use the active voice; avoid the passive voice. The active voice communicates power and conviction; the passive voice suggests uncertainty, lack of confidence, and disengagement. The passive voice is also often vague and wordy. What follows here are some examples of good, active phrases to use in your abstract. These phrases, which highlight your claim, will ideally appear in the first, penultimate, or last sentence of the abstract, but they should definitely appear somewhere. (And, yes, we like the use of "we" when it means "we the coauthors.")

"We demonstrate that . . . "
"We report . . . "
"We offer . . . "
"We argue . . . "
"We claim . . . "

Here are some examples of commonly used, uninformative, and wordy phrases: "We examined . . . " or, even worse, "X was examined." Still worse, "An experiment examined . . . " or "This research examined . . . " or "A study was conducted to examine. . . . " (You almost never need to say "X was examined, investigated, assessed, measured"; instead, that idea can usually be incorporated into the statement of the results.) Another such phrase is "Participants were presented with...." (Did you present them with a gift? Otherwise, participants *did* something – they read or heard or watched or reported.) Another is "We found an effect of X on Y" or "we found a relation between X and Y." (How nice, but what was the effect or the nature of the relation?)

And, finally, here's our favorite: "The theoretical and practical implications of these findings are considered." (We swear this sentence has appeared at least once in *Psychological Science* but we don't want to cite the source. We think the sentence means that they wrote a discussion section. We have also seen variations, such as, "The implications of these findings for X are considered." A more informative statement would be "These findings imply that....")

There are certainly other good ways to start an abstract besides using a *we* sentence. Here are two more good approaches.

1. A Question

Does knowledge about which objects and settings tend to co-occur affect how people interpret an image? (Davenport & Potter, August, 2004)

When language is correlated with regularities in the world, does it enhance the learning of these regularities? (Yoshida & Smith, February, 2005)

2. A Statement of Existing Theory, Practice, or Conventional Wisdom, Which Sets the Background Context for Your Claim

If you find it necessary to start with a statement about the findings of previous research, be sure to avoid the passive voice. Do not simply state, "Previous research has found X." With a little effort, you can figure out a better way to say it. Then immediately contrast this background with your claim. What is your addition, qualification, new approach, or resolution? Note that when referring to previous research, it is particularly good if you can describe a conflict in the previous literature that your research helps to resolve. The following are good examples.

Contemporary knowledge of infant cognition relies heavily on violation-of-expectation experiments. However.... (Newcombe, Sluzenski, & Huttenlocher, March, 2005)

The way people respond to the chance that an unlikely event will occur depends on how the event is described. (Koehler & Macchi, August, 2004)

It has become almost a maxim that "talking through" a problem is advantageous. (Lane & Schooler, November, 2004)

Now compare the following two fictional examples that accentuate some of the points just made.

Word wasting (bad): The latency to find a deviant visual pattern was measured as a function of the number of distractor patterns for two age groups – adolescents and adults. Both age groups detected the target stimuli more rapidly when there were fewer distractor stimuli.

Word saving (good): Both adolescents and adults found a deviant visual pattern more rapidly when it occurred among a smaller number of distractors.

Note that the first version expends words describing what was measured and mentioning that there were two different groups; the second version incorporates those ideas into the statement of results. The length difference: 20 words versus 41 words! Think what you could do with those extra 21 words in the rest of your 100-word abstract.

Next compare a published abstract that we believe is informative and compelling with a parody of that abstract that illustrates much of what we have said not to do (but that we have often seen in real articles). The abstract is from an article titled "Visual Recognition: As Soon as You Know It Is There, You Know What It Is" by Kalanit Grill-Spector and Nancy Kanwisher (February, 2005). It is 126 words.

Good (real) version: What is the sequence of processing steps involved in visual object recognition? We varied the exposure duration of natural images and measured subjects' performance on three different tasks, each designed to tap a different candidate component process of object recognition. For each exposure duration, accuracy was lower and reaction time longer on a within-category identification task (e.g., distinguishing pigeons from other birds) than on a perceptual categorization task (e.g., birds vs. cars). However, strikingly, at each exposure duration, subjects performed just as quickly and accurately on the categorization task as they did on a task requiring only object detection: By the time subjects knew an image contained an object at all, they already knew its category. These findings place powerful constraints on theories of object recognition.

Now consider how the authors might have introduced their work (but fortunately did not) using a slightly different set of 126 words:

Bad version: Many researchers have tried to determine the sequence of processing steps involved in visual object recognition. This issue was investigated by examining performance on three different tasks: within-category identification, perceptual categorization, and object detection. Each of these tasks was designed to tap a different component process of object recognition. Subjects were presented with natural images at varying exposure durations, and for each task we measured both accuracy and reaction time. Our results showed that, at each exposure duration, subjects' performance on the within category-identification task was slower and less accurate than on the perceptual categorization task, but that subjects performed just as quickly and accurately on the categorization task as they did on a task requiring only object detection. Implications of our findings are discussed.

Which of the two abstracts actually tells you something? Which makes you want to find out more? We hope you find the differences as striking as we do.

The bottom line on abstracts: When you think about how people use abstracts, you should realize that they are your first, best, and maybe only chance to make your claim. Be strong and be clear.

Title

Okay, perhaps we exaggerated when we said that abstracts are your first, best, and maybe only, chance to entice a reader. The honor of being the "first" – and sometimes, unfortunately, the "only" – goes to those few words immediately above your abstract: your title. Most of the lessons learned from writing abstracts are applicable to writing titles.

We agree with the *Publication Manual of the American Psychological Association* (2001, p. 10) that titles "should summarize the main idea of the paper simply and, if possible, with style." We don't, however, like the example the manual provides: "Effect of Transformed Letters on Reading Speed." That title illustrates what most undergraduates are taught in their research methods class: mention the independent and dependent variables. What it does not do are some of the other useful things that titles can do – including making your claim. Titles, like abstracts, can serve to entice and inform the reader; simply mentioning the variables, without revealing the direction of the finding or situating them within a larger issue or context, does neither.

Consider the following title: "Music Lessons Enhance IQ" (Schellenberg, August, 2004). From just those four words you know exactly what the researcher found; in contrast, "The Effect of Music Lessons on IQ" is seven words and much less informative. Notice that the original example and all the following examples do contain the key variables, but the variables are supplemented by an action word that reveals their relation: "Remembering a Location Makes the Eyes Curve Away" (Theeuwes, Olivers, & Chizk, March, 2005); "Reaction Time Explains IQ's Association With Death" (Deary & Der, January, 2005); and "Toddlers' Responsive Imitation Predicts Preschool-Age Conscience" (Forman, Aksan, & Kochanska, October 2004).

Not only can your title reveal your results, it can also reveal your claim. Theoretical claims are often appropriate for titles: "Fractionating Working Memory: Consolidation and Maintenance Are Independent Processes" (Woodman & Vogel, February, 2005); "Partial Awareness Creates the 'Illusion' of Subliminal Semantic Priming" (Kouider & Dupous, February, 2004); and "Visual Recognition: As Soon as You Know It Is There, You Know What It Is" (Grill-Spector & Kanwisher, February, 2005).

Practical claims are particularly good to have in titles as they create a broad appeal for your work: "Knowing Is Half the Battle: Teaching Stereotype Threat as a Mean of Improving Women's Math Performance (Johns, Schmader, & Martens, March, 2005); "The Symptoms of Resource Scarcity: Judgments of Food and Finances Influence Preferences for Potential Partners (Nelson & Morrison, February, 2005); or "When High-Powered People

Fail: Working Memory and 'Choking Under Pressure' in Math" (Beilock & Carr, February, 2005).

We are not advocating that all titles include the entire claim; many are too complex to be conveyed in so few words. Although it is definitely best to include a claim, clarity is of paramount importance.

One final note: although your primary goal is to have a clear and informative title, one that is also clever is even better. From recent years in *Psychological Science*, we especially like "Looking Forward to Looking Backward: The Misprediction of Regret" (Gilbert, Morewedge, Risen, & Wilson, May, 2004) and "Show Your Pride: Evidence for a Discrete Emotion Expression" (Tracy & Robins, March, 2004).

The bottom line on titles: A title is your first chance to hook the reader. As with the abstract, you need to balance clarity and brevity. Use the active voice; state what you found, not just what you investigated; and do your best to represent your claim.

Introduction

It is simple to make the case (as we just did) that claims should be present in abstracts so that researchers can find relevant papers and will be enticed to read interesting papers. In fact, many published papers do contain claims in the abstracts. It is more difficult to find claims made in the Introduction of a paper; however, we believe that it is no less important to make them there. We also believe that the reluctance to do so is misguided.

Why Are People Reluctant to Put Claims in Introductions?

We believe that authors are reluctant to put their claims in the Introduction because they think it ruins the suspense. Authors sometimes get caught up in developing the "story" of their research and then write as if their manuscripts were mystery novels. "What will happen if we do X? Stay tuned and we will reveal, clue by clue, how we solved the mystery." Authors get caught up despite the fact that, as writers of empirical papers, we know that the "story" as presented in a manuscript (i.e., the order of the experiments, the predictions, even the research question) is usually not the story of what actually happened when the research was done.

Why Should People Put Claims in Introductions?

Although Arthur Conan Doyle would have sold many fewer books were his mysteries solved on page 1, you are not writing a Sherlock Holmes mystery. In fact, the very reason that mystery writers put the "answer" at the end is why you need to put your claim at the beginning. Have you ever gotten to last page of a mystery novel, or the final scene of a movie with a "twist," and then felt that you wanted to go back to the beginning to see whether it all fit together? That is great for book or movie sales, but that is not the kind of time a reader wants to invest in reading your scientific paper. How everything fits together should be obvious all the way through.

In fact, psychologists know that reading something with an "advanced organizer" – a statement that tells you what something is about or where it is going – is much less taxing than reading something without one. You want to keep your readers focused and on task – and all on the "same page." You want to make it easy for them to follow your argument and understand what you are doing and why; you don't want them to have to keep seemingly unrelated pieces of information in their heads until you provide them with the unifying "twist" at the end.

Where Should People Put Claims in Introductions?

As with the abstract, the claim might appear in the first sentence of your Introduction, or you might have some work to do before you can get to the claim. You might first need to set up the background against which you can contrast your finding (e.g., explain existing theories or prevailing conventional wisdom). You might want to introduce the research area or problem in some engaging manner. Regardless, somewhere in the Introduction, before your reader starts wondering why she or he is reading about the search for intelligent life in the universe, you should make your claim.

Other Sources of Examples

Many excellent examples of strong ways to introduce your claim very early in your paper can be found in the work of professional science writers. The following are a few representative examples. Notice how the authors immediately get to the point of the research and what it shows. Also notice how much information is packed into every sentence. Although journal articles are typically much longer than these types of pieces, we think the direct approach is equally valuable there.

A part of the brain that's involved in sound processing shows pronounced activity when rhesus monkeys hear their comrades vocalizing but not when the same animals hear other sounds, a new brain-scan investigation finds. [Bower, B. (2004, February 14). *Science News, 165,* 109]

How quickly babies home in on the sounds of their native language during their first year may predict how quickly they learn new words, string together complex sentences, and acquire other language skills as toddlers. [Miller, G. (2004). *Science* (News Focus), *306,* 1127]

Three British men who suffered left brain damage that undermined their capacity to speak and understand language still possess a firm grasp of mathematics.... This observation dramatically illustrates the presence of separate brain systems for language and numbers. [Bower, B. (2005, February 19). *Science News, 167,* 117]

Babies exposed to lead in the womb may be at increased risk of developing schizophrenia as adults. [Pearson, H. (2004, February 17). *Nature Science Update*]

In Southern Asia, where an estimated 75 million children qualify as malnourished, lack of food may only be part of the problem. A prospective study in rural Pakistan finds that mothers who became depressed shortly before or after giving birth had babies far more likely to experience stunted growth and bouts of diarrhea than were babies with psychologically healthy mothers. [Bower, B. (2004, September 18). *Science News, 166,* 179]

Good examples of informative abstracts that make clear claims can also be found in the general journals *Science* and *Nature.*

The bottom line on introductions: Although it may seem like you are "giving away the ending" when you put your claim in the Introduction, a research article is not a mystery novel. By making it clear, from the very beginning, where you are going and what you found, you will help your readers to follow and evaluate your research.

Results

Although not everyone agrees with this recommendation, we believe that you can and should make modest claims in your Results section. It is not the place to make your big claims – only to state what you think your evidence directly shows. You should begin this section with a sentence or paragraph summarizing in a straightforward, non-technical way what you found. Knowing what the general results of the research are at the outset makes it immensely easier for the reader to comprehend the later detailed and technical description of your analyses.

Discussion

The Discussion is, of course, another place where your claim should be clearly stated. In fact, everyone agrees that it should be there, but many people fail to do it effectively. They err by just reiterating their results. The point of the Discussion is to bring it all together – your fascinating question, your delicate methods, and your lovely results – and to show that you have the goods to support your claim. You have fulfilled your promise. The Discussion is also often the place to make and justify claims about the applications of your findings to the real world. Such claims can make a strong ending to a paper.

We want to remind you that writing a paper is an iterative process. No one we know, except possibly the lead editor of this book, can write a paper from start to finish and then be done. Instead we might, for example, write the Method and Results first, then a draft of the Introduction. Next we might start the Discussion, but as we are trying to tie up everything, we might realize that we cannot make our claim as strongly as we would like because we are missing some supporting data. So, we might go back and run some new analyses on our data. Then we revise our Results and Discussion – and then the corresponding lead-in from the Introduction.

If, as we have suggested, you can step back from your own work and be ruthlessly critical during this iterative process, you will end up with a strong and coherent argument – and a claim of exactly the right size.

The bottom line on discussions: Be sure to have a crisp, succinct, statement of your claim in the Discussion. Your readers will feel satisfied with your work only if, at the end, they fully understand what you have claimed and how your claim is justified.

COMMUNICATING YOUR CLAIM IN A TALK

When you write a manuscript you have two very different goals: one is to do justice to your research, to be interesting, informative, and persuasive, and to make the claim the right size; the other is to get your manuscript accepted to a journal. In the best of all possible worlds, if you achieve the first goal, the second will follow.

When you give a talk you no longer have the goal of getting the talk accepted; that has already happened. You still, however, must do justice to your research, and in the limited time allotted. How you can best present your research, therefore, differs somewhat between a paper and talk.

Special Considerations in Giving Talks

Our advice regarding talks (especially the 15-minute kind) is that you be aware that it is difficult to communicate effectively in such a short period of time. You need to be selective in what you present, but you also have to be sure that the audience gets the big picture; you may have to sacrifice details, but never sacrifice audience understanding. (It may be important, for example, to give a concrete example of your materials, but not how you achieved a certain counterbalancing.) Preparing a short talk forces you to streamline your argument to its bare essentials. For that reason, giving a short talk on your research can be very helpful as a precursor to writing your manuscript.

Techniques for giving effective talks, and for making claims in talks, are much the same as for papers but somewhat less constrained. For titles and abstracts our advice is identical: an engaging title and an abstract that makes a strong, clear claim will draw a better audience than one that does not. The "rules" about when to make your claim in the actual talk are, however, less rigid. One respected colleague of ours insists that his students begin their talks with a "take-home message" (i.e., their claim) as a very early slide. This technique is certainly effective in helping the listener to follow the talk. On the other hand, we believe that the "unfolding mystery" technique – which we don't approve of in papers – can sometimes be used effectively in talks, in part because asking listeners to wait 15 minutes or so for the punch line does not seem excessive. A speaker can use various devices, such as reminders, humor, or rhetorical questions, to keep the listener engaged as the story is revealed. Of course, regardless of style, at the end of the talk, as in the Discussion section of a paper, you should always make a strong, clear statement of the claim and how it is supported by the work.

Capturing and Convincing Your Listeners

To capture your audience and to convince them of your claims and the importance of your work, it is important that they understand not only your basic problem and method, but also the participants' task and parallels to that task in the real world. Toward that end, it is important to avoid a kind of egocentrism in giving talks – an egocentrism that leads to presenting the research from only your own (i.e., the experimenter's) perspective. Abstract statements about designs, conditions, comparisons, and so forth are difficult for an audience to assimilate. What audiences need in order to follow your rationale and evaluate your claim is a description of the procedure from the participant's viewpoint, including concrete examples of trials, materials, and the typical sequence of events.

In addition to getting your listeners to imagine themselves being participants in your experiment, providing a real-world example or two that illustrates the problem your research addresses is also an effective way to get your listeners to resonate to the goals and importance of your research. The late Amos Tversky, who was famous for his ability to give compelling talks on complex decision-processes research, almost always began his talks by posing a real-world example or a heuristics-and-biases conundrum for his audiences.

Finally, talks provide a great opportunity for you to speculate about *possible* implications or applications of your research. Such speculations need to be clearly identified *as* speculations, but they can be provocative, motivating, and sometimes the main thing listeners will remember and seek you out to discuss. (Of course, speculations may be offered in papers too, but overly daring ones can later be quoted in embarrassing ways should they prove unwarranted.)

The Bottom Line on Giving Talks

Talks, like abstracts, are not full presentations of your research but, rather, are advertisements for your research (and, in fact, advertisements for you). If you need to err at all, err (slightly) in the direction of making your claims and speculations too bold. Be interesting and be persuasive, and demonstrate that you can make a strong, justified claim. A successful talk will get people interested and excited enough to remember you and to take the time to find and read, and maybe talk to others about, your research.

LAST WORDS

Here is a summary of our main points:

Work hard to clarify for yourself what your research contributes to psychology; only then will you be in a position to communicate it clearly to others. Giving a short (e.g., 15 minute) talk on your research before you write (or while you are writing) your paper might help you find the essence of your claim.

Avoid being timid or vague when stating your contribution: Being bold and clear is the best strategy for you, your research, and the field.

Make sure that your abstract (whether for a paper or a talk) – and your title, too, if possible – communicates your claim.

Make sure that near the end of either a paper or a talk you clearly state your claim and the support for it.

Good luck. We look forward to reading and hearing about your research.

AUTHOR NOTE

We thank the members of the Spellman Reasoning & Memory Laboratory, in particular Debby Kermer, for helpful comments on an earlier draft.

References

American Psychological Association. (2001). *Publication manual of the American Psychological Association* (5th ed.). Washington, DC: Author.

Brescoll, V., & LaFrance, M. (2004). The correlates and consequences of newspaper reports of research on sex differences. *Psychological Science, 15,* 515–520.

Cohn, M. A., Mehl, M. R., & Pennebaker, J. W. (2004). Linguistic markers of psychological change surrounding September 11, 2001. *Psychological Science, 15,* 687–693.

Davenport, J. L., & Potter, M. C. (2004). Scene consistency in object and background perception. *Psychological Science, 15,* 559–564.

Deary, I. J., & Der, G. (2005). Reaction time explains IQ's association with death. *Psychological Science, 16,* 64–69.

Friedman, O., & Leslie, A. M. (2004). Mechanisms of belief-desire reasoning: Inhibition and bias. *Psychological Science, 15,* 547–552.

Gable, S., Reis, H. T., & Downey, G. (2003). He said, she said: A quasi-signal detection analysis of daily interactions between close relationship partners. *Psychological Science, 14,* 100–105.

Grill-Spector, K., & Kanwisher, N. (2005). Visual recognition. As soon as you know it is there, you know what it is. *Psychological Science, 16,* 152–160.

Haldane, J. B. S. (1927). One being the right size. In *Possible worlds and other essays.* New York: Harper.

Klahr, D., & Nigram, M. (2004). The equivalence of learning paths in early science instruction. Effects of direct instruction and discovery learning. *Psychological Science, 15*, 661–667.

Koehler, J. J., & Macchi, L. (2004). Thinking about low-probability events: An exemplar-cuing theory. *Psychological Science, 15*, 540–546.

Lane, S. M., & Schooler, J. W. (2004). Skimming the surface. Verbal overshadowing of analogical retrieval. *Psychological Science, 15*, 715–719.

Lustig, C., Konkel, A., & Jacoby, L. L. (2004). Which route to recovery? Controlled retrieval and accessibility bias in retroactive interference. *Psychological Science, 15*, 729–735.

Markman, A. B., & Brendl, C. M. (2005). Constraining theories of embodied cognition. *Psychological Science, 16*, 6–10.

Mellers, B., Hertwig, R., & Kahneman, D. (2001). Do frequency representations eliminate conjunction effects? An exercise in adversarial collaboration. *Psychological Science, 12*, 269–275, 536 (erratum).

Newcombe, N. S., Sluzenski, J., & Huttenlocher, J. (2005). Preexisting knowledge versus on-line learning. *Psychological Science, 16*, 222–227.

Plant, E. A., & Peruche, B. M. (2005). The consequences of race for police officers' responses to criminal suspects. *Psychological Science, 16*, 180–183.

Singer, M. A., & Goldin-Meadow, S. (2005). Children learn when their teacher's gestures and speech differ. *Psychological Science, 16*, 85–89.

Smith, M., Franz, E. A., Joy, S. M., & Whitehead, K. (2005). Superior performance of blind compared with sighted individuals on bimanual estimations of object size. *Psychological Science, 16*, 11–14.

Tracy, J. L., & Robins, R. W. (2004). Show your pride: Evidence for a discrete emotion expression. *Psychological Science, 15*, 194–197.

Tse, P. U., Sheinberg, D. L., & Logothetis, N. K. (2003). Attentional enhancement opposite a peripheral flash revealed using change blindness. *Psychological Science, 14*, 91–99.

Yoshida, H., & Smith, L. B. (2005). Linguistic cues enhance the learning of perceptual cues. *Psychological Science, 16*, 90–95.

12

Critical Thinking in Clinical Inference

Thomas F. Oltmanns and E. David Klonsky

OVERVIEW

Every day, health professionals make decisions about issues that affect the well-being of their patients. These decisions can be called *clinical inferences*. This chapter explains how psychologists reach the conclusions they do, including a critical look at the validity of clinical inferences.

What types of inferences do psychologists make? Two common inferences involve diagnosis and treatment selection. Psychologists make decisions about the types of problems experienced by their clients, and they select interventions that are likely to be effective for treating these conditions. Psychologists make other important clinical inferences as well. In a criminal case, a judge or lawyer may ask a psychologist to predict whether a defendant will engage in violent behavior if released from custody. A patient recovering from alcoholism may want information about the probability that he or she will relapse. Diagnosis, treatment selection, violence prediction, and prognostic forecasting are all examples of clinical inferences made by psychologists in the course of clinical practice.

Critical thinking refers to the use of skills and strategies that make desirable outcomes more likely (see Chapter 1, this volume). In the context of clinical practice, desirable outcomes include the formulation of accurate diagnoses, effective treatments, and accurate predictions about future behavior. Valid clinical inferences can substantially improve people's lives, whereas invalid inferences can lead to prolonged psychological distress. Critical thinking is essential for achieving desirable clinical outcomes.

People engaged in the practice of psychology must think critically about the decisions that they make when they collect information about their clients, when they interpret that information, and when they select and evaluate approaches to treatment (McFall, 1991). Psychologists must define and measure the concepts that they employ in the most objective fashion possible. Psychologists' judgments and decisions should be based on the best available evidence, and they ought to consider that evidence from different points of view. What evidence supports the validity of assessment procedures that are being used to identify the presence of problems? Is there good evidence to indicate that a particular form of treatment will be helpful?

No one has had a greater impact on the discussion of critical thinking and clinical judgment than Paul Meehl (1920–2003), who is considered by many to have been the leading clinical psychologist of the 20th century. In one classic essay, Meehl (1973) explained that he had temporarily stopped attending case conferences because the conversations were often filled with sloppy patterns of thought. He noted, for example, that all evidence was frequently treated as being equally useful. "A casual anecdote about one's (demented) uncle as remembered from childhood is given the same group interest and intellectual respect that is accorded to the citation of a high-quality (research) study" (p. 228). One important feature of critical thinking involves the ability to distinguish between strong and weak evidence.

Meehl's plea for critical thinking in case conferences was a provocative and penetrating analysis of this field. In the following pages, we discuss a number of typical inferences that are involved in the process of working with individual clients. The chapter is organized around a set of five questions that lead to important clinical inferences: First, what is a mental disorder? Second, are diagnostic categories valid or meaningful? Third, are diagnostic decisions based on valid information? Fourth, is a specific form of treatment effective? Fifth, do psychologists make accurate clinical judgments? These are questions that are often raised implicitly rather than explicitly in the work of clinical psychologists. We raise them here, and summarize the inferences that follow, because they form the basis for many of the day-to-day activities in our field.

WHAT IS A MENTAL DISORDER?

The popular media have devoted considerable attention to issues that are concerned with mental disorders. One story that attracted a flurry of press coverage in 1998 was a concept that has been called "sexual addiction." Shortly after the public learned that President Bill Clinton had had an illicit sexual affair with a young White House intern, many newspapers, magazines, and television programs sought interviews with professional psychologists who offered their opinions regarding the president's behavior. Why would he risk his marriage, family, and career for a casual sexual relationship with someone on his staff? Was his misbehavior the product of a mental disorder? Or was this illicit relationship better viewed in terms of ethical, moral, or legal issues? When psychologists consider the nature of problem behaviors, they must begin with an inference about the nature of the problem. Does it fall under the general heading of mental disorders?

Many experts suggested that the president was suffering from a mental disorder, specifically "sexual addiction" (some called it "sexual compulsion," and one even called it the "Clinton syndrome"). The symptoms of this disorder were alleged to include low self-esteem, insecurity, need for reassurance, and sensation seeking (to name only a few). The public was warned that between 2% and 8% of American men suffer from the disorder, and one expert claimed that fully 20% of highly successful men suffer from sexual addiction. The public was also told that sexual addiction could be treated successfully with antidepressant medication and psychotherapy.

Most of the stories failed to mention that sexual addiction does not appear in the official diagnostic manual. That, by itself, is not an insurmountable problem. Disorders have come and gone over the years, and it's possible that this one might turn out to be useful. Perhaps it will be included in the next edition. We shouldn't reject a new concept simply because it hasn't become part of the official classification system (or accept one on faith simply because it has). The most important issue is whether people reading these stories ask critical questions when they consider a concept such as sexual addiction.

In order to view sexual addiction as a mental disorder, we have to ask ourselves, "What is a mental disorder?" We also have to consider specifically how the problem will be defined. Can it be identified reliably? To the best of our knowledge, no published studies have been concerned with the reliability of diagnosing sexual addiction. Another important question is whether this concept is more useful than other similar concepts. For example, narcissistic personality disorder includes many of the same features (such as lack of empathy). The same argument can be made for impulse control disorders, which also include compulsive gambling and fire setting (which have conceptual problems of their own). What evidence supports the value of one concept over another? In the next few pages, we consider two specific ways to think about mental disorders.

Harmful Dysfunction

One approach to the definition of mental disorder has been proposed by Wakefield (1999). According to this approach, a condition should be considered a mental disorder if, and only if, it meets two criteria:

1. The condition results from the inability of some internal mechanism (mental or physical) to perform its natural function. In other words, something inside the person is not working properly. Examples of such mechanisms include those that regulate levels of emotion and those that distinguish between real auditory sensations and those that are imagined.

2. The condition causes some harm to the person as judged by the standards of the person's culture. These negative consequences are measured in terms of the person's own subjective distress or difficulty performing expected social or occupational roles.

A mental disorder, therefore, is defined in terms of *harmful dysfunction*. This definition incorporates one element that is based as much as possible on an objective evaluation of performance. The natural function of cognitive and perceptual processes is to allow the person to perceive the world in ways that are shared with other people and to engage in rational thought and problem solving. The dysfunctions in mental disorders are assumed to be the product of disruptions of thought, feeling, communication, perception, and motivation.

There is, of course, room for argument about the specific nature of these mental mechanisms and the ways in which they are supposed to function naturally. At present, dysfunction is typically inferred on the basis of problem behaviors rather than specific tests that might be able to determine whether an internal mechanism has been disrupted. Consider, for example, the notion of sexual addiction. In order to be considered a form of mental disorder according to the harmful dysfunction view, its proponents would have to argue that the symptoms by which it is identified are produced by the failure of an internal mechanism to perform its natural function. This might mean than the person has an excessive sexual appetite, or it might mean that some mechanism that regulates actions based on sexual impulses is dysfunctional. Unfortunately, these concepts are currently undefined; the internal mechanisms that are presumably dysfunctional cannot be measured other than by monitoring the person's overt sexual behavior.

Psychologists and other mental health professionals do not at present have laboratory tests that can be used to confirm definitively the presence of psychopathology, because the processes that are responsible for mental disorders have not yet been discovered. Unlike specialists in other areas of medicine where many specific disease mechanisms have been discovered by advances in the biological sciences, psychologists and psychiatrists cannot test for the presence of a viral infection or a brain lesion or a genetic defect to confirm a diagnosis of mental disorder (Turkheimer, 1998). Clinical psychologists must still depend on their observations of the person's behavior and descriptions of personal experience.

Open Scientific Constructs

There is another way to define the concept of mental disorders. They can be described as *open scientific constructs* (Gorenstein, 1992; Meehl, 1972; Neale & Oltmanns, 1980). A hypothetical construct is simply an abstract, explanatory device or concept. In the case of behavioral disorders, a hypothetical construct is an internal event whose existence is inferred on the basis of observable behaviors and the context in which they occur. For example, we may find it useful to say that the trembling of a speaker's hands, her faltering speech, and her obviously speeded rate of breathing are explained by the hypothetical construct *anxiety*. The construct itself cannot be directly observed, but it is tied to overt behavioral referents that can be observed.

Hypothetical constructs do not exist. They are simply more or less useful. Their utility, or validity, is a reflection of the extent to which they enter into relationships with other constructs and related observable events. To return to the example of the trembling speaker, anxiety is a construct that is largely defined in terms of three classes of events: muscular movements (trembling, pacing, fleeing), physiological responses (speeded cardiovascular and respiratory rates, increased perspiration), and subjective reports (the experience of fear). This construct is useful to the extent that (a) these events are correlated and (b) the construct allows us to make predictions about the person's future behavior in particular settings. Thus, as Cronbach and Meehl (1955) argued, "Scientifically speaking, to 'make clear what something is' means to set forth the laws in which it occurs."

The validation of hypothetical constructs must obviously be an empirical process. In the case of sexual addiction, those people who suggest that it is a meaningful or valid construct would be expected to provide evidence to support its utility. Can it be identified reliably? Are there any other behavioral, physiological, or neurological measures that are able to distinguish between people who meet the definition of the disorder and those who do not? Does it provide better predictions of the person's future behavior than we would be able to make if we did not employ this concept (or if we viewed the person's behavior in terms of other constructs, such as narcissism)? Finally, are there any specific forms of treatment that are effective for this disorder? Evidence of this kind must be produced before it would be possible to decide whether or not sexual addiction is a valid construct.

Cultural Considerations

In order to think critically about the nature of mental disorders, we also have to recognize the extent to which their definition is influenced by cultural considerations (Lopez & Guarnaccia, 2000). The impact of particular behaviors and experiences on a person's adjustment depends on the culture in which the person lives. To use Wakefield's (1992) terms, "only dysfunctions that are socially disvalued are disorders" (p. 384). Consider, for example, the diagnostic manual concept of female orgasmic disorder, which is defined in terms of the absence of orgasm accompanied by subjective distress or interpersonal difficulties that result from this disturbance. A woman who grew up in a society that discouraged female sexuality might not be distressed or impaired by the absence of orgasmic responses. In that sense, she might not be considered to have a sexual problem. Therefore, this definition of abnormal behavior might lead us to consider a particular pattern of behavior to be abnormal in one society and not in another. Value judgments are an inherent part of any attempt to define "disorder" (Sedgwick, 1981).

ARE DIAGNOSTIC CATEGORIES VALID OR MEANINGFUL?

After a psychologist has decided that a person's condition involves some kind of mental disorder, the next step is to narrow the focus of that decision. *Diagnosis* refers to the identification or recognition of a disorder on the basis of its characteristic symptoms. Diagnoses help psychologists understand a patient's symptoms in the context of a coherent framework and choose appropriate interventions. In this section we address how a psychologist arrives at a diagnosis.

Caveats About Diagnosis

Several caveats should be mentioned before we move on to discuss specific types of mental disorder. One is that clinical psychologists sometimes treat people who do *not* qualify for a formal diagnosis. Marital therapy, family therapy, and sex therapy are examples of therapeutic procedures that do not focus exclusively on the problems of individual clients. People who experience serious difficulties in interpersonal relationships may not enter treatment because they are seeking relief from a mental disorder. Mental health services can be beneficial for people with a variety of problems. It would be naïve and misleading to suggest that the only important decision that clinicians make in evaluating a client is whether or not the person qualifies for a specific diagnosis. Nevertheless, a decision regarding the diagnosis of mental disorder is one important consideration in many clinical situations. In fact, some leading experts in the delivery of health care services have suggested that psychological treatments (as opposed to psychotherapy more generally defined) ought to be focused on the most serious forms of mental disorder (Barlow, 2004). Our chapter is intended to illustrate some of the elements of critical thinking that are involved in the identification of these conditions.

We should also point out that, in the field of psychopathology, diagnosis does not depend upon a causal analysis, and it does not imply that the psychologist understands the origin of the problem. Specific causes have not been identified for mental disorders. Psychologists can't "look under the hood" in the same way that a mechanic can examine the engine in a car. In the case of a mental disorder, assigning a diagnostic label simply identifies the nature of the problem without implying exactly how the problem came into existence.

Validity of Psychiatric Diagnoses

A simple explanation about how psychologists make diagnoses is that they consult diagnostic manuals, which contain sets of diagnostic criteria to be used in identifying the presence of disorders. The *Diagnostic and Statistical Manual of Mental Disorders* (*DSM*), published by the American Psychiatric Association (1980), is the manual most often used in the United States. It was developed in the middle of the 20th century, has been revised several times, and is currently known as *DSM-IV-TR* (American Psychiatric Association, 2000) because the latest version represents a text revision of the fourth edition. Another widely accepted manual, the *International Classification of Diseases* (known as the *ICD*), is published by the World Health Organization (1992) and is similar to *DSM-IV* in content and structure. We focus on the *DSM-IV-TR* for the purposes of this chapter.

The *DSM-IV-TR* contains lists of numerous disorders and the symptoms that characterize each disorder. Related disorders are grouped under umbrella categories such as Mood Disorders, Anxiety Disorders, and Personality Disorders. Guidelines for diagnosing each mental disorder are also provided by the manual. Consider the example of Narcissistic Personality Disorder (NPD), 1 of 10 personality disorders listed in the *DSM-IV-TR*. Nine symptoms, or criteria, are used to diagnose NPD, including "has a grandiose sense of self-importance," "requires excessive admiration," and "shows arrogant, haughty behaviors or attitudes." According to the *DSM-IV-TR*, someone exhibiting five or more of the nine NPD criteria has the disorder. After conducting a thorough psychological assessment of a patient, a psychologist can use *DSM-IV-TR* guidelines to determine if a patient meets criteria for NPD, or for any other disorder included in the *DSM-IV-TR*.

The process of making diagnoses may seem straightforward, but thinking critically means questioning the *DSM-IV-TR* diagnostic system (Kendell, 2002; Widiger & Clark, 2000). How was the list of disorders compiled? How were the criteria that define each disorder identified? In short, is the *DSM-IV-TR* a valid system for classifying and diagnosing mental disorders? The disorders in the *DSM* were originally derived from the consensus thinking of expert psychiatrists and psychologists. Revisions to the disorders and definitions were made as knowledge regarding mental disorders evolved, but many important issues are still open to meaningful debate. For example, many mental health professionals take issue with the *DSM-IV-TR* classification of personality disorders (Livesley, 1998). The manual lists 10 types of personality disorder, which are divided into three clusters: Cluster A (paranoid, schizoid, and schizotypal), Cluster B (histrionic, borderline, narcissistic, and antisocial), and Cluster C (avoidant, dependent, and obsessive-compulsive). This system contains several questionable assumptions, including the notion that personality disorders are best defined in terms of discrete categories, and that personality disorder categories listed in the same cluster are closely related to each other.

Thinking critically means evaluating these assumptions in light of empirical research. For example, studies show that people who meet criteria for one personality disorder tend to meet criteria for others as well (Klonsky, 2000; Krueger, 2002). Is a categorical classification system warranted in light of the frequent diagnostic overlap? Research also reveals that patterns of co-occurence among the personality disorders do not always conform to the three-cluster system. Studies show that people who exhibit features of borderline personality disorder, a member of Cluster B, often display symptoms of paranoid personality disorder, a member of Cluster A. Should the three-cluster system be discarded? If so, what should take its place?

Simple answers are not available for questions such as these. The key point is that one must think critically about diagnostic classification systems that psychologists use to make diagnoses. The "expert consensus" on which diagnostic manuals are largely based is fallible. Psychologists must keep open minds about the diagnostic systems they use, and constantly evaluate the emerging research evidence that inevitably will change how psychopathology is classified.

ARE DIAGNOSTIC DECISIONS BASED ON VALID INFORMATION?

Regardless of the diagnostic manual or classification system used, psychologists must obtain information of sufficient quantity and quality in order to make a diagnosis. Several methods are available for gathering this information. Thinking critically means knowing the strengths and limitations of various techniques, and understanding how psychologists determine if a technique provides valid data. Several assessment methods, and information about the validity of the data they provide, are described here.

A Critical Look at Different Psychological Assessment Methods

The unstructured interview, the most common technique employed by psychologists, involves the psychologist asking the patient numerous questions. The psychologist has the freedom to ask any questions, in any order, to understand the patient's psychological problems. Unstructured interviews have several advantages. Psychologists can tailor their questions to each patient's individual situation, and they can improvise as they obtain new information and pursue lines of questioning that were not anticipated. Another advantage is that unstructured interviews tend to foster comfortable, free-flowing conversations that help establish rapport between the patient and therapist. An important disadvantage, however, is that different psychologists will ask different questions and perhaps obtain very different information from the same patient. Therefore, if two psychologists interviewed the same patient, they could easily arrive at different diagnostic conclusions (an example of poor interrater reliability). There are several problems associated with the use of unstructured interviews in clinical practice (Zimmerman, 2003).

Alternatives to unstructured interviews are structured and semistructured interviews. Structured interviews contain questions relevant to a wide variety of diagnoses. These interviews are standardized, in that the same questions are presented in the same order to all patients. Semistructured interviews are similar to structured interviews but allow for the limited use of follow-up questions to clarify responses to the interview questions. Because the same questions are asked in the same order to all patients, different psychologists are more likely to obtain similar information and arrive at similar diagnoses for a given patient. In other words, interrater reliability is better for structured and semistructured than for unstructured interviews. Research also suggests that structured and semistructured interviews lead to better diagnostic accuracy than unstructured interviews.

A third method, self-report questionnaires, offers some of the benefits of structured interviews while avoiding the drawbacks. Self-report questionnaires are paper-and-pencil (and more recently computer-based) instruments that are completed by the patient. The most widely used self-report measure of personality and psychopathology is the Minnesota Multiphasic Personality Inventory (MMPI). As in structured interviews the same questions are presented in the same order to all patients, but self-administered questionnaires are less time consuming and can even be completed at home. Unlike patient responses to structured interviews, which are interpreted by psychologists and then scored, responses to self-report questionnaires are based solely on patient opinions. Because information derived from self-reports is not always accurate (Kolar, Funder, & Colvin, 1996), poor self-insight, defensiveness, and malingering on the part of the patient can limit the validity of these measures.

A final form of assessment involves projective methods. The most well-known projective test is the Rorschach Inkblot Test, which requires patients to interpret ambiguous images of various patterns and colors. Ostensibly, the manner in which the inkblots are interpreted yields important information about personality and psychological problems. For example, according to the Rorschach Comprehensive System, patients whose interpretations are informed in a particular manner by the color of the inkblots are more likely to suffer from depression (Exner, 1993). The advantage to projective tests is that they are less susceptible to impression management since participants do not know how their responses are being scored. An important disadvantage is that the reliability and validity of many Rorschach indices that relate patient responses to different types of psychopathology have not been supported by research (Woods, Nezworski, Lilienfeld, & Garb, 2003).

Validity of Psychological Assessment Methods

Standardized assessment instruments, including interviews, questionnaires, and projective measures, yield numerical scores that can reflect the presence of psychological problems. For example, high scores on Scale 2 of the MMPI, the depressive disorder section on structured diagnostic interviews, and the Depression Index of the Rorschach all supposedly indicate the presence of clinical depression. How do we know that they all measure the same thing? In other words, how are psychological tests validated?

Careful research is required to validate a psychological test and demonstrate that it identifies the people or problems it is intended to identify. For example, if an instrument for assessing depression is administered to two groups of patients, some with clinical depression and some with spider phobia, members of the former group should generate high scores with few exceptions, and members of the latter group should produce lower scores with few exceptions. If this is not the case – that is, if scores are comparable in both groups – it is unlikely that the instrument is a valid measure of depression. Psychological tests are routinely validated, revised, or discarded on the basis of this type of research.

Consider the examples of the MMPI and Rorschach to illustrate this process. The MMPI is considered one of the most valid psychological tests because its scales consistently perform as expected in research studies (Garb, Florio, & Grove, 1998). In contrast, research findings have led to questions about the validity of many Rorschach indices. Whereas a Rorschach thought disorder index reliably identifies patients with schizophrenia (Acklin, 1999), a disorder characterized in part by thought disorder, many other Rorschach scales do not perform consistently across studies. For example, a study found that many people without psychiatric disorders generate scores on Rorschach indices considered pathological by the Rorschach Comprehensive System manual (Woods, Nezworski, Garb, & Lilienfeld, 2001). This finding suggests that use of the Rorschach in clinical practice may lead to inaccurate diagnoses and inappropriate treatment selection. In addition, many Rorschach indices perform well in one study but then perform poorly when reexamined. As a result, some psychologists feel the Rorschach should not be used in clinical practice (Garb, 1998; Lilienfeld, Wood, & Garb, 2000).

IS A SPECIFIC FORM OF TREATMENT EFFECTIVE?

After clinicians have collected information about the nature of their clients' problems, they are frequently expected to provide therapeutic services. One of the most important functions of a diagnosis is to suggest a treatment that has been useful with clients who suffer from similar problems. Therefore, another important inference that clinical psychologists make is the decision to employ a particular form of therapy that will be helpful for a specific type of client. These decisions ought to be based on empirical evidence.

Clinical Experience Versus Research

Historically, many psychologists have relied primarily on their own training or clinical experience as a basis for selecting an approach to treatment. In other words, they use the therapeutic skills that they learned in graduate school or during their internship training. Practice with specific techniques inevitably leads to some success with specific clients, and these clinical experiences often reinforce the clinician's belief that his or her approach is effective. Unfortunately, extensive reliance on a series of case studies can be misleading. The most obvious limitation of case studies is that they can be viewed from many different perspectives. Any case can be interpreted in several ways, and competing explanations may be equally plausible. Another limitation of case studies is that it is risky to draw general conclusions about a disorder from a single example. How do we know that a specific individual is representative of the disorder as a whole? For these and many other reasons (see Chapter 6, this volume), hypotheses generated on the basis of case studies or personal clinical experience must be tested in research with larger, more representative samples of patients and the use of careful measurement procedures.

Many different procedures can be used to evaluate the effects of psychological treatments (Garske & Anderson, 2003). We do not intend to provide a review of that evidence in this chapter because the literature is so extensive (Chambless & Ollendick, 2001; Nathan, Stuart, & Dolan, 2000). Rather, we hope to raise a number of issues that should be considered when attempting to evaluate such studies. In order to determine whether an intervention is effective, the investigator must ask specific questions. What kind of treatment is being used for what kind of clinical problem? There are many different forms of psychotherapy, and it seems reasonable to expect that some are more beneficial than others. Some may actually be harmful, at least under certain conditions. Some types of mental disorder may be more responsive than others. The selection of a treatment approach must hinge on a critical analysis of the data regarding existing outcome studies.

Randomized Controlled Trials

The most well-accepted research design for use in evaluating treatment procedures is called a randomized, controlled trial (RCT). In this procedure, patients are randomly assigned to different conditions. One condition would be the treatment that is being evaluated, and the other condition is a control group of some kind. This might be a no treatment group (sometimes called a waiting-list control group) in which people do not receive any kind of active treatment for a period of several weeks. An alternative would be the use of a different kind of treatment (either medication or another form of psychotherapy) so that the investigators could determine whether one form of treatment is more effective than another. The use of a comparison group is extremely important because mental disorders are known to be episodic conditions. In other words, some patients in any study would be expected to improve over a period of several weeks, even if they do not receive treatment. The real question is whether the treatment in question produces better results than one might expect without that form of treatment.

One active ingredient in any treatment program may involve the patient's belief system. Does the person's condition improve primarily because he or she *expected* to get better? The use of placebo control groups in psychotherapy research is a difficult and controversial topic (Manschreck, 2001). Should we expect a treatment program to produce better results than a psychological placebo condition? In pharmacological research, a placebo is a substance that does not contain an active ingredient (such as a sugar pill) but that the person believes to be an effective form of medication. Years of research have demonstrated that, in a number of medical conditions, some patients improve as a product of their belief in the power of the treatment that they receive. That is a placebo effect. In psychotherapy, it is difficult to know exactly what kind of process would constitute an adequate placebo condition. It isn't possible to give someone a sugar pill. They have to engage in a series of interactions with a therapist, and they must *believe* that these interactions will be helpful to them. Some people have used generic supportive therapy as a comparison condition when evaluating treatments such as cognitive therapy or behavior therapy. If the people who receive the specific form of treatment show better improvement rates than the people who receive the placebo treatment (e.g., supportive therapy), then it is possible to conclude that the beneficial effects of the treatment cannot be attributed simply to a general expectation that therapy will be helpful. Critical thinking about treatment outcome studies involves a careful consideration of the possible role played by a client's expectations.

RCTs are useful because they allow the investigator to draw strong causal inferences. They follow an experimental design in which patients are randomly assigned to conditions. If differences are observed between the outcomes in different conditions, we can infer that one form of treatment is more effective than another (Jacobson & Christensen, 1996). Unfortunately, RCTs also have some important limitations. Perhaps most important is the fact that the conditions in which RCTs are conducted are artificial in many ways. In other words, they are carefully controlled and do not mirror closely the circumstances in which psychological treatments are delivered "in the real world." For example, patients in RCTs are carefully selected so that they do not exhibit a number of comorbid conditions. In most treatment settings, people with mental disorders do have a variety of problems. Furthermore, the treatments that are delivered in RCTs are highly structured and time limited (usually 8 to 14 sessions). Given these extensive differences between laboratory conditions and circumstances in real clinical settings, many people have questioned the "external validity" of results produced in carefully controlled, treatment outcome studies (Seligman, 1995; Westen, Novotny, & Thompson-Brenner, 2004). An important critical question is therefore whether psychological treatments that are evaluated in carefully controlled, experimental settings will be effective when they are applied in actual clinical practice.

Efficacy Versus Effectiveness

People who evaluate treatment results draw a distinction between RCTs, which are also known as *efficacy studies,* and *effectiveness studies* (Nathan et al., 2000). An effectiveness study is one that considers the outcome of psychological treatment, as it is delivered in real-world settings. Effectiveness studies can be methodologically rigorous in the sense that careful procedures are employed to identify the nature of the clients' problems and to measure changes in their adjustment during the course of treatment, but they do not include random assignment to treatment conditions or placebo control groups. In fact, comparison groups of any kind may be missing.

The distinction between efficacy studies and effectiveness studies is nowhere more clearly portrayed than in the debate over the results of a survey conducted by the editors of *Consumer Reports* (Seligman, 1995). In the early 1990s, the editors of this influential and widely respected publication distributed to a random sample of its readers a questionnaire that included questions about psychotherapy. They were asked questions about mental health problems that they may have experienced, whether they had received professional treatment for these conditions, and the success of any treatment that they had received. From the entire sample of 186,000 people who received the question, 7,000 people responded (less than a 4% response rate). Of these, 4,000 reported that they had received professional help for a mental health problem. Slightly more than half (54%) said that the treatment had helped "a great deal." Ninety percent said that it had been at least slightly beneficial. On the basis of these responses, the authors of the study were unable to identify any significant differences between different approaches to psychotherapy, although psychologists and psychiatrists and social workers were seen as being more helpful than marriage counselors. The investigators also concluded that long-term treatment was more beneficial than short-term therapy.

A critical analysis of the *Consumer Reports* survey would suggest considerable reason for caution in interpreting these results (Jacobson & Christensen, 1996). The study suffers from a number of important methodological weaknesses. One obvious issue involves the small percentage of people who agreed to participate in the study. In such a large sample, it seems obvious that many more people actually received some form of mental health treatment. It also seems possible that people who were less satis-fied with the treatment that they received might have been less likely to respond to the survey. Perhaps most important was the absence of any type of control group. There is no way to know how many people in this sample would have improved if they had received no treatment at all. Furthermore, measurement of improvement was based entirely on the clients' own self-report. Were their judgments of improvement accurate? And would people who had invested a lot of time and resources into long-term treatment be more likely to believe that the effort had been worthwhile? For all of these reasons, critical thinkers should be skeptical of the results of this study and others like it.

Evidence-Based Practice

The field of clinical psychology has become increasingly interested in the value of evidence-based practice. In other words, there is considerable sup-port for the notion that therapists should promote and employ therapies that have been demonstrated to work. The term that has come to be used in this discussion is *empirically supported treatments* (Chambless & Hollon, 1998). The important question, of course, is "What *kind* of evidence would qualify as support for the notion that a treatment has been shown to be effective?" Does it have to come from randomized controlled outcome study? At present, the answer is "no." In order to be considered a well-established empirically sup-ported treatment, a treatment must meet one of the following conditions:

1. There must be at least two good group design studies, conducted by different investigators, demonstrating efficacy in one or more of the following ways: (a) superior to pill or psychological placebo or to another treatment, or (b) equivalent to an already established treat-ment.
2. There must be a large series of single-case design studies demon-strating efficacy. These studies (a) must have used good experimental designs, or (b) compared the intervention with another effective form of treatment.

Serious discussions continue with regard to the nature of the evidence needed to establish that a treatment is effective. Although experimental effi-cacy studies remain the most substantial part of that support, many investi-gators have raised important questions about the assumptions involved in these designs (Westen et al., 2004). Critical thinkers should keep many of these issues in mind. For example, RCTs assume that treatment is aimed at a specific problem. In the real world, clients often present with multiple prob-lems or those that cross clearcut diagnostic boundaries. Treatments deliv-ered in RCTs follow carefully prescribed scenarios (often called *manualized treatements* because the therapists follow an outline for each session that is dictated by a treatment manual) and are ended after a rather small, fixed number of sessions. In the real world, treatments sessions often need to be more flexible in their content and duration. For these and other reasons, we should remain skeptical regarding the implications of RCTs as well as efficacy studies and case studies.

DO PSYCHOLOGISTS MAKE ACCURATE CLINICAL JUDGMENTS?

Two features of clinical practice are probably clear by this point in the chapter. First, psychologists have a tremendous responsibility to their clients. Psychologists routinely make judgments that can profoundly affect people's lives. Second, making these important clinical judgments is a complex process involving the integration and interpretation of many sources of information. In an ideal world, the judgments of mental health experts would be accurate most or all of the time. Unfortunately, this is simply not the case (Garb, 1998, 2005). In fact, research has documented a number of factors, often referred to as *biases* and *heuristics*, that interfere with clinical judgment (Garb, 1998; Turk & Salovey, 1988). Thinking critically about clinical inference requires understanding why mental health experts often reach incorrect conclusions. Consequently, the final section of this chapter reviews some of the biases and heuristics that lead to inaccurate clinical inferences.

Biases

Garb (1997) summarizes research on three biases that affect the validity of clinician's judgments: race bias, gender bias, and social class bias. In several studies the accuracy of clinicians' judgments about diagnosis, symptoms, personality traits, behavioral prediction, or treatment planning varied as a function of the patients' race, gender, or social class. For example, in two studies, clinicians were more likely to diagnose African American than Caucasian patients as having schizophrenia, even when data from structured interviews did not support a diagnosis of schizophrenia (Pavkov, Lewis, & Lyons, 1989; Simon, Fleiss, Gurland, Stiller, & Sharpe, 1973). A third study conducted at a psychiatric hospital had clinicians predict which patients would be rehospitalized within 2 years (Stack, Lannon, & Miley, 1983). This clinical judgment is ostensibly based on severity of mental illness, frequency of past hospitalizations, and social factors including homelessness and social supports. Nonetheless, results indicated a bias to forecast worst prognoses for minorities. Clinicians predicted that 63% of Caucasian patients and 81% of minority patients would be rehospitalized, but at 2-year follow-up the actual proportion of patients who had been rehospitalized was comparable for Caucasian and minority patients.

Research has also demonstrated gender bias in clinical judgments (Garb, 1997). For example, when mental health experts make diagnoses on the basis of case histories that are identical except for the designation of gender, women are more likely to be diagnosed with histrionic personality disorder and men with antisocial personality disorder (e.g., Ford & Widiger, 1989). Gender bias can affect clinical judgments about future behavior as well. McNiel and Binder (1995) asked clinicians to predict which of their patients would perform violent behaviors. The clinicians tended to overpredict violence for men and underpredict violence for women. In other words, men who did not become violent were often predicted to become violent, and women who did become violent were more often predicted not to become violent.

Cognitive Heuristics

Cognitive heuristics can be defined as simple, time-saving rules that people use to make decisions, solve problems, and form beliefs. For the most part these mental shortcuts serve us quite well in daily life. An example is the representativeness heuristic, which is the tendency to judge the category of membership of people or objects based on how closely they match the "typical" or "average" member of that category (Kahneman & Tversky, 1973). For example, if while you are driving you hear a siren and notice a white vehicle behind you with flashing lights, you will likely move out of the way to let the ambulance pass. The determination that the vehicle is an ambulance usually does not require us to notice the word *ambulance* written on the vehicle. Rather, we are able to make the judgment because the white vehicle with flashing lights and a siren resembles, or is representative of, our notion of the typical ambulance.

Although cognitive heuristics often lead to efficient, accurate judgments in everyday life, they can cause problems when they are applied incorrectly. For example, the representativeness heuristic might account for many of the instances of race and gender bias just described. Recall the study by Ford and Widiger (1989) in which clinicians were biased to diagnose men as having antisocial personality disorder, a disorder characterized by criminal behavior and a lack of empathy, even when the case histories could also have justified a different diagnosis. The clinicians may have unwittingly employed the representativeness heuristic by considering the typical antisocial patient to be male and thus diagnosing a disproportionate number of men as having antisocial personality disorder. Of note, Garb (1996) provides evidence that the representativeness heuristic affects the diagnostic conclusions reached by clinicians even when they are instructed to strictly adhere to *DSM* diagnostic criteria.

Another common heuristic is the availability heuristic. The availability heuristic occurs when people judge the frequency or likelihood of an event on the basis of how easy it is to think of an example of that event. For example, someone might choose to follow a new diet plan if he or she recalls a few friends who spoke well of the plan. In favoring and selecting the diet plan, this person would be basing the decision on how well the opinions of others could be recalled. Of course it could turn out that other friends or even nutrition experts had heavily criticized the diet plan. The availability heuristic can also affect the judgments of clinicians. For instance, many people believe that a person who is mentally ill is prone to violence, simply because they can easily recall examples of violent people who are mentally ill, such as Ted Bundy or John Hinckley (Turk, Salovey, & Prentice, 1988). Similarly, a clinician who often works with depressed people may overestimate the proportion of patients who are depressed and have a tendency to perceive and diagnose depression even if the depressive symptoms are subthreshold.

A third heuristic that may affect clinical judgment is the anchoring and adjustment heuristic. This heuristic refers to a tendency to form an initial impression and then insufficiently adjust that first impression in light of new information. This heuristic may account for the adage that it is important to make a good first impression. Once a bad impression is made, it becomes difficult to change or adjust the impression, even if it is unwarranted. In clinical settings, this heuristic may lead therapists to overvalue information obtained early in a diagnostic interview and ignore or undervalue information revealed later in therapy (Turk et al., 1988). This tendency could adversely affect case conceptualization and treatment planning.

The representativeness, availability, and anchoring and adjustment heuristics are just a few of the mental shortcuts that people use everyday and that can impede the formation of accurate judgments, including those of psychologists and other mental health professionals. Understanding the various biases and cognitive heuristics is necessary for improving clinical practice. Fortunately, a tremendous amount of effort has been devoted to exploring the effects of biases and cognitive heuristics on clinical judgment. Turk and Salovey (1988) and Garb (1998, 2005) provide excellent examinations of these issues.

CHAPTER SUMMARY

Clinical inferences refer to the judgments made by clinical psychologists in their practice of psychology, including diagnosis, prognosis, and the selection of appropriate treatments. Clinical psychologists must think critically about mental disorders, including whether mental disorders exist and how they can be identified reliably. Various diagnostic manuals and assessment methods have been developed to aid in the diagnosis of mental disorders. However, conceptions of disease and mental disorders evolve constantly, and clinical research often disputes the definitions contained in diagnostic manuals. In addition, a particular assessment method should only be trusted once research demonstrates that it provides reliable and valid data.

Critical thinking is also essential for selecting appropriate treatments. Randomized controlled trials, which follow an experimental design, remain the gold standard for evaluating the efficacy of particular treatments for particular disorders. Unfortunately, RCTs may not simulate real-world clinical environments, where psychiatric comorbidity is common and structured, time-limited treatments are not always feasible. Therefore, psychologists must use their best clinical judgment to apply research on large clinical populations to the particular patient they are treating.

Finally, clinical psychologists must think critically about the process of making clinical inferences. Biases and cognitive heuristics often lead people, including clinical psychologists, to make inaccurate inferences. Examples discussed in this chapter include gender and racial biases, as well as the representativeness, availability, and anchoring-and-adjustment heuristics. Understanding barriers to accurate clinical judgment can help psychologists avoid sloppy thinking and provide services that reduce suffering and improve people's lives.

References

Acklin, M. W. (1999). Behavioral science foundations of the Rorschach Test: Research and clinical applications. *Assessment, 6,* 319–326.

American Psychiatric Association. (1980). *Diagnostic and statistical manual of mental disorders* (3rd ed.). Washington, DC: Author.

American Psychiatric Association. (2000). *Diagnostic and statistical manual of mental disorders* (4th ed., text rev.). Washington, DC: Author.

Barlow, D. H. (2004). Psychological treatments. *American Psychologist, 59,* 869–877.

Chambless, D. L., & Hollon, S. D. (1998). Defining empirically supported therapies. *Journal of Consulting and Clinical Psychology, 66,* 7–18.

Chambless, D., & Ollendick, T. (2001). Empirically supported psychological interventions: Controversies and evidence. *Annual Review of Psychology, 52,* 685–716.

Cronbach, L. J., & Meehl, P. E. (1955). Construct validity in psychological tests. *Psychological Bulletin, 52,* 281–302.

Exner, J. E. (1993). *The Rorschach: A comprehensive system, volume 1: Basic foundations.* New York: Wiley.

Ford, M. R., & Widiger, T. A. (1989). Sex bias in the diagnosis of histrionic and antisocial personality disorders. *Journal of Consulting and Clinical Psychology, 57,* 301–305.

Garb, H. N. (1996). The representativeness and past-behavior heuristics in clinical judgment. *Professional Psychology: Research and Practice, 27,* 272–277.

Garb, H. N. (1997). Race bias, social class bias, and gender bias in clinical judgment. *Clinical Psychology: Science & Practice, 4,* 99–120.

Garb, H. N. (1998). *Studying the clinician: Judgment research and psychological assessment.* Washington, DC: American Psychological Association.

Garb, H. N. (2005). Clinical judgment and decision making. *Annual Review of Clinical Psychology, 55,* 3.1–3.23.

Garb, H. N., Florio, C. M., & Grove, W. M. (1998). The validity of the Rorschach and the Minnesota Multiphasic Personality Inventory: Results from meta-analyses. *Psychological Science, 9*, 402–404.

Garske, J. P., & Anderson, T. (2003). Toward a science of psychotherapy research: Present status and evaluation. In S. O. Lilienfeld, S. J. Lynn, & J. M. Lohr (Eds.), *Science and pseudoscience in clinical psychology* (pp. 145–175). New York: Guilford Press.

Gorenstein, E. E. (1992). *The science of mental illness.* San Diego: Academic Press.

Jacobson, N. S., & Christensen, A. (1996). Studying the effectiveness of psychotherapy: How well can clinical trials do the job? *American Psychologist, 51*, 1031–1039.

Kahneman, D., & Tversky, A. (1973). On the psychology of prediction. *Psychological Review, 80*, 237–251.

Kendell, R. E. (2002). Five criteria for an improved taxonomy of mental disorders. In J. E. Helzer and J. J. Hudziak (Eds.), *Defining psychopathology in the 21st century* (pp. 3–17). Washington, DC: American Psychiatric Press.

Klonsky, E. D. (2000). The DSM classification of personality disorder: Clinical wisdom or empirical truth? *Journal of Clinical Psychology, 56*, 1615–1621.

Kolar, D. W., Funder, D. C., & Colvin, C. R. (1996). Comparing the accuracy of personality judgments by the self and knowledgeable others. *Journal of Personality, 64*, 311–337.

Krueger, R. F. (2002). Psychometric perspectives on comorbidity. In J. E. Helzer and J. J. Hudziak (Eds.), *Defining psychopathology in the 21st century* (pp. 41–54). Washington, DC: American Psychiatric Press.

Lilienfeld, S. O., Wood, J. M., & Garb, H. N. (2000). The scientific status of projective techniques. *Psychological Science in the Public Interest, 1*, 27–66.

Livesley, W. J. (1998). Suggestions for a framework for an empirically based classification of personality disorder. *Canadial Journal of Psychiatry, 43*, 137–147.

Lopez, S. R., & Guarnaccia, P. J. (2000). Cultural psychopathology: Uncovering the social world of mental illness. *Annual Review of Psychology, 51*, 571–598.

Manschreck, T. C. (2001). Placebo studies: Lessons from psychiatric research. *Psychiatric Annals, 31*, 130–136.

McFall, R. M. (1991). Manifesto for a science of clinical psychology. *The Clinical Psychologist, 44*, 75–88.

McNiel, D. E., & Binder, R. L. (1995). Correlates of accuracy in the assessment of psychiatric inpatients' risk of violence. *American Journal of Psychiatry, 152*, 901–906.

Meehl, P. E. (1972). Specific genetic etiology, psychodynamics, and therapeutic nihilism. *International Journal of Mental Health, 1*, 10–27.

Meehl, P. E. (1973). Why I do not attend case conferences. In *Psychodiagnosis: Selected papers* (pp. 225–302). Minneapolis: University of Minnesota Press.

Nathan, P. E., Stuart, S. P., & Dolan, S. L. (2000). Research on psychotherapy efficacy and effectiveness: Between Scylla and Charybdis? *Psychological Bulletin, 126*, 964–981.

Neale, J. M., & Oltmanns, T. F. (1980) Schizophrenia. New York: Wiley.

Pavkov, T. W., Lewis, D. A., & Lyons, J. A. (1989). Psychiatric diagnoses and racial bias: An empirical investigation. *Professional Psychology: Research and Practice, 20*, 364–368.

Sedgwick, P. (1981). Illness – Mental and otherwise. In A. L. Caplan, H. T. Engelhardt, and J. J. McCartney (Eds), *Concepts of health and disease: Interdisciplinary perspectives* (pp. 119–129). Addison-Wesley: Reading, MA.

Seligman, M. E. P. (1995). The effectiveness of psychotherapy: The Consumer Reports study. *American Psychologist, 50*, 965–974.

Simon, R. J., Fleiss, J. L., Gurland, B. J., Stiller, P. R., & Sharpe, L. (1973). Depression and schizophrenia in hospitalized Black and White mental patients. *Archives of General Psychiatry, 28*, 509–512.

Stack, L. C., Lannon, P. B., & Miley, A. D. (1983). Accuracy of clinicians' expectancies for psychiatric rehospitalization. *American Journal of Community Psychology, 11*, 99–113.

Turk, D. C., Salovey, P., & Prentice, D. A. (1988). Psychotherapy: An information processing perspective. In D. C. Turk & P. Salovey (Eds.), *Reasoning, inference, and judgment in clinical psychology* (pp. 1–14). New York: The Free Press.

Turk, D. C., & Salovey, P. (Eds.) (1988). *Reasoning, inference, and judgment in clinical psychology.* London: Free Press.

Turkheimer, E. T. (1998). Heritability and biological explanation. *Psychological Review, 105*, 782–791.

Wakefield, J. C. (1992). The concept of mental disorder: On the boundary between biological facts and social values. *American Psychologist, 47*, 373–388.

Wakefield, J. C. (1999). Evolutionary versus prototype analyses of the concept of disorder. *Journal of Abnormal Psychology, 108*, 374–399.

Westen, D., Novotny, C. M., & Thompson-Brenner, H. (2004). The empirical status of empirically supported psychotherapies: Assumptions, findings, and reporting in controlled clinical trials. *Psychological Bulletin, 130*, 631–663.

Widiger, T. A., & Clark, L. A. (2000). Toward DSM-V and the classification of psychopathology. *Psychological Bulletin, 126*, 946–963.

Woods, J. M., Nezworski, M. T., Garb, H. N., & Lilienfeld, S. O. (2001). The misperception of psychopathology: Problems with norms of the Comprehensive System for the Rorschach. *Clinical Psychology: Science & Practice, 8*, 350–373.

Wood, J. M., Nzworski, M. T., Lilienfeld, S. O., & Garb, H. N. (2003). *What's wrong with the Rorschach?* San Francisco, CA: Jossey-Bass.

World Health Organization. (1992). *The ICD-10 Classification of Mental and Behavioural Disorders: Clinical Descriptors and Diagnostic Guidelines.* Geneva, Switzerland: Author.

Zimmerman, M. (2003). What should the standard of care for psychiatric diagnostic evaluations be? *Journal of Nervous and Mental Disease, 191*, 281–286.

13

Evaluating Parapsychological Claims

Ray Hyman

Imagine that you have been assigned to evaluate a parapsychological claim. The assignment could be from a journal editor or from a media outlet. Or it could come from a granting agency or an instructor. You might be faced with such a task in your role as a referee for a professional journal. Or you might take on the assignment out of curiosity.

How would you proceed? Your first step might be to decide on the scope of the parapsychological claim. Are you dealing with a specific claim based on one experiment? Or is the claim based on evidence from a series of experiments? Perhaps you want to assess the status of the entire field of parapsychology.

What, indeed, makes a claim "parapsychological?" The term *parapsychology* was borrowed by J. B. Rhine to refer to what previously had been called *psychical research*. With the new label, Rhine wanted to promote an experimental science. Previous to Rhine, psychical research had focused on field investigations of haunted houses, tests of spiritualist mediums, surveys of premonitory dreams, and other dramatic, but controversial, paranormal claims. Rhine wanted parapsychology to focus on quantitative evidence obtained in controlled, laboratory settings. Beginning in the 1930s, parapsychologists started accumulating experimental evidence for the existence of *extrasensory perception* (ESP) and *psychokinesis* (PK). According to the glossary in the back of *The Journal of Parapsychology*, ESP is defined as "Experience of, or response to, a target object, state, event, or influence without sensory contact." ESP includes telepathy, clairvoyance, and precognition. PK is defined as "The extramotor aspect of psi: a direct (i.e., mental but nonmuscular) influence exerted by the subject on an external physical process, condition, or object." In other words PK implies that humans can mentally influence the external world without physical contact.

Parapsychologists use the term *psi* to include both ESP and PK. They define *parapsychology* as "The branch of science that deals with psi communication, i.e., behavioral or personal exchanges with the environment which are extrasensorimotor – not dependent on the senses or muscles." To evaluate a parapsychological claim, two aspects of its definition have to be considered. The first is that parapsychologists define their field as a "branch of science." This implies that they base their claims upon scientific evidence. If you are going to evaluate a parapsychological claim, then, you should apply the criteria that you would use to judge any other scientific claim. For this purpose, the other chapters in this book should provide helpful guidelines. The following chapters are especially relevant: "The Nature and Nurture of Critical Thinking"; "Evaluating Experimental Research"; "Critical Thinking in Quasi-Experimentation", "Critical Thinking in Clinical Inference"; "Designing Studies to Avoid Confounds"; and "Evaluating Theories."

You will need additional guidelines to help you cope with parapsychological claims. This is because of the second important part of the definition. This states that parapsychology "deals with psi communication, i.e., behavioral or personal exchanges with the environment which are extrasensorimotor – not dependent on the senses or muscles." In the orthodox natural and social sciences, the goals are to develop, extend, and revise existing theories. The idea is to extend the scope of existing theories beyond the phenomena they already successfully encompass. The existing theories are used to predict and explain additional and, perhaps, more challenging, findings. Science is conservative in the sense of trying to make do with current theories when confronted with new data. If the new data appear inconsistent with the existing theory, the scientists first look for mistakes or errors in the new evidence. If the new information survives such scrutiny, then the scientists try to accommodate the deviant data by tweaking the existing theory. In those rare instances in which minor tweaking will not work, then major revisions of existing theory might be in order. A major revision or replacement of the existing theory will only occur, however, if a suitable alternative theory is available. The alternative theory must account not only for the new information but also for all the previous data that the older theory encompassed.

Parapsychology, as a science, is unique in its goals of deliberately seeking evidence for the limitations of the current scientific world view. The subject matter of parapsychology is the purported phenomenon of psi. If psi exists, it violates what the late philosopher C. D. Broad (1953) called the "basic limiting principles" of the scientific world view. These principles include the following: Causes cannot occur after their effects; information and forces diminish with distance; and mind cannot act on matter without the intervention of physical contact. Broad, who was a supporter of parapsychological claims, declared that "psychical research is concerned with alleged events which seem *prima facie* to conflict with one or more of those principles. Let us call any event which seems *prima facie* to do this an *Ostensibly Paranormal Event*."

Some General Considerations

Evaluating parapsychological claims, then, requires the application of standard scientific criteria as well as additional standards resulting from the peculiar status of parapsychology. Such evaluation requires dedication, time, patience, and resources. If you evaluate a parapsychological claim, I assume you want to do it as fairly and effectively as possible. This is hard work. It is no wonder that throughout the more than a century and a half of psychical research and parapsychology, informed criticism has been scarce. Critics have focused on a few select examples, usually the weakest cases; have misrepresented the evidence and the claims; and have been polemical. The parapsychological community has dismissed such criticism as irrelevant and prejudiced. The consequence has been that psychical research and parapsychology have suffered because of a lack of constructive criticism.

THE BASIC PLAN FOR THIS CHAPTER

No standard procedure exists for evaluating a parapsychological claim. At a very general level the basis for each claim is similar. The claim is supported by evidence that the guesses or the wishes of certain individuals correlate with a set of targets to a significant degree beyond chance. Moreover, all normal explanations for this correspondence have been ruled out by the experimental controls. At the level of the specific materials and methods, however, the basis for the claims vary over time and experiments.

Beginning in the 1930s, ESP claims were based mainly on the outcome of the card-guessing experiments by J. B. Rhine and his colleagues. Claims for PK were based on the outcome of dice-throwing trials in which individuals attempted to will certain numbers to land face up. At first these experiments relied on shuffling the cards and tossing the dice by hand. Later, mechanical procedures were introduced to mix the cards and throw the dice. The card-guessing and dice-throwing trials dominated parapsychological research for almost 40 years. Beginning around the 1970s, new technology and interests in altered states resulted in departures from the Rhine paradigm. Random event generators are now routinely used to generate targets or as a way to detect PK. Computers are used to control many aspects of the experimental procedure and sophisticated instruments are used to find physiological indices of psi. The statistical methods have also grown in sophistication and complexity (Hyman, 1985a).

Consequently, at the level of specific evidence, evaluating parapsychological claims has to change with the times as well as deal with the specifics of the technology, methodology, and the underlying logic of the argument. Coping with a given claim may require a completely different approach from dealing with another parapsychological claim. In this chapter, I try to provide some general guidelines not by precepts but by briefly describing a few specific examples of actual evaluations of claims. These examples will come from my experiences.

EXAMPLES FROM MY OWN EXPERIENCES

My first serious attempt to evaluate a parapsychological claim was almost 50 years ago (Hyman, 1957). I was asked by W. Allan Wallis, the editor of the *Journal of the American Statistical Association*, to review a book on parapsychological claims that was at the center of fierce controversy. In accepting this assignment, I did not realize the amount of time and effort that it would require. Since that time, I have been asked on several occasions to evaluate a parapsychological claim. In almost every case, I first declined on the excuse that I could not afford to take the time away from my other professional duties. I was then asked to suggest someone else to handle the assignment. Often, I was at a loss to think of someone who had the necessary background and who would put in the required time and effort to do the task effectively. On most of these occasions, I reluctantly changed my mind and accepted the task because I feared that it otherwise might be handled superficially.

As I mentioned, my first attempt to assess seriously a parapsychological claim was in 1957. A research chemist, George Price, had instigated an acrimonious debate with his lengthy review of the book *Modern Experiments in Telepathy*, by Soal and Bateman (1954), in the prestigious journal *Science* (Price, 1955). Price conceded that if Rhine's and Soal's psi experiments were conducted as reported, then they do indeed constitute a compelling case for the reality of ESP. He then explained that the truth of ESP would be incompatible with nine of the basic limiting principles of science. To handle this seeming dilemma, Price argued at some length to justify the following paragraph of his paper:

My opinion concerning the findings of the parapsychologists is that many of them are dependent on clerical and statistical errors and unintentional use of sensory clues, and that all extrachance results not so explicable are dependent on deliberate fraud or mildly abnormal mental conditions. (p. 360)

Science received several letters in response to Price's article. Many were angry. Some congratulated the journal and the author for their courage. The January 1956 issue of *Science* printed reactions by Soal, Rhine, a philosopher and a psychologist, and the physicist P. W. Bridgman. In the same issue, Price responded to these reactions and Rhine replied to Price's response.

This was the context in which the editor of the *Journal of the American Statistical Association* asked me to provide a second look at this debate. Wallis, the editor, believed that my experience as a magician along with my training in experimental psychology and statistics would make me ideally suited for the task.

My Review of Soal's Parapsychological Claims

To prepare for this assignment, I carefully read Soal and Bateman's *Modern Experiments in Telepathy*. I also consulted the original reports of the British experiments as well as the work of Rhine and his colleagues. Before this undertaking, I was familiar with parapsychological research, but only through secondary sources. Individuals who I respected had attacked parapsychological claims because they were based on poorly conducted experiments and erroneous statistical procedures. I was surprised to discover that most of the parapsychological experiments appeared to be well designed and used sophisticated statistics. They were certainly much better than the critics had portrayed them.

Soal and Bateman (1954) based their conclusions on more than 60,000 guesses obtained from two gifted subjects. Basil Shackleton's guesses were consistently better than chance over a period of $2\frac{1}{4}$ years. The authors quote the odds against chance as 10^{35} to 1. Mrs. Stewart's correct guesses over a period of 4 years were sufficiently accurate with odds against chance reported as 10^{70} to 1. Soal convincingly argued that the results could not be attributed to recording errors, optional stopping, improper selection of data, ad hoc tests of hypotheses, wrong statistical models, inadequate randomization of targets, or deliberate signaling between agent and percipient.

In my review (Hyman, 1957), I was impressed with the sophistication of Soal's statistical procedures and his attempts to make his data collection free from criticism. On the other hand, I was puzzled by the crudeness of the screening of the percipient from the agent and of the lack of some important details about the later experiments with Mrs. Stewart. However, I felt that these flaws could not explain the results because Mrs. Stewart showed an equal rate of success in six sittings in which she was separated from the agent by the English Channel. I wrote, at the time, "This successful long distance series is indeed fortunate for the argument of Soal and Bateman. It is only because of the outcome of this series, in this reviewer's opinion, that the entire set of 170 sittings becomes plausible evidence for nonsensory communication."

It was only some years later that I learned additional details about the long distance series that convinced me that they no longer could be taken seriously (Hansel, 1966). There were actually two sets of long distance experiments. The first, conducted by Hansel without the participation of Soal, produced only chance results. The second series, the one that I referred to in my review, lacked some critical safeguards that were essential for a properly controlled experiment. And it was not until 1978 that Betty Markwick (1985) published her sensational report that convincingly demonstrated that Soal had cheated on at least several of the sittings. Price, Hansel, and other vocal critics had earlier suggested that it was possible for Soal to have cheated. However, they had produced no direct evidence of such cheating. The scenarios that they suggested would have required that several important individuals collaborate with Soal. Even skeptics found this implausible.

Markwick's ingenious detective work involves two ironies. The first is that Soal's method of doctoring the data sheets did not require collaboration with anyone else and it was much simpler than the complicated scenarios that his extreme detractors had proposed. The second irony is that Markwick, who had been inspired by Soal, was trying to gather evidence to vindicate Soal when she unwittingly discovered the discrepancies in the data sheets.

Lessons from the Soal Affair

My first attempt to evaluate seriously a parapsychological claim taught me many things that have been useful in my subsequent evaluations. I have already mentioned that parapsychological claims are based on statistical and experimental evidence that is much more sophisticated than it is represented by many critics. To me this implies that the assessment of the evidence for psi requires equally sophisticated criticism. The responsible critic will either refrain from commenting on parapsychological claims or devote the necessary time and resources to evaluate the evidence with the respect that it deserves.

The surprisingly high quality of the parapsychological evidence, however, does not justify their claims. This is for at least two reasons. My judgment about the quality is a relative one. The research is of high quality in comparison with how it is commonly portrayed by its detractors. As I indicate in the paragraphs that follow, careful scrutiny of even the best parapsychological research reveals that it frequently departs from standards that parapsychologists themselves insist should be met for acceptable evidence for psi. These departures, to a disturbing degree, are ones that could, and should, have been easily avoided.

The second reason is that, because of the nature of the claims, parapsychological evidence requires a higher level of quality than does evidence for more orthodox scientific claims. Parapsychologists often complain that they are being held to a higher standard than are scientists working in other fields. Whether this is the case, I believe they have failed to realize how much their best programs of research contain flaws that should not be there. Rarely does a critic devote the necessary effort toward carefully assessing the quality of each experiment in a line of parapsychological research. Indeed, I can think of only two examples of such an undertaking (Akers, 1984; Hyman, 1985b). Both of these surveys required months of labor carefully scrutinizing hundreds of pages of technical and complex reports. In my case, I had to devote the major portion of my professional time to the task over a period of more than 6 months. In addition to that period of almost complete dedication to the task, some of my time for at least an additional 2 years was taken up by the task and some of its fallout.

Both Akers[1] and I, to our surprise, discovered that even the best parapsychological research did not survive this careful examination. Because such intensive scrutiny is demanding for both external critics as well as parapsychologists, parapsychologists understandably do not have a good grasp of the true quality of their best research. I believe that until Akers and I published our surveys, parapsychologists did not realize how much their best research failed to meet their own standards.

Another lesson I learned was how flexible the notion of confirmation or repeatability can be for parapsychologists. Soal's findings were universally hailed by Rhine and other parapsychologists as successfully vindicating previous parapsychological claims. Yet, Soal's findings, taken at their face value, differed from Rhine's findings in important ways. Rhine's card-guessing experiments, as well as the ESP research conducted in America, consistently found no difference in success rates with trials in which a sender is trying to convey the target symbol (telepathy) and trials in which no sender is involved (clairvoyance). The outstanding feature of Soal's work was that both his successful percipients succeeded only on telepathy trials and consistently guessed at chance levels on clairvoyance trials. Rhine's findings involved a large number of unselected subjects who seemed to display ESP to some degree. Soal's successful findings were restricted to just 2 out of his original 160 percipients.

At the time I first reviewed Soal's work, I had no way to know that it contained fatal defects. It was only 20 years later that Markwick fortuitously discovered the serious problems with Soal's data sheets. If this had not occurred, Soal's research might still be hailed by parapsychologists as one of the strongest supports for the existence of psi. In my many years of evaluating parapsychological claims, other information has sometimes accidently come to light that discredited a previously impressive example of evidence for psi. The lesson here is that in evaluating a psi experiment, we usually have to rely on the written report. Surprisingly, many reports reveal flaws. However, reports can cover up flaws and fail to supply key information that might reveal limitations of the evidence. Sometimes, as I have indicated, such limitations fortuitously come to light at some later time. The worrisome problem is that presumably some reports might successfully conceal fatal flaws.

The situation is not hopeless. Often, there can be other clues that raise questions about the claim. With hindsight, I realize several clues should have raised questions about Soal's work even before the startling revelations by Markwick. Careful study of the data revealed that both Shackleton and Mrs. Stewart produced successful guesses only when Soal was present. On those occasions when Soal was not present or when Shacklelton and Mrs. Stewart were tested in other laboratories, the results were always consistent with chance. This means that even Soal's colleagues could not

---

[1] Akers was working as a parapsychologist when he conducted his assessment.

replicate his findings. Furthermore, the discrepancy between the pattern of Soal's findings and that of Rhine's should have raised questions about whether the two sets of data were dealing with the same underlying phenomenon.

The Hyman–Honorton Debate

In 1981, I was invited to write a tutorial review on parapsychology for the international journal, *Proceedings of the IEEE* (Hyman, 1986). About the same time, I was invited to speak at the joint meetings of the Society for Psychical Research and the Parapsychological Association. These meetings were to be held in the summer of 1982 in Cambridge, England to celebrate the 100th anniversary of the founding of the Society for Psychical Research. Both assignments involved providing an overall critique of the field of parapsychology.

A fair assessment would examine parapsychological research at its best. I decided to evaluate the status of the claims for psi by looking at its strongest evidence. Accordingly, I contacted some major parapsychologists and asked them to suggest the most promising area of parapsychological research. Just about everyone told me that the best case for psi would be found in the ganzfeld psi experiments.

The first published experiment of this type used a recipient or subject who was isolated in a room with halved Ping-Pong balls taped over her eyes. While she reclined in a comfortable position, white noise or the sound of waves were fed into her ears. In this condition, apparently the subject enters a mild and pleasant altered state. Meanwhile, a sender who was given four ViewMaster reels selected one (presumably at random), placed it in the viewer, and observed the set of pictures for a given amount of time. While the sender was looking at the target pictures, the subject, who was in the ganzfeld state, was encouraged to vocalize any thoughts and images that came to mind. When the trial was over, the agent shuffled the target in with the three decoys. The sender then brought the packet of four ViewMaster reels to the experimenter. The experimenter had the subject look at all four reels and choose the one that best matched what she saw during the ganzfeld state (Honorton & Harper, 1974).

I contacted Charles Honorton, the parapsychologist who first published a ganzfeld psi experiment, and told him of my plan. He was delighted that a skeptic was willing to examine the growing body of research in the area. He told me he would see to it that I had access to every experiment in this area, both published and unpublished (at least the ones he knew about). I had requested his cooperation for this project during the summer of 1981. In January, 1982, I received from Honorton a package containing 600 pages of reports on the ganzfeld psi experiment. By Honorton's account, these reports described 42 separate experiments that had appeared from 1974 until the end of 1981. Approximately half of these experiments had been published in refereed journals or monographs. The remainder had appeared only as abstracts or papers delivered at meetings of the Parapsychological Association. Forty-seven different investigators, many of them prominent members of the Parapsychological Association, had participated in these experiments.

In an attempt to be as objective as possible, I devised a set of 12 categories of flaws that could be used to assess each experiment. Six of the categories concerned statistical defects such as multiple testing without appropriate adjustments of the significance level, use of the wrong statistical test, and the like. Six additional categories covered procedural flaws such as inadequate randomization, inadequate security, possibilities of sensory leakage, and inadequate documentation. To my surprise, only 3 of the 42 studies were free of flaws on the six statistical categories. The results were equally dismaying on the procedural flaws. Over half of the studies failed to safeguard adequately against sensory leakage. Every one of these 42 ganzfeld psi experiments exhibited at least one of the 12 flaws.

None of these flaws is esoteric. Each one of them points to an obvious standard that any parapsychologist would readily agree should be met in any acceptable parapsychological experiment. Keep in mind that my assignment of flaws depended upon the report as written by the experimenter. Because the writeups are done after the experiment has been completed, and they have to follow a standard format, the experiment as reported appears to be much better organized and conducted than is usually the case. You cannot be sure of how well an experiment was actually conducted without having directly observed it being carried out. Although we might expect the experimenter's accounts to be self-serving, it is surprising how many flaws I detected in the written reports.

My extended critique of these 42 ganzfeld psi experiments appeared in 1985 in a special issue of the *Journal of Parapsychology* (Hyman, 1985b). Honorton's equally detailed rejoinder appears in the same issue (Honorton, 1985). Although they are somewhat technical, you might find it worthwhile to read both. My first reaction was to submit a lengthy response to Honorton's rejoinder. But, I soon discovered that neither the skeptics nor the parapsychologists were taking the trouble to follow the subtleties of our debate. Instead, the skeptics assumed that I was correct and had discredited the ganzfeld experiments. The parapsychologists assumed Honorton was correct and had completely demolished all my criticisms. At this time I met Honorton at a conference and we discussed our differences. Although we each believed that the other had misrepesented the situation, we also were surprised to discover that we agreed on several points. Honorton agreed with me, for example, that the ganzfeld database was riddled with enough flaws (although we disagreed on just how badly) that, by itself, it could not serve to support a claim for the existence of psi. What was needed was independent and successful replication with experiments that were free of the flaws that I had uncovered. We wrote a joint paper in which we spelled out the standards that such new experiments should meet (Hyman & Honorton, 1986).

The Autoganzfeld Experiments

Honorton et al. (1990) published the results of 11 experiments that they claimed met the standards specified by Hyman and Honorton (1986). This set of experiments became known as the "autoganzfeld experiments" because most of the procedures and data collection were controlled by computers. The combined total of 354 ganzfeld sessions resulted in a hit rate of 32% compared with the chance expectation of 25%. Because the odds against such an outcome by chance were 500:1, the results were considered statistically significant. Bem and Honorton (1994) published a joint paper in which they reviewed the findings and the controversy over the original ganzfeld database and compared the autoganzfeld results with the earlier data. They concluded that the flaws that I had uncovered in the original database did not affect the outcomes. They also concluded that the autoganzfeld experiments had successfully replicated the original ganzfeld psi database.

In my comments on the Bem–Honorton article (Hyman, 1994), I disagreed with their conclusions. Where Bem and Honorton saw consistencies between the original ganzfeld database and the autoganzfeld experiments, I saw inconsistencies. For example, the targets in the original ganzfeld database were all static images. The targets in the autoganzfeld experiments were video clips, half of which were "dynamic" (action scenes accompanied by a sound track) and half of which were of static scenes. Significant hits were obtained only for the dynamic targets. The static targets, which were most consistent with those of the original experiments, produced only chance results. I pointed out other apparent discrepancies. Bem and Honorton based their claim that the two databases were consistent with each other on the fact that the average effect sizes were not significantly different from each other.

The fact that the average effect sizes were approximately equal in the two databases is meaningless. The average effect size in the original database is an arbitrary average across the contributions from several different laboratories and investigators who differ widely in the effect sizes they obtain. Some, like Palmer and Parker, consistently obtain negative or zero effect sizes. Honorton and his colleagues, on the other hand, consistently obtain relatively large and positive effect sizes. Because the different investigators contributed different numbers of experiments to the database, and because the effect sizes are heterogeneous, any average is arbitrary. By changing the number of studies contributed by each investigator or by altering the mix of investigators, a completely different average could be obtained. The average effect size for the autoganzfeld experiments is equally arbitrary. Only the dynamic targets showed a significant effect. Does it make sense to average the effect size from the dynamic targets with those from the static targets if they differ from one another?

The use of the autoganzfeld experiments as evidence for a successful replication of the original ganzfeld database or as evidence for psi becomes even more problematic in the light of my analysis of the original data. My evaluation of the original ganzfeld experiments relied solely on the individual written reports. When the autoganzfeld experiments were published, I agreed that they met the standards that Honorton and I had specified *with the possible exception of proper randomization of targets during the sending and the judging procedures as well as the possibility of inadequate safeguards against sensory leakage*. In preparing my rejoinder to their *Psychological Bulletin* article, I asked Daryl Bem (unfortunately, Honorton passed away before the publication of their joint article) if it were possible to obtain a copy of the original data.

My plan was to examine the distribution of target selections over the 330 or so sessions of the autoganzfeld experiments. Bem kindly sent me electronic copies of the autoganzfeld raw data. For some reason, the data did not include the information about target selections that I required for my analysis. So, I tried to use an indirect approach as a check on the adequacy of randomization. This indirect approach resulted in the discovery of some surprising patterns in the data that strongly implied that something artifactual had occurred in the experiments. The most suspicious pattern was the fact that the hit rate for a given target increased with the frequency of occurrence of that target in the experiment. The hit rate for targets that occurred only once was right at the chance expectation of 25%. For targets that appeared twice the hit rate crept up to 28%. For those that occurred three times it was 38%, and for those targets that occurred six or more times, the hit rate was 52%. Each time a videotape is played its quality can degrade. It is plausible, then, that when a frequently used clip is the target for a given session, it may be physically distinguishable from the other three decoy clips that are presented to the subject for judging.

Surprisingly, the parapsychological community has not taken this finding seriously. They still include the autoganzfeld series in their meta-analyses and treat it as convincing evidence for the reality of psi (Radin, 1997; Utts, 1991). In his discussion of my finding, Bem implies that this finding could be a fluke. He writes that, "Ironically, Hyman has been one of the most outspoken critics of parapsychologists who search through their data without specific hypotheses and then emerge with unexpected 'findings'" (Bem, 1994, p. 27). Bem's remark has some justification, but it misses the point that, regardless of whether my finding was a fluke, the autoganzfeld experiments were flawed because they did not preclude the possibility of sensory leakage. Later ganzfeld experiments carried out at the University of Edinburgh use duplicate video clips for the judging specifically to avoid this deficiency of the autoganzfeld experiments.

The Later Meta-Analyses of the Subsequent Ganzfeld Psi Experiments

The meta-analyses of the ganzfeld psi experiments carried out since the autoganzfeld experiments have confused rather than clarified the status of these studies as evidence for psi. Radin (1997) offers a meta-analysis of the ganzfeld experiments through early 1997. Including both the early and the later experiments, Radin's meta-analysis contains 2,549 separate ganzfeld sessions. The average effect size for this database corresponds to an overall hit rate of 33.2%, "with odds against chance beyond a million billion to one." Milton and Wiseman (1999) also conducted a meta-analysis of the ganzfeld studies carried out since the autoganzfeld experiments through early 1997. Thus, Milton and Wiseman's meta-analysis overlaps with that of Radin. Yet, where Radin concluded that the ganzfeld psi effect has been supported with astronomical odds beyond chance, Milton and Wiseman concluded that the average effect size in their meta-analysis was close to zero (corresponding to a direct hit rate of approximately 25.6%) and that the new ganzfeld experiments failed to replicate the original ganzfeld experiments.

How can two meta-analyses covering roughly the same time span come to such diametrically opposed conclusions? Further scrutiny provides an answer and also reveals the grave weaknesses of meta-analyses as a way to confirm claims about psi. For one thing, Radin included the original ganzfeld experiments and the autoganzfeld experiments in his meta-analysis. This provides him with a much larger database but is an illegitimate way to check on the replicability of the ganzfeld psi results. It is a form of "double dipping." By including the experiments whose replicability is under question, you are allowing them to be part of the replication. Obviously, if Radin wanted to show that the later experiments replicate the earlier ones, he should have excluded the earlier studies from his database. Beyond this, Radin and Milton and Wiseman did not include the same experiments in their respective databases. The volatility of the meta-analyses is evident when Radin is able to claim odds against chance of more than a billion to one whereas Milton and Wiseman, covering roughly the same period of research, report results consistent with chance.

I do not have space to point to even more problems with the two other meta-analyses of recent ganzfeld psi experiments (Bem, Palmer, & Broughton, 2001; Storm & Ertel, 2001). Each of these contain surprising defects. Bem et al., for example, provide a statistical test to show that the closer in design a ganzfeld study is to the Honorton and Harper original study, the higher its effect size. This is another example of "double dipping." Someone noticed that this seemed to be the case during an extended discussion of the Milton–Wiseman database. Once this pattern is noticed, after the fact, in a set of data, then it is legitimate to test for this pattern in a new and independent set of data. However, doing the test on the same data that generated the hypothesis is both circular and meaningless.

This brings up one of the serious problems with the way that parapsychologists are using meta-analyses to draw conclusions about the existence of psi. Meta-analysis, used carefully, can provide useful information and suggest hypotheses that can be tested on *new* data. To use the same data in a meta-analysis for both estimating the effect size and finding correlates of effect sizes as well as test for significance and drawing conclusions about correlates is a form of double dipping. It confuses exploratory research (which meta-analysis is) with confirmatory research.

The most serious drawback of the way parapsychologists use meta-analysis, however, is that almost every database that is used in parapsychological meta-analyses is heterogeneous. This means that the "average" effect size is an arbitrary and meaningless composite. It also means that the use of the Stouffer z to put confidence intervals around the mean effect size greatly exaggerates the true significance of the mean effect size and grossly underestimates the confidence interval that is placed around it. Indeed, it makes no sense at all to compute a mean effect size for a set of effects that obviously do not share a common size.

CONCLUSION AND LESSONS

I have described just a small sample of my experiences in evaluating parapsychological claims. I did most of these evaluations at the request of an editor, a government agency, or some other source. In almost every case, when I first looked at the basis for the claim, I was impressed by the seeming sophistication of the underlying research and puzzled by the baffling statistical outcomes. Further scrutiny, however, typically uncovered previously unnoticed, but serious, deficiencies in the data. Sometimes I could detect no obvious problems from the written report, but later information would become available, often fortuitously, that made the basis for the claim highly suspect. After almost 50 years in evaluating parapsychological claims, I have yet to come across one that could withstand careful and skeptical assessment.

Given my experiences, how is it eminent parapsychologists such as Jessica Utts (1991) and Dean Radin (1997) can claim that the existence of psi has been established beyond any doubt? Radin presents meta-analysis after meta-analysis that shows, in his opinion, that both ESP and PK have been shown to be real and the supporting evidence has been successfully replicated many times over. So how can I and other skeptics still deny the reality of psi? Radin devotes much of his book toward answering this question in cultural, social, and psychological terms.

The different assessments of the status of parapsychological claims, however, more likely are due to peculiarities of the parapsychological claim and the status of its evidence than to any psychological quirks of the skeptics. Unlike claims in other sciences, the claim for psi depends upon demonstrating that a correlation persists between a human guess or intention that is explicable neither by chance nor by normal sensory or motor connections. This places a very heavy burden upon the statistical testing and the procedures for excluding the possibility of any mundane sources for the obtained effects.

Statistical artifacts can creep into the experiments in a multitude of ways. Many of these are hard to detect from the written report, but as I have indicated, I found obvious possibilities for such artifacts in the original ganzfeld database and in subsequent ganzfeld experiments. Even the parapsychologists admit that it is impossible to eliminate the possibility of nonparanormal causes in a given experiment. The known possibilities are just too many to completely exclude. Previously unknown possibilities keep turning up, especially with the introduction of new equipment and techniques. These problems would not be so serious if the parapsychologists had independent ways to indicate the presence or absence of psi.

Unfortunately, the parapsychologists agree that they currently have no positive theory of psi. Instead, psi is negatively defined as any effect that cannot be currently explained in terms of chance or normal causes. In the 1930s, Rhine discovered the "decline effect" in psi scoring sheets. The decline effect referred to the fact that the early guesses in an ESP experiment tended to be above chance while the later guesses tended to be below chance. When the results were tallied for the experiment as a whole, they result was at chance. This was because the early positive hitting was canceled out by the later negative hitting. The decline effect was found to occur in a variety of ways. When the experimenter found evidence for the decline effect, this was taken as a marker for psi. However, when the decline effect was not found, this did not deter the parapsychologist from declaring evidence for psi if he or she found another kind of significant discrepancy from chance. Over the years, many other patterns were put forth as showing the existence of psi. The parapsychologists used the occurrence of one of these patterns as evidence for psi. Again, if none of these patterns showed up in the data, the parapsychologists were not discouraged. They would search for psi by finding some other deviation from chance. Even when they could not find a significant effect in their data, the parapsychologists did not declare that the psi hypothesis had been disconfirmed. Instead, they could and did argue that some unknown psi-conducive conditions were not operative. This creates the unfortunate situation in which it is impossible to falsify a parapsychological claim.

Moreover, it produces the "patchwork quilt fallacy." This fallacy occurs when the investigator uses any peculiarity that occurs in the data as a characteristic of psi. The unfortunate lack of a positive theory of psi encourages this fallacy. Despite the bold claim by Radin that psi is real and replicable, many parapsychologists recognize how elusive the evidence is. An interesting example of this fallacy is in Bierman's (2000) recent attempt to use the elusiveness of psi and the fact that effect sizes for any line of psi research decline over time as a property of psi. Bierman is just one recent example of parapsychologists turning what outsiders would perceive as failures in the search for psi into properties of psi.

Up to now, only two reliable findings can be found in the history of the search for psi. One is that effect sizes of previously successful programs in the search for psi decline to zero over time. To the cynic this indicates that as the experimenters improve the quality of their experiments, the previously successful results disappear because loopholes have been removed. To the parapsychologist this seems to be a peculiar property of psi. The other finding is the "experimenter effect." This refers to the fact that some experimenters consistently get large effect sizes, others tend to get moderate effect sizes, some get zero effect sizes, and still others tend to get negative effect sizes. Again, parapsychologists tend to see this as a property of psi. However, it raises serious questions about the scientific status of parapsychology. Science depends upon the publicness of its findings. If psi is something that can only be observed by certain privileged individuals, it becomes difficult to consider it as part of science.

The fact that effect sizes vary with experiments and experimenters not only makes the testing of average effect sizes meaningless. Combined with the fact that the parapsychologists do not have a positive or independent way to determine the presence or *absence* of psi, and with their use of consistent effect sizes across databases as evidence for a replicable phenomenon across experiments, the experimenter effect challenges the notion of such a unitary phenomenon. An effect size, by itself, is simply an observed difference divided by a standard deviation. Just because two effect sizes are the same size is no reason to assume that they represent the same phenomenon. Effect size gains meaning only in the context of other information and in terms of clear theoretical constraints.

Until parapsychologists can provide a positive way to indicate the presence of psi, the different effect sizes that occur in experiments are just as likely to result from many different things rather than one thing called psi. Indeed, given the obvious instability and elusiveness of the findings, the best guess might very well be that we are dealing with a variety of Murphy's Law rather than a revolutionary anomaly called psi.

References

Akers, C. (1984). Methodological criticisms of parapsychology. In S. Krippner (Ed.), *Advances in parapsychological research* (vol. 4, pp. 112–164). Jefferson, NC: McFarland.

Bem, D. J. (1994). Response to Hyman. *Psychological Bulletin, 115*, 25–27.

Bem, D. J., & Honorton, C. (1994). Does psi exist? Replicable evidence for an anomalous process of information transfer. *Psychological Bulletin, 115*, 4–18.

Bem, D. J., Palmer, J., & Broughton, R. S. (2001). Updating the ganzfeld data base: A victim of its own success? *Journal of Parapsychology, 65*, 207–18.

Bierman, D. J. (2000). On the nature of anomalous phenomena: Another reality between the world of subjective consciousness and the objective world of physics? In P. Van Loocke (Ed.), *The physical nature of consciousness* (pp. 269–292). New York: Benjamin.

Broad, C. D. (1953). *Religion, philosophy and psychical research*. London: Routledge & Kegan Paul.

Hansel, C. E. M. (1966). *ESP: A scientific evaluation*. New York: Scribner's.

Honorton, C. (1985). Meta-analysis of psi ganzfeld research: A response to Hyman. *Journal of Parapsychology, 49*, 51–91.

Honorton, C., & Harper, S. (1974). Psi-mediated imagery and ideation in an experimental procedure for regulating perceptual input. *Journal of the American Society for Psychical Research, 68*, 156–168.

Honorton, C., Berger, R. E., Varvoglis, M. P., Quant, M., Derr, P., Schechter, E. I., et al. (1990). Psi communication in the ganzfeld: Experiments with an automated testing system and a comparison with a meta-analysis of earlier studies. *Journal of Parapsychology, 54*, 19–24.

Hyman, R. (1957). Review of *Modern experiments in telepathy*. *Journal of the American Statistical Association, 52*, 607–610. (Reprinted in Hyman, 1989).

Hyman, R. (1985a). A critical historical overview of parapsychology. In P. Kurtz (Ed.), *A skeptic's handbook of parapsychology* (pp. 3–96). Buffalo, NY: Prometheus Books.

Hyman, R. (1985b). The ganzfeld psi experiment: A critical appraisal. *Journal of Parapsychology, 49*, 3–49.

Hyman, R. (1986). Parapsychological research: A tutorial review and critical appraisal. *Proceedings of the IEEE, 74*, 823–849.

Hyman, R. (1994). Anomaly or artifact? Comments on Bem and Honorton. *Psychological Bulletin, 115*, 19–23.

Hyman, R., & Honorton, C. (1986). A joint communiqué: The psi ganzfeld controversy. *Journal of Parapsychology, 50*, 351–364.

Markwick, B. (1985). The establishment of data manipulation in the Soal-Shackleton experiments. In P. Kurtz (Ed.), *A skeptic's handbook of parapsychology* (pp. 287–311). Buffalo, NY: Prometheus Books.

Milton, J., & Wiseman, R. (1999). Does psi exist? Lack of replication of an anomalous process of information transfer. *Psychological Bulletin, 125*, 387–391.

Milton, J., & Wiseman, R. (2001). Does psi exist? Reply to Storm and Ertel (2001). *Psychological Bulletin, 127*, 434–438.

Price, G. R. (1955). Science and the supernatural. *Science, 122*, 359–367.

Radin, D. I. (1997). *The conscious universe*. San Francisco: HarperEdge.

Soal, S. G., & Bateman, F. (1954). *Modern experiments in telepathy* (2nd ed.). New Haven, CT: Yale University Press.

Storm, L., & Ertel, S. (2001). Does psi exist? Milton and Wiseman's (1999) meta-analysis of ganzfeld research. *Psychological Bulletin, 127*, 424–433.

Utts, J. (1991). Replication and meta-analysis in parapsychology. *Statistical Science, 6*, 363–403 [Includes commentaries and Utts' rejoinder to commentators].

14

Why Would Anyone Do or Believe Such a Thing?

A Social Influence Analysis

Anthony R. Pratkanis

In the 1920s and 1930s, Oscar Hartzell conned untold millions of dollars from Americans mostly living in the Midwest (Rayner, 2002). His scam: Hartzell claimed to be heir to the Drake fortune – a multibillion dollar trust fund left by the famed explorer Sir Francis Drake. The catch: The British government refused to release those funds without a legal fight. Hartzell invited investors to help pay for the legal fees, and in return they would share the fortune upon victory in court. In the 1980s, Dr. John Ackah Blay-Miezah raked in over $250 million by using the same basic scheme (Jackman, 2003). Blay-Miezah claimed to be the sole beneficiary of the $27 billion Oman Ghana Trust created by Kwame Nkrumath, first president of Ghana, with money from his illicit smuggling operations. Of course, the fund was secret, the financial dealings complex, and thus Blay-Miezah needed investors to help him hire lawyers to release the funds. Blay-Miezah promised a 1,000% return on investment. Every year, Americans lose over $55 billion in telemarketing, investment, and charity scams (Pratkanis & Shadel, 2005).

In 1997, 36 men and women of a California group known as Heaven's Gate dressed in purple shrouds, black pants, and black tennis shoes and killed themselves to board a UFO tailing the comet Hale–Bopp. In 1995, members of Aum Supreme Truth placed bags of leaking sarin gas in the Tokyo subway system, killing 12 persons and injuring more than 5,500. In the early 1900s, a Russian group known as the Brothers and Sisters of the Red Death believed the world was about to end. The cult banned marriages, but members could engage in sexual activity provided that they immediately submitted themselves to the possibility of death by suffocation with a large red cushion.

In the early 1920s, Sir Arthur Conan Doyle, creator of Sherlock Holmes, published an article claiming that two young girls had managed to take photos of fairies. In actuality, the fairies were cutouts from a popular children's book that were posed in the photos (Randi, 1987). Similarly, people have deluded themselves into thinking that psychics can bend spoons with their minds; the future can be foretold by astrology or someone channeling a dolphin; planes and ships are disappearing in the Bermuda triangle; Big Foot, Yeti, and Nessie roam the Northwest, Himalayans, and Loch Ness; and space aliens abducted Betty and Barney Hill (Hines, 2003; Randi, 1987).

We human beings are capable of doing some very strange things and believing some very weird beliefs. By strange, I mean beliefs and behaviors that just don't stand up to a scientific and critical appraisal of the type described in this book. A scientific appraisal doesn't consist of merely putting on the trappings of science – the lab coat, jargon, and statistics (although you may need these things) – but instead engages the essence of science as put forth by Richard Feynman (1985): a bending over backward to prove oneself wrong. A scientific appraisal begins not by accepting a given explanation but with a search for alternative hypotheses, by asking, "What else can it be?" Then, an identification of the consequences of these hypotheses can be used to guide data collections and investigations to sort the bunk from the hypotheses that receive empirical support. The scientific enterprise places a premium on these principles: (a) Occam's razor or the simplest explanation with the least assumptions is best; (b) the burden of proof is on the claimant; (c) extraordinary claims require extraordinary proof; (d) there are no easy outs – null and disconfirming results are taken seriously (Greenwald, Pratkanis, Leippe, & Baumgardner, 1986); and (e) acknowledgment that we humans are error prone and need to take steps to help correct for our errors (for more detail see Baker & Nickell, 1992; Lilienfeld, Lynn, & Lohr, 2003; Sagan, 1995).

And the list of strange things we humans do continues. In 1988, after attending a Christian Youth meeting, Erika and Julie accused their father Paul Ingram of sexual molestation. Despite the lack of evidence, many (including for a time, Paul Ingram) became convinced of the allegations; Ingram was sentenced to 21 years in prison (Wright, 1994). An elderly woman in Oregon stayed home from work to wait for the prize patrol from Publisher's Clearinghouse (PCH), calling a local florist to see if the prize patrol had picked up her flowers. She had purchased many products from PCH in the belief that buying will increase the chances of winning and thought that this day was to be her day (Oregon v. PCH, 2001). People who suffer from aches and pains and from serious illness turn to unproven medical practices such as spine adjustments, crystals, psychic surgeons, therapeutic touch, faddish diets, and homeopathic remedies in hopes of a cure (Barrett & Jarvis, 1993). Similarly, those who seek relief from depression, anxiety, stress, or similar psychological states put their faith in "therapists" who roll them up in carpets to simulate a rebirth, claim their problems are due to something they did in a past life, or treat them with flower remedies or by tapping at so-called energy points (Lilienfeld et al., 2003; Singer & Lalich, 1996).

Why do people believe and do such things?

There is disagreement as to the correct answer to this question. In 2001, I was called by Oregon Senior Assistant Attorney General Thomas Elden to give my answer to this question in a preliminary injunction hearing involving PCH. The State of Oregon sought to prevent PCH from conducting business in Oregon using what the state believed to be misleading and deceptive practices. As part of my testimony, I was asked by Richard Mescon, an attorney representing PCH, if the woman who waited for the prize patrol was acting reasonably. Apparently, the woman still thought that buying would help her win the PCH sweepstakes even though she had been told by the office of the Attorney General that that was not the case. Specifically, Mr. Mescon asked, "Do you believe it is reasonable for a consumer when told by an Assistant Attorney General ... that buying will not help you win the sweepstakes, is it reasonable for that person not to believe the statement by the Assistant Attorney General?" (Oregon v. PCH, 2001, p. 615).

Implicit in Mr. Mescon's question is a theory of why people do and believe crazy things – those people are, at best, unreasonable people. In fact, a very common explanation of why people do strange things is that they are crazy or have something wrong with them. I gave a different answer to Mr. Mescon's question. To understand why anyone would wait for a prize patrol that is not coming, we must understand her or his social situation and the types of social influence in that situation. Let's look at these two classes of explanation for why people do and believe seemingly crazy things to help develop our critical skills in spotting and rejecting weird beliefs.

TWO COMMON (BUT MOSTLY WRONG) CRAZINESS THEORIES OF STRANGE BELIEFS AND BEHAVIORS

Myth 1: You Have to be Crazy to Do Crazy Things

Perhaps the simplest explanation for why people would invest in Drake's fortune or join a cult or try to cure cancer with a psychic surgeon is that they are insane, gullible, overly trusting, conforming, frail, stupid, mentally deficient, unreasonable, foolish, naïve, or some combination of these traits or their synonyms. Despite a widespread belief that certain people are more influenced than others, researchers have failed to find evidence for this claim. Beginning in the 1950s, researchers have employed a basic procedure of giving subjects a variety of persuasive tasks and individual difference measures and then (a) looking for an underlying factor of persuasibility and (b) correlating the subject's level of persuasion with personality measures (Hovland & Janis, 1959). In general, this research has not found an "influence" factor and has obtained only low (below .3) correlations between personality and persuasibility, which generally have not been replicable (Mann, 1959; McGuire, 1968; Segal, 1957).

A survey I conducted with my colleagues at AARP is illustrative (AARP, 2003). We contacted known victims of lottery and investment frauds along with a random control group of the general population and asked them questions designed to measure a range of personality characteristics such as locus of control, trust, propensity to confess, need for cognition, hypnotic susceptibility, and so on. None of these scales predicted victimization. Our research did find that con criminals were tailoring their pitches to the victim's psychological and other characteristics. For example, we found that victims of lottery fraud (which emphasizes luck) were higher in external locus of control than the general population, whereas victims of investment fraud (which emphasizes mastery of one's fate) were higher in internal locus of control than the general population. In many cases, con criminals profile their victims to find their Achilles' heal (and we all probably have one) to construct the exact pitch that is likely to be most effective with each victim.

Myth 2: People Who Do Crazy Things Must Be Infected by Some Crazy Influence

In the 1890s, George du Maurier's novel *Trilby* was all the rage. It told the story of a young girl named Trilby who was hypnotized and controlled by the evil Svengali. The tale captures people's darkest fears of being irrationally controlled by others and provides yet another explanation for why people do crazy things: Strange, exotic behavior must be caused by strange and exotic influence. This portrayal of exotic influence can be seen in the use of hypnotism in the movie *The Manchurian Candidate*, tales of subliminal messages inducing popcorn eating and coke drinking in the 1950s, and reports of brainwashing in Chinese POW camps during the Korean War.

The evidence for this crazy influence theory is also found wanting. First, terms like *hypnotized, subliminal seduction*, and *brainwashing* merely label the phenomenon; they don't explain it. Second, on closer examination, the magnitude of effects caused by these processes is not as large as they are touted to be. Hypnosis is not capable of producing the extreme behavior changes imagined by du Maurier (Spanos & Chaves, 1989); research on subliminal influence fails to replicate (Pratkanis, 1992); and only 21 POWs defected in the Korean War. Third, and more importantly, when these processes are examined more closely, they reveal normal influence processes. Hypnosis can readily be explained in terms of expectations and social roles (Spanos & Chaves, 1989); expectations are an important ingredient in subliminal influence (Pratkanis, Eskenazi, & Greenwald, 1994); and Chinese POW camps used a mixture of information control, group pressure, self-persuasion, and change of social identity (Schein, 1961).

A Dangerous Consequence of Believing in Craziness Theories

It is comforting to think that only crazy people or people infected by crazy influence are prone to believe and do strange things. We may think we are

invulnerable: "That couldn't happen to me; it only happens to the crazies."
But that comfort and feelings of invulnerability come at a cost – it may make
us even more prone to influence. In recent research conducted by Sagarin
and his colleagues (Sagarin, Cialdini, Rice, Serna, 2002; Sagarin & Wood,
in press), students were taught about the ways of persuasion, including how
to discern a legitimate from an illegitimate use of authority. When these
students were confronted with ads containing illegitimate authorities, the
training did not help them resist the dishonest ads. It is only when Sagarin
demonstrated to the students that they were capable of being fooled by an
ad misusing authority that the training was effective. The lesson: If we truly
want to hone our critical skills and not fall prey to influence, we need to
learn the ways of persuasion (what we will do in the rest of the chapter) and
to think that each of us could be vulnerable to undue influence.

SOCIAL INFLUENCE ANALYSIS

A social influence analysis of crazy belief and behavior begins with a premise:
No one gives their money to a con criminal or takes a quack cure or even
joins a dangerous cult. They think they are doing something else such
as making a wise investment, advancing their health, or joining a group
with positive aims. The question becomes: How do they come to think that
way?

The experience of intense social influence can be likened to a trip to an
amusement park. Consider one of the most popular rides at Disneyland –
The Pirates of the Caribbean. On this ride, you are seated in a boat and within
seconds are taken away to a different time and place where "it's a pirate's
life for me." In a very short time, everyone on the boat is waving their
arms, humming a pirate song, and imagining what it would be like to be
a swashbuckler. Few on that boat are thinking about the world they left
behind – whether they left their car lights on or if they locked their hotel
door. They are caught up in the power of the situation. An observer who
saw these people humming a pirate song and waving their arms but didn't
see the trappings of the ride – the music, the simulated pirates, the artificial
setting, the social influence, if you will – would think that these folks are
quite crazy. When we hear of someone investing in Drake's fortune, calling
a local florist to check up on the prize patrol, or claiming to be abducted
by space aliens, we see the crazy behavior but may miss the trappings of the
ride – the social influence that is taking place in that situation.

A social influence analysis begins with a description of the social influence tactics used in a given situation. By *social influence tactic* I mean any
noncoercive technique capable of creating or changing belief or behavior by appealing to the social psychological nature of a target of the influence attempt, whether this attempt is based on the actions of an influence
agent or the result of the self-organizing nature of social systems. Recently,
I reviewed the social influence literature and identified 107 experimentally

tested social influence tactics along with 18 ways to improve credibility (Pratkanis, in press). When one looks at situations that result in crazy beliefs and behavior, one typically finds the extensive use of many of these common and ordinary social influence tactics, along with the possible use of coercive tactics such as deception and power (e.g., control of critical resources to create a dependency relationship; Singer & Lalich, 1995). Such situations can be very powerful in inducing belief and behavior, especially when those tactics have been tailored in such a way to take advantage of our personal goals, desires, and characteristics (Pratkanis & Shadel, 2005). In the rest of this chapter, I review 20 social influence tactics that are common to situations producing crazy beliefs and behavior. Identification of these tactics and their typical effects is essential for understanding the power of the situation and for developing our own critical skills at appraising situations.

SOME COMMON INFLUENCE TACTICS FOR INDUCING SEEMINGLY STRANGE BELIEFS AND BEHAVIOR

Phantom Dreams

Most schemes that induce strange beliefs begin with the bait or what can be termed a *phantom* – an unavailable goal that looks real and possible with just the right effort, belief, or money, but in reality can't be obtained (Farquhar & Pratkanis, 1993; Pratkanis & Farquhar, 1992). Phantoms usually appeal to one or more of our basic desires: wealth, health, popularity, and immortality. For example, PCH offered a large sweepstakes prize. Hartzell and Blay-Miezah dangled large returns for risk-free investments. Doyle's fairies, the spoon-bender's "psychic power," and Heaven Gate's beliefs in UFOs all suggest the hope that supernatural powers exist and there is more to life than just death. Today's con criminals entice with such phantoms as winning a foreign lottery, solving a problem through a phony charity, providing for loved ones after one's death with a phony living trust, getting big payoffs by "investing" in coins and Internet gaming, and winning 1-in-5 prizes (Horovitz & Pratkanis, 2002). The delights of a phantom are designed to take advantage of our tendency for wishful thinking (Lund, 1925); skillful cons will profile a victim to find out which phantoms will have the biggest effects (Pratkanis & Shadel, 2005).

Research on phantoms reveals that the inclusion of a phantom in a choice set decreases the positive evaluation of other options. In other words, a phantom makes us less satisfied with what is possible in everyday life, and we become fixated on that prize. The phantom serves to trap us between a dream that is false and a life that is too dull and colorless. A phantom also can induce strong self-emotions; the denial of a phantom suggests that the self is lacking, resulting in feelings of frustration, relative deprivation, and self-threat. These emotions motivate a person to attempt to obtain the phantom prize.

The Altercast

Altercasting is an influence tactic in which the target of influence is placed in the exact social role that increases the effectiveness of the influence attempt. More formally, altercasting describes a social interaction in which an ego (e.g., source of influence) adopts certain lines of action (i.e., self-descriptions, mannerisms, impression management, etc.) to place the alter (i.e., target) into a social role that specifies an interpersonal task (i.e., message acceptance or rejection). Once a person accepts a role, a number of social pressures are brought to bear to ensure the role is enacted, such as expectations and sanctions for role violations. Any influence attempt is more or less effective depending on what roles are invoked and how the appeal makes use of the responsibilities and privileges inherent in each role. Trust is a function of the role set.

An example of the use of altercasting can be found in the pitch of a con criminal we will call Tyler (Pratkanis & Shadel, 2005). At age 24, Tyler was quite successful at getting people to send in money for a nonexistent prize. He did this by playing three different characters on the telephone. He'd begin his pitch by playing a young and anxious salesman: "Hi Mr. Jones, this is Tyler. Congratulations, you've walked away with one of the biggest awards we've ever given away. My boss wants to get on the phone to congratulate you. I'm a little nervous, because he's my boss." Next, Tyler would congratulate Mr. Jones, pretending to be an executive vice president of marketing and speaking with a British accent and an air of authority. Then Tyler would again play the young and ever anxious salesman, introducing a new character who would be coming to Mr. Jones's house to take photos. The final character spoke in a southern drawl as a "good old boy" and admiring friend who just happened to have the same last name as Mr. Jones.

By playing three social roles, Tyler altercast the victim into three different roles that he could call upon throughout his scam as needed. When Tyler played the role of VP of marketing, he became an authority – a person who is perceived to have a legitimate right to command others. For example, Bickman (1974) found that a man dressed as a guard could successfully order passersby to pick up a paper bag, give a dime to a stranger, and move away from a bus stop (compared with when the man was dressed as a civilian or milkman). The authority altercast is used by cult gurus and psychics who claim to have a special status. The police and clergy told Paul Ingram that he had molested his daughters. Con criminals will pretend to be police officers, lawyers, bank presidents, U.S. Marshals, clergy, CEOs, IRS agents, and even the Attorney General of Ohio to enact their crimes (Pratkanis & Shadel, 2005).

When Tyler played the Southern photographer, he became a likable friend to the victim. We tend to help our friends and not question what they have to say (Pratkanis, 2000; in press). A sense of friendship can be created by sharing similarities, mutual self-disclosures, fleeting interactions, attitudinal agreement, and appearing to be on the target's side. PCH used both the friendship and the authority altercast in their mailings. The woman who waited for the prize patrol had received mailings from Dorothy Addeo (a PCH employee), who as a friend complained that the woman had not won a prize and then advocated on her behalf to the PCH authorities responsible for sweepstakes winners.

Finally, when Tyler played the anxious young salesman, he took the role of a dependent to altercast the victim into the role of responsibility; the person on the other end of the phone would then be afraid that if he or she didn't do what Tyler said, he might lose his job. Pratkanis and Gliner (2004–2005) provide an example of the dependency altercast; we found that a child, who altercast a target into the role of responsible parent, was more effective at arguing for nuclear disarmament than an expert (although the expert was more effective than the child on technical matters). The schemes by Oscar Hartzell and John Ackah Blay-Miezah make use of the dependency altercast – they are depending on investors to help get back the lost fortunes. So too was Sir Doyle a victim of this altercast. How could two young innocent girls make up a story about fairies? Doyle must defend their honor. (I should note that the selling of strange beliefs is not limited to the three roles used by Tyler. For example, another ploy is to place the target in the role of expert. See Pratkanis & Shadel, 2005; Pratkanis & Uriel, 2005; for additional examples, see Pratkanis, 2000; Pratkanis, in press.)

Granfallooning

According to the novelist Kurt Vonnegut, a granfalloon is "a proud and meaningless association of human beings" such as a Hoosier, Buckeye, devotee of Klee, or Nazi. Once an individual is altercast into a social identity, social influence follows in at least two ways. First, influence is based on the unit relationship established between the target and the identity. The social identity provides a simple rule to tell the individual what to believe: "I am a ____ [fill in the blank with an identity] and we do and believe ____ [fill in the blank with identity-related behavior and belief]." Second, in specialized cases, some identities become important as a source of self-esteem and locate a person in a system of social statuses. In such cases, influence is based on a desire to stay in the good graces of a positive group and avoid the pain of associating with a derogated identity (Turner & Pratkanis, 1998). Granfalloons appear to be remarkably easy to establish (Abrams, Wetherell, Cochrane, Hogg, & Turner, 1990; Tajfel, 1981) and have the added advantage of creating outgroups and enemies that can serve as a scapegoat for the group's failures.

During the Drake's fortune scam, "Drake clubs" sprang up in small towns; these clubs consisted of investors talking amongst themselves about their cleverness (and the stupidity of others). One church of "investors" even went so far as to fire their minister for opposing contributions. Cult leaders give their members new names, distinctive clothing, special diets, and, of course, new enemies to hate. As one cult leader put it, "Don't use your little mind inside. Use your big mind, the collective family's mind. We're your mind." (Pratkanis & Aronson, 2001, p. 309). Often, quack psychotherapists create groups of believers that meet regularly to reinforce belief in the therapist and therapy. Proponents of Big Foot, space alien abductions, and similar beliefs have conventions and form groups of self-sustaining believers. Finally, Erika and Julie Ingram belonged to a church and participated in group seminars such as Heart-to-Heart where child abuse was frequently discussed.

Self-Generated Persuasion

One of the most effective means of influence is to design the situation subtly so that the target generates arguments and persuades herself or himself of a proposition. For example, during World War II, Lewin (1947) was able to get Americans to eat sweetbreads (organ meats) by having them form groups to discuss how they could persuade others to eat sweetbreads. Self-generated persuasion is effective because it induces a target of influence to generate as many good arguments about a course of action as possible and to try to refute any counterarguments the target might come up with. In addition, self-generated arguments come from a very credible source.

How do the purveyors of strange beliefs use self-generated persuasion? Cult leaders will immediately send new recruits out to proselytize for the group and in the process convince themselves of the value of the cult. After providing a worthless treatment, sellers of quack medicine ask questions such as, "What's better? Your eyes are brighter." A polite response is to describe something that has gotten better and, not coincidentally, persuade one's self that maybe that treatment actually did some good. Early séances were conducted in the homes of prominent citizens who were then charged with recruiting their friends to the meeting. The trick to doing a cold psychic reading is to throw out lots of vague details about the person and then have that person fill in (self-generate) why those details apply to her or his life. Retailers of so-called nutritional and health products will recruit customers to serve as sales agents. By trying to sell the product, the customer-turned-sales-agent becomes more convinced of its worth. Sometimes a con criminal will just ask a potential victim to self-generate arguments for the criminal's cause. As one con on an undercover tape asked (Pratkanis & Shadel, 2005), "Why do you trust me, Sarah? Just answer why you trusted me." Sarah then went on to tell John why she trusted him.

Social Consensus

Social consensus or what is commonly called "getting on the bandwagon" occurs when it appears that everyone is doing "it" or supports a position, and this causes others to join in and agree (Asch, 1951; Cialdini, 2001; Milgram, Bickman, & Berkowitz, 1969). Social consensus invokes two psychological processes. First, a consensus provides *information* or social proof about what to do and think via a simple rule: "If other people are doing it, it must be correct." Second, consensus provides *normative* influences or social pressure to agree and get on the bandwagon. In other words, people don't want to feel left out or worry that they are doing the wrong thing.

The social consensus tactic is a popular one for promoting strange beliefs. For example, hawkers of quack medicines and psychic phone services feature testimonials of people who have found what they are looking for. Mass media coverage of UFOs, Big Foot, and haunted houses usually contain witnesses who speak for the legitimacy of the event. PCH's advertising described others who had won the big prize. Those who invested in the Drake fortune told their friends. To make it appear that everyone wants in on a deal, fraudulent telemarketers will say things like: "Lots of people calling . . . ," "Most investors coming in at 25–50K," and "Everyone is calling your name."

Another way that con criminals create a false sense of social consensus is with a shill – a confederate who seemingly spontaneously acts on the deal the scammer is offering. Here is how one con did it in a prize scam (pay a fee to win a prize). He found a legitimate businessman who had sent in $399 to win a $2,000 prize. On this rare occasion, the con criminal let the man win the prize. In return, he required the man to sign a release that would allow other "customers" to contact him and to tell them about his winnings. Unsuspectingly, this honest businessman became a shill for the con criminal, singing his praises to unsuspecting victims. Another, less costly method is for the con criminal to give out a phone number of a supposedly satisfied winner or customer. The number belongs to the con criminal's associate, who pretends to be someone else.

Commitment and the Rationalization Trap

Securing a commitment to a course of action increases the likelihood that a person will comply and perform that behavior (Cialdini, 2001). For example, Wang and Katsev (1990) increased recycling behavior merely by obtaining a commitment to recycle from community members. The creation of strange beliefs often involves a process of escalating commitments in which a small or false commitment is secured, which then elicits more commitments (and stranger behavior) in an attempt to justify prior actions. An initial commitment can be obtained by using the foot-in-the-door technique in which the target agrees to a small and seemingly innocent first request (e.g., small investment in Drake's fortune, attending a cult dinner, a free "health checkup," a small PCH purchase) that serves to increase the probability of agreeing to a larger request (e.g., larger investments, recruiting for the cult, purchase of a health regime, and more and more PCH purchases). Con criminals use another way to secure an initial commitment: They will pretend that they have talked to the victim before and assume that the victim has already agreed to the deal. A third trick is known as bait and switch, in which the person (target) agrees to a deal that is then later changed to his or her disadvantage.

At the heart of the use of commitment to secure strange belief and behavior is the rationalization trap (Pratkanis & Aronson, 2001; Pratkanis & Shadel, 2005). For example, consider a person who has just sent money to what every indication appears to be a fraud. This person is faced with two discrepant thoughts: "I am a good and capable person" but yet "I just sent my money to a scammer." These dissonance thoughts can be resolved in one of two ways. First, and perhaps most common, is to deny that the scam is a scam. For example, when Oscar Hartzell was brought to justice, his victims protested the court proceedings, and the U.S. attorney prosecuting the case was booed and spat upon on his way to the trial. Cult members, proponents of unproven therapies, and advocates for Big Foot, UFOs, Nessie, and Yeti often argue adamantly for the rightness of their cause. It is this route of dissonance reduction that most directly answers Mr. Mescon's question on why even an Assistant Attorney General could not convince the woman who waited for the PCH prize patrol that buying won't help you win. A second way to resolve this dissonance is to change one's belief about one's self – "I am not a good and capable person after all." Sadly, fraud victims are often left with a reduced sense of competency and self-worth that can result in depression and even suicide.

The Projection Tactic

One way to cover one's tracks when the heat is on and to get away with a misdeed is to employ the projection tactic – accusing another of the negative traits and behaviors that one possesses and exhibits with the goal of deflecting attention away from one's own misdeeds and toward the accused. We (Rucker & Pratkanis, 2001) conducted four experiments in which subjects were informed that a misdeed was committed (e.g., lying about intentions, invading another country, cheating on a test) and, in the experimental treatments, one of the protagonists in the story accused another of the misdeed. In these four experiments, we found that projection was effective in increasing the blame placed on the target of projection and decreasing the culpability of the accuser. In addition, the effects of projection persisted despite attempts to raise suspicions about the motives of the accuser and providing evidence that the accuser was indeed guilty of the deeds.

Oscar Hartzell was a master at the use of the projection tactic. The Drake fortune scam was not invented by Hartzell but by his employers, Sudie Whittaker and Milo Lewis. Hartzell took over the scam by spreading a story that Whittaker and Lewis were crooks and that he would help save the investors from them. Early in his scam, a Mrs. Scheid filed a complaint with law enforcement in an attempt to get her money back. Hartzell informed the investigating officer that it was the other way around – Mrs. Scheid owed him money – and the police officer left impressed with Hartzell's righteous anger and recommended no further action in the case.

Some additional examples of the use of projection: In the 14th century, Bishop Pierre d'Arcis contested the authenticity of the Shroud of Turin, and was accused of being motivated by greed and a desire to possess the shroud by those who sought to make money off of the shroud. Proponents of unproven health and mental health regimens who rake in the cash for worthless treatments often accuse doctors and clinicians of being motivated only for the money. It is common in telemarketing fraud for the con criminal to accuse either the victim or other con criminals of being a liar.

Additional Influence Tactics

It is impossible to describe all the tactics that can be used to manufacture strange beliefs and behavior in this short chapter. However, Table 14.1 lists additional influence tactics and describes how they are used to promote strange beliefs (see Pratkanis, in press, for more information about each tactic).

WHY DON'T WE JUST SEE THROUGH THESE MANIPULATIVE GAMES?

When the social influence tactics behinds scams, cults, quack medicine and therapies, phony psychics, and other sources of strange beliefs are laid out, they often look so obvious and manipulative. Why don't people see through these schemes? One of the defenses raised by PCH at the Oregon preliminary hearing was just this argument – people can and should see through attempts at deception and manipulation and thus PCH's marketing communications could not be viewed as misleading. To support this defense, the lawyers for PCH introduced the concept of a "schemer schema" advanced by Friestad and Wright (1994). The basic notion of Friestad and Wright is that consumers learn to identify and interpret advertising and sales presentations and that knowledge allows them to cope and adaptively respond to these persuasion attempts. In other words, consumers learn that marketing communications are designed to sell and persuade, and they use this knowledge to keep themselves from being fooled. There are a number of reasons to suspect that even if people possess a schemer schema it provides limited if any benefits in defending against influence attempts.

First, mass media researchers find evidence for a third-person effect (Davison, 1983): a tendency to believe that the mass media will have a greater effect on others than on oneself. It is as if we all say, "I will not be influenced,

TABLE 14.1. *Some Additional Influence Tactics Used to Promote Strange Beliefs and Behavior*

Tactic	Description
Comparison point or set	Options are evaluated by comparison to salient alternatives with an advantage gained by making certain comparisons more salient. Example: a criminal selling fraudulent coins will mention other coins that are less attractive.
Control information flow	Selective presentation of facts through censorship, self-censorship, or other means. Example: cults convene in secluded locations.
Define and label an issue	How an issue is labeled controls and directs thought that then impacts persuasion. Example: a lawsuit against quack medicine is defined as "anti-freedom of choice" not "pro-consumer protection."
Door in the face	Asking for a large request (which is refused) and then for a smaller favor. Example: Con criminals will ask for a large amount to secure a prize and then reduce that amount.
Emotional seesaw	Inducing a change in emotions (happy to sad or vice versa) increases compliance. Example: used in cults and to extract confessions.
Expectations	Expectations guide interpretations to help create a picture of reality that is congruent with expectations. Example: a belief in the Bermuda triangle leads to the mistaken perception that disasters are common in the locale.
Fear appeals	Fear is aroused and a simple, doable recommendation for eliminating the fear is suggested. Example: a patient is diagnosed with a made-up disease such as "candidiasis hypersensitivity" to sell a cure.
Misleading questions	Ask questions to structure information and to imply certain answers. Example: False memories of child sexual abuse can be elicited by symptom questionnaires.
Norm of reciprocity	Provide a gift or favor to invoke feelings of obligation to reciprocate. Examples: a con criminal does a favor for the mark; a quack doctor provides a "free" exam.
Repetition	Repeating the same information increases the tendency to believe and to like that information. Example: a politician repeating the refrain, "governments are inefficient."

Tactic	Description
Scarcity	Scarce items and information are highly valued. Example: There is a conspiracy to limit information about UFOs.
Storytelling	A plausible story serves to guide thought and determines the credibility of information. Example: con criminals embed their pitches into complex stories.
Vivid appeal	Vivid (concrete and graphic) images can be compelling. Examples: alien abductions, Bermuda triangle, and haunted houses are usually described in searing detail.

but others may very well be persuaded." Earlier, I noted that teaching about the ways of persuasion did little to prevent persuasion unless the person felt vulnerable to influence (Sagarin et al., 2002; Sagarin & Wood, in press). The research on the third-person effect indicates that most of us understand the media is out to persuade, but believe it will impact the other person and not ourselves. Without acknowledging our personal vulnerability to influence, we are less likely to use our knowledge about influence (schemer schema) to defend ourselves.

Second, propaganda and flim-flam often go undetected if it agrees with our beliefs and attitudes. We use our attitudes as a heuristic to make judgments about the truth or validity of a claim (Pratkanis, 1989; Pratkanis & Greenwald, 1989). For example, Thistlethwaite (1950) found that invalid syllogisms were more likely to be rated as valid if the person agreed with the conclusion, and Lord, Lepper, and Ross (1979) observed that a persuasive argument was perceived as more valid by those who agreed as opposed to disagreed with the content. Thus, we may not recognize agreeable falsehoods as bunk and conversely falsely believe that disagreeable truths are false.

Third, it is much harder to recognize ulterior motives and manipulation when one is the target of influence as opposed to an observer – a fact I observe in my classroom and Campbell and Kirmani (2000) obtained in experiments. In my social influence course, students learn many of the influence tactics described in Pratkanis (in press) and can pass an exam on those tactics. Students then go shopping and, on occasion, have reported that the salesperson didn't use any of the tactics described in class. For example, one student reported that "the salesman at the car lot was so nice [altercasting], he didn't use any tactics. Instead, he just asked me why I liked a particular car [self-generated persuasion]. The salesman agreed with me [altercasting] and noted that that was why that model was selling like hotcakes [social consensus]." This elicited giggles from the other students, who immediately pointed out the influence tactics used in the situation. The student quickly realized what had happened and then went on to accurately report on other influence tactics used during the visit to the car lot. Campbell and Kirmani found the same phenomenon in their experiments. When people are the targets (as opposed to the observers) of influence or cannot devote their full attention to a pitch, they tend to be very poor at identifying ulterior sales motives.

Fourth, even if an influence tactic can be identified, we may not take enough action to actually mitigate that influence. For example, Urbany, Bearden, and Weilbaker (1988) found that consumers exposed to an exaggerated reference price (e.g., a $319 television set that supposedly normally sells for $799) quickly saw through the tactic (i.e., didn't believe the TV cost $799), but nonetheless viewed the offer as better when the exaggerated price was included than when it was not.

Fifth, forewarned does not equal forearmed unless it leads to a plan on how to respond to an influence attempt (Cialdini & Petty, 1979; Wood & Quinn, 2003). Forewarning of persuasive intent is effective in increasing resistance to influence when the forewarning induces the target to prepare to counterargue the persuasive appeal; without such preparation, forewarning does not increase resistance. Thus, knowing that an influence agent is out to persuade (a schemer schema) does little good unless it induces a person to prepare to counter that appeal.

Finally, as Toris and DePaulo (1984) found, suspicion that a deception may occur often leads to cynicism (believing that everyone is lying) but not skepticism (the ability to sort a lie from the truth).

HOW TO ACTUALLY REDUCE YOUR SUSCEPTIBILITY TO UNWANTED INFLUENCE

Given that believing you are invulnerable to influence and can see right through it won't reduce your susceptibility to unwanted influence, what will? Here are a few tips that you can employ (see also Pratkanis & Aronson, 2001; Pratkanis & Shadel, 2005).

Know the ways of persuasion. Knowledge of influence tactics is the first step to developing a critical appraisal of the situation. But remember that knowledge alone will not help unless you also believe that you can fall prey to those tactics.

Monitor changes in your emotions. If all of a sudden you are feeling strong emotions in response to a communication, ask "Why?" Look for things such as social influence tactics that might induce emotions. Use a change in emotions as a cue to start asking questions about the situation.

Take control of your thoughts. One of the primary goals of an influence agent is to control the way you think about an issue. As a counter, you need to think for yourself. One way to stimulate thought is to ask, "What else can it be?" when confronted by a claim. This will give you a pool of explanations for any given event that can then be tested through empirical observation and other means.

Ask critical questions. Ask, What does the source of information have to gain? If the deal is so good, why doesn't he or she take the deal? What are the arguments for the other side? What other options do I have? Where else can I get additional information?

Have a plan for dealing with unwanted influence. Such a plan may consist of how to get off the phone when a fraudulent telemarketer calls, how to exit an intensive influence situation, or preparations for dealing with an upcoming persuasive message.

Promote fair and ethical influence. Given the significance of social influence for a democracy and for a capitalist system, it is important to ask, "What types of influence are appropriate in our society?" and to take action to ensure proper forms of persuasion. This is exactly what Senior Assistant Attorney General Thomas Elden and his colleagues in other states did when they brought a suit against PCH. After the Oregon preliminary injunction (but before a judge could rule), PCH came to a settlement with Oregon and other states. In this settlement, PCH agreed to pay $34 million in restitution, consumer education funding, and other fees, to run corrective advertising to counter the belief that "buying helps you win," and to never again use specific marketing communications that might mislead people to think they have won a prize when no prize has been won.

References

AARP. (2003). *Off the hook: Reducing participation in telemarketing fraud.* Washington, DC: Author.

Abrams, D., Wetherell, M., Cochrane, S., Hogg, M. A, & Turner, J. C. (1990). Knowing what to think by knowing who you are: Self-categorization and the nature of norm formation, conformity, and group polarization. *British Journal of Social Psychology, 29,* 97–119.

Asch, S. E. (1951). Effects of group pressure upon modification and distortion of judgment. In H. Guetzkow (Ed.), *Groups, leadership and men* (pp. 177–190). Pittsburgh, PA: Carnegie Press.

Baker, R. A., & Nickell, J. (1992). *Missing pieces.* Buffalo, NY: Prometheus Books.

Barrett, S., & Jarvis, W. T., (1993). *The health robbers.* Amherst, NY: Prometheus Books.

Bickman, L. (1974). The social power of a uniform. *Journal of Applied Social Psychology, 4,* 47–61.

Campbell, M. C., & Kirmani, A. (2000). Consumers' use of persuasion knowledge: The effects of accessibility and cognitive capacity on perceptions of an influence agent. *Journal of Consumer Research, 27,* 69–83.

Cialdini, R. B. (2001). *Influence.* Boston: Allyn & Bacon.

Cialdini, R. B., & Petty, R. E. (1979). Anticipatory opinion effects. In R. E. Petty, T. M. Ostrom, & T. C. Brock (Eds.), *Cognitive response in persuasion* (pp. 217–235). Hillsdale, NJ: Erlbaum.

Davison, W. P. (1983). The third-person effect in communication. *Public Opinion Quarterly, 47,* 1–15.

Farquhar, P. H., & Pratkanis, A. R. (1993). Decision structuring with phantom alternatives. *Management Science, 39,* 1214–1226.

Feynman, R. P. (1985). *Surely you're joking, Mr. Feynman.* New York: Norton.

Friestad, M., & Wright, P. (1994). The persuasion knowledge model: How people cope with persuasion attempts. *Journal of Consumer Research, 21,* 1–31.

Greenwald, A. G., Pratkanis, A. R., Leippe, M. R., & Baumgardner, M. H. (1986). Under what conditions does theory obstruct research progress? *Psychological Review, 93,* 216–229.

Hines, T. (2003). *Pseudoscience and the paranormal.* Amherst, NY: Prometheus Books.

Horvitz, T., & Pratkanis, A. R. (2002). A laboratory demonstration of the fraudulent telemarketers' 1-in-5 prize tactic. *Journal of Applied Social Psychology, 32,* 310–317.

Hovland, C. I., & Janis, I. L. (Eds.). (1959). *Personality and persuasibility.* New Haven, CT: Yale University Press.

Jackman, I. (2003). *Con men.* New York: Simon & Schuster.

Lewin, K. (1947). Group decision and social change. In T. M. Newcomb & E. L. Hartley (Eds.), *Readings in social psychology* (pp. 330–344). New York: Holt.

Lilienfeld, S. O., Lynn, S. J., & Lohr, J. M. (Eds.). (2003). *Science and pseudoscience in clinical psychology.* New York: Guilford Press.

Lord, C. G., Lepper, M. R., & Ross, L. (1979). Biased assimilation and attitude polarization: The effects of prior theories on subsequently considered evidence. *Journal of Personality and Social Psychology, 37,* 2098–2109.

Lund, F. H. (1925). The psychology of belief. *Journal of Abnormal and Social Psychology, 20,* 174–196.

Mann, R. D. (1959). A review of relationships between personality and performance in small groups. *Psychological Bulletin, 56,* 241–270.

McGuire, W. J. (1968). Personality and susceptibility to social influence. In E. F. Borgatta & W. W. Lambert (Eds.), *Handbook of personality theory and research* (pp. 1130–1187). Chicago: Rand McNally.

Milgram, S., Bickman, L., & Berkowitz, L. (1969). Note on the drawing power of crowds of different size. *Journal of Personality and Social Psychology, 13,* 79–82.

Oregon v. Publisher's Clearinghouse. Preliminary Injunction Proceedings, No. 00C-10706. (C. C. Marion County 2001).

Pratkanis, A. R. (1989). The cognitive representation of attitudes. In A. R. Pratkanis, S. J. Breckler, & A. G. Greenwald (Eds.), *Attitude structure and function* (pp. 71–98). Hillsdale, NJ: Erlbaum.

Pratkanis, A. R. (1992). The cargo-cult science of subliminal persuasion. *Skeptical Inquirer, 16,* 260–272.

Pratkanis, A. R. (2000). Altercasting as an influence tactic. In D. J. Terry & M. A. Hogg (Eds.), *Attitudes, behavior, and social context* (pp. 201–226). Mahwah, NJ: Erlbaum.

Pratkanis, A. R. (in press). Social influence analysis: An index of tactics. In A. R. Pratkanis (Ed.), *The science of social influence: Advances and future progress.* Philadelphia: Psychology Press.

Pratkanis, A. R., & Aronson, E. (2001). *Age of propaganda: The everyday use and abuse of persuasion* (Rev. ed.). New York: Freeman/Holt.

Pratkanis, A. R., Eskenazi, J., & Greenwald, A. G. (1994). What you expect is what you believe (but not necessarily what you get): A test of the effectiveness of subliminal self-help audiotapes. *Basic and Applied Social Psychology, 15*, 251–276.

Pratkanis, A. R., & Farquhar, P. H. (1992). A brief history of research on phantom alternatives: Evidence for seven empirical generalizations about phantoms. *Basic and Applied Social Psychology, 13*, 103–122.

Pratkanis, A. R., & Gliner, M. D. (2004–2005). And when shall a little child lead them? Evidence for an altercasting theory of source credibility. *Current Psychology, 23*, 279–304.

Pratkanis, A. R., & Greenwald, A. G. (1989). A socio-cognitive model of attitude structure and function. In L. Berkowitz (Ed.), *Advances in experimental social psychology* (Vol. 22, pp. 245–285). New York: Academic Press.

Pratkanis, A. R., & Shadel, D. (2005). *Weapons of fraud: A source book for fraud fighters.* Seattle, WA: AARP.

Pratkanis, A. R., & Uriel, Y. (2005). *The expert snare as an influence tactic: Surf, turf, and ballroom demonstrations of the compliance consequences of being altercast as an expert.* Unpublished manuscript, University of California, Santa Cruz.

Randi, J. (1987). *Flim-flam.* Buffalo, NY: Prometheus Books.

Rayner, R. (2002). *Drake's fortune.* New York: Doubleday.

Rucker, D. D., & Pratkanis, A. R. (2001). Projection as an interpersonal influence tactic: The effects of the pot calling the kettle black. *Personality and Social Psychology Bulletin, 27*, 1494–1507.

Sagan, C. (1995). *The demon-haunted world.* New York: Random House.

Sagarin, B. J., Cialdini, R. B., Rice, W. E., & Serna, S. B. (2002). Dispelling the illusion of invulnerability: The motivations and mechanisms of resistance to persuasion. *Journal of Personality and Social Psychology, 83*, 526–541.

Sagarin, B. J., & Wood, S. W. (in press). Resistance to influence. In A. R. Pratkanis (Ed.), *The science of social influence: Advances and future progress.* Philadelphia: Psychology Press.

Schein, E. H. (1961). *Coercive persuasion.* New York: Norton.

Segal, J. (1957). Correlates of collaboration and resistance behavior among U.S. Army POWs in Korea. *Journal of Social Issues, 13*, 31–40.

Singer, M. T., & Lalich, J. (1995). *Cults in our midst.* San Francisco: Jossey-Bass.

Singer, M. T., & Lalich, J. (1996). *Crazy therapies.* San Francisco: Jossey-Bass.

Spanos, N. P., & Chaves, J. F. (1989). *Hypnosis.* Buffalo, NY: Prometheus Books.

Tajfel, H. (1981). *Human groups and social categories.* Cambridge, England: Cambridge University Press.

Thistlethwaite, D. (1950). Attitude and structure as factors in the distortion of reasoning. *Journal of Abnormal and Social Psychology, 45*, 442–458.

Toris, C., & DePaulo, B. M. (1984). Effects of actual deception and suspiciousness of deception on interpersonal perceptions. *Journal of Personality and Social Psychology, 47*, 1063–1073.

Turner, M. E., & Pratkanis, A. R. (1998). A social identity maintenance theory of groupthink. *Organizational Behavior and Human Decision Processes, 73*, 210–235.

Urbany, J. E., Bearden, W. O., & Weilbaker, D. C. (1988). The effect of plausible and exaggerated reference prices on consumer perceptions and price search. *Journal of Consumer Research, 15*, 95–110.

Wang, T. H., & Katsev, R. D. (1990). Group commitment and resource conservation: Two field experiments on promoting recycling. *Journal of Applied Social Psychology, 20,* 265–275.

Wood, W., & Quinn, J. M. (2003). Forewarned and forearmed? Two meta-analysis syntheses of forewarning of influence appeals. *Psychological Bulletin, 129,* 119–138.

Wright, L. (1994). *Remembering Satan.* New York: Knopf.

15

The Belief Machine

David J. Schneider

THE BELIEF MACHINE

Human minds are belief machines. Put raw data into the proper slot and out pops a belief, all polished and ready for action. We believe what we can and give up our beliefs reluctantly. Lest this seem hyperbole, let us observe the belief machine in its purest form – a 3-year-old child. Long before cute little kids can tell right from wrong, illusion from reality, truth from fiction, they believe everything is just what it seems to be – everything is on the level. Parents and, later, schools spend considerable time trying to convince the growing belief machine to modify its input–output routines. We teach children that some things are illusionary, that the truth of important things lies well beneath the surface of sensory experience, and that we should consider before we declare our beliefs.

Fortunately all this effort is often effective, but unfortunately it sometimes is not. The great philosopher-psychologist William James put it most directly: "As a rule we believe as much as we can. We would believe everything if only we could" (James, 1890/1950, p. 299). More recently, Daniel Gilbert (1991) has pointed out even well-educated adults tend to accept what they experience at face value unless they make a deliberate effort to think more deeply about perceived realities. The belief machine can be tweaked and overridden, but it's always on idle waiting to do its thing.

What we believe is not always correct, unfortunately, and an education that encourages critical thinking is a vital tool in dividing the true from the false. Psychology courses can be particularly useful in that regard, and among the lessons we hope you take away from such courses is that our beliefs have fragile relationships with reality and that we should sometimes be skeptical of their validity. We also hope that studying psychology helps give you the tools you need to evaluate the beliefs of others and more importantly your own. It's not that all your beliefs are false, but just that you ought not take their validity for granted.

WHAT BELIEFS ARE

Certainly since the time of Plato, the psychological and logical status of beliefs has been debated and chewed over. Since it does not serve present purposes to get lost in philosophical thickets, I adopt a rather commonsensical definition. *Beliefs are ideas or mental content that we take to be true or accurate.* When I say I believe that the sun will rise tomorrow, I am simply asserting that this statement will be validated in a factual sense. Likewise, my belief that Politician A would make a great president asserts what I take to be a political truth, good enough for me, whether or not I could prove it to your satisfaction.

From time to time we make distinctions between beliefs that have truth value in the sense that they could be validated through formal or informal empirical tests and those that rest more on faith or cultural validation. My computer either does or does not exist at this moment, but your belief that God exists or not is not the sort of thing likely to be shown to be true or false, at least during your lifetime. But even empirical testing does not completely rescue those beliefs that are subject to it. As philosopher David Hume alerted us 250 years ago, we hold some beliefs that will likely be confirmed in the future but whose logical justification today is in doubt. On the basis of past experience I believe that the lecture hall will be reasonably populated when I start my lecture tomorrow, but it is possible that all the students will decide to sleep in and the room will be empty. Because what has happened is not a perfect guide to what will, such inductive beliefs rest on fragile logical grounds.

Normally these kinds of issues do not concern us. We have millions of beliefs, most of which we never question. Admittedly sometimes we are acutely aware that some of our beliefs have an uncertain and unknowable relationship with empirical truth, although usually we manage quickly to get on with our lives. However, even for the most open-minded of us, beliefs are the epitome of self-centered cognition because each of us is convinced that our beliefs are true. You may think that some of mine are based on false information, ridiculous premises, and illogical thought processes, but it certainly doesn't seem that way to me. You may claim that my belief is false, but it makes no sense for me to say that my present belief is so. Yesterday I believed that the sky was yellow, but today I realize the error of my ways and declare it to be blue (or for that matter pink). However, at exactly that moment when this new blue version of truth enters my consciousness, the old idea that the sky is yellow ceases to be my belief. I could, of course, say that I used to have the false (and silly) belief that the sky is yellow, but it is nonsensical to say that I believe the sky is yellow when I know that to be untrue. Self-disavowals of beliefs must involve the past tense. Beliefs can also be related to the future. An atheist on her death bed may wish with all her might to believe that God exists, and she may or may not actually have a late conversion experience. But she can't fake it; at the point of her death she either does or not believe.[1]

HOW BELIEFS ARE VALIDATED

Personal Experience

Most of our beliefs are never questioned, but when they are, we must have some sense of why we think them to be true. Beliefs are derived and validated roughly in one of four major ways. First, they may be based on personal experience. My belief that I have 10 toes is redemonstrated each time I shower or put on a clean pair of socks. Although I suppose I first learned this important fact about human, and especially my human, anatomy when I was taught to count piggies by my mother, the truth of this belief today has been confirmed countless times by everyday experience. The perceived validity of many of our beliefs rests heavily on our experiences or of those we trust. It's not as if we have any other choice; it would be a poorly calibrated mental machine that did not rely on experience. How else could we learn? However, as we shall see, there are problems.

Cultural Effects

Second, we may believe something because we have been encouraged to do so by culture and its agents. It is an open question whether humans would arrive at a belief in God from their own experiences, but it is certain that people stumbling around the byways of experience would not produce beliefs that exactly matched Catholic dogma or the teachings of the Koran. Whatever experiences people have, their religious beliefs are shaped to a large extent by what they have been taught. At a more mundane level, probably the vast majority of our beliefs about the truth of even verifiable facts is based on explicit teaching and informal cultural tuition rather than direct experience. I have no experiential evidence that the earth is more or less round, that the moon is generally 385,000 km from the earth, that cobra bites are painful and potentially deadly, or that Australians are beating the heat while I am trying to keep winter blasts at bay. Although I could create experiences that validated these beliefs, I am content to believe without direct experience what I have been told about weather patterns, charming

---

[1] In that regard, some readers may be familiar with Pascal's wager. The crude version of his argument was that if one believes God to exist and this turns out to be false, no great harm is done. But if one believes that God does not exist and God does, then one is subject to whatever presumably harsh punishments God holds out for unbelievers. Thus, the cost-effective belief would be that God exists. However, even rational justification does not always produce belief, and the lifelong atheist who recognizes the rationale still may not be able to pull off this mental slight of hand.

facts about astronomy, and the dangers of cobras. We depend heavily on people who know more than we do, not only for our religious and moral beliefs but also for much of what we take to be hardcore truths that are subject to empirical test.

Deductions From Other Beliefs

Third, each of us has what we might call a core belief system, built on basic religious, political, and ideological beliefs that we rely on to give meaning to our lives and experiences. Many, but not all, of our more peripheral beliefs are related to these core beliefs in a more or less logical way. So a political conservative who believes in the importance of individual initiative will have quite different beliefs about homeless people than the political liberal whose core beliefs are built around structural reasons for economic inequalities. In some ways the world looks quite different to a conservative Christian than to an atheist or a devout Muslim. Beliefs spawn beliefs.

Emotions and Motives

Fourth, some beliefs are pure figments of imagination, driven largely by motives and needs. That's what gives beliefs a bad name. For thousands of years, philosophers and poets have been warning us. Julius Caesar said it best and most directly: "Men willingly believe what they wish." Or consider the ancient philosopher, Demosthenes: "Nothing is easier than self-deceit, for what each man wishes, that he also believes to be true." To quote the poet John Dryden, "With how much ease we believe what we wish," or the more familiar quote from Shakespeare, "Thy wish was father, Harry, to that thought."

Most of us could find the odd belief wandering around in our mental household that basically seems more due to desire than logic or empirical experience. For example, we would not find it strange to discover that beliefs in an afterlife or miracle cures increase in the terminally ill. But even motivated beliefs, erroneous as they may be, have strong roots in the total belief system and are not totally a result of desires run amok. When our wishes create beliefs, the belief machine is clever enough to gather up other beliefs in a supporting role. A man who desperately wishes he could contact his dead wife to remind her how much he loved her (or to ask where the peanut butter is stored) will come to rely on other beliefs about life after death, all of which are consistent with his deeply felt religious beliefs.

Yes, our motives do sometimes lead us to manufacture strange beliefs, but what I'll call *motivated beliefs* garner support from cultural belief systems, experiences, and logical relationships with other beliefs so that in the end it becomes hard to divorce emotions from other normal cognitive and social processes. Furthermore, cultural and physical realities set limits on how far our needs can push us around (Kunda, 1999). No matter how much I would like to own a high-powered sports car, I cannot convince myself that I actually own one or even that I especially deserve one (or for that matter could drive it properly even if I did). We have terms such as *insane, crazy,* and *paranoid* for people whose beliefs are totally at odds with the realities others of us endorse.

Whereas desires may affect what we believe and how strongly, most of our beliefs, and surely the most important ones, have some sort of emotional charge. These emotions are often what turn our beliefs into behaviors. If I didn't care about my belief that Politician A would make a better president than Politician B, there would be no point in voting. It is worth noting that even false beliefs can lead to productive behavior. You may erroneously believe, as it turns out, that whether you get an A or a B in your psychology course will make a difference in your life, but even so this belief will motivate you to work hard. I often work hard preparing lectures on the perhaps dubious belief that my students will learn as much as I hope they will. So in the final analysis, although we recognize that motivated beliefs may say more about the person who holds them than the realities of the world, we should not assume that the mix of motives, desires, and beliefs is inevitably bad.

Beliefs Are Complexly Validated

As many of these examples have illustrated, it is often impossible to separate out the various reasons why we believe something. Although we can suggest that beliefs have one source or another, in fact all our beliefs are part of a piece of clothing, cut from the whole cloth of experiences and stitched together with threads of culture, support from others, and consistency with other beliefs. In a way that's what education is all about. At their best, educational institutions and informal tuition help with the cutting and stitching by providing solid empirical foundations, logical relations, and criteria for evaluating our beliefs. Education does not always get it right, but it tries.

WHY BELIEFS ARE SOMETIMES FALSE

Unfortunately none of these ways we have of generating and validating beliefs guarantees that they will be correct. In fact each of the sources has built-in defects that sometimes lead to mistaken or false beliefs. Sometimes these beliefs are so out of touch with accepted realities that we call them *anomalous beliefs* or, more popularly, *crazy beliefs* (Zusne & Jones, 1989).

Those of us who teach psychology courses often find ourselves confronting beliefs about humans that are almost certainly false and certainly based on less than satisfactory evidence. Over my many years of teaching, I have discovered that at least some students believe that astrology can predict the future, we use only 10% of our brain to reason, women are less rational and worse drivers than men, almost all poor people are lazy, homosexuality is created when boys are seduced by older men, people really can communicate through ESP, astrology really does tell a lot about personality, dreams forecast the future, so-called recreational drugs are harmless, people commit more crimes during a full moon, depressed people can cure themselves by just thinking happy thoughts, and, in one sad case, that people can fly. Some people believe that aliens from UFOs abduct humans, Satanic cults murder thousands of babies every year, the Holocaust did not occur, the United Nations is trying to take over the government of the United States, and mediums can contact the dead (Shermer, 1997). False and silly beliefs are not in short supply, because unfortunately the belief machine does not have an accuracy routine.

What would lead people to hold such beliefs that have little or no supporting evidence and that are almost certainly false? Much as we would like to think differently, there is no special psychology of anomalous beliefs – they are formed in much the same ways as our everyday beliefs. They are based on experience, cultural support, logic, and emotion, just as are all beliefs. Each source is valuable, but when relied on too much and without checks from the other sources can produce anomalous beliefs.

More specifically there are four main problems. First, such beliefs are often based on individual experiences that are corrupt in some way. Second, anomalous beliefs often rely much too heavily on cultural assumptions and values as well as on perceived social support. Third, people's ideological beliefs, often supported by a larger culture, can also create strange beliefs. Fourth, to the extent such beliefs have an empirical base (i.e., can theoretically be tested), they are often at odds with scientific explanations and data.

Experiential Factors

Most of us arrogantly think that our own experiences are trustworthy reflections of reality, but what we often fail to realize is that our experiences are never pure, never completely in touch with external reality. In recent years, cognitive and social psychologists have documented a huge array of what are usually called *cognitive biases* (Gilovich, 1991; Piattelli-Palmarini, 1994; Plous, 1993). In addition, our emotions, wishes, and desires may affect how we process information (Kunda, 1999). Rather than detail a list of such biases, let me mention just a few that are most likely to affect our beliefs.

Experiences Are Parochial and Limited
One is that experiences are parochial. We view life through a picket fence, seeing only parts of it at any given time. Each of us gets to experience only bits and pieces of reality, and it's sometimes hard to knit all this together properly. My experience with young Asian Americans is that they are smart, polite, and a bit diffident. A policeman I know who works with Asian street

gangs assures me that the Asian men he knows are neither shy nor polite, and he's not willing to bet on smart. It's not that either of us is wrong but just that we have had different experiences.

Another variation on this theme is that we often give far too much weight to single experiences. This is the bugaboo of medical cures. A person suffering from cancer tries the old cure of eating ground-up pearls in wine, and a few days later he is seemingly cured – or so he believes. But, of course, before prescribing this admittedly expensive recipe for a loved one who has just been diagnosed with cancer, we ought to ask some questions. First, and most important, has the cancer really disappeared? People with cancer can have their ups and downs, and maybe he drank the concoction on an upswing. Also his momentary revitalized heath may be due more to his desires to believe in the cure than in any direct physical cause. But assuming that the cancer has disappeared or slowed its advances, we should understand that this could be due to several causes, many of which we do not fully understand. The fact that we're not sure why something happened isn't license to invent whatever cause comes to mind. Generally there are many reasons why people get sick or healthy, and we need to examine many cases in an experimental study to find out which are the most effective.

We Ascribe Too Much Meaning to Random Events

A related problem is that we often give too much meaning to random events and coincidence in our lives. The belief machine passionately hates randomness and does everything in its power to give meaning even to those things that don't deserve it. So, you note from reading the newspaper that during the last full moon there were several more murders than usual and an increase in traffic accidents to boot. Surely this is proof enough that the moon affects our behavior.

However, life is not constant and level; it produces hills and valleys in most everything, including violent deaths. If you think about it, we can't expect murder rates to remain exactly the same from week to week. Without doubt there are times when mayhem of all sorts occurs during full moons, and because this is so striking we tend to remember it well. However, there are also full-moon periods that are peaceful and quiet, and we tend to ignore or forget about these.

Another problem with focusing on single events (the period when full moon and numerous murders coincide) is that we privilege one explanation over others. There are lots of reasons why murder rates go up and down from week to week, including weather, frustration with the success of the local sports team, economic uncertainties, perhaps full moons; selecting moon phases without considering the other potential causes allows you to read too much into the data you have. Because individual case studies or individual experiences (which this is) always have problems of this kind (Stanovich, 2004), we need to enlarge our sample. So if we looked at murder rates during the full moon over a 5-year period, we might find that murder rates go up during such periods sometimes and go down at others. Overall there is no relationship between moons and much of anything except tides (Kelly, Rotton, & Culver, 1985–1986).

Sometimes striking coincidences attach themselves to popular explanations, and the belief machine insists that the explanation is correct. I have personally never had a dream that a close relative was about to die, although I've had plenty of dreams and have lots of dead relatives. But should that experience happen to me, I'm confident that I would have to use all my mental resources to overcome the efforts of the belief machine to convince me that dreams predict the future. Yes, personal experiences are striking and convincing, but that's all the more reason to mistrust them.

Experiences Are Filtered

Another problem with relying on experiences is that they are heavily affected by previous beliefs, expectations, memories, even language, and often in ways that satisfy our desires and fit nicely with what we already believe. In the world of psychologists, "I saw it with my own eyes" does not cut it, because what we call experiences are hardly unadulterated raw data, perfectly attuned to reality. Some of this processing occurs at a relatively low level and automatically with, say, color constancy or transforming two-dimensional retinal images into three-dimensional representations. But once we begin to label our experiences and fit them into our larger meaning systems, all bets are off.

The belief machine likes to ensure mental tranquility and consistency, so we protect our beliefs from molestation in various ways (Kunda, 1999; Moskowitz, 2005). For example, we tend to seek out and expose ourselves more to information consistent with our beliefs (Frey, 1986). That's one reason it's so hard to change voting preferences during elections – Republicans listen only to Republican candidates and Democrats to like-minded candidates. People tend to remember information that is consistent with their beliefs and often to have less access to disconfirming information (Olson, Roese, & Zanna, 1996). We tend to evaluate evidence consistent with our beliefs as more valid than is information that is inconsistent (Lord, Ross, & Lepper, 1979). As the theory of naive realism (Robinson, Keltner, Ward, & Ross, 1995; Ross & Ward, 1996) suggests, we also tend to denigrate inconsistent information by seeing it as biased. Most of us firmly believe that we are in touch with reality, and therefore people who disagree with us must have poor information, be biased or even deluded by their needs and emotions. My beliefs cannot be false, although I'm inclined to think yours are if they disagree with mine.

Experiences Require Interpretation

Another reason why we ought not blindly trust our personal experiences is that the belief machine has a wonderful way of carving up the meaning of our experiences so they can be made to fit whatever belief slot the belief machine is featuring that moment. One major reason why horoscope predictions so often come true is that we interpret experiences to fit. My horoscope predicts that I will meet a new friend today, and now that I think about it, this morning I did meet a person who seemed like a good candidate for a developing friendship. Surely that counts. Or maybe I was home alone all day, but yesterday I met the friend of my dreams. So the horoscope was off by a day. Big deal. A prediction of financial success could be confirmed by anything – the stock market going up, an unexpected raise, or a friend giving me back $10 I loaned him. One assumes that ghosts come in all shapes and sizes, but counting vague shapes on the wall, strange sounds in the middle of the night, and half-dreams that someone is talking to you ensures that we all have ghostly experiences. If a belief in ghosts is what your belief machine is recommending, I'm sure you can find the odd experience in support.

People with different belief systems often interpret and label the same things differently. For example, fans of one sports team may see the actions of their players and those of the opposition quite differently than do fans of the other team (Hastorf & Cantril, 1954). A welfare policy may be an economic safety net to a liberal but a government giveaway to a conservative. Anytime I teach a large class I am always surprised that some students report it to be interesting and others boring. Did they take the same class?

When beliefs guide experiences, the latter are likely to support the former. That's one of the things that makes stereotypes so harmful (Schneider, 2004). A person who believes that African Americans are lazy can usually find some way to manipulate and organize his or her experiences to create supporting evidence. Prejudiced people often interpret the behavior of someone from a racial minority in a different manner than do those who are less prejudiced (Wittenbrink, Gist, & Hilton, 1997).

Cultural and Social Factors

No one needs reminding that culture doesn't always push the right beliefs. History is filled with discarded beliefs once fervently endorsed by nearly everyone but seen as perfectly silly by subsequent generations. We no longer believe that bloodletting is a cure for much of anything, that witches roam our streets, that magnets can cure mental and physical disorders. Still, while it is easy to show that public opinion is sometimes wrong, we should not fall into the error of assuming that it is never correct. On average, I suspect (but cannot prove), cultures more or less get it right at least for their time and place. Despite the fact that many of my culturally ordained beliefs of today will seem peculiar to my great-great-grandchildren, those beliefs work pretty well for me in the present. So I will continue to go to my physician and take the medications she prescribes even though I suspect that in a century or so this will seem quite primitive, indeed perhaps flat out wrong. We're stuck with the beliefs we have, even though we know they may likely be false, because we have no other choice.

Yes, silly beliefs sometimes result from cultural indoctrination, but cultures, and for that matter our friends and neighbors, are not engaged in some diabolical conspiracy to lead us down the paths of error. It's just the ways things work out. Cultures have to stand for something – a culture that endorsed everything and allowed us to believe whatever we wished would not be doing its job. Nor are we conforming sheep when we rely on culturally sanctioned beliefs. To be sure, sometimes we believe what other people tell us because it is comfortable or because we fear ridicule for our disagreements. But mostly we accept what we are taught or other people tell us for the best of reasons, namely that, at least within a particular time and context, cultural beliefs are far more often right than wrong and, within that context, good guides to behavior.

However, the downside is that most of us do not get fully exposed to the wide range of options available within a culture, not to mention across cultures. Parents, schools, and other socialization agents present a restricted menu of intellectual options, and as adults we associate with people at work, in our neighborhoods, at our churches and synagogues, who share our basic beliefs.

When the belief machine gives too much weight to social and cultural support, anomalous beliefs can pop up. The person who wants to believe that Satanic cults molest and kill innocent children can easily find books giving firsthand reports of such goings on (I personally have a dozen or so such books in my library). The Internet also has many sites devoted to the dangers of Satanic cults. Some churches sponsor speakers who give flamboyant testimonials of these evil enterprises, and when Geraldo announces on national television that possibly 1 million babies a year are killed by Satanists, fantasy becomes reality. Those who believe in UFO alien abductions have relevant workshops, Internet sites, and books galore. Militant right-wing conspiracy theories are supported by some conservative talk show hosts. When Larry King presents known fake mind-readers and mediums as genuine, some otherwise skeptical people figure there must be some truth to the ideas because he would not present it otherwise. Smoke and fire.

The social nature of anomalous beliefs is seen most clearly in rumors surrounding ideologically conditioned fears. Witchcraft fears in 16th- and 17th-century Europe resulted in the deaths of thousands of innocent people. More recently we have had our own witchcraft crazes; during the 1980s several dozen daycare workers were accused of sexually molesting children in their care, and although some of these cases may have been genuine, most were, in hindsight, not. Usually these cases resulted from one or two parents reporting possible abuse, which was then fanned into a frenzy by the police, media, social workers, and psychologists who were convinced that such abuse is routine (Pendergrast, 1995). Another instructive case occurred in a small town in New York, where citizens transformed a few counterculture teenagers into a Satanic cult within a few weeks (Victor, 1993).

Ideological Factors

As these examples make clear, such beliefs do not arise in a mental vacuum. Most anomalous beliefs would soon wither away if not supported by others and tied in with larger ideologies. The belief machine nourishes beliefs that are consistent with our ideologies.[2] There is nothing sinister about this. We all have religious, political, economic, and scientific beliefs that, among other things, provide us with filters and criteria for evaluating the truth of beliefs. Since I believe strongly in the validity of modern physics, I am highly skeptical of claims that pyramids release hidden energies, but another person who is more inclined to mysticism than science would probably have the opposite belief. Furthermore, my beliefs about such matters encourage me to judge any alleged evidence in support quite critically, whereas our mystical friend would not be so critical. Someone whose religious beliefs include the idea that Satan is among us doing his evil things will surely be more predisposed to believe in the existence of Satanic cults – after all Satan needs helpers – than those who are less inclined to supernatural explanations. Right-wing militia groups who believe that evil forces are taking over American society have well-developed core beliefs about the values of individualism, patriotism, government control, and usually racial superiority that help support their beliefs that using force to fight the government is reasonable and just.

Unfortunately, when the belief machine overemphasizes ideologies and allows them too much freedom, it fosters anomalous beliefs. When we think of political or for that matter religious extremists, we are usually referring to people whose beliefs are dictated by their ideologies to a much larger degree than by other hooks into reality. Terrorists whose beliefs are out of touch with accepted ethical realities and usually the practicalities of political change are one salient example.

The Importance of Science and Accepted Standards for Validation

In our culture, science is usually seen as the arbitrator of truth for issues that fall within its domain, but unfortunately many people are ignorant of and skeptical about the value of science. Science does not, of course, have all the answers. It cannot tell us for sure whether God exists, whether income

---

[2] The term *ideology* now has a somewhat negative connotation as a vaguely deviant set of beliefs held by other people. I am using the term in its original (and still dominant) meaning as an organized set of beliefs or concepts. Thus, religions, political persuasions, and beliefs in capitalism as well as socialism are all ideologies.

taxes are too high or low, or whether the Houston Astros will ever win a World Series. And even in those domains that are genuinely scientific, all educated people understand that scientists are not immune to error. It's both mildly amusing and humbling to look at science books from a century ago – amusing because scientists believed some fairly simple-minded things and humbling because our descendants in 2105 will look at our science with equal amusement. That having been said, science has a really fine batting average. Moreover, at least during the past four centuries or so, it has had a consistent record of self-correction, although sometimes with unseemly slowness. The reasons we no longer believe that sperm contain little children ready to do their thing inside the womb is because science marches on. The history of our understanding of human reproduction is filled with errors, some actually amusing, but in the end we can tell a more or less linear story of how each of us got from there to here.

It is too much to ask that all of our beliefs be consistent with scientific knowledge, but when our beliefs are wildly inconsistent with it, alarms should go off because the belief machine is heated up and about to explode. Anomalous beliefs are usually dramatically unscientific and have more to do with magical thinking than with reality testing (Zusne & Jones, 1989). Science teaches us to reject beliefs that the world is flat, people live on the moon, that our thinking is controlled by little people in our heads. We do not believe these things because even those of us with limited scientific background and curiosity understand that such beliefs violate major physical and biological laws. If someone discovered trolls in a cave tomorrow, it is going to take a bunch of scientists by surprise.

We're not all scientists, of course, so what's the nonscientist to do? Because science is sometimes wrong, we don't exactly feel we are on safe ground in *completely* trusting it. Still it's the best guide we have for beliefs that fall within its domain. Science helps us at three distinct levels. First, it provides models for how to think about issues clearly and systematically. Second, it provides models for how to test claims that can indeed be tested empirically. Third, it provides a systematic body of knowledge that more or less defines what is normal. Let's demonstrate by considering astrology.

Clear Thinking

Scientists are not, of course, the only people who think clearly, nor are they perfectly immune from fuzzy thinking of their own. Still, approaching a problem scientifically usually leads to productive questions that often have answers. In the first instance it helps us evaluate the adequacy of theories. From a scientific perspective we require that good theories be clear and consistent. The first problem with astrology is that there are lots of logical inconsistencies, not to mention profound disagreements among different astrology systems about how to use the relevant data to make predictions (Culver & Lanna, 1988). Much of astrology is based on ancient Babylonian theories and observations, and since the earth's orientation in space changes (that is, the North Pole points in different directions over time), the astrological signs of the zodiac are no longer aligned with the constellations that gave them their names 2,000 years ago. So whereas the sun was at one point in the constellation of Scorpio during the month of November (hence people born at this time are named Scorpios), now it is in the constellation of Virgo during this period. Modern astrology therefore is based on outdated concepts (Culver & Lanna, 1988; Zusne & Jones, 1989). Trusting a theory that is so temporally out of whack makes about as much sense as trusting your physician were she to suggest that your humors were misaligned (as ancient doctors believed). Moreover, even if we overcome this problem, different astrologers use different systems to make their predictions; it would be a scandal if two engineers could not agree on what basic physical principles to use in building a bridge. Scientists don't always agree, but they usually don't disagree about such fundamental matters.

Since astrology was not taught in your high school, you can be forgiven if you were unaware of these problems. But you can still think rigorously, just a scientist would, about the issues. Suppose you believe that your astrological signature has affected your personality. Now I encourage you to think about what that must mean. A perfectly reasonable question that anyone (scientist or not) could come up with might be to ask when this influence took place. Conventionally, according to astrologers, it took place at the time of birth. Then you might ask what it means to be born. When your mother starts her contractions, when the doctor says the baby is coming, your little head pokes its way out, when your whole body emerges, when the doctor or nurse clears your lungs so you can start breathing comfortably? You do not have to have a doctorate in physics or biology to pose these questions and to understand that astrology's vague responses to them indicates a mushy core to the theory.

A person with rigorous common sense might go on to ask how the effect manifests itself. If somehow the position of the planets affects you as you emerge from your mother's body, why can't it affect you earlier, say at 8 months of gestation, when you are ignorant of what is about to befall you? Why not 2 days after birth? In other words, what is so special about birth in this scheme of things? And speaking of that, why not at conception? That's a discrete event, and given that your genetic identity is set at that point, isn't that a more meaningful time for influence to take place? As you pose these sorts of questions you might well consider that astrology doesn't take them into account, because when it was invented people didn't know much about conception or the laws of physics.

Recipes for Testing

You don't have to be a scientist to recognize the importance of testing predictions. Astrology does make predictions; at the crudest level your sign is supposed to predict your personality. For example, Leos (my sign) are sup-posed to be assertive and leaders much like the lion that gives them the name. So let's do a systematic study – that's what we do to test predictions. We'll get a whole bunch of people – college students will work just fine for this – and give them personality tests that measure assertiveness. Then it is a simple matter to see whether the Leos actually score higher on these tests than others, say Virgos. Well, guess what? Such tests have been done many, many times (I've done them myself in large Intro Psych classes), and the personalties of people with different signs do not differ significantly more than chance (Zusne & Jones, 1989).

Astrologers also claim to be able to predict the future or at least to give us information about favorable and unfavorable times for certain activities. Of course, we have to make sure they give us exact predictions. Saying that July 1 is a favorable financial time for a Leo isn't very exact, because almost anything could be made to confirm that prediction. When astrologers are forced to make exact predictions (which they hate to do, by the way) they almost always fail. Again, you don't have to be a trained researcher to know that. If astrologers could make accurate predictions about good financial times, they'd all be rich.

The Fit With Existing Science

One important rule that governs all science might be called *connectivity* (Stanovich, 2004) or sometimes *convergence*. This simple rule says that new scientific discoveries must be consistent with previous scientific theories. People with little knowledge about the history of science often think that it proceeds through gigantic leaps forward, so that the Newtons, Darwins, and Einsteins use their genius to fashion new scientific theories that completely overthrow old and outmoded ways of thinking about the world. However, science almost never progresses this way. New theories and discoveries build on prior science and can largely accommodate it. For example, although Galileo and Newton did propose radical new ways of thinking about the world, their proposals were built on a fairly extensive database of physical phenomena. Furthermore, they did not so much discover gravitation as show how it operated systematically, and what they overthrew was not previous science as much as it was muddled philosophy masquerading as science. The earlier belief that things fall to the ground because it is in their nature to do so is not a scientific statement any more than saying students fail to study hard enough for exams, because, well, it's in their nature to do so. Arguments that conclude that something happens because it's all in the essence are almost always incomplete and wrong (Stanovich, 2004).

The main problem with astrology (and for that matter with ESP) is that there's no way to account for how it might work. Astrologers are vague about this (again vagueness being a telltale sign), usually referring to some sort of occult forces unknown to science, but within the world of physics, gravitation must do the work because the other forces known to modern physics (electromagnetic and the strong and weak forces inside atoms) cannot. To be sure, Neptune and all the other planets did have a particular alignment at the moment of my birth; there is some tiny but presumably measurable gravitational pull from Neptune on my body now and at the time of birth. But the effects of that pull are so tiny that it's hard to imagine that they could affect anything. Indeed, the gravitational pull of the doctor who helped deliver me is far greater than any effects from such distant planets. It just doesn't add up. Similarly, those who believe in ESP have no way to explain how my thoughts get to your head or how things that might happen tomorrow make their way into my present dreams. No such explanations fit the science of today and almost certainly not that of tomorrow.

Science Doesn't Have All the Answers

One common response to this sort of criticism is that science doesn't "have all the answers," and that just because in the early days of this century we can't figure out how heavenly bodies do their astrological work or how thoughts migrate from one mind to another doesn't mean we won't be able to explain such effects in the future. Although this argument cannot be absolutely refuted, it is vacuous and it fails to understand how science works. It is vacuous because it is a claim that could made about anything, those we think we understand and those we do not. Suppose Jon argues that biological inheritance has nothing to do with DNA but rather is guided by some master alien force. You might tell Jon that this is nonsense because it fits no known laws of science, and his response is that "Well, science doesn't have all the answers." Yeah, and . . . ?

Obviously there are many important things science does not attempt to explain and a good many others for which it has incomplete knowledge. But whatever new forces that can affect humans at birth and transport ideas across space will have to fit with what we already know. That's the way science progresses. A discovery of some force that can affect personality at birth would require a complete revamping of physics, much as discovering that a previously unknown hormone that precisely dictates the time of our death would require a whole new biology.

I might add, somewhat in passing, that not only do ESP and astrology fail almost every known test of physical science, but also those of biology. Not only do we not have any idea how thoughts can get from one brain to another, but as far as we know there are no brain or for that matter liver parts that send such thoughts or receptors that decode them. Nor are we likely to discover brain bits that respond to gravitational forces from Neptune.

The Problem of Pseudoscience

Unfortunately the lure of scientific respectability is so strong that many anomalous beliefs claim scientific respectability. However, such claims almost always fall short because either the theories are vacuous or the data not reliable. Science is largely a public endeavor, and it is part of a community effort. Among other things, that means that not only are the results of scientific experiments and observations publicly reported, but also that enough detail about how the results were obtained (the methods) are also public, such that any independent person with the right training and equipment can replicate the results. Usually the data claimed in support of anomalous beliefs cannot be replicated independently by using well-established methods. Astrologers sometimes have major battles over how to make their predictions, which is not a good start for something that pretends to be science.

Another feature of legitimate science is that it has hypotheses that lead to concrete predictions, predictions that can be tested through experiment or systematic observation. Just because someone claims that their theory is scientific doesn't make it so. For example, so-called creationist science, which claims that the theory of evolution is wrong, makes no predictions that can be easily tested (Shermer, 1997). To say that God planted the extensive fossil record used in support of evolutionary theory may or may not be true, but it is impossible to verify. Similarly, just because astrologers use numbers and equations and wrap their ideas in the mantle of science does not mean that the theories represent true science.

Misleading Science

A more common problem is that results or ideas of science are presented in such a way that they are misleading. Advertisers take advantage of our noncritical approach to science in many ways. The attractive spokesperson dressed in a lab coat seems authoritative. He certainly looks like everyone's stereotype of a scientist, and as he speaks for his product, graphs flow across the screen showing marked reduction in whatever ailment is affected by the product. Of course what they don't tell you is that many other products may be equally or even better at reducing symptoms. The claim that no aspirin is recommended by doctors more than X brand does not mean that brand X is the most recommended – it may be that Y is recommended just as often or that doctors do not recommend pain relievers by name so that none are recommended. True science doesn't need flashy graphs or serious-looking spokespersons or media exposure at all.

One ought also to be wary of someone trying to make a profit by throwing around lots of scientific jargon. For example, there is a notion that people somehow use only a small part of their brains (the usually quoted figure is 10%) and that various programs or exercises can help individuals recruit unused portions to improve intelligence and creativity. In the first place this claim is ludicrous on the face of things because the brain is an expensive organ to run (it uses approximately 20% of the energy expended by the body), and it's unlikely that evolutionary forces would have operated to produce such waste. It's also fairly silly because it rests on a false metaphor, namely that the mind can be strengthened much like a muscle.

But somehow the 10% use is an appealing idea for many, and so programs exist that claim they will double or even triple your brain power (presumably so that you now use 20% or even 30% of your brain). The programs might consist of various memory and other intellectual exercises, and people who complete these programs often do show gains in various reasoning tasks. But, of course, that has nothing to do with using more of your brain. Obviously neural connections have been changed in relevant parts of the cortex, but it is highly unlikely that there is a huge hunk of cortex sitting idle that suddenly springs to life. Whether or not the exercises are useful has nothing to do with unused parts of the brain. To be sure, the claim seems scientific because we all know that the study of the brain is Real Science, but in reality it is nothing more than advertisers using pseudoscience.

WHY THIS IS IMPORTANT

Why should we care? After all most of us are, almost by definition, satisfied with the beliefs we have. So I believe in astrology; big deal – harmless fun isn't it? However, believing in astrology is a big deal if its predictions lead me to do things not in my best interests. Moreover, a belief in astrology creates a mind set that gives personal experiences more credibility than the huge weight of scientific evidence. I suppose no one is really harmed if you are convinced that your dream 2 weeks ago accurately predicted your uncle's unexpected death the next day, but I suspect your aunt might have a critical anxiety attack if you phone her to tell her about your latest dream of her unfortunate demise.

But a more important reason is that it is, of course, imperative that we bring as much rationality as possible to bear on problems in an increasingly complex society. As it is, many problems are slipping out of our grasp because of their complexity, and this process can only be accelerated if our bag of solutions is filled with the garbage of false and unsubstantiated beliefs. Whether you think of yourself as a political liberal or conservative (or something in between), you can find plenty of public policies, liberal or conservative, that are guided by largely incorrect beliefs.

For example, although the data are somewhat ambiguous, there is no clear evidence that the death penalty deters murder or that long prison sentences deter most crimes; such effects if they exist (and I believe they do not) are tiny (Feldman, 1993). Yet, common sense and political agendas about the effectiveness of harsh penalties continue to guide our criminal justice policies, and often create solutions that do more harm than good, especially to members of racial minorities (Tonry, 1995). Furthermore, as the recent report on intelligence failures before 9/11 and the invasion of Iraq point out, erroneous beliefs can lead to catastrophic errors (Radford, 2004).

These and many other examples show that bad beliefs lead to bad policies, which create more harm than good.

BELIEFS AS BETS

Unfortunately the belief machine is too mechanical and stupid to provide hints as to which of your beliefs are true and which are not. The world might be a better although less interesting place if there were a National Bureau of Correct Beliefs to which we could turn for ultimate answers. There are, however, some standard tests you can employ. Probably the safest and quickest test is that if a belief sounds too good to be true, then it probably isn't true. Yes, it would be nice if drinking tomato juice or watching comedies could make cancers go away, but such claims ought to be treated with the same caution as you would a letter announcing that a man in Nigeria is holding $10,000,000 for you. If it's too weird to be true it's probably false. Of course, what is weird to one generation may be established beliefs to the next; beliefs that men would go to the moon or people would communicate via computers would have seemed weird indeed a century ago. But be careful, because there were far more weird beliefs of a century ago that were false and silly. Of all the things that are promised today, it is a safe bet that the great majority of these will never be practical, a few will be practical but inconsequential, and only a tiny number truly transforming. Under these circumstances the betting person would win big time by simply seeing strange beliefs for what they are. If beliefs violate established theories and procedures in science, beware. If a belief is totally out of whack with what most people believe, you should have a good look at your belief machine. As I have stressed, beliefs too good to be true may still be so, weird beliefs are sometimes correct, and science, common sense, and consensus don't always get it right. However, anomalous beliefs fail one and usually several of these tests. A properly calibrated belief machine would assess beliefs against each of these criteria, but it often fails at that task.

Think of beliefs as being bets. You are a betting person whether or not you realize it. If you would rather drive the 400 miles to your grandmother's house for Thanksgiving than fly, you are betting that you will be safer in a car than in the air (based on a false belief in this case). In effect when you signed up for the psychology course you may be taking, your belief that you would learn more interesting and important things by taking the course than by taking an English course or by taking no course at all caused you to bet on the psych course. Selecting a college or a career is a bet, as is voting.

Life is a betting game, and bets are guided by beliefs. The person who believes that the day will warm up so she wouldn't need a sweater is a betting sort of person just as much as if she bet on Silly Putty in the fourth race at Aqueduct. If I were given to gambling (which unfortunately I am not), I would want my bets to be based on the best odds I could find. Life decisions are mostly far more important than whether you can beat the house at blackjack. Some of the decisions you and I will make will be bad bets because we lacked important information and failed to use that at our disposal. But a person who wanted to win at the game of life would certainly want to act on the basis of the most accurate beliefs he could muster. Thus, the ultimate answer to the question of why beliefs matter is that those whose belief machines lead them astray will lose more of life's bets. Misery may love company, but it positively adores a corrupt belief machine.

References

Culver, R. B., & Lanna, P. A. (1988). *Astrology: True or false?* Buffalo, NY: Prometheus Books.

Feldman, P. (1993). *The psychology of crime.* New York: Cambridge University Press.

Frey, D. (1986). Recent research on selective exposure. In L. Berkowitz (Ed.), *Advances in experimental social psychology* (Vol. 19, pp. 41–80). Orlando, FL: Academic Press.

Gilbert, D. T. (1991). How mental systems believe. *American Psychologist, 46,* 107–119.

Gilovich, T. (1991). *How we know what isn't so: The fallibility of human reason in everyday life.* New York: The Free Press.

Hastorf, A. H., & Cantril, H. (1954). The saw a game: A case study. *Journal of Abnormal & Social Psychology, 49,* 129–134.

James, W. (1950). *The principles of psychology* (Vol. 2). New York: Dover. (Original work published 1890)

Kelly, I. W., Rotton, J., & Culver, R. (1985–1986). Moon was full and nothing happened. *Skeptical Inquirer, 10,* 129–143.

Kunda, Z. (1999). *Social cognition: Making sense of people.* Cambridge, MA: The MIT Press.

Lord, C. G., Ross, L., & Lepper, M. R. (1979). Biased assimilation and attitude polarization: The effects of prior theories on subsequently considered evidence. *Journal of Personality & Social Psychology, 54,* 74–85.

Moskowitz, G. B. (2005). *Social cognition.* New York: Guilford Press.

Olson, J. M., Roese, N. J., & Zanna, M. P. (1996). Expectancies. In E. T. Higgins & A. W. Kruglanski (Eds.), *Social psychology: Handbook of basic principles* (pp. 211–238). NY: Guilford Press.

Pendergrast, M. (1995). *Victims of memory.* Hinesburg, VT: Upper Access.

Piattelli-Palmarini, M. (1994). *Inevitable illusions: How mistakes of reason rule our minds.* New York: John Wiley.

Plous, S. (1993). *The psychology of judgment and decision making.* New York: McGraw-Hill.

Radford, B. (2004). Senate Intelligence Committee highlights need for skeptical inquiry. *Skeptical Inquirer, 28,* 12–14.

Robinson, R. J., Keltner, D., Ward, A., & Ross, L. (1995). Actual versus assumed differences in construal: "Naive realism" in intergroup perception and conflict. *Journal of Personality and Social Psychology, 68,* 404–417.

Ross, L., & Ward, A. (1996). Naive realism. In E. S. Reed, E. Tuiel, & T. Brown (Eds.), *Values and knowledge* (pp. 103–135). Mahwah, NJ: Erlbaum.

Schneider, D. J. (2004). *The psychology of stereotyping.* New York: Guilford Press.

Shermer, M. (1997). *Why people believe weird things: Pseudoscience, superstition, and other confusions of our Time.* New York: Freeman.

Stanovich, K. (2004). *How to think straight about psychology* (7th ed.). Boston: Allyn & Bacon

Tonry, M. (1995). *Malign neglect: Race, crime, and punishment in America.* New York: Oxford University Press.

Victor, J. S. (1993). *Satanic panic: The creation of a contemporary legend.* Chicago: Open Court.

Wittenbrink, B., Gist, P. L., & Hilton, J. L. (1997). Structural properties of stereotypic knowledge and their influences on the construal of social situations. *Journal of Personality & Social Psychology, 72,* 526–543.

Zusne, L., & Jones, W. H. (1989). *Anomalistic psychology: A study of magical thinking* (2nd ed.). Hillsdale, NJ: Erlbaum.

16

Critical Thinking and Ethics in Psychology

Celia B. Fisher, Adam L. Fried, and Jessica K. Masty

INTRODUCTION

The contributions of those in the field of psychology to society are in part based upon trust. The public places its trust in psychologists for their capacity to offer scientific knowledge and services that contribute to individual and social welfare. The public trusts psychologists to use acceptable scientific methods and to honestly report their research results. The legal system trusts psychologists to provide accurate and unbiased expert testimony during court proceedings. Finally, clients place their trust in psychologists who provide psychotherapy to maintain confidentiality, practice within the limits of their competence, and to give quality care. Psychologists who publish false results, violate confidentiality, or testify in court or practice in areas outside their training competence jeopardize the public trust in psychology as a discipline.

Professional ethics is concerned with doing what is right. In the discipline of psychology, doing what is right is associated with conducting oneself in ways that aspire to satisfy a number of moral principles. For example, psychologists make a commitment to conduct themselves in ways that maximize benefits and avoid harms to those with whom they work. They promote honesty in psychological science, teaching, and practice and strive to fulfill their role responsibilities to society. Finally, they treat people fairly and respect the dignity and worth of all with whom they work. In effect, psychologists are "active moral agents committed to the good and just practice and science of psychology" (Fisher, 2003, p. 237).

To help ensure that psychologists act responsibly, the American Psychological Association (APA), the largest association of psychologists in the world, requires its members to be familiar with and adhere to the APA Ethical Principles of Psychologists and Code of Conduct (APA, 2002a), known as the APA Ethics Code. The Ethics Code provides a set of general ethical principles as well as specific standards of conduct that can help psychologists prevent ethical problems and solve ethical dilemmas. However, psychologists often come up against complex ethical problems in which adherence to and knowledge of the APA Ethics Code alone do not provide a clear ethical path. Ethical dilemmas are present in all disciplines and psychology is no exception. When an ethical dilemma emerges, there are often many choices that may be ethical; identifying alternative solutions and selecting the most appropriate actions requires critical thinking.

Critical thinking, which refers to the cognitive skills involved in reasoning, making thoughtful inferences and judgments, and solving problems, is a complex endeavor when it comes to making decisions about ethical dilemmas. Because no set of rules, including the APA Ethics Code, can offer psychologists definitive "black or white" answers to complicated problems, critical thinking in psychology often involves making decisions in areas that are "shades of gray" (Halpern, in press). Therefore, finding the best solution to an ethical dilemma requires a careful consideration of context, guided by the psychologist's unique experiences as well as relevant professional values and legal boundaries. Knowledge of the APA Ethics Code and state and federal regulations for the conduct of responsible science and practice provides only one first step for ethical decision making. This chapter discusses additional steps that must be taken to ensure that psychologists' decisions reflect the standards of the profession and merit public trust.

Critical thinking about ethics requires a flexible thinking style. It involves careful analysis, creativity, and practical thinking skills. Some general skills for critical thinking in ethical decision making include the ability to acquire new information and to integrate it with previously learned concepts. Critical thinking also involves the ability to generate alternative solutions to a problem from old and new information and the ability to weigh the advantages and disadvantages of potential courses of action. The psychologist who is confronted with an ethical problem must have the ability to generate alternative solutions to the problem as well as the skills to evaluate and select the actions that will maximize benefits and minimize negative consequences. A complementary skill requires psychologists to be able to evaluate the feasibility of alternative solutions; that is, solutions that can be effectively implemented. Critical thinking in ethical decision making also requires a commitment to and competence for monitoring and evaluating the consequences of the selected solution to ensure that no unanticipated harm has come to the individuals involved; and to generate new alternatives to correct the harm when feasible. As you can see, thinking critically about ethics and ethical decision making is a multistep process that can be adapted for a wide range of problems and contexts. This chapter outlines some of the professional guidelines and values that psychologists use to make ethical decisions, describes an ethical decision-making process, and illustrates the application of critical thinking and ethical decision making to specific cases.

THE APA ETHICAL PRINCIPLES AND CODE OF CONDUCT

The development of a dynamic set of ethical standards for psychologists' work-related conduct requires a personal commitment and lifelong effort to act ethically; to encourage ethical behavior by students, supervisors, employees, and colleagues; and to consult with others concerning ethical problems. (APA, 2002b, Preamble)

The APA Ethics Code provides a set of ethical principles to which psychologists must aspire as well as a set of specific enforceable standards that require or prohibit specific behaviors. In other words, the Ethics Code is not simply a set of rules but rather a guide to help psychologists make decisions that promote the welfare of those they serve.

Aspirational Principles and Enforceable Standards

The Ethics Code is composed of two parts: five aspirational principles and over 100 specific enforceable standards governing work-related behavior. The five aspirational principles are the moral backbone of the profession and represent the values that psychologists, in their everyday work, strive to fulfill. The standards in the Ethics Code are derived from these principles. The standards articulate specific rules that psychologists must follow. They are directly related to psychologists' behaviors, applicable to all work-related activities, and enforceable by the APA and many state laws governing the activity of psychologists. All of the APA Ethics Code standards and principles can be found on the APA's Web site, at www.apa.org/ethics (APA, 2002a). In the list that follows, we describe the five aspirational principles and provide examples of specific enforceable standards derived from each principle.

A. Beneficence and Nonmaleficence

This principle directs psychologists to aspire to conduct their work in ways that maximize good results and minimize harms. Psychology as a profession strives to help people understand themselves and others through research, therapy, education, or consultation and to help improve the condition of society.

Enforceable standard: In most situations psychologists are prohibited from providing psychotherapy to students over whom they have direct teaching authority, because such a dual relationship is likely to impair the psychologist's objectivity and effectiveness and could lead to exploitation (APA Standard 3.05: Multiple Relationships).

B. Fidelity and Responsibility

People who work with psychologists must be able to trust them. Whether it is a client, research participant, or student, psychologists establish relationships based upon trust. Psychologists must be aware of their roles in and obligation to society and accept responsibility for their behaviors.

Enforceable standard: Teaching psychologists must provide students with course syllabi that accurately describe the course content and requirements. If for legitimate reasons a professor must change the curriculum during the semester, he or she must alert students to these changes and give them ample time to fulfill course requirements (APA Standard 7.03: Accuracy in Teaching).

C. Integrity

Psychologists are required to be honest and truthful in the science, teaching, and professional practice of psychology. They strive to keep their promises and make only those commitments they are likely to be able to keep.

Enforceable standard: Psychologists do not plagiarize or otherwise misrepresent research findings in any way. In doing so, psychology would jeopardize the trust of both the public and the scientific community in its findings, thus reducing psychology's ability to help others through its work (APA Ethical Standards 8.11: Plagiarism and 8.10: Reporting Research Results).

D. Justice

Psychologists must take steps to provide all people with fair, equitable, and appropriate access to the benefits of science, education, and treatment. To do so, psychologists must recognize their own prejudices and not allow them to interfere with their work-related duties.

Enforceable standard: Psychologists cannot deny academic admission or employment to an individual solely because that individual accused someone or was accused of sexual harassment. This does not prevent psychologists from taking action if they discover that the complaint was frivolous or that the individual had indeed engaged in the harassment (APA Standard 1.08: Unfair Discrimination Against Complainants and Respondents).

E. Respect for People's Rights and Dignity

Recognizing and respecting individual differences is a central theme in psychology. Not only do psychologists seek to understand how people differ, their methods for doing so must also respect these differences. Psychologists must consider how cultural, individual, and role differences may affect their work with others and consider such differences in ways that permit them to respect the rights of all individuals to privacy and self-governance.

Enforceable standard: When a psychologist is asked to conduct a mental health assessment of persons for whom English is a second language, he or she must ensure that the assessment methods are appropriate to the individual's language preference and competence and that the tests are valid for the person's cultural group (APA Standard 9.02: Use of Assessments).

APA PRINCIPLES AND STANDARDS AND THE CASE OF MS. THIN

Sometimes psychologists confront a situation in which an action that meets the goals of one moral principle appears to conflict with the goals of another principle. In this situation, critical thinking skills are necessary to determine which of the moral principles is more salient to the specific context. For example, informing relatives that a psychotherapy client is suicidal may protect the immediate welfare of the client, but also violate his or her right to privacy and self-determination. This seeming conflict among principles is called an *ethical dilemma*. Whether in research, teaching, consulting, or practice, psychologists face ethical dilemmas like this that require critical thinking for effective ethical decision making.

Rather than a static set of rules or a formula for solving ethical dilemmas, the APA ethical principles and enforceable standards provide guidance for psychologists as they navigate through an ethical dilemma. As we have discussed, in ethics, critical thinking requires, among other things, the ability to view a dilemma from multiple vantage points without allowing personal bias to interfere with judgment (Meltzoff, 1998). As we discuss in greater detail later in this chapter, it also requires familiarity with existing ethical standards and relevant laws as well as the ability to generate and compare alternative solutions that can resolve the dilemma. Critical thinking can also help psychologists anticipate and avoid ethical dilemmas before they arise. Unfortunately, too many professionals, including psychologists, consider the consequences of their decisions only after dilemmas arise. Those who can use critical thinking skills in psychology will be able to identify and consider the key components of a situation to ensure that preventable harm does not occur and to remediate harm when it does occur, thus meriting the trust of those with whom they work. In the following paragraphs we present an ethical dilemma faced by a clinical psychologist and the relevant APA ethical principles and standards she must consider as she attempts to resolve the dilemma.

Dr. Donna Know, a psychologist in private practice, has an initial consultation with a potential new therapy client, Ms. Thin, who appears to have a serious eating disorder. Although Dr. Know had excellent doctoral training in treating depression and anxiety disorders, she has no formal training or experience treating eating disorders. Should Dr. Know accept Ms. Thin as a client?

Stakeholder Perspectives

There are certain key points that Dr. Know must critically consider in making an ethical decision. First, she needs to consider her potential client's state of mind and potential perspectives on any decisions that would be made. Persons who will be directly affected by a psychologist's actions are *stakeholders*. Sometimes there is only one stakeholder in a psychologist's work (i.e., a young adult to whom a psychologist is providing vocational counseling). Frequently, there are multiple stakeholders. For example, the stakeholders of a research project involving children in a school include not only the children, but also the parents of the children, the school staff, the scientific community, and people or groups that stand to benefit or be harmed from the information derived from such research.

Getting back to the case of Ms. Thin, imagine if you were Ms. Thin and suppose you have been afraid to seek therapy. Now that you have finally taken the plunge and found a psychologist with whom you have rapport, you want to get on with the therapy and not shop around for another therapist. How would you feel if Dr. Know told you she could not see you as a client? Suppose Dr. Know did decide to take you on as a client; would you want to know whether she had sufficient training to help you with your problem? If she failed to tell you she had no experience working with individuals with eating disorders, would you continue to trust her if your condition was not improving?

What if Dr. Know told Ms. Thin about her lack of experience: Would her responsibility for providing competent services end with informing Ms. Thin about her limitations? Would this be perceived as professionally responsible by Ms. Thin? Would it meet the aspirational principle of fidelity and responsibility?

Competence

Under most conditions, the APA Ethics Code prohibits psychologists in all fields from providing services, teaching, or conducting research in areas in which they have not had the appropriate training (Standard 2.01: Standards of Competence). Why do you think there is such a general rule? Psychologists can only benefit those with whom they work if they have the specific knowledge and skills to address the work challenge. Ms. Thin did not initially decide to go to Dr. Know's office to find a friend. Rather she came to find a professional who was trained to help her solve her problems. According to Standard 2.01, Dr. Know should refuse to accept Ms. Thin as a client because she lacks any training in treating eating disorders. It is probably in the best interest of Ms. Thin, who may be at risk for very serious health complications due to her illness, to be referred to another clinician who specializes in treatments for eating disorders. However, the reader should note that Dr. Know's narrow educational background is probably rare. In reality, the APA requires that psychology doctoral program curricula be broad and comprehensive in order for the program to be accredited. Therefore, there are many psychologists with broad educational experiences that cover a variety of disorders and treatment modalities. Although it may be preferred, it is not necessary for all individuals to be treated by specialists. The key here is that the psychologist know his or her own limitations and consult other professionals or refer patients to other clinicians when it is in the best interest of the patient to do so.

Terminating Therapy

There are many reasons why psychologists may be ethically bound to terminate psychotherapy. According to APA Standard 10.10: Terminating Therapy, psychologists should not continue seeing a client if the client is not likely to benefit from the treatment, if the client has improved to the extent that he or she no longer needs the therapy, or would be harmed by continued service. However, simply refusing to help Ms. Thin may also be harmful if it deters her from seeking help elsewhere. Thus another step in solving this ethical dilemma is for Dr. Know to discuss with Ms. Thin the reasons she cannot see her and provide Ms. Thin with the names and contact information of other therapists who are trained to work with individuals with eating disorders.

Providing Therapy in Underserved Areas

Let's imagine there is one more wrinkle to this ethical dilemma. Dr. Know practices in a small rural township in which she is the only mental health professional within 500 miles of where Ms. Thin lives. If Dr. Know cannot accept Ms. Thin as a client, there is the strong possibility that she will not receive treatment for this serious health disorder. What should Dr. Know do? Under these circumstances there is another portion of Standard 2.01 that permits psychologists to provide psychotherapy to individuals for whom other mental health services are not available, as long as the psychologists have related training and they make reasonable efforts to get the training, supervision, or experience necessary to provide competent services. Thus, under these special circumstances, Dr. Know may provide psychotherapy to Ms. Thin as long as she makes reasonable efforts to obtain the competence required. She might accomplish this by seeking supervision via telephone or the Internet from a qualified expert in eating disorders, reading appropriate training materials, and attending professional workshops on eating disorders. It would also be incumbent on Dr. Know to carefully assess over time whether Ms. Thin is being helped, harmed, or not benefiting from her services so that other means of helping the client can be arranged.

STEPS IN ETHICAL DECISION MAKING

Although it is imperative that psychologists familiarize themselves with the APA Ethics Code and follow professional standards, familiarity with the APA Ethics Code alone is not enough. As indicated in the case of Ms. Thin, often the problems with which psychologists are confronted are complex

TABLE 16.1. *Fisher's Eight-Step Decision-Making Model for Ethics in Psychology*

1. Develop and sustain a professional commitment to doing what is right.
2. Acquire sufficient familiarity with the APA Ethics Code general principles and ethical standards to be able to anticipate situations that require ethical planning and to identify unanticipated situations that require ethical decision making.
3. Gather additional facts relevant to the specific ethical situation from professional guidelines, state and federal laws, and organizational policies.
4. Make efforts to understand the perspective of different stakeholders who will be affected by the decision and consult with colleagues.
5. Apply Steps 1–4 to generate ethical alternatives and evaluate each alternative in terms of moral theories, general principles, and ethical standards.
6. Select and implement an ethical course of action.
7. Monitor and evaluate the effectiveness of the course of action.
8. Modify and continue to evaluate the ethical plan if necessary.

Source: From Fisher (2003).

and do not fit neatly under a particular standard. Therefore, in order to find solutions to complicated dilemmas, psychologists must have a knowledge of, and commitment to, moral values for ethical practice. They also must have the ability to integrate these values in thinking critically about the problem in order to discover the most appropriate and ethical solution.

Because people and their life experiences are intrinsically unique, a psychologist may be confronted with a situation he or she has never encountered before. This new problem may be due to an unforeseen event or an individual's unexpected reaction to some event. What are psychologists to do when they realize that by following one standard they may be violating another? How does the psychologist decide which strategy to adopt when two ethical principles are seemingly in conflict?

Fisher (2003) has proposed an eight-step model for ethical decision making that emphasizes critical thinking based upon a "goodness of fit" between the potential ethical alternatives, the psychologist's role, and the needs of the stakeholders (see Table 16.1). The model also draws upon the motivation of psychologists to act ethically and their ability to critically evaluate alternative actions, and continue to evaluate the consequences of the ethical decision once it is made.

Step 1: Develop and sustain a professional commitment to doing what is right. Ethical psychologists "do what is right because it is right" (Josephson Institute of Ethics, 1999). This commitment to principled behavior and virtuous practice reflects a degree of moral character in the professional that propels him or her to make the "best" choices for clients, research subjects, and students. Although different psychologists may give preference to different virtues, most believe that kindness, care, and compassion are personal characteristics essential to making ethical decisions. The ethical psychologist strives to be conscientious by trying to determine what is right and by putting forth every effort to behave accordingly. The virtuous psychologist also is discerning; he or she uses contextual information and sensitivity to understand each situation as thoroughly as possible in order to make good judgments. Additionally, the morally responsible psychologist values prudence and uses practical wisdom to resolve problems. A lifelong dedication to morals and virtues becomes a firm foundation from which psychologists can face a variety of ethical challenges.

Step 2: Acquire sufficient familiarity with the APA Ethics Code general principles and ethical standards to be able to anticipate situations that require ethical planning and to identify unanticipated situations that require ethical decision making. To work competently and responsibly, psychologists need to be familiar with the ethical values and standards regulating their field. They must be aware of common ethical questions and be able to identify situations in which ethical dilemmas may arise so that harm and injustice can be avoided. When ethical challenges do surface, the APA Ethics Code and ethical standards should be viewed as tools that psychologists can use to guide them toward good decision making. Facility with these tools enables psychologists to create plans of action that will help them anticipate and avoid problems, and more easily use their critical thinking skills to solve ethical dilemmas as they occur.

Step 3: Gather additional facts relevant to the specific ethical situation from professional guidelines, state and federal laws, and organizational policies. It is insufficient for a psychologist to know and abide by the APA Ethics Code alone, as laws and professional or organizational guidelines may limit the course of action the psychologist may be able to take. Very few APA ethical standards explicitly require that psychologists act according to federal or state laws, but the violation of such laws may harm those with whom the psychologists work and have punitive consequences for psychologists and their institutions. There are federal regulations or state laws governing all fields of psychology. For example, psychologists conducting federally funded research involving human participants must comply with the Code of Federal Regulations, Protection of Human Subjects (U.S. Department of Health and Human Services, 2001) and those researching animals must comply with the Health Research Extension Act of 1985 (Public Law 99-158) that regulates humane care of animals. Practitioner psychologists must be familiar with and adhere to specific state laws governing licensed psychologists. Industrial-organizational psychologists conducting employment testing must be familiar with the Americans With Disabilities Act of 1990. Therefore, psychologists need to gather additional facts about relevant laws and rules in order to make a critical evaluation of ethical alternatives.

Step 4: Make efforts to understand the perspective of different stakeholders who will be affected by the decision, and consult with colleagues. Ethical decisions made by psychologists in mental health clinics, research laboratories, college campuses, or business settings may differentially affect various stakeholders. In addition, how stakeholders react to the actions of psychologists may be dependent upon their cultural, educational, economic, and other back-ground characteristics. In some situations, an experienced psychologist will know a great deal about the values and needs of members of these pop-ulations. At other times it will be essential to actively explore stakeholder perspectives. It is also important to note that for any one ethical dilemma, multiple stakeholders like parents, children, and schools may have very dif-ferent views of the psychologist's role and be differentially affected by the psy-chologist's decisions. Before making an ethical decision, psychologists must familiarize themselves with and critically evaluate stakeholder expectations and potential consequences of possible solutions to an ethical dilemma. An understanding of stakeholder perspectives will help the psychologist gener-ate alternative ethical solutions.

An important resource for placing stakeholder views in the appropriate perspective is to consult with colleagues. It is important for psychologists to have colleagues with whom they can discuss complicated issues. Clini-cal psychologists can engage colleagues with specific expertise in ethics or members of their state psychological association as consultants to explore difficult issues in practice; psychology researchers may turn to members of their institutional review board with questions regarding the ethics of their research projects; teaching psychologists can draw upon the expertise of their chair, dean, or more experienced colleagues. Consultants can help colleagues illuminate new points of view, anticipate unforeseen obstacles, and provide general support for the psychologist. Additionally, it is a valu-able experience for psychologists to articulate their own decision-making process in the company of professional peers. In doing so, psychologists become explicitly aware of their own critical thinking process, which con-tributes to better decision-making over all (Halpern, in press).

Step 5: Apply Steps 1–4 to generate ethical alternatives and evaluate each alter-native in terms of moral theories, general principles, and ethical standards. A chief component of critical thinking is the ability to generate and evaluate alter-native solutions to a problem. When a psychologist is committed to doing what is right, knows the APA Ethics Code and relevant laws, and has an understanding of stakeholders' points of view, the psychologist has a solid background upon which to build a series of possible plans of action. The psychologist should generate as many potential solutions as possible, and then evaluate each of them in reference to APA aspirational principles and ethical standards, state and federal laws, the diverse needs and expectations of stakeholders, and the practical aspects of the situation.

Step 6: Select and implement an ethical course of action. After critically eval-uating each alternative, psychologists should choose the most appropriate course of action and apply it. The critical thinking involved in this selec-tion includes comparing each alternative on the various dimensions just discussed, weighing the harms and goods that will emerge from each alter-native for each stakeholder, and evaluating the certainty of the harms–goods assessment and whether new information is required. During this comparative process, new solutions may emerge that combine elements of the different alternatives. Once the best course of action is identified, in some situations it may be appropriate for psychologists to explain the decision to stakeholders and let them know that their needs have been considered.

Step 7: Monitor and evaluate the effectiveness of the course of action. It is not enough for psychologists to implement a plan of action. Often, actions have unforeseen consequences and even ethical decisions made with the best intentions may need to be reevaluated. An ethical decision put into action is a dynamic process. Psychologists may wish to consult stakeholders to ensure that the plan is working and that no troublesome unforeseen events have occurred. As the course of action unfolds, it is important to continue to monitor the decision in relation to the APA Ethics Code, relevant laws, and intended and unintended effects on stakeholders.

Step 8: Modify and continue to evaluate the ethical plan if necessary. Psychologists are not fortune-tellers. It is not always easy to foresee the consequences of a decision that may affect multiple individuals. Sometimes, promising solutions have unintended negative effects. When a course of action has not produced desirable results, psychologists should attempt to modify the plan of action and monitor and evaluate the new plan's progress and consequences. Again, psychologists should consult colleagues, refer to the Ethics Code and state and federal laws, and seek stakeholder feedback to ensure that the best possible (and most ethical) solution is chosen in light of the new information. Modifications to each version of the plan should be made until the most suitable solution for the problem is found.

ETHICAL DECISION MAKING IN A CLINICAL CONTEXT: THE CASE OF DAN GEROUS

Dan Gerous, a college student, just learned that some of the students in his dorm are spreading rumors that he is HIV positive. He has been seeking help from Dr. Tell, a psychologist at the college counseling center, for the depression and rage he is experiencing as a result of the bullying and isolation he feels in the dorm. Dan tells Dr. Tell that at the next dorm party he is going to spike some drinks with the drug Ecstasy to get back at some of the students. Although Dr. Tell attempts to change Dan's mind, she is unable to sway him from this plan. Dr. Tell is concerned about the welfare of the other students, but is also aware that by notifying others of Dan's plan, she is breaching client–therapist confidentiality and stigmatizing Dan even more among the other students. What course of action should the counselor take?

Let us suppose that Dr. Tell's first attempt at dissuading Dan through discussion during the counseling session did not work. Dr. Tell needs to use her critical thinking skills to formulate a new plan. She wants to protect the other students from harm (APA Standard 3.04: Avoiding Harm), but she

also has an obligation to whenever possible protect the confidentiality of
those with whom she works (APA Standard 4.01: Confidentiality). Her ethical dilemma involves two competing professional guidelines. Dr. Tell must
rely on the ethical decision-making model to help her critically evaluate
which course of action is the most appropriate one to take in this case.

Initial Steps in the Decision-Making Process

Dr. Tell is aware that this situation requires a difficult ethical decision. She
must take principled action as a professional who is courageous, caring, and
prudent. She is committed to doing what is right (Step 1). Dr. Tell is familiar
with the APA ethical principles and standards (Step 2). She recognizes that
the aspirational principles of beneficence and nonmaleficence conflict in
this situation. If she takes steps to protect the other students from harm, she
will harm her relationship with her client and expose Dan, at minimum, to
peer antagonism and possibly university punitive actions. She is also aware
that she must identify the APA ethical standards most relevant to the situation. Standard 4.01: Maintaining Confidentiality stresses the psychologist's
primary obligation to protect the information her client has told her in
confidence. But in this case, Standard 4.05: Disclosures also applies. The
disclosure standard permits, but does not require, psychologists to disclose
confidential information when this action is necessary to protect others from
harm. Another standard, Standard 3.04: Avoiding Harm, also leads to seemingly contradictory decisions. Preventing Dan from harming his dorm mates
by disclosing the information to authorities will most likely result in negative
peer reaction and potential university punitive action. Dr. Tell checks the
policies of the counseling center and appropriate state laws for additional
guidance (Step 3). She finds that the university counseling center defers
to the APA for standards of practice and that her state laws permit professional discretion in these situations. Dr. Tell decides she needs additional
information. She calls Resident Director (RD) to find out if there is indeed
a party planned in the dorms that evening. She protects Dan's privacy by not
telling the RD why she is asking. The RD confirms that approximately 20
students will attend the party. Dr. Tell also calls the head of campus security
to find out more about university policy concerning students suspected of
harboring illegal drugs in the dorms and whether students have an option
to release drugs to the security office without punitive action.

Without mentioning Dan's name, Dr. Tell then consults the director of the
counseling center to discuss options. The supervisor and Dr. Tell examine
the implications of several alternatives (Step 5). Dr. Tell could attempt to
arrange a second meeting with Dan to try to dissuade him from the course
of action. However, if this did not work she would have to have another
option and, out of respect for Dan, inform him of what that option would
be. Additional options would be informing the Resident Director of Dan's

plans and working with her to prevent Dan from attending the party or canceling the party altogether. The former action would involve violating Dan's confidentiality by revealing that Dan was a client at the counseling center and by revealing his plans, both told in confidence. Once notified of the details, the RD would be required by university policy to initiate a formal investigation to determine whether Dan did indeed have illegal drugs in his dorm room, and this in turn could lead to Dan's suspension or expulsion. Both these actions would tend to stigmatize Dan more among his peers and further exacerbate his psychological problems. Dr. Tell and the counseling center director also recognize that permitting the party to go ahead without taking any action would compromise the APA ethical principles of fidelity and responsibility to students at the university.

Selecting, Monitoring, and Evaluating a Course of Action

After discussing these alternatives, a specific course of action emerges (Step 6). Dr. Tell will contact Dan for an emergency session. At that session she will attempt to dissuade him from his plan and ask him to destroy any drugs that he has in his dorm room. If he appears committed to carrying out his plan, Dr. Tell will explain her obligation to protect other students from harm and inform him that if he does not change his mind, she will notify the Resident Director that it has come to her attention that illicit drugs will be brought to the dorm party with potentially serious consequences for the students and urge the Resident Director to cancel the event and all other parties in the dorm until the matter is resolved. She lets Dan know that although she will take action to stop his plan, she will not reveal his identity to the Resident Director. She also recommends that Dan begin to attend counseling sessions more frequently so that they can together develop a plan to remove the drugs from his premises and work on positive ways he can address his anger and depression.

Dr. Tell initiates this alternative. She meets again with Dan, who agrees not to go to the party and to return for counseling the next day. At the next meeting she discusses with Dan what she learned from campus security about university policy with respect to how he could destroy or anonymously send the drugs over to the security office. Finally, Dr. Tell arranges to meet with Dan 3 days a week and to provide him with an emergency phone number to use if he feels his anger is again getting out of hand.

Dan agrees to go along with Dr. Tell's plan and begins to meet with Dr. Tell 3 days a week. Dr. Tell checks with the Resident Director to inquire if there had been any untoward events at the dorm and is relieved to find out there had not been (Step 7). Dan also tells Dr. Tell that he destroyed the drugs. After a 2-week period, Dan informs Dr. Tell that he is having constant thoughts about harming the students who are making fun of him. Dr. Tell concludes that she needs to take additional steps (Step 8). With

Dan's permission, she contacts a psychiatrist who will meet with Dan to determine whether medications may help to stem his anger and obsessive thoughts about harming others while he is being helped in counseling. Over the next few weeks, Dan's obsessive thoughts about harming others decrease. Dr. Tell continues to see Dan a 3 days a week. As the end of the semester approaches she helps Dan make arrangements to see a private clinician during the summer.

ETHICAL DECISION MAKING IN A RESEARCH CONTEXT: THE CASE OF DR. NICE

A group of researchers wants to study aggression in boys with conduct disorders. The principal investigator, Dr. Nice, designed a study that would take place at a local psychiatric hospital in-patient unit for adolescent males. The study involves asking each boy to play a competitive game against a peer and observing and recording the types of aggression that surface during the competitive play. Because these boys are being treated for exhibiting dangerous behaviors in the community, Dr. Nice expects to see a great deal of aggression come out during the game. He is excited that this experiment will allow him to measure the boys' tendencies to act aggressively in a realistic setting, because that will enhance the potential usefulness of the study results to service providers. However, knowing how violent these boys can be, he is also concerned that the boys could get carried away and might become overly aggressive and possibly hurt one another while living together on the hospital unit. Frequent fighting among the boys would compromise their treatment and would necessitate the premature termination of the research study. As Dr. Nice thinks more about this project, he begins to realize that the current research design will probably produce very good results, but it might jeopardize the treatment of the patients if they become angry and violent as a result of having participated. How can Dr. Nice balance his safety concerns for the research participants with his commitment to conducting a valid psychological experiment that produces a relatively accurate representation of how these children show aggression in competitive situations? (Adapted from Fisher, Hoagwood, & Jensen, 1996.)

Initial Decision-Making Steps

The researchers in this case are confronted with the challenge of doing good research and protecting their research subjects from harm. This is a difficult ethical issue that many researchers face. Often, important research questions have been left unanswered because the topics are socially sensitive or dangerous to study. In such cases, researchers must engage in critical thinking and responsible decision-making practices to ensure that the most ethical research design is chosen.

The fact that Dr. Nice is carefully planning the research project indicates he is dedicated to doing what is right (Step 1). He wants to conduct good research, but knows that the welfare of the research subjects cannot be compromised in order to create a better study. Dr. Nice is familiar with APA Ethics Code Standard 3.04: Avoiding Harm, which mandates that psychologists protect those with whom they work and take measures to avoid (or minimize) any potential harm (Step 2). He is also aware of federal regulations for the protection of research participants that require investigators to maximize research benefits and minimize research harms (Step 3). Even though Dr. Nice does not know for a fact that his experiment will cause the boys to fight more with each other, he understands that the project increases the *risk* that this will happen. So he begins to think of ways in which he can minimize the potential harm to the boys at the hospital.

Dr. Nice organizes a focus group composed of the hospital's therapists and the boys' parents to get their opinions regarding the value of this research and the possible effects this experiment may have on the patients (Step 4). The therapists on the unit encourage Dr. Nice to conduct this type of research, because they feel it is important to learn more about aggression and violence in children with behavioral disorders and the implications for treatment. However, the therapists and parents also express serious concerns regarding the low frustration tolerance and volatile mood states of the children. They are concerned the boys who compete against each other may end up fighting with one another after the "game" is over. Parents are also worried about the effect that losing will have on their children's very low self-esteem and frustration levels.

Dr. Nice and his research team brainstorm about alternative ways to tap into aggression without actually pitting the boys against each other in a game (Step 5). They realize that in order to arouse their aggressive natures, the boys do not need to engage in competitive play against each other, they just need to *think* that they are playing against an opponent. Dr. Nice amends his research design so that each boy plays a game against the computer rather than against another patient (Step 6). However, to try to keep the study realistic and the boys invested in the game, the researchers could tell each boy that he is playing the game against an "opponent" in the adjacent room. Although this design simulates the competitive environment that Dr. Nice is aiming for, it would require deceiving the boys. Under APA Standard 8.07: Deception in Research, such deception is permissible only if the deception is justified by the potential importance of the research results, no other alternative methods are feasible, and the research will not cause physical pain or severe emotional distress.

The computer program the boys play allows each child to retaliate against his opponent by sending shrill noises through his headphones or by delivering a mild shock. The frequency with which these measures are administered will provide the researchers with a quantitative measure of aggression. Since the boys believe that they are playing the game against a live person in the next room, they should behave relatively naturally. In response to focus group concerns, as a further precaution, Dr. Nice decides that in order to prevent the boys from being tempted to seek out their opponents once the experiment is over, the boys will be told that the opponent is from a different hospital unit. The focus group was additionally valuable for Dr. Nice because a new idea came up that he had not thought of: designing the game so that the boys would start to lose in the middle of the game (thus arousing potential aggressive feelings) but all the boys would win against the opponent at the end. Dr. Nice believes he has found an appropriate balance between protecting the boys and good science. By utilizing the deceptive procedures the experiment can produce valid results about aggression in behaviorally disturbed boys without inciting aggressive behaviors against peers.

Implementing, Monitoring, and Evaluating the Decision

Dr. Nice begins the research study. He stays in continuous touch with hospital staff and parents to see if there is any postexperimental aggression on the unit that is tied to the boys' playing the game (Step 7). He also notes that the boys seem really happy to win as the game ends. In compliance with APA Ethical Standard 8.08a: Debriefing, when the game is over, Dr. Nice explains the purpose of the study to the boys, describes the deception, and gives them an opportunity to ask questions. He doesn't notice any particularly negative reactions when the boys leave the study. However, hospital staff report the boys were observed telling others that they had been made fools of and were heard discouraging other boys from participating in the research.

Although the number of fights on the unit did not significantly increase as a result of the study, some distress was observed in the form of grumblings and minor opposition toward staff. Dr. Nice seems to have successfully prevented additional outbreaks of violence on the unit by incorporating deception in his research design. However, he did not anticipate that debriefing the boys about the deception would cause problems in the patient–staff or participant–researcher relationships. He halts the progression of the study at this point to modify the plan (Step 8).

On the basis of staff feedback, Dr. Nice reevaluates his decision to debrief. He is aware that APA Ethical Standards 8.08b and 8.08c require psychologists to take reasonable steps to reduce postexperimental harm when they become aware of it. The standards also permit psychologists to withhold debriefing information if debriefing would cause the participant harm. Dr. Nice decides that humane values justify withholding study information when it comes to telling each boy that he won the game, and chooses not to debrief the boys about winning or losing. Because children often take losing very hard, Dr. Nice feels justified in allowing the boys to think they won in order to keep distress at a minimum. He consults with staff and parents about this plan and they agree. In the study modification, the boys play the game and are congratulated for winning. Then each child is thanked for helping the researcher understand how boys like him play competitive computer games. The boys are also assured that their attacks on the opponent were very mild and did not hurt.

Some time has passed since the initiation of the study, so the children who participated in the first round of the study have been discharged from the hospital. This is an advantage for the researchers, as the current inpatients have not been informed about or dissuaded from the study by the past participants, allowing the researchers to recruit new participants and to maintain the deception in the research. Dr. Nice is pleased to discover, when monitoring the effectiveness of his revised project, that no patient distress is being reported and fights on the unit have not increased. However, hospital staff note that the boys are asking questions about the nature of the project once they have participated. In response, Dr. Nice agrees to give a short presentation to the boys following completion of the experiment to help them understand how they have aided the researchers in learning more about behavioral disorders. The boys are interested to discover how research helps others and how they had been collaborators in this quest for knowledge. Upon seeing such a positive response from the children, Dr. Nice feels confident that maintaining deception and not debriefing specifically about the deception were good solutions to the ethical dilemmas. Although perhaps not appropriate in other situations, deception without debriefing was necessary in this case to protect the welfare of the boys on the unit while allowing the researchers to procure valid data from the experiment.

CONCLUSION

Ethical decision making in psychology is a dynamic process requiring sustained effort and well-developed critical thinking skills. Effective critical thinking about ethical dilemmas requires the motivation to be ethical; familiarity with professional standards and relevant laws; consultation with stakeholders; the ability to generate and select among alternative solutions; competence to implement an ethical plan; and dedication to monitoring and evaluating the selected course of action and, if necessary, making amendments to the original plan. Critical thinking skills are necessary to identify and understand the perspectives of others and anticipate the consequences of different courses of action without personal bias. Ethical practice is ensured only to the extent that psychologists are aware of ethical issues and standards and are committed to the aspirational principles of the field. The responsible conduct of psychology requires not only a commitment to doing what is right but also the motivation and courage to critically evaluate the adequacy of past ethical decisions. It is also part of the psychologist's ethical responsibity to generate new means of achieving psychology's primary goal: a commitment to increasing scientific and professional knowledge in ways that improve the conditions of individuals. This service will, in turn, merit society's continued trust in the profession of psychology.

References

American Psychological Association. (2002a). *Ethical principles of psychologists and code of conduct.* Retrieved January 19, 2005, from www.apa.org/ethics.

American Psychological Association. (2002b). Rules and procedures: October 1, 2001 [Ethics Committee rules and procedures]. *American Psychologist, 57,* 626–645.

Americans With Disabilities Act of 1990, 42 U.S.C.A. § 12101 *et seq.* (West 1993).

Fisher, C. B. (2003). *Decoding the Ethics Code.* Thousand Oaks, CA: Sage.

Fisher, C. B., Hoagwood, K., & Jensen, P. S. (1996). Casebook on ethical issues in research with children and adolescents with mental disorders. In K. Hoagwood, P. S. Jensen, & C. B. Fisher (Eds.), *Ethical issues in mental health research with children and adolescents* (pp. 135–238). Mahwah, NJ: Erlbaum.

Halpern, D. F. (in press). The nature and nurture of critical thinking. In R. J. Sternberg, H. Roediger III, & D. Halpern (Eds.), *Critical thinking in psychology* (pp. 1–22). New York: Cambridge University Press.

Health Research Extension Act of 1985, 42 U.S.C.A. § 289a (West 2003).

Josephson Institute of Ethics. (1999). *Making ethical decisions.* Marina del Rey, CA: Author.

Meltzoff, J. (1998). *Critical thinking about research.* Washington, DC: American Psychological Association.

U.S. Department of Health and Human Services. (2001, December). *Code of federal regulations: Protection of human subjects.* (Title 45, Public Welfare, Part 46). Washington, DC: U.S. Government Printing Office.

17

Critical Thinking in Psychology

It Really Is Critical

Robert J. Sternberg

In this book, distinguished theorists and researchers in psychology have explored the role of critical thinking in psychology. The conclusion I come to is that critical thinking is critical in and to psychology. In this final chapter, I summarize some of the "critical" lessons readers can learn from having read the book.

HOW YOU SAY IT IS OFTEN AT LEAST AS IMPORTANT AS WHAT YOU SAY

Our parents socialize us into the importance of putting things in a positive and constructive way, and of saying things in the "right" way. These skills should be part of our socialization in psychology as well. For example, Halpern (Chapter 1, this volume) points out that although two questions – "Do you favor or oppose allowing students and parents to choose a private school to attend at public expense?" and "Do you favor or oppose allowing students and parents to choose any school, public or private, to attend using public funds?" – essentially ask the same thing, the percentages of respondents responding in favor of vouchers differed by 22%, depending on how the question was asked. Similarly, Schwarz (Chapter 4, this volume) shows that how survey questions are framed has an enormous impact on how they are answered. Even using a scale of −5 to +5 versus 0 to 10 had a large impact – a difference of 21% – in the way a question about success in life was answered.

　There are many other examples besides these two. Piaget (1972) gave children piles of marbles, where he might have, say, eight blue marbles and six green marbles. He would ask children in a class-inclusion problem whether there were more blue marbles or marbles. Children would become confused with the wording, figure he meant to ask whether there were more blue marbles or green marbles, answer "blue marbles," and get the problem wrong. Piaget thereby reached the wrong conclusion about children's cognitive abilities because of the way he framed the questions he asked.

The importance of saying things right extends beyond just surveys and experiments. Reviewers of articles and grant proposals in psychology often say things in a destructive rather than constructive way, at times attacking the person rather than his or her ideas (Sternberg, 2003). The result is that authors, especially young ones, become discouraged, and may find it difficult to focus on or even find the substance of the critiques they receive. As scientists, we need to be careful not only in our scientific statements, but in the statements whereby we evaluate the scientific work of others.

THE MOST DIFFICULT CRITICAL EVALUATION TO MAKE IN PSYCHOLOGY IS OFTEN OF ONESELF

I was fascinated by Halpern's citation of a study showing that low-ability students greatly overestimated their knowledge in comparison with that of others (Kruger & Dunning, 1999). In my and my colleagues' work on implicit theories of intelligence (Sternberg, Conway, Ketron, & Bernstein, 1981), we found that the large majority of people rated themselves as above average in intelligence – the infamous Lake Wobegone Fallacy, after the mythical village in which everyone is above average. The problem for us in psychology is that if we are unaware of and fail to think critically about our own weaknesses, we cannot correct them or compensate for them.

I believe careers are most often derailed by people's unawareness of their own shortcomings. None of us is great in everything. Some of us are better in research, others in teaching, others in administrative work. And even within these broad categories, there is a lot of room for difference. People differ in their talents for different kinds of research. But if we fail to analyze our own strengths and weaknesses, we are likely never to achieve our goals in our careers. In my own life as a professional, I have recognized many weaknesses, some of which I have attempted to correct, and others, to compensate for.

OUR CAUSAL EXPLANATIONS TEND TO BE INCOMPLETE AND SOMETIMES CONFUSING

We all know that correlation does not imply causation, and that, to draw causal inferences, it helps to have a controlled experimental design. But Shadish (Chapter 3, this volume) discusses "inus" conditions, in which causal explanations are insufficient but nonredundant parts of unnecessary but sufficient conditions (Mackie, 1974).

The basic issue here is that issues of causation are far more complex than even our experiments sometimes allow us to grasp. For example, someone learning a new fact can depend on multiple sources of causation, at biological, cognitive, contextual, motivational, and other levels. Any one "cause" of learning is likely to be part of the story of causation, but not the full story. Many psychological phenomena occur under some circumstances but not others.

Where this issue becomes especially important is when a researcher claims to have found *the* cause for a psychological phenomenon. In psychology, a cause is mostly likely to be one whose effect depends on other variables, and that is limited to one level of analysis. The same, of course, can be true in multiple fields. For example, the cause of a car starting can be described in terms of internal-combustion mechanisms, but also, the turn of a key, a driver's state of mind upon turning the key, or the need to go to work that can lead the driver to start the car in the first place. There is no one unique cause of the car starting, just as there is no one unique cause of how people learn, forget, become happy, or become anxious.

What makes drawing causal inferences even harder is that our samples are often limited. As Schwarz (Chapter 4, this volume) points out, we often use convenience samples that are unrepresentative in various degrees of the population of interest. Our results may have little to tell us about the populations to which we claim to generalize. For example, very few investigators are interested in generalizations to populations of college sophomores, yet often these are the only ones we test. They are probably even less interested in generalizations to populations of white rats, but other studies are limited to such samples. In drawing conclusions, we have to be careful about the generalizations we make. Case studies can tell us a great deal, but as Martin and Hull (Chapter 6, this volume) point out, they are fraught with challenges when one tries to generalize from them. Our goal should, of course, not be to draw no conclusion at all, but rather to be careful in the conclusions we do draw.

EVEN SCIENTISTS ARE SUSCEPTIBLE TO INFORMAL LOGICAL FALLACIES, SUCH AS CONFIRMATION BIAS

We would like to believe that scientists live in a Popperian world in which they propose ideas and then diligently try to falsify them. But they do not live in such a world, as Shadish (Chapter 3, this volume), Risen and Gilovich (Chapter 7, this volume), Dennis and Kintsch (Chapter 9, this volume), and Sternberg and Grigorenko (Chapter 5, this volume) point out. On the contrary, like everyone else, psychologists are susceptible to informal logical fallacies, perhaps the most notorious of which is confirmation bias. Scientists, like most others, want to show that they are right, not wrong, in their beliefs.

Confirmation bias can be pernicious in a number of respects. It can lead scientists to interpret ambiguous data as supporting their position more strongly than the data actually support it. It can also lead them to view data that are harmful to their position as more ambiguous than they actually are. And it can lead them to view with suspicion those whom they view as "foolish" enough to disagree with them.

How do we overcome confirmation bias? There probably is no foolproof way. But one very good way is to recognize our own susceptibility to it, and to seek it out in ourselves and, of course, others.

Informal fallacies of the kind discussed by Risen and Gilovich (this volume) in all likelihood build on each other. For example, when trying to explain a psychological phenomenon, the availability heuristic can enter into one's thinking. In availability, we are susceptible to preferring explanations that come more easily to mind. And what explanations of a phenomenon in which we are interested come more easily to mind than our own? So we may prefer our own explanations, simply because they most readily come to mind and thus feel comfortable to us.

Some of the worst examples of confirmation bias are in research on parapsychology (see Hyman, Chapter 13, this volume). Arguably, there is a whole field here with no powerful confirming data at all. But people want to believe, and so they find ways to believe, despite the recalcitrance of the data.

ALL INVESTIGATIONS IN PSYCHOLOGY ARE SUSCEPTIBLE TO CONFOUNDS

As Shadish, Schwarz, McDermott and Miller, and Sternberg and Grigorenko all point out in this volume, our explanations of psychological phenomena are often based on confounded research. Some confounds, such as order effects, are more blatant. But others are very subtle. For example, people of different ethnic groups may differ in socioeconomic status, type of socialization, type of acculturation, native language, number of years of schooling, and a number of other variables. How does one disentangle all of the variables that may be associated with ethnic group? When one finds an effect of ethnic group, is it ethnic group, per se, that is responsible for the result, or some other variable confounded with it?

One of the most difficult entanglements in psychology has been that between heredity and environment. It is exceedingly difficult to disentangle these two sources of variation. There are methods that can be helpful, such as the method of separated identical twins, but even these methods have their limitations, such as the confounding variable that identical twins tend to be placed in similar, and hence correlated, environments, so that effects that may appear to be a result of genetic factors may, in fact, not be a result of such factors.

Roediger and McCabe (Chapter 2, this volume) point out that we always have to be careful regarding the possible generalizations of our work. Does it generalize across tasks? Does it generalize across situations? Does it even generalize across participants? Often, psychologists are careless in assuming work will generalize beyond what is reasonable to assume, given our research.

No method in psychology can give us results that guarantee valid inferences. As a result, the best thing to do is to study psychological phenomena by using multiple methods, in the hope that the multiple methods of analysis will converge on the same results. Different methods have different strengths and weaknesses, and when they are combined, they tend to average out each other's strengths and weaknesses.

THERE IS NO GREAT CONSENSUS ON WHAT MAKES A THEORY GOOD

We would like to believe we know a good theory when we see one. But what is a good theory? Dennis and Kintsch (Chapter 9, this volume) have proposed a number of sensible criteria for critically evaluating theories. But, in truth, psychologists disagree with respect to which criteria they care about, and how they weight them. For example, some theorists value parsimony, but for theorists whose theories are computer programs, parsimony is not possible in any great degree. Other theorists (including Dennis and Kintsch) value creativity, but theories can, of course, be creative and wrong, or uncreative and largely correct. Almost everyone values data-supported theories, but oddly enough, many of theories taught in psychology, including introductory psychology, have little data attached to them. For example, the psychosocial theory of Erik Erikson is typically taught in the absence of any supportive data whatsoever.

In my view, the worst problem we face is generalizability. In physics, it is likely that the atoms we test in the United States will be the same as the atoms we test in Kenya. But the people of the United States and Kenya may differ, on average, in many ways, a great deal of which are only poorly understood. So our ability to generalize will be limited by the samples and also the kinds of materials we use. As my colleagues and I have shown in our own work (Sternberg, 2004), conceptions of intelligence differ widely around the world, and the adaptive skills people bring to bear on tasks differ widely as well. But many researchers have a rather narrow view of how adaptive skills should be measured, preferring measures derived and, for the most part, validated on very restricted groups of peoples.

WE TEND TO UNDERESTIMATE THE ROLE OF PERSUASIVE COMMUNICATION IN PSYCHOLOGY

Jordan and Zanna (Chapter 10, this volume) point out the tremendous role persuasive communications play in psychology and other sciences. We would like to believe that creative ideas sell themselves, or that good experiments speak for themselves. Often, they don't. We have to sell the ideas, the experiments, or whatever else we may have to offer. Indeed, my colleagues and I have argued that the more creative an idea is, the harder it will be to sell it (Sternberg & Lubart, 1995; see also Spellman, DeLoache, & Bjork, Chapter 11, this volume).

In my experience, the biggest mistake students make in presenting the results of their research is to present masses of uninterpreted data. Results sections quickly can become incomprehensible as readers struggle to make sense out of the voluminous data there presented. As readers struggle to distinguish the forest from the trees, they may become frustrated, and give up altogether. As a result, data that might have a substantial impact end up having less effect than they should.

Jordan and Zanna (this volume) present many suggestions for how one can increase the persuasiveness of one's writing. One key suggestion is making clear the new contribution of your work (see also Spellman, DeLoache, & Bjork, this volume). Researchers often assume that if they can recognize what is new, so can readers. But readers will tend not to know the specialized literature as well as the author does, and may see as splitting hairs the distinctions that to an author appear major. Do not assume readers will see the importance of what you do. Without bragging, explain why your work is important. What is especially important when making your claim is that what you have to present really is, in fact, new. It is important that you know where your results fit into the existing literature, and where they go beyond that literature (Spellman, DeLoache, & Bjork, this volume).

It is important, in making your claim, that you do not go too far beyond your data. Reviewers are often ready to pounce, not on what you have found, but on what they see as your exaggerated claims for what you have found. If you are going beyond the data, it usually behooves you to show that you know it.

THE SAME ERRORS THAT APPLY TO THEORETICAL AND EXPERIMENTAL WORK APPLY TO CLINICAL WORK AS WELL

The chapter of Oltmanns and Klonsky (Chapter 12, this volume), with very little revision, could have been about scientific research rather than about clinical practice. Although some psychologists think that research and practice are two different domains, in many ways, they are not. Clinicians are case-study action researchers who use their scientific skills to make diagnoses and prescriptions for cures. Researchers often may need clinical skills in doing case studies (see Martin and Hull, Chapter 6, this volume), and they certainly need clinical skills in dealing with the various administrators, both inside and outside the university, with whom they come into contact.

Oltmanns and Klonsky (this volume) point out how we can easily become blind to the meaning of what we do. For example, applying a diagnostic label to someone gives us understanding at only the most superficial level of the kinds of problems the person may have. We can make the mistake of believing that a label is explanatory, when in fact it is merely descriptive.

This book has brought together many different strands of thought regarding critical thinking in psychology. The principal lesson of this varied work is that it is easy to become snookered not only by others' lapses of critical thinking, but also by one's own lapses.

We tend to view critical thinking primarily in terms of skills. But attitudes, or dispositions, are at least as important as skills. Someone may have the skills needed to think critically, but simply fail to apply these skills to the problems he or she confronts. So it is important to have the disposition to think critically. This means that, when you confront a problem, you ask yourself whether you are thinking critically about it.

Gilbert (1991) proposed an interesting distinction whereby he differentiated between Cartesian and Spinozan views of how people process new information when they receive it. The Cartesian view, he argued, is that people receive new information and critically process it simultaneously. The Spinozan view is that when people receive new information, they tend to believe it. To think critically about its validity requires an extra step, one that people often are unwilling to take. Gilbert argued that the Spinozan view better represents how people really think. I agree with him. Critical thinking requires not only one additional step, but typically, several. Unless you self-consciously apply these steps, you are unlikely to think critically about what you hear. Here are some questions you can ask yourself when confronted with an assertion of unknown validity:

1. Is what you have been told intuitively plausible?
2. What evidence has been offered to support it?
3. How many different kinds of evidence are there?
4. How strong is the evidence?
5. What kinds of evidence could show the assertion to be wrong?
6. Has any attempt been made to disconfirm the assertion?
7. Does the assertion fit with other theories or facts of which you are aware?
8. What are the consequences of believing the assertion if it proves to be wrong?

Note that, in each case, it is not only how well you answer the question that matters (skills), but also your asking yourself the questions (dispositions) in the first place that matters. Critical thinking is up to you. Having read this book, you are in an excellent position to do it, and to do it well!

References

Gilbert, D. T. (1991). How mental systems believe. *American Psychologist, 46*(2), 107–119.

Kruger, J., & Dunning, D. (1999). Unskilled and unaware of it: How difficulties in recognizing one's own incompetence lead to inflated self-assessments. *Journal of Personality and Social Psychology, 77,* 1121–1134.

Mackie, J. L. (1974). *The cement of the universe: A study of causation.* Oxford, England: Oxford University Press.

Piaget, J. (1972). *The psychology of intelligence.* Totowa, NJ: Littlefield, Adams.

Sternberg, R. J. (2003). To be civil. *The APA Monitor on Psychology, 34*(7), 5.

Sternberg, R. J. (2004). Culture and intelligence. *American Psychologist, 59*(5), 325–338.

Sternberg, R. J., Conway, B. E., Ketron, J. L., & Bernstein, M. (1981). People's conceptions of intelligence. *Journal of Personality and Social Psychology, 41,* 37–55.

Sternberg, R. J., & Lubart, T. I. (1995). *Defying the crowd: Cultivating creativity in a culture of conformity.* New York: The Free Press.

Author Index

Subject Index